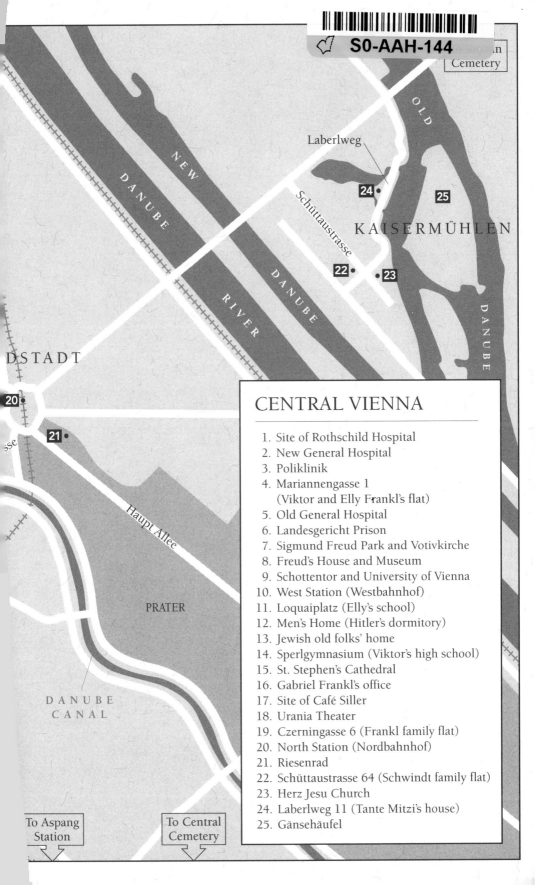

Cemetery

OLD

Laberlweg

Schüttaustrasse

NEW

DANUBE

DANUBE

RIVER

DANUBE

24

25

KAISERMÜHLEN

22

23

DANUBE

DSTADT

20

21

Haupt Allee

PRATER

DANUBE
CANAL

To Aspang
Station

To Central
Cemetery

CENTRAL VIENNA

1. Site of Rothschild Hospital
2. New General Hospital
3. Poliklinik
4. Mariannengasse 1
   (Viktor and Elly Frankl's flat)
5. Old General Hospital
6. Landesgericht Prison
7. Sigmund Freud Park and Votivkirche
8. Freud's House and Museum
9. Schottentor and University of Vienna
10. West Station (Westbahnhof)
11. Loquaiplatz (Elly's school)
12. Men's Home (Hitler's dormitory)
13. Jewish old folks' home
14. Sperlgymnasium (Viktor's high school)
15. St. Stephen's Cathedral
16. Gabriel Frankl's office
17. Site of Café Siller
18. Urania Theater
19. Czerningasse 6 (Frankl family flat)
20. North Station (Nordbahnhof)
21. Riesenrad
22. Schüttaustrasse 64 (Schwindt family flat)
23. Herz Jesu Church
24. Laberlweg 11 (Tante Mitzi's house)
25. Gänsehäufel

When Life
Calls Out
to Us

Doubleday

NEW YORK LONDON TORONTO

SYDNEY AUCKLAND

When Life Calls Out to Us

THE LOVE AND LIFEWORK OF
VIKTOR AND ELLY
FRANKL

Haddon Klingberg, Jr.

PUBLISHED BY DOUBLEDAY
a division of Random House, Inc.
1540 Broadway, New York, NY 10036

DOUBLEDAY and the portrayal of an anchor with a dolphin
are trademarks of Doubleday, a division of
Random House, Inc.

Library of Congress Cataloging-in-Publication Data

Klingberg, Haddon.
When life calls out to us: the love and lifework of Viktor and Elly
Frankl / Haddon Klingberg Jr.—1st ed.
p.   cm.
Includes bibliographical references.
1. Frankl, Viktor Emil. 2. Frankl, Elly, 1925– .
3. Jews—Austria—Vienna—Biography.
4. Holocaust, Jewish (1939–1945)—Austria—Vienna.
5. Holocaust survivors—Austria—Vienna—Biography.
6. Psychiatrists—Austria—Vienna—Biography.
7. Logotherapy. 8. Vienna—Austria—Biography. I. Title.
DS135.A93 F725 2001
943.6′13004924′00922—dc21
2001028643

Maps by Travis Klingberg
Book design by Gretchen Achilles

ISBN 0-385-50036-X (alk. paper)
All Rights Reserved

PRINTED IN THE UNITED STATES OF AMERICA

October 2001

FIRST EDITION

1   3   5   7   9   10   8   6   4   2

to Jan

Contents

CONTENTS

PART THREE:

Viktor and Elly Together, 1946–1997

Author's Note

ODDLY ENOUGH, THE origins of this book can be traced back to a long automobile tour of Chicago and a conversation the following morning.

The drive around the city began in the late afternoon of Saturday, May 22, 1993. Viktor and Eleonore Frankl had come to Chicago from their home in Vienna—he to give a lecture, but mainly to be with Elly when she received an honorary doctorate from North Park University. My wife Janice and I were hosting the Frankls, who stayed at a hotel near our home in Evanston.

After the Saturday morning ceremony in which Elly was honored, the Frankls had returned to their suite to rest. Viktor was eighty-eight, Elly twenty years younger. Following his usual afternoon snooze, he phoned us to ask for a ride around Chicago. It was a balmy spring day and there was little traffic. The drive lasted five hours, but we didn't see much and I was the only one who ever got out of the car—and that only to refuel after nightfall.

We spent the whole time swapping stories. The time flew by as the Frankls reminisced about their long lives, the Hitler years, and a half-century of love, work, and travels. There were poignant moments, of course, but jokes and laughs abounded. Just before dropping the Frankls at their hotel, I asked them, "Certainly someone in Vienna has recorded these stories of yours?" No, no. They didn't have the time for it, since back home they were always working on Viktor's brainchild, logotherapy. Plenty has been written about logotherapy and its keystone—the search for meaning—but Jan and I thought: what a pity if the Frankl personal stories are lost. But that was not up to us, so we let it be and slept through the night.

Early the next morning I drove the Frankls to the airport to meet the Japanese host for their Tokyo flight. On the way there Viktor took me by surprise. "Don [my familiar name], Elly and I were talking last night. We want to tell you that, if you will come to Vienna, we will make time to tell you our stories—as much as we are able to do, since we don't know how much longer I will live."

As I drove away from O'Hare Airport, it dawned on me that I was alone with this. If I did not record their stories no one ever would, and there might not be much time. So using money left from the sale of my motorcycle, the following month I was in Vienna with tape recorder and camera—my mission, to capture the stories. I had barely a clue about what I was getting into.

Over a period of seven years the project widened and deepened. Recording anecdotes turned into gathering the Frankl love story itself and recreating its context. A mere inkling of writing something evolved into this book. Thanks to grants, loans, and breaks from university teaching, I returned to Vienna whenever I could and accumulated more than a hundred hours of audio recordings of intimate conversations with the Frankls—literally thousands of recollections, opinions, impressions, stories, jokes, and anecdotes. These I indexed on minidiscs and in a vast computer database.

In addition, the Frankls towed me around Vienna to see the places of significance to them, and I tagged along to dinners with friends and family, even to appointments with their doctors. By the end I had taken eleven hundred slides of the Frankls, their places, people, and documents. I mixed with a lot of other people and conducted interviews with more than thirty of them in Europe and the United States. For the historical context of the Frankl story I dug through libraries, archives, Holocaust museums and memorials, and the Internet. I visited the sites of the four concentration camps where Viktor was held prisoner. In Vienna, I wandered in the Frankl neighborhoods over and over and began to feel their story.

What makes this book one-of-a-kind is the time I spent with the Frankls in conversation and in their daily lives. Our talks, day after day, week after week, were free-flowing and lively—never a boring moment even in sessions lasting six hours. Elly said, "Don, we look forward each time to your coming. You are the only one in the whole world with whom we are so open. It is so easy, and we enjoy it." Viktor chimed in, "But you elicit all that. We feel no inhibition to tell whatever can be told at all. We have no hesitation whatsoever. Like nobody else in the whole world you understand our life *and* our work."

Near the end of this book I will tell more about how I came to be its author, though why remains mysterious even to me. Perhaps what Elly said after Viktor's death is the best explanation we have: "But Don, it's you that Viktor talked to as to no one else. And it is the same for me. I would not talk this way with anyone else. Something happened between us—it is the same when you meet someone you are going to marry. You meet a real friend. You cannot choose. You have to take it or not to take it. . . . You know Viktor in a very unusual way. I was always present when you talked with Viktor and he was completely open, but to no one else. To him family was always a private affair, as if it was of no interest to anyone else."

Viktor Frankl never found time for professional biographers who approached him over the years. Occasionally he granted interviews, but he was busy and became impatient. In one such interview in 1974, Frankl insisted at the outset that the concrete situations of his past be used as a way of "helping people, without preaching at them." That insistence was the same in 1993 when we started. Apparently my inclusion of Elly as a full partner in the story-gathering was novel for the Frankls, but I knew early on that what I was being given to tell was primarily a love story.

Because the Frankls lived through the Hitler years, I was drawn inevitably into the real and retrospective gloom of Holocaust literature and into the never-satisfying debate over how that horror could have happened at all. I became aware of the immense written material on that era and of the bitter controversies regarding it. I discovered material that included the careful work of scholars who, aware of their own biases, handle data with genuine respect. I found other "scholars" who were really crusaders—screening their sources and slanting them to manufacture one case or another, scarcely able to conceal their political and personal motivations. Two well-researched tendencies in us humans are starkly evident in the work of some scholars and academics: *confirmation bias* (seeking information that supports one's beliefs and ignoring information that disconfirms) and *belief perseverance* (hanging onto beliefs in the face of contrary evidence—one no longer even considers opposing perspectives). I knew that nearness to subject (in my case, to the Frankls) would diminish objectivity; what I learned is that scholarly distance from subject per se is no assurance whatsoever of objectivity or freedom from bias.

I am neither a Holocaust scholar nor historian and this book is neither comprehensive nor critical biography. Rather, it is an unabashedly sympathetic rendering of their story as Viktor and Elly told it to me. But I am no ghostwriter for the Frankls. Throughout the project I maintained a measure of independence, interviewing whom I would and searching where I thought it prudent. In the end I combined a number of key elements in this book:

- telling the love story of Viktor and Elly for the first time;

- using the reflections of the mature Frankls from our conversations;

- drawing out the main themes of logotherapy;

- reweaving what I garnered from sources and other interviews into the Frankl story and its historical context; and

- offering my own perspectives, as person and psychologist, based upon what I learned.

Distilling the recorded conversations with the Frankls was a particular challenge. First, though we spoke in English, predictably the Frankls slipped into German whenever we were fishing for the best English words. Frequently I offered English reformulations, which they readily affirmed or amended. Second, the recordings are marked by good-natured banter and hundreds of digressions; that and numerous telephone and doorbell interruptions made tracking the story more daunting and interesting. Third, a particular anecdote might occur in conversations at two or more points over the years of interviewing, sometimes with additional details but never contradictory—a testimony to the Frankls' memories and integrity.

The sheer volume of recorded material made verbatim transcriptions untenable, and reading such would be too tedious anyway. So I merged discussions of the same substance, indicating where the breaks were significant. I also smoothed the English while preserving the Frankls' unique speaking styles. Only in the prologue did I take the liberty of piecing together one neighborhood walk from various actual strolls and chats.

My confidence grew when those closest to the Frankls said that I was portraying Viktor and Elly just as they were. One such instance occurred when I spent some hours in California with the late Joseph Fabry, who was born a Viennese Jew and became an author on logotherapy, Frankl translator, founder and longtime head of the Institute of Logotherapy in Berkeley, and editor of *The International Forum for Logotherapy*. Since

1963 he had been closely associated with Viktor. At the end of our day together Fabry said to me, "You are just the right person to write this story."

The book is constructed for a range of thoughtful readers. Those new to Frankl and to logotherapy may find the background in the introduction helpful. A reader who is interested only in the story may pass over that background and the endnotes, staying with the text, photographs, and maps. Beyond that, a reader may go into the citations and the sources themselves and plunge into Frankl's own writings. Those with particular interest in logotherapy may find their understanding of it enriched by the personal story of the Frankls, a story that may provoke in others a curiosity about logotherapy.

One thing is certain. The story is new, both in its telling and its detail. The nearest kin learned new things from the manuscript and even Viktor and Elly found out more about one another in our conversations— "Elly, you never told me this before" and "Viktor, I didn't know about this until now."

I hope that in reading you will not merely learn about the Frankls but that you will meet Viktor and Elly and know them; and that by the concrete situations in their story your spirit may be buoyed to pursue the meaning of your own life until you find it.

When Life Calls Out to Us

Introduction

THIS IS THE story of Viktor and Elly Frankl and of their influence on the world that shaped them. Because of them, countless people have been uplifted. Many who found life empty, even in the most enviable circumstances, have found meaning. Others in terrible and inescapable situations have discovered that life still can be worth living.

This is a love story. The story of a man who could scarcely believe that the love of his life was waiting for him after he had lost everything. The story of a woman as much surprised to find in this unlikely man the love of her life. But it is more than that, since the affection that grew between them was not centered in itself. Rather, their love was directed at the world and toward a cause outside, beyond itself.

It is a story that speaks to the new century from the wisdom of the old. We live and love, hope and fear, labor and laugh, celebrate and mourn, make peace and war, meet and part, suffer and die. Through it all we yearn for happiness, and we desperately hope that those we love will find it, too. For many in our era, happiness has become the greatest of all goals and treasures.

As a result we have been chasing happiness through self-discovery, self-enhancement, self-fulfillment, self-improvement, self-indulgence. We have been trying to increase our self-awareness and self-understanding, to become more self-affirming. Through self-help we have boosted our self-acceptance, our self-esteem, and our self-concepts. We learned to believe that we are okay just the way we are. We reassured ourselves that looking out for number one is really the right thing to do. And as we acquired the self-love we formerly lacked, some of us became disillusioned when the people we loved did not love us back as we thought we deserved. Some of us were disillusioned when those closest to us got in the way as we pursued our own happiness.

In affluent countries from the 1920s on, the age-old search for happiness became the endeavor of *individuals* and at the same time turned inward. This form of the pursuit was encouraged at home, in school, even in church of all places. But by midcentury a small Austrian man was summoning us to a different chase. His call was first heard after fascism and nationalism had dragged Planet Earth through a second horrific war.

Before the Nazi SS deported him from Vienna to his first concentration camp, Frankl had written most of his first book, *The Doctor and the Soul.*[1] During his two years in that camp Frankl continued to work on the manuscript secretly. Just before his transfer to Auschwitz, he sewed the manuscript inside the lining of his coat. But there the coat was confiscated in exchange for a still shabbier one, and all the pages were lost.

When Frankl returned to Vienna after the war, he immediately reconstructed the lost manuscript, adding a brief chapter about the concentration camps. When his friends read it, they persuaded him to write more about his experiences. So early in 1946, just before he met the love of his life, Frankl wrote his second book, *Man's Search for Meaning.*[2]

To find him, we go to Vienna at midcentury and encounter him in his own home. He is in his fortieth year and dictating that second book at a furious pace. The third-floor room is unfurnished and dreary, and the bombed-out windows are still boarded up. He barely survived two and a half years as prisoner in four Nazi concentration camps and, though he had been a vigorous man, the hideous circumstances of those years subdued him. Now the floodgates are open and he paces the room, formulating and reformulating sentences, agonizing over the best word to use. Working in shifts, three women harness the torrent of his utterances in shorthand. Their only breaks come when he slumps into a chair, sobbing. In nine days the small book is finished.

At that time no one imagined how it would speak to the spiritual longings in people everywhere. Yet more than a half a century later *Man's Search for Meaning* endures as a worldwide bestseller. Philosopher Karl Jaspers called it "one of the great books of mankind." In 1991 the United States Library of Congress/Book-of-the-Month Club survey of lifetime readers named it one of the ten most influential books in America.

What Frankl wrote about in his first two books has come to be known as "logotherapy." He coined the tag from two Greek words, *therapeuo*—to heal or to make whole—and *logos*. *Logos* has many meanings in Greek, including word and statement, but Frankl chose it because it also means *reason, meaning*. So logotherapy is "healing through meaning" or "becoming whole through meaning."

Logotherapy was Frankl's creation and it consumed him. When he and Elly married, her deep love for him drew her into his cause and she joined him in it. For this Viktor loved her as deeply in return. Their devotion to one another became a dedication to the world. From logotherapy we learn to forget about self, and put our whole heart into someone or something greater. In the love story of Viktor and Elly Frankl we see how they did that, in their way and in their time.

PRIOR TO THE Nazi deportation of the Frankl family from Vienna to the camps in 1942, Frankl as a young psychiatrist already had assembled the elements of what came to be called the third Viennese school of psychotherapy.[3] The first was Sigmund Freud's psychoanalysis, marked by the "will to pleasure" and by Freud's ingenious expedition into the unconscious and its sexual and aggressive forces—"depth psychology." The second school was the individual psychology of Alfred Adler, distinguished by the "will to power"—striving to overcome feelings of inferiority in our relations with other people. Throughout his life Frankl remained respectful of Freud and Adler and acknowledged that their work formed the foundation of his own.[4] At the same time, he said that he could see even more than they. After all, Frankl quipped, even a dwarf standing on the shoulders of a giant can see farther.

Frankl created the third approach and originally called it "logotherapy and existential analysis."[5] And since, in his view, meaning is found beyond and not within oneself, he was advancing a "height psychology." By the 1930s he was insisting that what human beings need—uniquely—is to discover meaning in existence, to find someone or something to live for. He called it the "will to meaning," and often quoted Nietzsche's line: he who has a why to live can endure almost any how. Frankl dubbed the failure of large numbers of persons to find meaning the "mass neurosis of the modern age," and called the emptiness they experienced the "existential vacuum."

With logotherapy Frankl challenged popular ideas as well as favorite notions in psychiatry, psychology, and religion. He lifted our sights from

the dismal psychoanalytic journey inward with its unmasking of our boil-
ing desires. He also drew us away from the path that leads to artificially
inflated self-esteem and the hollow promise of limitless personal growth
and joy.

Man's Search for Meaning appeared in English in 1959 through the
efforts of Gordon Allport of Harvard, who wrote its preface. At first glance
it may appear to be a grandparent to the vast brood of books on self-
improvement and happiness for which we Americans have developed such
a raging appetite. With a closer look, however, Frankl's writings seem outlandish in comparison to the modern lore of self-fulfillment.

Frankl was a major voice in humanistic psychology—a loosely connected array of approaches that arose in the United States in the mid-
twentieth century. It counteracted the dehumanizing tendencies of both
psychoanalysis and behaviorism, which predominated at the time, and offered a more optimistic and less deterministic view of human nature.
Frankl anticipated the distortion of humanistic psychology into the
American "human potentials movement." That movement asserted that
we all have the right to personal happiness as well as virtually limitless potential to attain it. A central feature of the movement became the acqui-
sition of wealth because of the perception that it too is necessary for life
at its best without waiting. One of the forms of the will to power is what
Frankl called "the will to money."[6,7]

The human potentials movement, in which the influence of Adler is
clear, may be traced in part also to the writings of Carl Rogers (1902–87)
and Abraham Maslow (1908–70), American psychologists who exalted
personal growth and self-actualization. On the popular front, two famous
New York clergymen, Harry Emerson Fosdick (1878–1969) and Norman
Vincent Peale (1898–1993), preached and published a religion of positive
thinking and human possibilities. At the same time, others within organized religion began to spread the word that God is on the side of those
who seek self-fulfillment above everything—"becoming all God wants
you to be and getting all God wants you to have."

Even in their graves, Fosdick and Peale must be outraged over how far
today's popular preachers have pushed religious selfism.[8] And can Rogers
and Maslow rest in peace as they witness the aftermath of a social movement in which more and more people are obsessed with themselves and
their rights? At the extremes, the human potentials movement has left
many in the clutches of an individualism that plays a role in the loss of

community, in the breakdown of marriages, and in boredom, promiscuity, loneliness, greed, addictions, abuse, and other forms of violence. Of course the movement is too far-reaching and socially complex to blame or credit Adler and these four honorable people for it. Surely they never intended to encourage the disregard of neighbors, the betrayal of spouses, and the right to happiness no matter whom we hurt. In retrospect at least, we can see that the pursuit has outrun concern for world, nation, community, neighbor, and even for family.

The experience of Viktor Frankl set him on a different course. As he wrote his first two books, he was no lucky optimist in the postwar United States, where opportunity offered "the American dream" to anyone who would go for it. Rather, he was a poor and lonely Austrian Jew writing in the rubble of a shattered European city. His unborn child had been lost in a forced abortion under Hitler; his father and mother, brother and sister-in-law, mother-in-law and wife of only a year had recently been slain in the deathcamps—as he nearly was himself—along with six million Jews and fifteen million others whom Hitler and the National Socialists despised as dangerous or undesirable.

To Frankl, the human potentials movement and its promise of boundless individual growth and happiness were a pipe dream from the start. To him it was wishful fancy to gloss over the guilt and pain and death that go with being human, to sidestep our personal responsibility to others and the world, to overlook the capacity of people to suffer courageously—even to bring good out of unavoidable adversity—and to ignore the fact that all human beings are capable of extraordinary evil as well as extraordinary good. One of the areas in which this belief drew the most controversy to Frankl is the notion of "collective guilt."

As soon as he was liberated from the deathcamps—before the human potentials movement ballooned and decades before Holocaust literature became popular and profitable—Frankl took a public stand against collective guilt, which blames all German people for the Nazi terror. Despite some fair-minded critics and vicious attacks from others across the years, Frankl was irrepressible that people of every race, every faith, and every society have the full potential for good as well as for evil. Every group is proud of its decent folk and disgraced by its brutes and villains. Indeed, each of us is saint and scoundrel waiting to happen, depending upon a complicated interplay of influences, decisions, and graces. Though a baffling and deadly fusion of factors led to the Holocaust, Frankl held that the basic problem lay not in German character alone, but in human character—in how easily we are influenced by situations and how far we will go to please tyrants when they promise us privilege, protection, prosperity, and pride in ourselves and our own kind.

When it comes to suffering, self-fulfillment teaching tends to evade, deny, or trivialize it as something abnormal and fleeting. Frankl not only underscored suffering as a normal part of human experience, but he asserted the real possibility of finding meaning in it *when it cannot be avoided.* In the Holocaust he himself faced incomprehensible evil and loss—after that he was never able to offer a quick fix, to suggest seven easy steps to perpetual joy, or to spell out the secrets for health-wealth-happiness. Rather, he summoned the human spirit to its triumph in love, in service, and even in suffering.

This helps to explain why *Man's Search for Meaning*, unlike so much self-improvement literature, endures and defies barriers of race, religion, culture, and politics. Though it is rooted in a great European intellectual tradition, it has been translated into nearly thirty languages including Spanish, French, and Afrikaans; Japanese, Chinese, Russian, Korean, Hebrew, and Persian. While people read less and less as suffering intensifies, still this book finds a home even in societies where people suffer on a wide scale. It inspires readers in cultures and circumstances wherein much of the modern self-enhancement literature—if it could be comprehended at all—would be viewed as superficial, sad, and peculiarly American.[9]

In affluent countries, multiple editions of *Man's Search for Meaning* persist, despite the assertion that no one, given some years, will escape the tragic triad of human experience: guilt, pain, and death. Indeed for many in the world, at least at times, life seems to consist of little more than suffering and dying. The book is treasured by persons who are ill—and even near death—and it circulates among the people of hospice who care for them. Prisoners sentenced to life or to death pass on copies to one another. People in menacing circumstances read it over and over, and others who had once lost heart now purchase copies by the dozen to give away.

Even as the book comforts the afflicted, it afflicts the comfortable.[10] Its message strikes a chord with overprivileged students and with women and men who are fit and doing very well indeed. They say it leaves them wanting better, realizing that merely acquiring things to live the good life for one's own sake is not what it's cracked up to be. Even the most outwardly fortunate may have the means but no meaning. One may crave and acquire more to live *on* when there is not much to live *for*. And what, at the end of the day, can make life really worth living unless there is something—a cause, a love, a person—worth dying for?

ONE OF THE hopeful signs amid the selfism of our time is a widespread spiritual yearning.[11] To be truly human is to be spiritual, Frankl said, and he was prophetic regarding this yearning. Before and since the Holocaust he distilled the essence of a person to *spirit, freedom, responsibility*.[12] However, the usage of certain words made it difficult for Frankl to explain in other languages what he meant by human spirit.

In English the words *spirit, soul, spiritual*, and *spirituality* traditionally bear religious overtones. What we need to understand is that, in German, the words *Geist* (mind, spirit), *Seele* (soul), and *geistig* (intellectual, spiritual) do not mean anything religious. Had Frankl been writing about things specifically religious, he would have used the word *geistlich*, which means sacred—religious and spiritual in that sense.[13] Thus Frankl was readily understood when he talked about the mental and spiritual dimensions unique to humans—believers and agnostics alike. Frankl would not have objected to the idea that spirituality can be pursued apart from religion, an idea that characterizes some contemporary notions of spirituality. Secular as well as religious people are openly aspiring to spirituality in its various forms. Our finest medical schools are producing literature and workshops on "spirituality and healing" as never before. Psychiatrists and psychologists are boarding the moving train of spirituality, healing, and wholeness. Recent publications from the American Psychological Association show how seriously religious issues and spiritual aspects of psychotherapy are now being taken.[14]

When Frankl started writing about human spirit in the late 1920s, the situation was different. He was in Freud's living shadow in Vienna, and Freud was attacking religion. With the passage of time, the prophetic claims of Frankl have become more piercing. Somehow in advance of contemporary trends, he already was challenging any "spirituality" that might be forged around self. Instead Frankl fixed on the chief manifestation of human spirit: *self-transcendence*—whereby persons rise above themselves, their limitations and circumstances. One becomes fully human and truly spiritual only in transcending self and going outward to the world, to others, to God if one chooses.

For Frankl, since spirituality is in its essence self-transcendence, it brings with it human freedom. But it is not freedom *from* as much as freedom *to*. We are not free from our biological nature, whether instinctual drives, genetic legacies, or the functions and malfunctions of our brains and bodies. Nor are we free from the grasp of social, developmental, and environmental influences. But we are free to take a stand toward these, even against them. We are free to do what we will with the cards we are dealt, to choose what response we will make to fateful events, to decide what cause or persons will receive our devotion.

And this *freedom to* carries an *obligation to*. Frankl described logotherapy as "education toward responsibility"—each of us is responsible for something, to someone. By using our freedom to act responsibly in the world, we uncover meaning in our lives. It is only when our will to meaning is frustrated that we settle for the pursuit of personal pleasure (Freud), or for financial and social success (Adler).

When a person exercises spiritual freedom and responsibility, there follows a host of effects: peace of mind, good conscience, and contentment. But these occur naturally—as by-products, so to speak. But pursuing any of these directly makes their attainment improbable or impossible, he said. There is nothing quite like striving for peace of mind to keep one edgy. To center one's effort on achieving a good conscience may lead to hypocrisy or guilt—or both. To make health one's chief aim may bring on something akin to hypochondria. For Frankl, these are not ends to be pursued for their own sake or even for one's own good. Instead, they ensue naturally for persons who live for something else, for something greater.

Since we are by nature spiritual, and therefore free and responsible, it is no wonder that we require something to live for. It is unbearable for us to suffer when there is no meaning in it, and we find it loathsome to go on when there is no point in doing so. Frankl also clearly stated that when we suffer from meaninglessness itself—the existential vacuum—it is a mark of personhood. He would tell a person deep in a spiritual crisis of meaninglessness that such a crisis is no sign of mental illness, but a human *accomplishment*.[15] Longing for life to make sense, yearning after something really worth living for, is no sign of psychological disorder. Rather, it reveals the human spirit in its most authentic and honest hours, for when we have a *reason* for peace or a good conscience, we no longer worry about them. It is not really happiness that we want, but rather something to be happy about.[16]

Prologue

IT IS JULY 1996, and I am back in Vienna to collect more of the story of Viktor and Eleonore Frankl. Using my summer break from university teaching, I meet with them at their home each day, and sometimes we go out to visit places of significance for them. Even though he is ninety-one and she seventy, they both are quick-minded and vigorous, taking afternoon walks each day for air and exercise.

Earlier today they invited me to walk with them, but I reminded them that I could not since a student from Chicago was arriving to visit Vienna and me. "Bring him along!" they urged.

When I met Ryan's train at West Station, he had been rereading a book by Professor Frankl and was hoping for a chance to meet him. Ryan is a twenty-one-year-old history major touring Europe with some college friends whom he left behind in Budapest. When I mentioned the option of the afternoon walk, he blurted, "Now that is excellent!"

After Ryan settled in, we headed for the Frankl place. On the way he wanted to know what their life is like in this city. I told him that venerable old Vienna is the only place they have ever called home. After the Hitler years and the concentration camps, Frankl was one of very few surviving Jews who returned. Through the decades since the war, honors have been heaped upon him here, but in other ways he has been disregarded and even resented. So the Frankls have mixed feelings about Vienna, and many times Viktor has been asked why he ever came back. Ryan rightly recalled that Sigmund Freud lived near the Frankls' neighborhood for nearly fifty years and often complained about the city. But he left it only when Hitler came, escaping to live his last year in freedom in London.

Ryan and I turn into Mariannengasse and stop at the first door. It opens to an old, six-story residential building, frayed but still handsome.

We go in, hike three flights of stairs, and ring a deafening doorbell at flat 14. Dr. Elly Frankl comes to the door, welcomes us, apologizes because they are not quite ready, and asks for a few moments. I insist that Ryan and I wait in the foyer with our dusty shoes.

"Okay then," she says and disappears.

The foyer is spacious, with a soaring ceiling and creaking parquet floor of bygone design. Through the open door to the hallway I point out to Ryan the elevator built for two. Its shaft is wrapped in steel and glass panels, a modern insult to the graceful old stairway coiling around it. The marble-like steps are chipped here and there and worn front and center by the foot traffic of a century. The railing has been smoothed by a million sliding hands. The original stained glass windows in the stairwell are still lighted by the sun, but their pastoral scenes of swans swimming and orchids blooming clash with the city surroundings.

The Frankls appear in the foyer, ready to go. Without small talk, they welcome Ryan cordially and usher us at once into the hallway. Frau Frankl shuts the narrow half-door behind us, then locks it twice. The double doors are white, and only the glass and brass have been spared the thick layers of glossy paint. Over the art nouveau protective bars on the doors she slams shut an outer iron gate with more locks—ever since they were burglarized, she says.

The Frankls take the elevator, Ryan and I the stairs. At the ground floor the elevator still leaves six steps down to the street-level corridor where we rejoin the Frankls, ambling across the original floor of blue-green and gold tiles. We pass through a white archway before reaching the exit doors, solid and reinforced against both weather and wars. A marker on the building dates it to 1903.

The four of us step into the sunshine on Mariannengasse, a short street here in the Ninth District of Vienna. It is a sticky July day, and the dust has barely settled in the torn-up street. Slow-moving construction crews arrive at nine, linger over lunch, then leave for the day at two. The Frankls and their neighbors are forced to give up cooking and hot baths for a week or two at a time so that the residential gas pipelines can be re-reconnected. The evenings in Vienna resound with waltzes and the mornings with jackhammers. In this Roman Catholic city, so strewn with altars and statues, it's a wonder that no shrine has been erected to the "Saint of Perpetual Demolition." One wonders if generations of citizens have peered into the same ditches.

Our walk is in an area that is home to the University of Vienna clinics. They boast centuries of medical advances and notable physicians—Freud the most famous and controversial of them. But this afternoon the area seems heedless of its history. Autos and trucks dodge rumbling streetcars, and mopeds zoom around belching diesel tour buses. On the sidewalks and in the establishments, shoppers and shopkeepers speak in a babble of languages, since refugees from the formerly Communist states to the east are still flooding the city.

The Frankls are walking arm-in-arm. Partway down the block Professor Frankl points out a courtyard that is unchanged from horse-and-buggy days. Then we move to the edge of the sidewalk to avoid the tables of a pizza place. Across the street stands the imposing Allgemeine Poliklinik, a relatively small city hospital with some of the greatest doctors' images looking down from its façade. Frankl tells Ryan that in this hospital he was chief of neurology for twenty-five years following the Holocaust.

At the corner of Mariannengasse and Pelikangasse, Professor Frankl grabs Ryan's arm and points upward and to the right where the new General Hospital looms into the sky on the hill beyond. Turning back and left, we duck under scaffolding and evade an outdated two-wheeled cement mixer. A vendor of medical supplies displays in window after window the scalpels and paraphernalia only a surgeon could love.

We turn left again, this time onto Alser Strasse. It is a broad and spirited thoroughfare where one can exchange foreign currency for schillings, and with schillings buy shoes, cigarettes, lottery tickets, guitars, music albums, watches, posters, computers, Italian ice cream, audio mixers, Bibles, nudie magazines, Mozart chocolates, apple strudel, and Stiegl beer. Window-shoppers joke about what missing body parts might be replaced by the prosthetic devices on display, or about what portions of the human physique might be shored up with the straps and trusses for sale. For those whose sagging is spiritual, one can pick up a religious icon in the next shop.

The Frankls point down the street to McDonald's and tell us how much they like cheeseburgers, minus the mushy bread. And a bit farther down Alser Strasse is the very church where in 1827 Franz Schubert poured out his grief at the coffin of Ludwig Beethoven, his idol. The following year Schubert made his own grave near Beethoven's, as if to rest in eternal awe of him. Ryan, the durable history buff, is enchanted.

Across the street from the church is the original sprawling complex of the General Hospital that dates back to 1693. Sigmund Freud, Alfred Adler, Gabriel Frankl, and his son Viktor each studied medicine here in his turn. Its vast courtyards are still crisscrossed by outdoor sidewalks. As recently as the 1980s, patients were still being wheeled on gurneys from building to building out-of-doors. But now the rambling structures are temporarily abandoned and await their destiny, probably as university offices blended with a shopping mall for the well, the healed, and the well-heeled.

The Frankls, as old lovers do, reminisce that they stroll today much as they did when they were young. After they first found one another they walked here as survivors of World War II, which had claimed their kin, exhausted their means, and left their city in shambles. Down this same Alser Strasse they had strutted in the warm evenings of 1946, he in his girls' white socks, the holes darned shut, and in his only pair of white undershorts. Nevertheless he had thought himself quite fashionable and fortunate even to be wearing them as his outer garment, the fly stitched closed by Elly. They had been that poor, but happy to be alive.

Through the decades since then, these two have been seen apart so seldom that they have been called "The Siamese Twins of District Nine," although almost no one notices them now. Even though Viktor and Elly have walked here and lived in the same nearby flat for fifty years, no one greets them on this day. Some youngsters, possibly jaded already, mock them rudely simply because they are old.

They are a pair of real characters—"originals"—who simply do things their own way, making life frustrating and interesting for those who know them. Viktor reflects more seriously, "Today, here on Alser Strasse, people think that we're just some old couple. Maybe I was a professor or something like this. But nobody knows." Elly agrees, "I think we look a little crazy even. We are always walking here, but nobody knows about us. Maybe no one cares."

But then simultaneously they remember a lady who always stops to greet them. She is deeply distressed about her husband's recent stroke. Yet whenever they meet, the lady sets aside her worry and speaks to the Frankls cordially and respectfully, as if from a kindlier former time or possibly out of a cheerful obedience to some holy book.

The consumers on Alser Strasse, clutching at parcels, and the commuters dashing mindlessly to chronic destinations would never believe who these old lovers are or what they have seen in their time. Who would guess where they have been, what they have done, or how many letters daily arrive at their door to which they daily reply? Even if a gentle stranger should stop to listen, she might never suppose that the fantastic stories these two are telling could be true. Who would believe that this man—of no imposing physical stature, indifferent toward possessions—is pursued by high society, venerated by lowly people around the world, and hated by cranks who phone to threaten his life, even in his old age?

Or who would believe that the rosary beads in the woman's brown shoulder bag had been handed to her by Pope Paul VI in a private audience with her Jewish husband and her? Even more far-fetched may seem the fact that this woman, of no fame whatsoever, was once mobbed in an adoring frenzy in faraway Brazil. The crowd literally tore off the dress she was wearing, as if the shreds of fabric they stole were holy remnants of a saint or martyr.

Viktor Frankl, a Viennese gent from way back, is accustomed to the city chaos. He speaks clearly and assuredly but, because he is nearly blind, walks cautiously. Age is disguised by his ruddy, youthful complexion. His vaulting forehead yields to flowing white hair parted center and combed straight back, though at the sides it is ruffled from repeated removals of eyeglasses. His height is much nearer five feet than six, not unusual in his generation.

For the most part, what he wears is traditional. The jacket of his blue-gray suit, tailored at the back with a decorative fabric belt, has no collar—a holdover style of Austria. Suspenders hidden by the jacket keep his loose-fitting trousers aloft. His walking shoes, with sticky composite soles, are well worn. His white shirt is open at the collar, ever since he yanked off his necktie for an afternoon nap. The coat pocket near his left shoulder bulges with a second pair of imposing eyeglasses, part of a dark lens showing. Even in the dazzling sun he has not yet thought to swap them. Overall Professor Frankl is slightly rumpled from the heat of day.

From an old city native like Frankl, one would expect to hear a dense Viennese dialect, *Wienerisch*. But there are only traces of it—though he can use it with comic exaggeration. His German is sophisticated, yet precise and plain. No pointless words. No petty chatter. No gripes. Not even one. He can shift without effort into English of an almost literary sort; even young Austrians with worldly ambitions do not speak this way. Instead of a commonly overstated Viennese courtesy, we see in this man a startling medley of outspokenness and grace. Here on the street, even with an audience of only three, he is charming and humorous; his dialogue is witty and intelligent. He clowns, doing an impression of a famous lecturer with a squeaky voice. He almost bumps into a woman passerby who steps out of his way to avoid his showing off. That hazard avoided, Professor Frankl seizes Ryan by the arm again and signals that we should stop and listen.

"Wait-a-minute-wait-a-minute," he insists. There is mischief in the old man's eyes as he launches into a joke.

"Two Israelis are headed for Tel Aviv in a military airplane. As they are flying the pilot announces that the plane will not stop at Tel Aviv after all; rather they will be continuing to Jerusalem. But he has radioed ahead and recommends that the two parachute down to the Tel Aviv airport. The pilot has even arranged for a jeep to meet them when they reach the ground."

Frau Frankl stands just behind her husband now, snickering impishly in anticipation of the punch line. He continues.

"So the two guys put on the parachutes and when the pilot gives the signal they jump out of the plane. But neither one can get his parachute to open. As they are falling faster and faster, one says to the other: 'Now watch. When we reach the ground there won't be any jeep to meet us either!' "

Having raised his voice for the last line, Frankl beams with pleasure at the punch line as he turns away. But Frau Frankl raises a mock complaint, "Sometimes I think if I hear that joke one more time I will cry."

"All the better!" Frankl shouts. "Often I kiss away her tears. So now all I have to do is tell this joke—then she will cry and I get a chance to kiss her again!"

Frau Frankl waves him away with a smirk. "Never mind."

As conversation eases along, the names of some Frankl friends turn up. Ryan stops short when he hears that Frankl and the late German existentialist Martin Heidegger were friends.

"No way!" Ryan blurts, then blushes. He holds back a question about how a Holocaust survivor could be a friend of Heidegger, who was a Nazi, wasn't he?

Elly—now she insists that Ryan address her this way—tells us that two of her husband's heroes are Bishop Fulton Sheen from the early days of American black-and-white television and—from the age of living color—Captain Kangaroo.

What?

Frankl chimes in, "Yes, really. I love them! I have personal autographs from both of them. Elly can show you. Ryan, are you too young to know Bishop Sheen? He gave absolutely clear, wonderful lectures using a blackboard! Whenever we were in America, I would not miss him *or* Captain Kangaroo on television."

Elly Frankl is ever watchful of Viktor as he walks along, even though he can be touchy about help he has not solicited. They are similar in height and frame, but her clothing is neat—earth tones on a summer dress that complement her hair, which is brown to sandy with hints of red and graying at the sides. She seems unaware of her natural elegance. Her eyes glisten and she defies the day's heat even while she gripes about it, as the Viennese do.

In her native German one can hear cadences of *Wienerisch*. Her English is very good, and among older Austrians—even the highly educated—this is unusual. This is still more surprising since, as she tells Ryan, "I came from a poor family and had no chance to go to university." In whatever language, Elly is plainspoken, natural. Occasionally she catches herself being too blunt and interrupts herself with a twinkling apology—"I shouldn't say this, but . . ." And then she says it anyway.

Elly holds her own in brisk dialogue with her husband. Warmhearted, she reveals the depth of her feelings on a matter with a homespun range of emotional expression. Her laughter is easily stirred—from a girlish titter to hysterics desperate for oxygen. When Elly makes a major point, she exaggerates it as well as her motions. In a moment of particular sorrow or joy, her eyes fill or even flow.

As we walk, Elly launches a diatribe about how badly Viktor is treated by certain others. But when Viktor injects a humorous counterpoint, she laughingly acknowledges the keenness of his insight. Both are playful. He quips, then grins boyishly as he awaits her retort. She laughs, shaking her head from side to side, "Oh well, what can you do?" Then, better than theater, they move on to the next exchange.

Just as we turn left again from Alser Strasse, the Frankls begin bickering with a startling sharpness—they can argue fiercely in German or English, depending on who is listening. Ryan looks alarmed as the spat cranks up. Neither one is winning. Each remains convinced, but soon the Frankls are distracted and simply drop the matter, as though they had been overrating its significance all along. What Ryan doesn't realize is that squabbling is almost an art form with the Frankls. Even when they seem to snap at each other, it is their normal quick-paced way of interacting.

As we turn again into Mariannengasse and approach their *Haus*, Ryan asks, "Why doesn't your name appear next to your doorbell, like all the rest? Are you trying to hide from people?"

"Of course not!" the alert Viktor rebuts. "Someone has stolen the nameplate! We put new ones there but they disappear again and again. It's unbelievable."

The Frankls do not suggest that Ryan and I return to their flat with them, so our parting is at hand. They muster from their weariness a tender farewell. The old professor shakes our hands carefully, each in turn. Elly embraces Ryan and me almost simultaneously.

"We enjoyed each minute," she says.

Viktor urges, before turning away, "Don, you will call us in the morning, yes? We'll be together again tomorrow if heaven permits. *Auf Wiedersehen.*" Then they enter the corridor of their building and—arm-in-arm—walk toward the six steps, fade from our vision, and vanish into the elevator built for two.

Ryan and I head back to Alser Strasse and toward the city center for dinner. He is pensive as we walk. Then he stops me, and I listen as he mulls over the afternoon walk with the Frankls. He says, with obvious feeling, "This isn't the first time Frankl has got me thinking. I guess there isn't much one person can do in the world, but what a mess if I spend my whole life thinking about myself, feeling sorry for myself. I'd love to do something really worthwhile for somebody else, and I think a lot about what to do with my life. I don't want it to be a waste."

PART ONE

Viktor Frankl

1905–1946

CHAPTER 1

Beginnings for a Century and a Boy, 1905–1915

SOME PEOPLE ARE born in tranquil places and are formed by gentle events within family, clan, and village. The life of Viktor Frankl and the twentieth century began and ended together, but in his time events were anything but gentle. His years were embedded in his family and in the city of Vienna, and also in the momentous events and international firestorms that overwhelmed them. He was destined to face the best and the worst of the age, and his life can be understood only against the backdrop of time and place.

Five years before Viktor's birth, the century had begun on a soaring note. Science, technology, and industry promised a bright future for humankind. Decades of relative peace had lulled people away from the dread of war. In Paris, the Universal Exposition of 1900 symbolized the wonders of the world to come. Transported on a near-miraculous moving sidewalk, visitors stepped on and off at will to see one dazzling display after another. Pavilions awash in electric lights exhibited technological marvels that fired everyone's imagination. With the Industrial Revolution spreading from Britain and America to the world, anything seemed possible!

If science and technology sent expectations soaring, so did the hope of prosperity and a better life for everyone. In 1900 many believed that education, literacy, and enlightenment would bring an end to wars in a new society of nations. At last all common people would attain the individual rights for which they longed. Communities, and even continents, would be linked by mechanized mass transportation on rail and sea, by motorized vehicles, and even by flying machines. Communication through newspapers and by wire would shrink the world into a family and—believe it or not—radios were about to start plucking news, music, and amusement from waves floating wireless in the wind. Entertainment was transformed as new movie houses began to show pictures that moved and soon would talk.

As the century opened, London was running not only its first motorbuses and subways, but also a huge chunk of the world—an empire so farreaching that, as the saying went, the sun never set on it. Western empires ruled half the world from Europe to Africa to Asia and back.

When Viktor Frankl was born in Vienna in 1905, the city was still one of the majestic capitals of Europe and the imperial seat of the Austro-Hungarian Empire—a vast union of many national groups without a common language. On the surface at least, Vienna shared the hopes of the new century, and its cobblestone streets, still clapped by the shoes of horses, bustled in anticipation of the new era. "The Ring," which surrounds Vienna's old inner city, is the royal boulevard of palaces and parks, music halls, theaters, museums, hotels, office buildings, businesses, and shops. Whether in a horse-drawn streetcar or carriage, or in a newfangled motorcar, riding the Ring in 1905 would remind one of the grandeur of Paris and Rome. From looking at the city's splendor no one would guess that the power of the monarchy and the unity of the empire were crumbling.

In music, Vienna stood alone in greatness. But the visitors who poured into the city from around the world did not come just for concerts. The University of Vienna was a hub of intellectual ferment and creativity, and visiting professors from other countries came to learn the latest from its celebrity faculty. Other visitors, with the means required, were patients coming to Vienna in search of the best that medical science could offer.

To put it simply, the city was simply grand when Viktor was born. More than any other metropolis, Vienna was sheltered and refreshed by vast surrounding forests. Among the hillside vineyards, large gardens were groomed for festive dining and drinking. There, dizzy patrons slurred through familiar songs as musicians moved from table to table, serenading locals and visitors alike. The Vienna Woods was sanctuary for citizens and tourists hooked on hiking, wine, and waltzes, in whatever order.

The city bore its share of the change and catastrophe that engulfed the world. As people of privilege and power danced and drank to celebrate the arrival of 1900, dismal masses of the poor huddled far from the flow of champagne. In Russia, czars lived in shameless luxury among millions of impoverished subjects, and the fault lines of a social earthquake were visible. China was a cauldron of social and political unrest. In Europe, chipper as it seemed, nations were arming themselves with novel technology for battle. Each political alliance was confident that war now would be quick if necessary and won if waged.

If the new century were to be so wonderful, why were the governments of Europe so edgy, so tied up in military alliances? In such a beautiful time—the "belle epoque"—why by 1914 were twenty-five million men trained for battle? Why were the nations developing machinery for mass killing? Technology was making carnage possible on a scale unknown before, both in war and in the holocausts' perpetrated by governments on their own people.

But our story begins before World War I, when the citizens of Vienna were still rather optimistic. Gabriel Frankl and Elsa Lion, the parents-to-be of Viktor, had just married—February 24, 1901—in the main synagogue on Seitenstettengasse.

Gabriel hailed from the little village of Porolitz (Pohorelice, today in the Czech Republic), about fifty miles north of Vienna and just off the main road to Brünn (Brno). His father and mother, Jakob and Regina Frankl, lived in the house at 445 School Street, upstairs from the toolmaker shop of a brother. Jakob provided for his household as a bookbinder, and the dwelling was crowded already when Gabriel was born there March 28, 1861. The elementary school he attended was not even a block down School Street, which today is a cobblestone alley much as it was then.

As a teenager Gabriel moved to Vienna and attended high school in Leopoldstadt, a city district. During his time there the high school moved to a new location in the Kleine Sperlgasse. From then on it was called the *Sperlgymnasium*. A *Gymnasium* in Vienna was similar to an American high school, but students started at a younger age and advanced further toward university. Attendance for eight years was typical.

Elsa Lion, much younger than her husband-to-be, was born February 8, 1879, to Jakob and Regina (Wien) Lion—that the same first names are shared by Viktor Frankl's maternal and paternal grandparents seems a notable coincidence. Elsa did have a famous ancestor in a long line of rabbis, however. He was High Rabbi Löw [Lion] (1520–1609) of Prague. For centuries his grave has been the most venerated in the ancient Old Jewish Cemetery there. As head of a Talmudic school in Prague, Rabbi Löw became famous for his scholarly work and also for his mysterious powers. It is told that he fashioned "the Golem" from clay, put a parchment or stone tablet in its mouth, and it became a living being. In legend and film, and in the literature of Gustav Meyrink and others, the Golem is portrayed variously as a buffoon or as a genuine protector of the Jews. In any case, the Golem went crazy and had to be subdued and reduced again to clay by Rabbi Löw.

Elsa's birthplace was in the winemaking region of Prague where foreign embassies are located today. In a man's world, less attention was paid to her heritage and so less was remembered.

As bride and groom, Elsa and Gabriel Frankl hunted for an apartment in the already familiar Leopoldstadt—the mainly Jewish Second District of Vienna. Together with Brigittenau (District 20), Leopoldstadt—defined by the Danube River to the east and by the Danube Canal which cuts through the city to the west—was once dubbed "Matzo Island" because of its many Jews. There the newlyweds found a flat at Czerningasse 6. It was in a busy, desirable street of mostly residential buildings, running nearly parallel to the broad Prater Strasse—both leading to the famed Prater park.

All three of the Frankl children were born in the tiny Czerningasse flat. Walter August, firstborn, was two and a half when the second child was due and, on the day of Viktor's birth, Gabriel and a very pregnant Elsa were spending a sunny Sunday afternoon in a typically Viennese way: chatting, reading, and sipping at a coffeehouse. The popular Café Siller on Postgasse was a short walk from home, just across the Aspern Bridge and near the canal.

Elsa felt her first contractions that afternoon, so she and Gabriel left the Siller quickly and returned to their home in Czerningasse. Since their flat was on the top floor, as always they had to climb the five long flights of winding concrete stairs. Before the day was out, Elsa gave birth to a second son. They named him Viktor Emil. It was March 26, 1905. Within the family they called him "Vicky."

The Frankls' flat was very modest, at door 25 just off the highest stairwell landing. They had only two rooms, plus kitchen and foyer. A dining table in the bedroom was used for meals. Four years after Viktor's birth, Gabriel and Elsa and their two sons made room for a daughter, Stella Josefina. In addition to this family of five, for several years a young girl lived in as a helper, sleeping on a divan in the foyer. Such an arrangement was common even in families of limited means, since many poor immigrant girls obtained room and board in exchange for their domestic help.

The household relied on Gabriel's salary, drawn from his steady employment in the monarchy, first as a parliamentary stenographer for ten years and then, for thirty-five years, as assistant to Minister Joseph Maria von Bärnreither of the department of child protection and youth welfare. By the time the Frankl children were born, Gabriel's income was "little but certain."

More than twenty years earlier in 1883, Gabriel had been forced to drop out of medical school for financial reasons after completing five years and everything except the *Rigorosa*—a series of comprehensive exams. In light of this we can understand Gabriel's delight when his three-year-old Vicky began to talk about being a physician someday, maybe even a navy doctor.

Elsa was mother and homemaker in the manner of the time, and the nurturing of the children and the emotional security of the family can be traced largely to this warmhearted and able woman.

Viktor and his siblings, Walter and Stella, thrived in family and neighborhood and attended the elementary school just down the street at Czerninplatz. Their apartment building at Czerningasse 6 was large and square, its four sections surrounding an inner courtyard, open to the sky above (as it still is today). There the Frankl children played, and Elsa could watch them from their fifth-floor windows above. Vicky was rather frail, and as he grew he was always more interested in talking about ideas than in playing competitive games.

The family went often to the Prater, only a fifteen-minute walk from home. After many years as a private imperial hunting reserve, the Prater was open to the public by 1770. The Haupt Allee was a three-mile, tree-lined promenade straight through the park where people strolled or sat on benches. The Prater was fairgrounds, public gardens, circus, zoo, and amusement park all wrapped into one and dotted with restaurants and wine gardens. The 1905 Baedeker guide to Austria-Hungary describes the Prater as "the favourite haunt of the humbler classes, especially on Sunday and holiday afternoons... when many fine horses, elegant toilettes, and handsome faces will be observed."[2]

In 1896 the world's grandest Ferris wheel, the *Riesenrad*, had been constructed and quickly became a symbol of the city. Its enclosed cars, each carrying a dozen people or more, made a slow revolution. Passengers could walk around inside to catch various vistas of the city. Today the views from the top of the *Riesenrad* are still spectacular. And while the wheel remains a city symbol, the sprawling Prater now hosts a more seedy amusement park—no place for children to roam free, and not a place to sit long in lofty conversation as Freud and many other intellectuals once did. While Gabriel was at work, Elsa often took their little ones to the Prater, staking out a circular bench where she could sit with other women. There Vicky and his playmates spent long hours in the huge sandbox at the center, in view of their chatting mothers.

Vicky also accompanied his mother on errands in their neighborhood. Sometimes they walked hand-in-hand down Schmelzgasse and past a favorite pastry shop. Occasionally they could afford a treat called *Schaumschnitten:* a sweet dessert on a crust, with two inches of fluffy whipped egg whites and sugar topped with a thin layer of chocolate— Vicky's favorite. Near the pastry shop one day he abruptly stopped his mother to ask, "Mama, what is the meaning of the navel?" Giving her no time to venture an explanation, the little boy offered his own. "But mama, I know already the meaning of the navel! It is a decoration on that boring flat stomach—an ornament to make it more interesting." This imaginative theory recalls that in many of Vienna's older dwellings there is a cup-like ornament placed at the center of high ceilings—similar to a mount for a chandelier but of no function whatsoever except decoration. In the conversation, a precocious child already was asking about meaning, purpose.

IT IS POSSIBLE, by stepping back to particular times in Viktor's boyhood, to glimpse the world around him and the drama of which he was becoming part. The year of his birth provides one such vista. Sigmund Freud had received his MD degree in 1881, and since 1891 had been living and writing at his famous Berggasse 19 address.[3] In 1905, fifty-year-old Freud published his *Three Essays on the Theory of Sexuality,* which outraged Victorian sensibilities with its frankness about sexual perversions and claims of sexuality in infants and children. At the same time, thirty-five-year-old Alfred Adler was already closely associated with Freud and psychoanalysis.[4] (Adler had completed his medical degree in 1895 and had continued with a residency at the Vienna Poliklinik Hospital near the university.) The Adlers were living not only in Leopoldstadt, but at Czerningasse 7—a building directly across the street from the Frankl place.[5] The Czerningasse entrance led to Adler's new medical office, while the family quarters were further in, overlooking Prater Strasse on the other side of the block.

In 1902, Adler had become one of four founding members of Freud's Vienna Psychoanalytic Society. Two years before that Adler had left his Jewish faith rather painlessly and, together with his daughters, was baptized in the Protestant Church in Dorotheergasse, First District. This may have suited Freud who—while he kept his own Jewish identity—did not want his psychoanalysis to be regarded as something exclusively Jewish. By 1905, Adler was one of Freud's most trusted followers, going at least weekly from Leopoldstadt across the inner city to the Freud home in the Ninth District. Adler frequented the Café Siller, walking the same short route to the coffeehouse that the Frankls used. During all this, little Vicky Frankl was born in the building just across the street from the Adler home.

Another slice into time that offers insight into the unfolding story may be taken in 1911. The Great War had not yet erupted, so some circles of Viennese psychiatry were obsessed with their own internal skirmishes. Now fifty-six, Freud was writing, receiving visitors, listening to his patients patiently, and puffing his cigars perpetually. The Adlers had moved away from Czerningasse to finer quarters in the First District, even closer to the Café Siller. Within Freud's Psychoanalytic Society some of the faithful were growing weary of particular ideas of Freud, and he met their early resistance with inflexibility and attempts at control. Adler, for example, had become disenchanted over the psychoanalytic preoccupation with sex as the basis of neurotic suffering. He was more a social activist than an intellectual and had definite ideas of his own. These Adler expressed in some crucial papers read before the Society in 1911.

The tensions mounted and the differences became too great to reconcile. Adler and several others left Freud's group and went off to form their own Society for Individual Psychology. For Freud, 1911 was a watershed year. His hopes shifted to Carl Jung, the Protestant psychiatrist of Zurich. In 1909, Jung had been a companion on Freud's only visit to the United States—to attend a conference and to receive an honorary doctorate at Clark University in Worcester, Massachusetts. They arrived in New York, disembarked from their ship and, before heading to the conference, did the town: Central Park, the great museums, Chinatown, Columbia University; they even caught some of the rides at the Coney Island amusement park. After the sessions and ceremonies at Clark, Freud, Jung, and others spent four days in a rustic cabin in the Adirondack Mountains of

New York State. Jung entertained the others by singing German songs, but already there were tensions between Freud and Jung—nudged forward on the transatlantic crossing when they had interpreted each other's dreams. Jung was put off by Freud's secrecy and by what he judged an unscientific defense of personal authority. The strain between them grew, and four years later their professional and personal relationship was finished. Freud's first "crown prince" (Adler) and now his second (Jung) had betrayed him. Both went off to start rival movements.

Adler's group took on an energy of its own. Their meetings at the Café Siller were now beyond Freud's active influence. Adler regularly held court with his disciples, engaging them in discussion together with patients he invited. The Frankls were aware of Adler's medical practice in Czerningasse and the gatherings at the Siller, even as six-year-old Vicky was running lighthearted to and from school.

Another man was living in obscurity in District 20 (Brigittenau), right next door to Leopoldstadt on the same "island." Twenty-two-year-old Adolf Hitler had a room in the massive new hostel for five hundred indigent men. The citizenry complained that the facility was too fine and fancy for its undeserving occupants. (The building is today still a men's home, looming as large as ever along Meldemannstrasse.)[6]

The young Hitler from Linz had come to Vienna in 1907, an eighteen-year-old in search of his future. He lived here and there in the city before resorting, in his near poverty, to Meldemannstrasse. Despite some artistic talent, especially for architecture, the Academy of Fine Arts had denied his application for admission. He deeply resented this. To keep himself alive he shoveled snow in front of the Imperial Hotel on the Ring for tips and peddled his sketches on the streets. He seemed innocent enough and at the time his name evoked no negative sentiments whatsoever. Though many of his housemates liked him, they would have scoffed if anyone had suggested that in just over twenty years this touchy youth would be chancellor of Germany and helmsman of the Third Reich. But young Adolf did show early signs of his gifts as a crusader, practicing his harangues on the men who happened to be in the trendy new lounges of the hostel. And he was defining his hatred of the Jews, inspired in some measure by the recent Mayor Karl Lueger in Vienna.

Young Adolf became increasingly malcontent, radical, and eager to get out of Vienna, and in May 1913 left Meldemannstrasse and slipped across the border to Munich without notifying the Austrian military draft.

He planted his feet in Germany at last, and Munich felt like home to him. There he honed his hatred and his fanatical edge. His rapid rise to power in Germany became a most implausible tale.

When Hitler left Vienna, Vicky Frankl was eight years old plus two months and living in the adjoining district. The Great War was drawing near. At the end of June 1914 an international crisis changed everything for Europe, for Vienna, and for the Frankls. The heir to the Austrian throne was assassinated in Sarajevo and, due to the wick of international treaties the incident ignited World War I, which spread like a windblown fire in a brittle forest. It seemed as though the nations were itching for a fight, and at first there was jubilation in the streets. Eager men and boys waited in long lines to enlist for something so exciting: a chance to be heroes at home while traveling the world. Apparently people believed that a war would settle old scores internationally and do it in record time. But it dragged on and on; as the years passed it became clear that no one would win this, the so-called "war to end all wars." The Frankls and their neighbors watched the monarchy unravel. Though the century was still young, the innocent, happy years were gone. This was the century in which—people remembered—anything would be possible.[7]

BECAUSE HE HAD attended medical school decades earlier, Gabriel Frankl knew the university district well. Sometimes when he had business near there, he took his little son along, possibly to encourage Vicky's interest in medicine. As they walked they passed the Anatomical Institute (still there today—the very building in which Gabriel and his classmates had dissected cadavers in the basement anatomy labs). Its pungent odors wafted out the open windows to the street, so most pedestrians walked on the opposite side of Währinger Strasse to avoid the stench. But not young Viktor. To Gabriel's surprise, Vicky actually tugged him across the street *toward* the anatomy cellars and directly *into* the smells—exercising his freedom to oppose the impulse to flee. Near the end of his life Viktor remembered how, in this incident, he "enjoyed exerting the power of the spirit to overcome the normal reaction—even at the age of seven or eight."

During the same years, Vicky's father was working in the second-floor government offices at the corner of Wollzeile and the Ring, directly across the square from a famous coffeehouse, the Café Prückel. They remain today, and between them stands a stone monument to the handsome, influential, and anti-Semitic Karl Lueger, Catholic mayor of Vienna from 1897 to 1910. Directly across the Ring is the lush Stadtpark, a public common with lawns and flower gardens, graceful walkways, benches, and statues of Franz Schubert and of Johann Strauss II playing his violin. Many times, at the entrance to the Stadtpark on the Ring, Vicky waited for his father to come out after work.

Upon meeting, the two headed for home. On the way they repeatedly played a favorite walking game. Because the Museum of Applied Arts was a structure required for the game, they passed in front of it. Today the museum exterior still descends to a ledge where it meets the sidewalk. The ledge is barely knee-high to an adult, and its top is flat and wide enough to walk on. To play the game, Vicky walked on this ledge behind and to the right of his father who remained on the sidewalk. Gabriel Frankl would hold the end of his walking stick under his arm while Vicky followed, holding its handle. Then Vicky could "drive" his father by pushing the cane forward or pulling it back to speed up or slow down and, by turning the cane, could steer his father to the left or right. The memories of this game remained with Viktor all his life.

AFTER ATTENDING THE same high school—the *Gymnasium* with perhaps two or three hundred students—both Freud and Gabriel Frankl became medical students only a few years apart at the university. Given their parallel educational journeys and Freud's eventual fame, Gabriel certainly knew of Freud even though at first none of the Frankls had direct contact with the Freuds. By the time Viktor was born the Freuds had been living for over twenty years in other more upscale districts of the city.

Because so many Jews were living in Leopoldstadt, the sting of anti-Semitism was moderated there, but the Freuds and Frankls certainly felt it. The anti-Semitism in Vienna affected all Jews more or less directly in various areas and eras. Prior to World War I the Frankl family, like the Freud family, had come south to Vienna from Moravia—Gabriel Frankl was only five years younger than Sigmund Freud. The families were part of what the anti-Semites of Vienna called the Jewish invasion,[8] and the city was getting nervous about it. The Jews were coming mainly from Eastern Europe and settling in Leopoldstadt, where the thriving and diverse Jewish community grew dramatically.

Gabriel and Elsa Frankl were pious Jews, eating only kosher food, fast-ing for Yom Kippur, and praying daily. They were not Orthodox, however, and increasingly observed their faith in a manner similar to the Reform Jews in America. Although the Frankls experienced flashes of anti-Semitism in the city, they also benefited from the respect and kindness of non-Jewish friends and associates.

An example of this occurred when Gabriel, as assistant to von Bärnreither, went with him to his country estate to take dictation for a book the government minister was writing on prison reform. In the first days von Bärnreither was puzzled that his assistant ate so little, even declining entire meals. When he asked why, Gabriel explained that his kosher diet forbade him to eat many foods on the table. Thereafter von Bärnreither sent his coachman into town twice every day to buy fresh kosher foods for Gabriel from a little Jewish market.

On the other hand there were officials who did not respect Gabriel and his religious practices. As a government employee with stenographic skills, Gabriel was frequently called upon to take minutes at business meetings. On one occasion a certain bureau chief asked Gabriel to take minutes, but he refused because the meeting was to take place on Yom Kippur. The bureau chief threatened that there would "be consequences" if Gabriel did not staff the meeting. He steadfastly refused nevertheless.

Years earlier Gabriel's medical studies had been aborted because he could not obtain a scholarship to prepare for the comprehensive exams. Such scholarships were granted almost routinely, and it is most probable that Gabriel's application was rejected because he was a Jew.

As an adult, Viktor insisted that his childhood sense of security and contentment was not diminished by discrimination. Living in Leopoldstadt, he was one among many Jewish students at school. His brother Walter, at the age of eight or so, was once offered some wine. Walter firmly refused, announcing, "I am an anti-Semite of alcohol." The strange expression came from a child confusing the German word *Antisemit* with *Antialkoholiker*—the term for teetotaler. This humorous word combination nevertheless indicates that even a very young Jewish boy was hearing, if not fully understanding, the word *Antisemit*.

FROM DAY TO day as I met with the Frankls, I updated them regarding my visits to places they had told me about. I had photographed the Stadtpark and the route that little Viktor had taken home with his father after work, and had been amazed to find the scenes exactly as Viktor had described them despite his virtual blindness: the ledge along the museum wall, the Lueger statue, the Stadtpark, the building where his father worked, Café Prückel, and the route home over the Aspern Bridge to Czerningasse. Elly was fascinated, since the story of those father-son homeward walks was new to her.

The family flat in Czerningasse also cradled many a memory for Viktor. He recalled that once in their little apartment he walked in on his father praying. Describing this, Viktor told me of the Jewish ritual that his father repeated each morning with the phylacteries: the long strap wound around the left arm, with a small leather box attached near the heart and another strapped to his father's forehead (the *Tefillin*). Viktor precisely explained that the scrolls in the small capsules had been penned by certain pious scribes who alone could write the holy words: "Hear, O Israel, the Lord our God, the Lord is One God; and you shall love the Lord your God with all your heart and with all your soul and with all your strength. These commandments that I give you today are to be placed on your heart . . ." (the *Shema Israel*).

"My father may have invited me, I suppose. But I remember as a child that once I came upon him in his morning prayers. I approached him and asked him to allow me to kiss the Dear Lord. I was five or six years old, and I knew that the capsule containing the scroll was made by someone just for such private prayers. Nevertheless—I remember it clearly—I identified the box and scroll with God. When I kissed them I kissed the Dear God. It was no mere symbol. At a primitive level of understanding, it *was God that I kissed*. For me at that time there was no difference between the symbol and the symbolized One. . . . But still I knew that the symbols themselves were man-made."

"And Viktor," Elly prompted, "you started doing these prayers each day after the war, or . . . ?" Viktor's eyes twinkled and he almost laughed. "Do we have to confess *everything?*" I reminded him that this had slipped out in a long conversation we had when we were together in our home in Chicago and perhaps he remembered it. "*Ja, ja*. I started doing the prayers when I was required to as part of my confirmation at the age of thirteen. . . . At that time I also learned that to hold a service, a minimum of ten Jewish men must be present. There has been a drama by an American playwright, and it was played here at the Theater in der Josefstadt—Elly, you were there too—a wonderful story."

"*Ja, ja.* I remember it."

"If I rightly remember," Viktor proceeded, "somewhere in New York nine Jewish men had gathered for a service, but the tenth was ill or something. I think they went out to the street and found a stranger who happened to be a Jew, but the man was absolutely atheistic, a young intellectual. But they didn't care, so they implored him to come with them: 'We need you, just for twenty minutes or so'—I don't dare to say, 'For heaven's sake' [Viktor laughing]. At the end of the story the man was converted again to his own faith—a wonderful play. One cannot find plays like this any longer in the theater. Everything now seems so shallow. What is being staged these days is so stupid, just nonsense."

"The main thing is that someone is naked," Elly added.

The play of which they were speaking is *The Tenth Man.*[9] On reading the play, set in a synagogue in Mineola, New York, I thought it could have been written by Viktor or for him. He must have delighted in its quips ("Americans, you know, are frantic about being happy") and humor (for example, one of the pious Jews remarks that the young atheist had fallen so far from his Jewish roots that he was probably no longer circumcised either). In the play, the meaning of life is questioned. And the Jewish men summon a respected rabbi to exorcise a demon from a girl who is mentally ill. All of this and the return of the young intellectual from nihilism to his Jewish faith link up solidly to Viktor's own personal journey.

One day Viktor was describing how during his childhood his father insisted that he go along on day hikes in the Vienna Woods. He complained that they were long and tedious, but his father dragged him and other family members along nonetheless. Viktor hated it.[10] I asked him if there might have been an element of revenge when he pulled his father across Währinger Strasse into the stink of the anatomy labs. He just smiled. In any case, those traumatic hikes in the woods did not extinguish his love of the outdoors.

Viktor reminisced about his boyhood vacations with his family in Porolitz, the little Czech town where his father was born. They went there often in summers and, when the war years came, the only holiday breaks away from Vienna that the family could afford were the short trips to Porolitz. The Frankls could stay there with kin at no cost and still enjoy the beautiful countryside and a change of pace. Viktor easily recalled it. "In Porolitz is the cemetery, and I remember the old wall that surrounded it. Ten or fifteen years later—after I had grown up—I went to Porolitz again and this time the wall seemed so *small.* I was very much impressed by this."

Another recollection came to Viktor from the time when he was little, not yet four and on a family vacation. A funeral was announced for 3 P.M. on a summer day. He ran down the main street in Porolitz shouting passionately to the townsfolk, "The cemetery is starting! The cemetery is starting!"

Elly offered a suggestion regarding Porolitz. "Viktor, we should tell Don about your cousin Fritz in Brünn, in Brno." Turning to me, she said, "He is eighty-eight and has himself lived a very interesting life. He is Jewish and was married to a Christian lady, and she hid him through the Hitler time in a closet—for years."

Viktor elaborated, "Even her parents, living in the same house, did not know that Fritz was hidden there! Only at midnight or later did he dare to go out to the streets for a little exercise." Then Elly updated the story.

"He is rather famous now in Czechoslovakia because they are making TV movies about his life. He kept a diary while in the closet all those years—as Anne Frank did—and now he has sold it or given it to a museum."

"Don, you should go and see Fritz," Viktor urged. "He could show you around Porolitz even. He no doubt can tell you some stories about our time together during the First World War and even after." Seeing an opportunity, Elly moved toward the phone. "Fritz knows all about Viktor's family and Porolitz, and he can show you everything. I can even call him right now." I nodded and she dialed for Fritz, who answered and perked up at the idea of the visit. We agreed on a time later that week when I would visit him.

I rented a car and made the short drive to meet Fritz Tauber at the once illustrious Slavia Hotel in Brünn. When I saw him I thought he was so similar to Viktor in appearance that I might have picked him out of a crowd: another meticulous gent, nearly ninety—and the only person still living who had known Viktor as a boy.

Fritz was dressed precisely in suit and tie and had with him a new, tan leather briefcase, which he held close. On the drive south to Porolitz from Brünn, he showed me the contents of the briefcase, piece by piece: his birth certificate; school report cards of 1913–18 with his father's signatures; a photograph of Fritz at age nine with his sister. I found myself looking into the life of a man I had known only for minutes, a life traced

by the keepsakes he had brought along. He lifted up his notice to report
for deportation to the concentration camps, number 474. He told me that
the day after receiving it, in December 1941, he went into hiding at the
urging of his ex-wife, in her home. Next he showed me his yellow star, the
very one he was to wear as Jewish identification, then a sheaf of photo-
copies of some of the 869 pages from his diary, 1941–45, which he had
written in the closet—equivalent to as many as 3,000 typewritten pages.
He said the original diaries are safe in the Jewish Museum in Prague, and
expressed the hope of having them reach an American publisher someday.
Fritz took from his case a videotape, which he explained was a duplicate
of several hours of interview he had granted in Porolitz to a crew from
Steven Spielberg's Shoah Foundation, a project to record the oral history
of the Holocaust from still-living survivors.

"You see, I was less afraid during the Hitler years because the diary
was my friend. But nobody who was not alive in that time can imagine the
atmosphere, what it was like. You cannot imagine it. We lost six years with
the Nazis, and we who survived them lost over forty years more under the
Communists—half a lifetime. My [ex-] wife died fourteen years ago, and
I miss her more and more. And so is my whole life now gone."

"These are lonely years for you, Fritz. You have so many memories of
bad things as well as wonderful things."

"Yes, yes. . . . Don, I want to tell you that Viktor telephoned me recently. I was not prepared for it, you see; when I answered he started
singing, in Czech, a song we used to sing together in our childhood. I told
Viktor that he and I are the last of our family—so many were killed. It is
sad, but we are the last."

We turned off the main road and entered Porolitz. The approach, with
the bridge into the village center, was just as Viktor had described it. Fritz
directed me to the house of his own birth and childhood. We parked the
car in order to walk about. I knew by his demeanor that we were touching
things all but sacred to him. When I took out my camera, Fritz struck a
pose against the backdrop of his boyhood home on School Street. On the
ground floor, he said, was once the family toolmaker shop; they had lived
on the second floor, which is now vacant and owned by a very old man living in Brünn.

As Fritz looked down the alley toward his old school building he said,
shaken with emotion, "My memories come back to me now as if it were
only yesterday. I see before my eyes my childhood, a very nice and good

and happy time. My father died in 1918 at age thirty-four from Spanish flu, and my mother was a good woman—you can't imagine. It looks very different in Porolitz now, though the old house, the school, and the cobblestones are very much the same as a hundred years ago. All through my life I can see the finger of the Lord. And so now is gone my whole life."

When I asked Fritz what he and Viktor had done as boys when they were together here, he pointed at the doorway to the house. "So often Viktor and I sat right here, on these steps. He told me fairy tales and stories and jokes. We went also into the forest and played there—that was our life. In the evenings, when the weather was warm, whole families sat in front of their houses on both sides of the street, talking with neighbors. A few hundred Jews lived together with a few thousand Christians with no trouble; it was harmonious in Porolitz before Hitler."

Fritz did not remember or was too much the gentleman to mention what I had learned elsewhere about the Frankl brothers. There is in Porolitz a very old church with a high steeple, the town's most visible landmark. Vicky and his older brother Walter liked to climb the steeple together on their vacations in the village. The view of the countryside from there was striking, and the boys blended a little of themselves into the scenery. Occasionally they urinated into the steeple's rain gutters and watched the flow, beneath the smiling eyes of angels—and under the scowls of saints who are in heaven by grace alone.

Necessity may explain quite a different misconduct of Walter, Viktor, and cousin Fritz. In the era of World War I, food shortages were widespread. Near-famine conditions existed in the cities, but farms surrounded Porolitz. The boys used to steal corn from the edges of nearby fields and begged for snacks from local farmers to quiet their raging appetites. Only once did Viktor fill his empty belly with sour pears. He got very sick and never ate them again even to fight off hunger.

"Viktor has told me," I said to Fritz, "about the desperate situation in Vienna during and after the First War . . . he said that everyone in the family learned to survive with little, and to understand what it was like to be poor."

"Yes, yes. It was desperate here also in Porolitz. After the war we did not even have coal for heat. But somehow we survived it."

Fritz and I chatted all the way back to Brünn. I learned that he lived alone and was lonely. I thanked him for giving life to Viktor's boyhood, and for opening up their story, and his own. As we parted I felt the sadness in him. His last words to me were, "I hope you will come again to see me. If you do come again, I hope I am alive then. And when you see Viktor and Elly, give them my best greetings. Good-bye. Bye-bye."

I drove back to Vienna that evening, and the next day delivered those best greetings as I told Viktor and Elly about my time with cousin Fritz. I mentioned how Fritz had remembered so clearly the phone call from Viktor when he sang the Czech song from their childhood. Viktor explained that he had learned it at the end of World War I from Czech soldiers who were tromping through Porolitz. It was a marching song about a recruit who had met "a totally black girl"—whether African or camouflaged or gritty from war—and he loved her dearly. Viktor whistled the entire tune, followed by singing it in original Czech.

On another occasion when the Frankl family was together the mood was jovial. They all were interested in my visit with Fritz, and so I got going on it again. "When Fritz was showing me the family house in Porolitz, he mistakenly told me that Viktor was born there and lived the first year of his life there." The place broke into laughter when Viktor clarified, "He should have been telling you about the house where I was *not* born!" Elly jumped in, "It was also the house where you did *not* spend the first year of your life! Viktor, tell Don about the society you started with Fritz in Porolitz."

"Fritz Tauber and I, in the town where he was born, founded an organization which we called 'The Alliance of Seekers of Small Benefits' [Viktor here used the more ambiguous original Yiddish words, *Club der kleinen Rebbach-Sucher*]. One of the donors to our Alliance was the son of the Porolitz baker. My elder brother Walter would join us in singing operatic songs in the street. Then out would come the baker's son with slices of fresh bread for us—one of the 'small benefits.' And so we tried to find various sources for such benefits, for gaining something. So I jokingly suggested that we organize the Alliance."

At the end of that particular visit in Vienna and on the plane home, I started to reflect on my experiences in Austria and the Czech Republic. Back in Chicago, and only a month after the day I spent with Fritz Tauber in Porolitz and Brünn, I received word from Vienna that he had died suddenly. I remembered that on that day I had offered to drive Fritz to his home but he, for whatever reason, preferred to return to the Slavia Hotel with me and take the streetcar from there. I thought, as I watched him walk toward the tracks with that briefcase of treasures tucked under his arm, "Oh, what he has seen in his time. Viktor and Elly were right. Fritz has helped me understand their story." After the news of his death, I listened to my recordings and viewed photographs of my day with Fritz, reliving the scenes and sentiments of those hours now sealed by the closing of a courageous human story. Fritz was a humble, grateful, perhaps stubborn person, and hints of clever rascal still showed through in the last weeks of his life. But despite his hope, he would not be there when I returned. And cousin Viktor was now alone with his boyhood memories.

CHAPTER 2

High School and Worlds Beyond,
1916–1924

IT WAS 1916 when Vicky Frankl completed elementary school at the *Volksschule* in Czerninplatz. The First World War had been raging for nearly two years, and times were miserable even in places that were not battlefields. The economic drain on the nations was ruinous and widespread shortages and outages were normal. Like most families, the Frankls barely got by. On many school days Vicky took his turn for the family by leaving home at 3 A.M. to go to the Landstrasser market; there he took his place in a line of people waiting to buy bread or whatever they could with whatever means they had. Even in winter, sometimes in bitterest cold, Vicky waited until 7 A.M., when his mother arrived to take his place in line so he could go to school.

When the war ended in 1918 the hardships continued as the world emerged from its most catastrophic conflict. Labor strikes in Vienna only made matters worse, and shipments of food to the city from other countries often never got through. As the monarchy collapsed, the new German and Austrian republics were formed. Fortunately for the Frankl family, they could count on Gabriel's salary. But the poorest of the city lived in starvation conditions, and procuring coal was impossible for many who needed it desperately in winter. Even the majestic hotels were unheated, and many newborns died in hospitals because of the cold.[1]

Competent Jews stepped into the postwar leadership vacuum in Vienna, but the anti-Semitism of the city smoldered and hissed as before. Fear of a Jewish takeover of more of the press, government, and business was deepening.

The three Frankl children—Walter, Viktor, and Stella—each in turn attended the *Volksschule* down the street. Stella continued at a different high school, but Walter and Viktor went to the *Sperlgymnasium,* the same high school formerly attended by Sigmund Freud, then by their father, and finally by Alfred Adler. During Freud's years it was located at Tabor Strasse 24, where Gabriel Frankl also went to school. Freud and Gabriel had been at the *Sperlgymnasium* together for two or three overlapping years—in an era when teachers remained in their jobs for decades. Certainly Freud, Gabriel Frankl, and Alfred Adler had some of the same teachers. After Freud's graduation and before Gabriel's the school was relocated to Kleine Sperlgasse 20, where the buildings stand today largely unchanged. Behind the boys school and across the yard was the girls school, a building marked now by a plaque identifying its role in the deportations of the 1940s.

Viktor's brother had a mixed experience at high school. Walter did not take to academia, earned mediocre grades, and eventually dropped out to pursue his interest in architecture. According to the family he was a good artist with a particular flair for interior design. Early in school he showed some inclination for drama also. Sister Stella, like Walter, was not the academic type and she turned to fashion, women's clothing especially. She sketched designs for dresses and even did some in watercolors. Perhaps there was in the family a propensity for the artistic, since Viktor developed an aptitude for drawing caricatures. But his ardent intellectual quest— well under way in high school—was unique and his siblings were poles apart from him in their pursuits.

In the fall of 1916, eleven-year-old Vicky enrolled for his first term at the *Sperlgymnasium*. He was a good student, though often tardy and preoccupied with his own interests. He focused most keenly on things that were not required at school, once begging his parents for money to buy a book on everyday physics—the physics of the kitchen. On another occasion Vicky actually begged for money on the street so he could buy a certain book by Goethe. His interest in Goethe diminished, however, when his teachers demanded the same reading of him. His grades could have been better, and they never gauged what the boy was learning through his intense concentration on things he liked.

During his eight years at the *Sperlgymnasium*, each school day Vicky scurried from the family flat, raced across the broad Prater Strasse, down Schmelzgasse and Grosse Sperlgasse to the school. It was a ten-minute run but seldom did he get to school on time. Vicky learned to justify his tardiness with a dubious maneuver. Repeatedly on his overdue arrivals, Vicky went directly to the lectern and explained, "Please excuse me, sir. I know

I am late. But you see it is because I am not on time, and that is why I am
tardy once more." The tone of his voice implied that he was offering a reason for being late. The preoccupied and half-attentive teacher accepted the
explanation and waved Vicky to his seat, continuing the lesson of the hour.

The Frankl family was close-knit, and its five characters were a study
in differences and similarities. Walter grew tall with a large frame and
Stella, though the youngest, became almost as big. Viktor was small. That
may be why he recalled with some satisfaction that once—as an exception—he got the better of big brother Walter in a tussle. None of the three
was naturally athletic. Stella did take to dancing, however, and liked outdoor activities occasionally. At least once she sped down a snowy hill standing behind Viktor on a single borrowed ski—though he himself was
ill-equipped for strenuous sport. Indeed, as a young child Vicky was not
only short but spindly and weak. His peculiarly small legs were cause for
concern, and the family doctor warned that he should never play soccer—
a restriction not particularly distressing for Viktor. But he remembered
well his competition in a high school fencing tournament using a foil he
had acquired somehow. Still it was not until he discovered mountain
climbing later on that he fully defied, on Alpine cliffs, his apparent physical limitations.

Walter and Stella as they matured through high school became in appearance more like mother Elsa, herself not obese but a substantial
woman. It was she who enfolded her family in affection and attention. She
was a woman devoted also to her husband Gabriel, openly expressive of
her feelings. Viktor often described his mother as kindhearted, deeply devout, and the very incarnation of human warmth.

Yet Viktor identified more with his father and looked the part with his
lean, straight profile. Once past childhood Viktor became even more like
his father temperamentally: self-disciplined and resolute, and more ready
to convey his love as fidelity than through physical contact. Father and son
were Spartan in manner, careful with money and with time. Since they
were both private with regard to religion, neither was ever fanatical or
pushy about it. Nevertheless Gabriel was deeply rooted in his faith and so
he was able to face life with confidence and hope. Viktor was grateful for
what he called his own inborn optimism,[2] and he was genuinely proud to
be so much like Papa.

Some of Gabriel's characteristic reserve melted away when he was
with Stella. They understood one another and drew out the best in each

other, as a parent and child may do. Often they went together on errands, talking and listening like old friends. It might be said that brother Walter was not as agile with close relationships. He was a practical joker, and in working with his hands he was both creative and skillful. Apparently he also showed flashes of leadership among his peers, as when he organized the cast for plays during vacations in Porolitz. By everything I have ever heard, Walter was a good boy and a thoroughly decent man to the day of his untimely death.

Even within the family it was said that no one would imagine that Viktor and Stella were brother and sister. Viktor was dark and wiry and tended to be frail even as a young adult. Stella could have passed for a blond and blue-eyed Scandinavian, robust and imposing. Other contrasts between them played out over their lifetimes, shifting in some measure as they aged. She was a very social person and knew lots of people in the neighborhoods where she lived, and she found pleasure in prattle. In contrast, Viktor shunned small talk and could hardly tolerate social chatter with strangers or acquaintances—what he relished was the give-and-take of a swift, logical dialogue, even in high school. When Viktor became impatient with Stella it was usually over her perfumes or her simple interests, which to him seemed silly. Though she was not dull, Stella lacked intellectual curiosity. She never read much, not even what her brother Viktor wrote later on—except perhaps *The Unconscious God*, which he dedicated in 1948 "to my sister."[5] According to the Frankls in Vienna and Stella's family in Australia, Stella was immensely proud of Viktor and she defended him whenever she heard him criticized, as if he could do no wrong.

Although at casual glance Stella seemed much more like mother and Viktor like father, when it came to adversity both lived out the stoic temperament so characteristic of their father, facing the blows of fate with composure and courage. Outliving brother Walter, neither Viktor nor Stella ever became especially sentimental and remained cheerful people. They teased and bantered and both treasured good jokes—in the family, cheerfulness and humor went hand-in-hand. Later in Stella's life her daughter Liesl—who never knew her uncle Walter—readily identified the comic capacity that Stella and Viktor had in common. And she recalled that the humor need not be proper—offbeat or vulgar one-liners were just fine as long as they were clever and well placed.

The jokes in Viktor's repertoire were many and, as his sense of humor ripened, he used the same word-care and precision in telling them whether they were respectable or unrefined. Usually he did not tell jokes one upon another, preferring that they emerge from the context of conversation—he had a knack for using jokes to illuminate a point. However, if Viktor wanted to tell a joke for which there was no context, sometimes he would create one just so he could tell the joke.

When I reflect on the Frankl family there comes to mind a German saying, which I heard many times in Vienna. It is a kind of tribute to the parents and ancestors of a person: "He comes from a good stable." Walter, Stella, and Viktor came from a good stable and, though we know little about their grandparents, certainly there are sturdy, upright people in the lineage. That helps to explain the decency and humanness of the five Frankls even in the face of the calamities to come. And as we center on Viktor's journey, one of the marks of it is his enduring fondness and esteem for his parents. To the day of his death he was mindful of them in a manner we seldom see in modern times. Over his life span Viktor honored his mother and his father, in keeping with one of the great commandments of their faith.

OVER SOME TOLERANT objections among his family, the mature Viktor was open with me about his sexual awakening as a young boy. Even before his puberty, the live-in domestic helper, whom Viktor described as well built, allowed him and his older brother—together or separately—some delicate explorations. Sometimes when the parents were out of the house she went to bed nearly naked and the boys could see her genitals as she pretended to be asleep. At other times she permitted the boys to remove the clothing below her waist and to fondle her as she "slept" on the floor.

> Eventually I came to understand the relationship between sex and marriage, and this even before I became aware of the connection between sex and propagation. I was probably in junior high school when I decided that, as a married man someday, I would try to stay awake, at least for a while, so I wouldn't miss having sex with my wife while we were "sleeping together." Are people so stupid, I asked myself, that they miss something so beautiful while they are sleeping? I was determined to enjoy it fully awake.[4]

THE PRATER WAS significant throughout Viktor's boyhood. As a child, on one of his many walks along its lanes, Viktor imagined that one day he would write a book that would help many people. But he would not become famous for it, since he would not attach his name to it. It is not widely known that Viktor attempted to have the first edition of *Man's Search for Meaning* published anonymously in 1946. But for the second edition Frankl, yielding to pressure from friends and colleagues, allowed his name to appear on the cover.

As he started his teens, Viktor was going more frequently to the Prater alone. When he did go in the company of school friends it was not for sport or simply to hang around with them. Rather, he went there in order to engage them and others in discussions about great thinkers or new ideas. This became a high school pastime for him and the interactions—on the park benches or walkways—circled increasingly around philosophy and the new discipline of psychology. He was filling his notebooks. But what stirred Viktor? What ideas drew him?

While his fascination with things medical never diminished, new worlds opened up to Viktor as he discovered philosophers who wrestled with questions that already were taking hold of him. Through the standard Austrian curriculum he learned about the ancient Greeks—Socrates, Plato, and Aristotle—and his excitement was provoked. In fact one of Viktor's teachers started calling him "Mr. Philosopher." The security provided by his family allowed Viktor to chase his interests. In doing so, however, he missed out on much of what typically occupied and entertained his schoolmates. But he didn't seem to notice or care as he mulled over possible relationships between philosophy and the new science of psychology. He picked up on psychology outside of school—through his own reading, attending public lectures, and through the ferment of ideas in a great city. He organized in notebooks what he was learning, then clarified and concentrated it. Increasingly he saw connections and conveyed his discoveries to his less-focused schoolmates, whether in the hallways, play yards, classes, or in the Prater.

He kept an eye on announcements of open lectures. In the evenings Viktor attended adult education classes in psychology. Like any active boy he liked to sleep in, but on many weekend mornings he would be up at dawn to make his way across town for lectures on psychoanalysis at the

Ottakring *Volkshochschule*. Though Freud and psychotherapy became the most exciting discoveries for young Viktor, he also was enticed by applied and experimental psychology, perhaps because of their close ties to physiology and medicine. He learned about the psychogalvanic reflex phenomenon, as it was called at the time. More recently the same phenomenon has been called simply the GSR (galvanic skin response), an aspect of EDA (electrodermal activity). Viktor found out that when a person is stirred up, there are changes in the rate at which electrical currents are conducted along the surface of the skin, especially on the hands and forehead. This skin conductance is one of the measures now used in "lie detection," which is based on the theory that lying causes bodily arousal in a way that telling the truth does not. When lying we might be able to mask more obvious signs of arousal—such as heavy breathing or sweating—but, as the theory goes, we cannot hide subtle signs of arousal of which we are not even aware. Skin conductance is one of these, though lie detection by such means is questionable. What fascinated Viktor about the GSR phenomenon was the link between physiology and psychology: tracking imperceptible changes on the skin's surfaces that originate with something psychological and emotional!

Viktor brought a demonstration of skin conductance into his classroom at the *Sperlgymnasium*. After recruiting a volunteer, Viktor connected his classmate to a borrowed galvanometer, which projected onto the wall a meter that indicated any changes in the GSR. When Viktor cleverly said the name of the volunteer's girlfriend in front of the class, the pointer on the wall jumped. Viktor thought it a good thing that the room had been darkened for projection so that his volunteer was spared the embarrassment of blushing. But the GSR was not the only information Viktor brought to his school.

In Vienna—where Victorian taboos regarding sexuality were still severe—controversy had erupted over Freud's bold new assertions about the predominant role of sex, even in infants! As everywhere and always, plenty was going on out behind the barn and in the bushes among Viennese in spite of the sexual taboos of the time. Freud's ideas about sexuality were scintillating to the boys at the *Sperlgymnasium*, and Viktor established himself as a reliable source of information about these elements of psychoanalysis.

So while other boys were eyeing the girls and playing soccer, Viktor was tripping off to hear more lectures at Wagner-Jauregg's University Psychiatric Clinic. He was soaking up psychoanalysis directly from Freud's own disciples, particularly Eduard Hitschmann and Paul Schilder.

THIS STORY IS not about great philosophers and scientists. They crop up, however, since Viktor's life cannot be understood apart from the ideas that permeated education during his developmental years. Just as he was beginning to develop a critical capability, Viktor was overtaken by the negative and pessimistic vision of certain philosophers and scientists whose views seemed to be verified by the ongoing war.

On a particular class day, when Viktor was about thirteen, he was sitting in his assigned seat at the *Sperlgymnasium*. The science teacher was pacing among the rows of students as he lectured.[5] Then he made a statement that mirrored the cynicism of the time. "In the final analysis, life is nothing more than a combustion process, a process of oxidation." Though it was proper to raise one's hand to be called upon by the teacher, Viktor jumped up at the statement and confronted the teacher with his question. "Sir, if this is so, then what can be the meaning of life?" The teacher had no answer, perhaps because he actually believed what he had said. This incident shows Viktor already struggling against the notion that life is "nothing more than." It also may be an early instance of Viktor's impetuous manner in confronting ideas to which he objected.

In any case, it was around this time that Viktor entered a personal crisis, what he later called "my atheistic, or rather agnostic, period." While he did not plunge into a debilitating despair, the crisis was a serious stretch of searching, questioning, with even some spells of hopelessness. And it was of defining significance for Viktor.

Prior to the crisis, things had seemed relatively simple. Now values and meaning were up for grabs, and the pessimism Viktor experienced was out of character for him. He yielded to the belief that life is pointless and futile, and he experienced some of the dehumanizing effects of that belief. Though Viktor was troubled intellectually, there was no eclipse of his fascination with psychology, whether as a laboratory science or as Freud's new psychotherapy. Viktor's comprehension of both psychology and medicine ultimately was enriched by the shake-up he was going through. He was realizing for the first time—in an existential way—how deadly was the cynicism he was facing. His struggle forced him to confront the question of what really makes a person human after all. As a result, his formerly naive vision of psychiatry—as a vocation which combines medicine, psychology, and philosophy—may have taken on both new weight and new luster for him.

Viktor's quest intensified as he read and listened. Dogged by the question of life's meaning, his natural optimism was hijacked for a time by his apprehension over the loss of faith and the shattering of traditional values during the seemingly endless war.

By the time he was fourteen he was reading Wilhelm Ostwald (1853–1932), the German physical chemist, and Gustav Theodor Fechner (1801–87), physician, physicist, and one of the founders of experimental psychology. Scientific psychology by then was standing on its own feet as a kind of stepchild of philosophy (pondering the questions) and physiology (investigating by new scientific methods)—both converging on human nature and behavior. As he pieced together streams of thought, he expanded his notebooks, filling their pages, zooming toward certain themes and caring less about grades and particular subjects at school. In 1974, Derek Gill, British author and biographer of Elisabeth Kübler-Ross, expressed amazement that Frankl had begun his philosophical quest at the age of thirteen and that—after the war ended in 1918 and certainly by 1920 when Viktor turned fifteen—he was doing some philosophizing of his own.

At that time Viktor began corresponding with Professor Freud, who was living at the now-famous Berggasse 19 address in the university district. Taken in by psychoanalysis, Viktor became a Freudian as much as a young student could. As he came upon articles that he thought would be of interest, he mailed them to Freud. Each time Freud replied within two or three days with a handwritten postcard. This correspondence continued for several years, though all of it was lost later when the SS deported the Frankls.

When Viktor was seventeen he went to the Prater to write a particular paper for school. This time, tapping into his own interests as usual, he titled the paper, "On Mimic Affirmation and Negation"—and what he wrote shows that Viktor had already taken in a good deal of psychoanalysis. He thought Freud might be interested in the paper and sent a copy to him. Viktor was astounded when Freud wrote back: "I have sent your paper on to the *International Journal of Psychoanalysis.* I hope you have no objection." Two years later the article appeared therein.[6] That was 1924, the year in which Viktor graduated from the *Sperlgymnasium*, when his senior paper also clearly showed his psychoanalytic tilt.

While he latched onto Freud as to no other, at the same time Viktor began his lifelong connections to existentialism, a European movement in philosophy that arose in reaction to other dominant philosophical and scientific systems of the time. The existentialists, a large group of loosely related thinkers, stressed the uniqueness of each person, existing in the actual circumstances of the here-and-now. In an unfriendly world, the individual might be isolated and alienated, but still was free to make decisions, to take stands, and to be responsible for them. The writings of the Danish philosopher and theologian Søren Kierkegaard (1813–55), once they were translated throughout Europe, became a seedbed from which existentialism grew. By the time Viktor was in high school, Friedrich Nietzsche (1844–1900), who had been inspired by the German writer Arthur Schopenhauer (1788–1860), became another source of what came to be known as existentialism.

The works of Schopenhauer, Nietzsche, and other existentialists had a refreshing ring of authenticity in troubled times, of challenge to old and established ways of thinking. Though some existentialists were attempting to counteract the nihilism of which Viktor was now aware, in himself and all around him, others fed into the nihilism (from the Latin *nihil*, nothing) that rejected religion and traditional values.[7] The pessimistic existentialists undercut faith in life's meaning. It was said that values are nothing more than creations of the feelings and individual preferences of people living in a hostile world. Everything is arbitrary and unintelligible. There is no objective reality, nothing above and beyond, no one and no thing transcendent. Any talk of ultimate meaning is self-delusion. In so harsh a world, into which we are thrown, we may strive to make of our lives what we can, but to what end? Those existentialists who were fundamentally pessimistic, atheistic, and negative seemed to carry the day. While the rash of suicides among Vienna's high school students was connected to their exacting exams and to social and sexual problems, thoughtful young people were also affected by the spreading nihilism of the time.

Whatever the motives of Schopenhauer, Nietzsche, and other philosophers, whatever they saw wrong with religion, whatever social and historical tides they were attempting to stem, whatever they tried to do to offset nihilism, they also fostered pessimism. And it spread first among philosophers and scientists and then onward to the everyday lives of reflective people—and the young Viktor began to see nihilism as a threat not only to his own personhood but to the whole of society.

Fortunately, there were existentialists whose viewpoints were more positive and even religious, and these also were spreading by the 1920s when Viktor was in crisis. Martin Heidegger (1889–1976), the great German philosopher, was somewhat more optimistic or at least wanted to be. He was concerned about nihilism and its effects. Gabriel Marcel (1889–1973), the French playwright and philosopher, became a believing Roman Catholic after serving with the Red Cross in World War I. Marcel, critical of his dismal existentialist countryman Sartre, learned from his own experience how indispensable was a commitment to others and about the role of faith and hope. For a few years Marcel even accepted the tag "Christian existentialist."

Back in Germany, Karl Jaspers (1883–1969), himself a psychiatrist, stressed moral attitudes and behaviors and allowed for something signifi-cant beyond and beside us, even for a transcendent Being. Martin Buber (1878–1965), the Jewish mystic and writer who had been born in Vienna and educated at its university, never fit the mold of atheistic, negative ex-istentialism. Rather, through his own exploration of Jewish Hasidism he found himself renewed by the spiritual riches of that heritage and devoted himself to invigorating the faith of Jews everywhere. Out of his obsession with the necessity of genuine encounter among human beings—*I and Thou* his most famous book—Buber was even active in promoting good re-lations between Jews and Arabs. So Viktor, undercut by the pessimism of the day, also experienced a hearty philosophical diet which began to revive his hope that life could have meaning after all.

By the time of his graduation from high school Viktor was not only torn by nihilism and tossed about among the existentialists, but his thor-oughgoing enchantment with psychoanalysis was also heading into rough seas. He began to see that nihilism ties in to particular ways of looking at human nature. What we think about being human has everything to do with how we understand life, how we behave, and ultimately how we treat one another. He gradually became convinced that the human spirit is what makes us uniquely what we are, though reductionists—those who reduced life and human nature to "nothing but"—denied, ignored, or discounted any such spirit.

Thanks to other philosophers and teachers,[8] Viktor in time would emerge from his nihilistic crisis. He no longer simply accepted what he heard and read but began to forge his own convictions. As his crisis had come on gradually, so he overcame it gradually during the years of his medical training.

In 1980, seventy-five-year-old Frankl addressed the First World Congress of Logotherapy in San Diego, California, on this subject. These are his own words.

> But what about the contention that each founder of a psychotherapeutic school in the final analysis describes in his system his own neurosis and writes in his books his own case history? Well, I am not entitled to speak, in this context, of Sigmund Freud or Alfred Adler but as far as logotherapy is concerned, I gladly and readily confess that as a young man I had to go through the hell of despair over the apparent meaninglessness of life, through total and ultimate nihilism. But I wrestled with it like Jacob with the angel did until I could "say yes to life in spite of everything," until I could develop *immunity* against nihilism. I developed logotherapy. It is a pity that other authors, instead of immunizing their readers against nihilism, inoculate them with their own cynicism which is a defense mechanism . . . that they have built up against their own nihilism.
>
> It is a pity because today more than ever the despair over the apparent meaninglessness of life has become an urgent and topical issue on a worldwide scale. Our industrial society is out to satisfy each and every need, and our consumer society even creates some needs in order to satisfy them. The most important need, however, the basic need for meaning, remains—more often than not—ignored and neglected. And it is so "important" because once the will to meaning is fulfilled, human beings become happy, but also become able and capable of suffering, of coping with frustrations and tensions, and—if need be—are prepared to give their life. . . . On the other hand, if the will to meaning is frustrated, they are equally inclined to take their life, and they do so in the midst, and in spite, of all the welfare and affluence surrounding them. . . .[9]

Viktor believed, in fact, that the ultimate outcome of nihilism is a devastating one. In 1954, less than a decade after his liberation from the deathcamps, he wrote the following for the introduction to the first English edition of his first book, *The Doctor and the Soul*:

> If we present a man with a concept of man which is not true, we may well corrupt him. When we present man as an automaton of reflexes, as a mind-machine, as a bundle of instincts, as a pawn of drives and reactions, as a mere product of instinct, heredity, and environment, we feed the nihilism to which modern man is, in any case, prone.
>
> I became acquainted with the last stage of that corruption in my second concentration camp, Auschwitz. The gas chambers of Auschwitz were the ultimate consequence of the theory that man is nothing but the product of heredity and environment—or, as the Nazi liked to say, of "Blood and Soil." I am absolutely convinced that the gas chambers of Auschwitz, Treblinka, and Majdanek were ultimately prepared not in some Ministry or other in Berlin, but rather at the desks and in the lecture halls of nihilistic scientists and philosophers.[10]

There was an incident in Viktor's young life that may illuminate the riddle of human nature. On a summer day the Frankls took me to visit Elly's childhood neighborhood. On the way in a taxi, we were crossing the Reichsbrücke, one of the main bridges across the Danube. Viktor, ever the commander in chief on these tours, turned around from his front seat in the cab.

> There is a story associated with this bridge. During WWI, I had to come to Kaisermühlen—where we are going now—to get one-eighth of a kilogram of flour. Everything was rationed, and I had one coupon from his Excellency Minister von Bärnreither, the boss of my father. And I could use it. So I was walking, with no money for the streetcar, and about here I was suddenly stopped by four or five young rowdies, about twelve years old as I was. They surrounded me as if to attack me. Their first question was, "Are you Jewish?"
>
> And I remember clearly that I answered by a question: "Yes, but does this mean I am not also a human being?" By this question I disarmed them, and they didn't hurt me and let me go. It

was a human appeal to their own humanness, as it were, making them immediately conscious of their responsibility to behave, confronted with another human being, in a human way. . . . This is my only memory of Kaisermühlen, except that years later we went for picnics at Gänsehäufel.

At once a Jew and a human being. As we have seen, there were people and philosophers who helped Viktor out of his intellectual quagmire. But one of the most powerful saving influences of his life is still understated. Early in high school Viktor had his Bar Mitzvah and by it entered into Jewish adulthood and personal responsibility for the commandments. One of the great commandments was that he should honor his mother and father. They were at once Jews and human—faithful Jews whose real human presence remained with Viktor long after their deaths and until his own. And though Gabriel and Elsa entered the tempest of the 1940s alongside Viktor, and perished therein not far from him, they lived on mysteriously in him, the public psychiatrist and private Jew. Viktor's anchor was set in the faith and hopefulness of his parents.

It is now clear from research on "modeling" that the example we actually live out in front of our children is far more powerful than what we say to them. Viktor's father and mother were people for whom substance mattered more than appearance. I am convinced that there was no thing and no one that so braced him for the future than these simple portraits: his mother Elsa, warmhearted, loving, and pious in the simplest and best way; and a humble and honorable Gabriel Frankl, with a black leather strap wound around his left arm, on his forehead and near his heart little leather boxes holding Holy Writ, and on his lips each morning without fail, the *Shema*—and also this morning greeting to the Most High: "*Modeh ani*—I thank You—King everlasting and eternal, for having mercifully returned my soul to me. Great is Your Faithfulness."

CHAPTER 3

Medicine, Freud, and Adler,
1924–1934

THE SUMMER OF 1924 was a transition time for Viktor. He had just completed high school by doing well on his *Matura*—the grueling exams that Freud, in his own school days, called "the martyrdom." In the fall Viktor was to start medical school at the University of Vienna while continuing to live with his family in Czerningasse. The deprivations of the years following World War I were easing during the lull before the economic depression. In some places the Roaring Twenties were underway, but the nations of Europe were still climbing out of war's aftermath. There was growing apprehension, especially in Europe, over Germany's industrial recovery and its failures to meet its reparations obligations set by treaty at war's end. In Vienna, as elsewhere, things were stabilizing somewhat, though the times were still marked by unemployment, economic problems, anti-Semitism, and fierce political rivalries.

During that summer Viktor, along with most people, was unaware of the implications of what was taking place in Germany just north of the Austrian border. Some thirty-five miles west of Munich and 280 miles west of Vienna is the town of Landsberg, on the Lech River. There, thirty-five-year-old Adolf Hitler was locked up in the Landsberg jail. After sneaking from Vienna to Munich in 1913 he had volunteered and served acceptably in the German army in World War I. While signs of Hitler's anti-Semitism had emerged during his boyhood and youth in Austria— first in Linz, then in Vienna—it was in Munich that it took on its ultimate character as a venomous crusade.[1] Since the end of World War I, Hitler had been attracting a following for his radical agenda. His charisma was becoming more crass and his harangues more defiant and caustic. In 1923, Hitler thought the time had come to overthrow legitimate authority in Munich. So he flexed what political muscle he had in the famous beer hall

Putsch of November 8. Some of his comrades in revolution were seriously injured or killed by police gunfire while Hitler, with minor injuries, was only arrested. He was demoralized by his misjudgment and the failed mutiny, and during his first weeks in the Landsberg prison he starved himself. But he soon rallied, recovered, and took up his causes again. In April 1924 he finally was tried and sentenced to the balance of a five-year prison term. For high treason, that was a slap on the wrist.

In his prison cell Hitler turned to creating his political autobiography, *Mein Kampf.* While writing, he hardened in his convictions that the Jews were no mere pest, but a conspiracy that threatened the German nation and its culture. In addition to fuming over the "Jewish question," Hitler was enraged by the humiliation of Germany in the war and under the Treaty of Versailles. Bolshevism and Wall Street were also favorite targets of his diatribes.[2]

As prisoners go, Hitler was well off: a room with a river view, associates to assist him with his book, and a stream of gift-bearing visitors. And just as Viktor was starting his first Christmas vacation as a medical student in Vienna, Hitler was released at Landsberg after serving less than a year of his sentence. Then he resumed his climb to the helm of the Third Reich.

Very early in Viktor's time at the university, while wrestling with the tensions between Freud and Adler, he was also entering new circles of acquaintance. His admiration for two prominent physicians, Rudolf Allers and Oswald Schwarz, grew steadily. The two were researchers with medical specialties, and both had broad interests that included psychology. Simultaneously he came under the spell of the writings of philosopher Max Scheler. Viktor found, to his relief and delight, that this philosopher fueled a reevaluation of what was happening to him. Scheler (Germany, 1874–1928) shed new light for Viktor on the affirmation of life. Not so much an existentialist, Scheler was a phenomenologist in the tradition of Edmund Husserl. Son of a Jewish mother and Protestant father, Scheler was converted to the Roman Catholic Church and for a time his writings reflected this faith affiliation. Though his religious orientation shifted over time, as it did with many philosophers, Scheler's writings caught Viktor at a crucial time—two books especially: *Formalism in Ethics and Non-Formal Ethics of Values* and *On the Eternal in Man.* Scheler integrated emotions and human thought, and was broadly interested in personal and religious experiences. His lucid, understandable writing about values, ethics, and love drew so many readers that he became one of the most popular philosophers of the 1920s. Viktor owed many pinnacles of insight to Scheler, and these "aha" experiences of discovery he later called "spiritual orgasms." One of these revelations was seeing through "reductionism"—explaining complex matters by pointing to some simpler underlying cause or process—and another was realizing that it is not we who question life but rather life that asks questions of us.

Once Viktor began to see through reductionism he realized how common was the practice among thinkers and scientists of "reducing" human beings to just one element or another. Now he caught professors and writers, again and again, focusing so intently on one aspect of a person that they, in fact, were no longer looking at a human being at all. Instead they had reduced the person to nothing but a bundle of physical tissue ruled by appetites (biologism), or to nothing but a psychic creature pushed by needs (psychologism), or to nothing but a social creature driven to compete (sociologism).

DURING 1924, FREUD was himself unnerved by international and Viennese politics, but he was writing book after book and his fame was spreading. Just a year earlier *The Ego and the Id* had been published, which young Viktor had devoured along with the earlier *Beyond the Pleasure Principle* (1920)—two small but significant books.

Freud was not a big man physically, but he was gifted with extraordinary energy. In addition to writing he was analyzing his patients, negotiating the troubled waters of psychoanalytic politics, and coping with local and international visitors and correspondence. The Freud flat at Berggasse 19 was both home and workplace. For any real respite he relied on his long summer vacations away from the city.

Even though Viktor was more than flirting with Adler's psychology, he still was interested chiefly in psychoanalysis. So he wrote to ask Professor Freud about joining the Vienna Psychoanalytic Society. He received another postcard from Freud, this one urging him to contact his loyal disciple Paul Federn (1871–1950)—Freud's "Apostle Paul." A meeting was arranged.

During a 1993 afternoon with the Frankls, Viktor described his watershed interview.

Paul Federn's son Ernest is here in Vienna, an eminent psychoanalyst in the small group of orthodox Freudians. When I started medical school in 1924, Paul Federn was the secretary of the Vienna Psychoanalytic Society. Paul was a tall man, bald and with a black beard and very dark, shadowy eyes. I asked him for a meeting and he invited me to come to him. And so I sat in his waiting room for about ten minutes, and then he appeared at his office door. "Please?" And so I said, "My name is Viktor Frankl and Professor Freud has referred me to you to explore the possibility of joining the Society as a member."

He invited me to come in and to sit down across from his desk. And then, with his dark eyes, he looked into my eyes for about two minutes without speaking a word. He seemingly wanted me to react—as a test to see how I would behave. And as he looked into my eyes, I took it, and looked back at him. Then he asked me a question about why I had come, and immediately after he asked me, "And what about your neurosis?" [Viktor was impersonating Federn, demonstrating both his slow speech and eerie demeanor.]

In a cool manner I reacted by saying, "My goodness, I wouldn't speak of a neurosis, but I certainly would admit I am somewhat of an anal character." With such objectivity, in a detached manner, I had confessed that I was an anal character in strictly psychoanalytic terminology. "After all, I certainly have some characteristics of pedantry and orderliness, of compulsive cleanliness—these signs of an anal character."

Federn was impressed by my professionality and objectivity at the age of nineteen, by my openly admitting that I was neurotic—in strictly psychoanalytic terms. Then he urged me to wait for membership and to finish my medical studies in a normal sequence without being distracted. After all, he said, if you are lying down on a couch for years, and if you don't have problems, you *create* them!

So I left Federn's office with this advice and went to the Kanalpark—at that time there was a small park along the Danube Canal—and I sat down there. I was deeply stirred and, as it were, the scales fell off my eyes, and it became clear to me: What kind of a science is psychoanalysis if you can't judge it on rational grounds, but you have to be indoctrinated first before you can agree with it? Decades later Sir Karl Popper said that both Marxism and Freudianism are not scientific approaches because they are dependent on extra-scientific conditions. Unless you are the son of a common laborer you cannot understand Marxism. Unless you have undergone five years of training analysis you cannot understand, even less agree with, psychoanalytic doctrine. This is pure psychologism, not to say psychopathologism. It was after my meeting with Federn that I first realized, what kind of science can this be?

By the next year I had become an Adlerian. Adler's psychology is simple, but it is rational. It overdoes things and exaggerates things—inferiority feelings and the like—but it is rational.

It is no wonder that Federn urged the young Frankl to finish his medical studies before joining the Freudian Society. What is remarkable, however, is that Freud had referred a nineteen-year-old to Federn in the first place. Even if Viktor had been interested in the months of training analysis the Society required, and even if Federn had urged it, he was taken up with his studies at that point.

BEFORE BEING DECLARED illegal by the SS, the Social Democratic Party was the leading political force in Austria between the world wars. In fact, the city became known as "Red Vienna." There was constant jockeying for power, but the Social Democrats—not to be confused with other parties in Austria or with Hitler's National Socialists (Nazis) in Germany—had programs of reform aimed at distributing opportunity and advantages more evenly to ordinary citizens. Housing was a major focus. In the decade starting in 1923 over 60,000 units were built by the government, most of them with affordable rents. Today a train to Heiligenstadt station, or a ride on streetcar D, will take a visitor to the Karl Marx Hof, a development of 1,400 flats that seems to stretch endlessly alongside the rails. Built 1927–30, it is the most dramatic visible and enduring sign of Red Vienna's program, though other housing projects abound in the city.

For the Frankls and others Jews in Vienna, buildings were not the main attraction of the leftist Social Democrats. Rather, it was the absence of anti-Semitic planks in the party platforms—a notable exception at the time—and a relative evenhandedness toward minority groups. Consequently most Jews voted for the Social Democrats, even if they viewed the party as the best of a bad lot. But there was no such thing as "the Viennese Jew." Instead of a cohesive community, there were many Jewish factions and groups ranging from liberals, to nationalists who were more ethnic than religious in orientation, to extreme orthodox sects. When I described this to a Jewish friend in Chicago he simply responded, "So what's new?"

During the years of the Austrian-Hungarian monarchy, Viktor stressed, many Jews came to Vienna from Poland. But since Germany was not part of the monarchy, the influx of eastern Jews affected Vienna dramatically, and much anti-Semitism in the city targeted them. And the social and cultural differences among Jews in Vienna were extraordinary. Some were wealthy, many were middle-class, many others very poor. There was a clear split between the Galician, or eastern, Jews, mainly from Russia and Poland, and the majority western Jews, many of whom looked down on the Galician immigrants.[3] "Polish Jew" was a disparaging designation even when used by other Jews from Hungary and Austria. Though in Vienna they were a deeply divided people and never mustered a united front, the Jews comprised a significant minority in 1923: at 200,000 they were nearly 11 percent of the city population; in the Leopoldstadt district nearly 40 percent; and in the Alsergrund—the university district—25 percent.[4] The social complexity is overwhelming when one considers the varieties of Jews trying to live out their lives in a diverse, anti-Semitic city which was over 80 percent Catholic—and Vienna itself was deeply split among aggressive political parties from extreme left to radical right.

The Frankl family were faithful Jews of no extreme and Viktor himself, in high school, was caught up in the Social Democratic movement. It was the likely thing for a Jewish boy from such a family in such a time and place. During Viktor's active involvement in socialist circles he became acquainted with Bruno Pittermann (1905–83), a teacher and politician of the Social Democratic Party who after World War II became vice chancellor of Austria. Pittermann became a friend to Viktor and was very kind, even coming from his law practice nearby to bring food to the Frankls in Czerningasse during the pinched times before Hitler. Viktor, as a high school student, was for a spell spokesman for the Young Socialist Workers of Austria. And the socialist agenda lined up rather neatly with the Adlerian agenda. The enthusiasm Viktor felt for the Adlerians, once he separated from psychoanalysis, arose partly from their social agenda, which the Freudians never adopted. The Adlerians were setting up child guidance clinics everywhere they could, not only in Vienna. Adler was immensely practical, aiming his efforts at the problems of children and youth and at defects in the educational system. He was trying to find realistic ways to deliver psychological services to the greatest number. Viktor's own development was shaped partly by the Adlerians' pragmatism and broad concern for people—that was significant for him, though his active participation in politics was brief.

But it takes more than the socialist agenda to explain Viktor's shift into the Adlerian camp. It was also that, as his confidence in psychoanalysis waned, Adler's individual psychology was the only tangible option in the brand new field of psychotherapy. While a senior in high school, Viktor visited Adlerian guidance clinics. At one of them Dr. Hugo Lukacs, an Adlerian psychiatrist-neurologist from Hungary, introduced Frankl to Adler. Lukacs became for Viktor a principal mentor in individual psychology and Adler a direct and personal influence.

In 1911, twelve years earlier, Freud had expelled Adler from his Vienna circle because of heretical and independent views. Adler was now firmly in command of his own growing federation and the expanding influence of his "individual psychology." He was holding forth with his disciples at the Café Siller among other places, and as a medical student Viktor began to meet with them—at the same café in which Viktor almost had been born. After the sessions, Viktor often extended discussions with Adler by accompanying him on his short walk home to his family residence, then at Dominikanerbastei 10 in the inner city.

Not far into medical school, Viktor was making a name for himself in the city and among the Adlerians. At the age of twenty his brief article, "Psychotherapy and Worldview: A Critical Examination of Their Relationship," was published in the Adler journal. It shows that Frankl has clearly moved away from psychoanalysis, that he is writing along Adlerian lines, and that—notably—his own thinking about meaning, values, and transcendence is underway. A year later his much longer article, "On the Psychology of Intellectualism," explored the tendency of some neurotic people to intellectualize their predicaments, to engage in exaggerated mental activity. Viktor is not anti-intellectual, but rather critiques types of intellectual*ism* as practiced by intellectual*izers* (or "intellectualists")—a phenomenon observed by psychotherapists. He suggests counteractive strategies. In the article some twists of concept and phrase appear, such as would become a hallmark of Frankl's writing and speeches. For example, "One can never get to know oneself through observation, but one can indeed do so through *action*. Do your duty, and you will know what is in you. What, then, is your duty? That which *everyday life* asks of you."[5] Both articles reflect his Adlerian orientation and give insight into his youthful and transitional thought at the time—and the seeds of logotherapy can also be seen. Of these early articles, written by Viktor when he was fifteen, or even twenty-five, he said, "I would not authorize those papers today, over fifty years later"—though when he said that to me it was more than *seventy-five* years after his first publications. But still, those early articles give clues about what is to come.

Due to Viktor's involvement with the Young Socialists, the Adlerian child guidance clinics, and his certification in individual psychology under Lukacs and Erwin Wexberg, at the age of twenty-one he was giving lectures on sexuality, suicide, and meaning in life—and even was traveling abroad. He gave an address at the International Congress of Individual Psychology in Dusseldorf in 1926, and on a stop in Berlin he lectured at the Society for Individual Psychology. Then at Frankfurt, Viktor marched with large groups of banner-waving students to a huge hall where he addressed the Young Socialist Workers. (In retrospect the mature Viktor thought it almost laughable that he was doing all that at the age of twenty-one.) In Berlin he met Wilhelm Reich, a well-known socialist and psychoanalyst who had some very odd ideas, and they drove around Berlin in Reich's open convertible for hours talking about suicide and the sexual problems of young people. Viktor in the same period gave lectures in Budapest, Zurich, and also in Prague, where he met Professor Otto Pötzl. Pötzl figures into the Frankl story as few others.

Viktor met Sigmund Freud in the winter/spring of 1925/26 when Freud was surviving terrible personal setbacks and experiencing the "detachment of old age." When Viktor first saw sixty-eight-year-old Freud, he thought the bowed, slow-moving figure was "a really old man." No wonder. Even with Viktor's awareness of the bickering and bad blood among Freud's disciples, he did not know what Freud was going through with his family and health. By this time Sigmund and Martha had suffered the passing of their adult daughter Sophie Halberstadt,[6] Freud's "Sunday child" who at her death was pregnant with her third child. But nothing prepared Freud for the anguish that came over him at the loss of Sophie's four-year-old child, little "Heinele" (Heinz Rudolf Halberstadt, 1919–23). "I don't think I have ever experienced such grief;

perhaps my own sickness contributes to the shock. I work out of sheer necessity; fundamentally everything has lost its meaning for me."[7] A couple
of months later—in August—Freud's "best niece," only twenty-three,
unmarried and pregnant, committed suicide.[8] His nephew Teddy
drowned in Berlin the same year.[9] If this were not enough, in early 1923
Freud was diagnosed with cancer of the jaw and palate.[10] The disease was
so terrible that Freud considered suicide and even talked with his physician about it.[11]

Viktor met Freud unexpectedly one day after he finished at the university and went as usual to catch his homebound streetcar at the
Schottentor, a tram interchange. As Viktor was waiting in the cold, he
looked upon the open space and gardens that slope upward toward the
neogothic Votiv Church with its distinctive twin spires. The space and gardens today are called Sigmund Freud Park. Behind the church were the
sprawling General Hospital and university clinics from which Viktor had
just come.

Near the Schottentor, Viktor noticed an aging gent heading toward the
park, using a walking stick with a silvery handle. Recalling photographs,
Viktor thought to himself, "That looks just like Professor Freud, but it cannot be—not this old guy in such a dark old overcoat and shabby, worn-out
hat." From their correspondence and from the fame of the address, Viktor
knew that Freud lived at Berggasse 19, which is today the Freud Museum.
Viktor watched the old man and wondered if he might head toward
Berggasse, up a few blocks and to the right of the Votiv Church and down
the hill from Währinger Strasse. Viktor decided to follow the unlikely figure, and he did—right into Berggasse.

In lectures throughout the world in his later life, Viktor described this
chance meeting and dryly added—to the delight of audiences—that "in
this way I became a so-called follower of Freud."

Once certain that this was Freud, Viktor caught up with him and addressed him with proper Viennese manners toward a professor. "Excuse
me, sir, but do I have the honor to speak to Professor Freud?" "Yes, I am
he." "My name is Viktor Frankl, and . . ." "Just a minute, just a minute,"
Freud interrupted. "Viktor Frankl. Second district, Czerningasse number
6, apartment 25, right?" From their correspondence Freud remembered
the address exactly. The two conversed for a time, Viktor mentioning to
Freud a book he had found on the death instinct by Lagrange. Freud was
excited about this, and suggested to Viktor that he write a book review for

his literary publication *Imago*. That was the only time Viktor talked with Freud.

One might wonder why, with their ongoing correspondence and Freud's publication of Viktor's short article, they did not meet more than this. But at that time great deference was shown to professors by young students. Even in 1963, when I was a student at the University of Vienna, we rose to our feet when the professor entered the classroom. I cannot recall ever seeing students casually socializing with professors the way we did in America. Viktor recalled that once, as a medical student, he sat opposite the well-known psychoanalyst Paul Schilder on a long train ride to Dusseldorf. When I asked if he had talked with Schilder, Viktor replied, "He was reading a book on mathematics. Anyway, why would he be talking with a student?" Given this, it would have been unthinkable back in 1925 for Viktor to impose upon Professor Freud and highly unusual for Freud to initiate their social contacts. Freud was an extremely busy man, making it even more remarkable that he wrote postcards to young Viktor.

Despite Viktor's delight in meeting Freud, he was already affiliated with the Adlerians. Whether Adler had been thrown overboard by Freud or jumped the psychoanalytic ship was not so important to Viktor as to find someone who dared to voice discontent with Freud's ideas, especially the relentless focus on sexuality and the reduction of nearly everything human to unconscious dynamics. Adler, while not the writer or intellectual giant that Freud was, gave Viktor a refreshing new way to think about human nature and about psychotherapy.

When Viktor first turned to the Adlerians he was welcomed by them and embraced by Adler in 1924. Hugo Lukacs was not the only key influence on Viktor. The two other physician-philosophers we have already mentioned became Viktor's respected teachers—Rudolf Allers and Oswald Schwarz. During 1925–26, Viktor assisted Allers at his physiological lab on Schwarzpanierstrasse, testing reaction time and the effects of caffeine. Though Viktor learned some negative effects of caffeine, nevertheless throughout his life he continued to use strong coffees to jump-start his days and his lectures.

Schwarz was a urologist at the Poliklinik Hospital—where Adler had once worked in ophthalmology—and was one of the founders of psychosomatic medicine. Both Allers and Schwarz met regularly with the Society of Individual Psychology and Viktor recalled how important these two were to him in grappling with Adlerian psychology.

"Schwarz resided across the street, on Alser Strasse. When Hitler came in, both Karl and Charlotte Bühler were professors of psychology here. Then she emigrated to Sweden, as did Schwarz at first, but he went on to London as I remember it. From London he wrote me a blue airmail letter and lamented that he was very desperate because the whole atmosphere in London was nothing for him. Nobody listened; no one was interested in our [Vienna] efforts to set up an existentially-oriented psychotherapy." Ultimately Schwarz took his own life.

Viktor's relationship with Allers endured even after Allers moved to Georgetown University in Washington. But it was while both Allers and Schwarz were still in Vienna that they led the challenge to Adler's insistence on certain ideas. Viktor recalled that "Adler was angry when they defected. And when I took sides—partially—with Allers and Schwarz in front of Adler, it cost me my head."

The event to which Viktor referred was the dramatic meeting with Adler that doomed their association with each other. But first, some background.

When young Viktor Frankl walked away from psychoanalysis, he owed a debt of thanks to Adler. But before long he started to see in Adler a dictatorial style with regard to Adlerian orthodoxy. And what was stunning to Viktor, as his own viewpoints sharpened, was the realization that Adler, like Freud, was a reductionist. That is, Adler's system, however different from Freud's, reduced human thought and behavior to one basic drive: striving to overcome social inferiority and defects of whatever kind. So Adler now had replaced Freud's psychologism with one of his own. Adler even went so far as to view sexual disorders as symbolic in the striving for superiority. No wonder Freud banished Adler. After all, for Freud any neurosis, any psychological distress, is ultimately traceable to unconscious sexual and aggressive forces.

Allers and Schwarz were direct in pointing out Adler's new reductionism. As they became more disenchanted with individual psychology, Viktor was inspired both by their insight and their courage. During the preceding year Viktor had given his youthful Dusseldorf speech, and in it he had challenged the Adlerian notion that each symptom in a neurosis is an alibi, an excuse—a means to an end. Rather, Viktor asserted, sometimes these "symptoms" or signs of distress are in fact an immediate expression of one's innermost life, a true self-expression rather than a signal of some underlying neurosis. This was against Adlerian orthodoxy.

Once Viktor saw through Adler's psychologism, however, he still believed that the society could rescue itself from reductionism. But Adler became controlling and defensive toward his critics. Viktor recalled that "Allers and Schwarz, my teachers whom I admired, were against psychologism and reductionism and the one-sidedness of the Adlerians. They announced that they would leave the society." The momentous meeting of the society took place in 1927[12] and was fixed in Viktor's memory.

Adler himself was present when Allers and Schwarz presented their divergent views to the society. Viktor sat next to a lady and close to Adler in the front row. When Allers and Schwarz had delivered their revolutionary statements, they announced their departures from the society and left, never to return. "Adler knew that this lady and I were critical of his rigid orthodoxy, and he also knew that I was under the influence of Allers and Schwarz. . . . Adler was expected to take the rostrum and comment on these renegades. For two or three minutes nobody moved, a painful silence. . . . Finally Adler rose to comment, but first he turned in contempt to the lady and me and said, 'Now, you heroes?' "

In the awkward situation Viktor felt that he must take a stand, that Adler was calling for this. He explained that he subscribed to much of what Allers and Schwarz were saying, but that there was no need to leave the society. The differences could be embraced within the Adlerian circle—together they could overcome psychologism and reductionism. When Viktor had finished, Adler stood up and ridiculed what he had said about the spiritual dimension in humans and about its significance. Adler made a reference to innocent children being killed in war, and how did Viktor's argument about some kind of spiritual harmony square with that? Viktor left the meeting even as Adler was mocking what he had said. He remembered that at the rear of the hall some psychoanalysts were enjoying the ruckus within the Adlerian camp, especially the defections of Allers and Schwarz. The disciples of Adler were betraying him, just as Adler had betrayed Freud.

After that encounter, by Viktor's own account, Adler never spoke to him again. Not even to return a greeting. Whenever Viktor approached Adler's table at the Café Siller, Adler ignored him or even left the table. At first Adler sent some indirect messages that Frankl should leave the society. Some months later Adler finally banished Viktor in the dictatorial style of Freud, and Viktor had to give up editing his own popular Adlerian journal (*Der Mensch im Alltag*). Though the personal relationship between Adler and Frankl was over, Viktor prized his enduring friendships with foremost Adlerians, including Rudolf Dreikurs, and with Alexandra, Adler's own daughter. She wrote this in 1980.

> Dr. Frankl and I were part of a group of friends who often met in Vienna. Viktor joined the scientific meetings, held under the chairmanship of my father, Alfred Adler, and his remarks were always original and gave rise to many discussions.
>
> I particularly enjoyed my personal contact with him. . . . I left Vienna in 1935 and was terribly distressed to hear that he had been caught by the Nazis and thrown in a concentration camp. I read his books and reports about these years and find them among the most impressive I have read.
>
> It was with great pleasure for me and my husband to have him as a guest, together with a group of some 20 friends, at my apartment in New York, a few years ago, when I felt the same personal closeness as I did during our joyful encounters in Vienna.[13]

There was no doubt that the positive example of Adler's social commitment affected Frankl. The Adlerian child guidance clinics, where Viktor learned individual psychology, provided a model for setting up suicide prevention services, which became a favorite Frankl project. He actually helped organize suicide prevention centers for youth in Vienna as increasing numbers were taking their own lives. The rash of suicides appeared to be related to the dreaded school report cards. Within families the pressure to succeed on school exams was severe. But students also frequently reported sexual problems such as anxiety about masturbation.

Of the prevention services to youth, Viktor recalled that "Wilhelm Börner, who had married a cousin of my father, had started a youth counseling (*Jugend-Beratung*) program in Vienna, with worldwide acknowledgment for suicide prevention. Decades later Erwin Ringel, an Adlerian or whatever, took credit for much of this and was very well known." Viktor recruited professionals in the city to volunteer their time to young people. The consultations and assistance given were to be both free and confidential. The psychiatrists, physicians, psychologists, and clergy opened their offices or homes for particular hours each week, and local newspapers carried announcements of the program. Posters were put up across the city: "It is never too late." On it was a who's who of professionals in Vienna, together with their addresses and drop-in hours—no fees whatsoever. Among them: Börner, psychoanalyst August Aichhorn, developmental psychologist Charlotte Bühler, the prominent Adlerians Rudolf Dreikurs and Erwin Wexberg, and others. There on the list is also medical student "Viktor Frankl, Czerningasse 6, apartment 25, Saturdays 3 to 4 P.M." In addition to this he was given office space in the administrative center for the Ninth District at Währinger Strasse 43. There he was available for drop-in visits by students during certain weekday afternoon hours, and he could link up students with the professionals on the poster and with former teachers, social workers, retirees, and so on who also were volunteering their time. And, Viktor had enlisted Professor Otto Pötzl to be honorary president of the Vienna program.

The model for the youth suicide prevention program was exported far beyond Vienna. In fact, on Viktor's first lecture tour to Dusseldorf, Berlin, and Frankfurt as well as on trips to Prague, Budapest, and other cities, he consulted on how to set up suicide prevention services.

THOUGH VIKTOR WAS interested in the politics of psychotherapy, he was after all—as Federn had reminded him—a medical student. He was taking a full course load in one of the world's great medical schools and in the oldest university in the German-speaking world. Before long he was observing surgical procedures in preparation for performing them.

Upon seeing his first abdominal cut, Viktor had to leave the operating room for fear of fainting. He was also apprehensive at first when he watched lumbar punctures, but when he did a spinal tap himself it was no problem for him. The same thing happened in surgery: when he made his own incisions it went smoothly and without distress. His theory was that mere observers have time to put themselves in the place of the "victim"; but the one doing the surgery is preoccupied with the procedure itself.

Viktor's laboratory work had a social downside, however. At Viennese performing arts centers, one could and can purchase a low-cost ticket for a *Stehplatz*—a place to stand. When the Frankls went to concerts or plays, all they could afford was standing room at the back. While in medical school Viktor occasionally went straight from his labs to performances at the opera or music halls, or at the *Volkstheatre*. This was his own description: "I was coming from the Anatomy Institute on Währinger Strasse, stinking from corpses. In the theater everybody moved away from me, making free space around me in the front row of the standing section. Proudly I occupied the front row almost alone. But not for too long a time because I was asthenic—slim and not strong—and I was prone to orthostatic collapse, fainting from standing for a long time. For most performances I missed the second or third act because I had to rush to the coatroom to lie down on the floor for some minutes to recover. So I never saw the whole show—I had to guess how it ended!"

As he progressed toward specialization in psychiatry, Viktor benefited from Vienna's progressive methods and from his work in the first facility in Europe exclusively for treating mental patients.[14] In 1784 the Narrenturm had been opened as part of the General Hospital and called the *Tollhaus*—the madhouse. That sounds terrifying, and it was. In those days a favorite weekend outing for some Viennese was a tour of the *Tollhaus*, where they could gaze through small windows at the lunatics in their locked cells. Yet the humane treatment of the mentally ill advanced rapidly in Vienna, and by the time of Viktor's education the city was one of the best places for treating both medical and psychological disorders. Today visitors to the madhouse museum can look into the same cells, much as they were, but now without inmates.

Medical education then as now required earning the medical degree and completing a series of placements for training in a specialty. In that way one became eligible for licensure to practice medicine. Frankl was granted his MD degree in 1930 and continued with training placements in neurology and psychiatry. His first assignment was off-campus and brief. For roughly a month he observed (*hospitieren*) at the Rosenhügel Neurological Hospital located on the outskirts of the city just a bit southwest of Schönbrunn Palace, the vast summer place of the former Hapsburg dynasty. The exteriors of the Rosenhügel buildings there have not changed much, and even with the growth of Vienna the setting remains relatively quiet and rural in feeling. While Viktor was there the first press photograph was taken of him, in connection with the suicide prevention program. The program's success was gaining attention as suicides among Vienna's youth diminished sharply to virtually no incidents. In the photo Viktor is very thin and somewhat disheveled, with dark-rimmed glasses, dark tousled hair, and a crumpled white medical smock.

Following Rosenhügel came more vital and longer-term assignments. The first of these was an internship of less than a year in the department of psychiatry in the school of medicine. Here he came under the supervision of Professor Otto Pötzl, the prominent brain pathologist-psychiatrist and former head of neurology at Charles University, Prague's famous German-speaking institution. Professor Pötzl already knew Viktor since they had met when Viktor went to Prague in 1926 to lecture on the youth counseling program. Viktor had known, when he visited Pötzl at Charles University, that Pötzl would be moving soon to Vienna as professor of neurology and psychiatry. What neither could have known, with a difference of nearly thirty years in age, was that they were at the start of a unique and enduring professional and personal association.

After being in Vienna for a relatively short time, in 1928 Pötzl was appointed chief of the University Psychiatric Clinic on Lazarettgasse as immediate successor to Julius von Wagner-Jauregg (1857–1940). Wagner-Jauregg was a Nobel Prize Laureate in 1927 for his dramatically effective treatment of paresis, a syphilitic illness leading to insanity and death. His radical method involved infecting the paresis patient with malaria—the first of the "shock therapies."

Wagner-Jauregg was a research psychiatrist and as such resisted psychoanalysis as completely unscientific, though he later allowed lectures on the topic. His assessment of Adler's individual psychology was similar. Earlier, Wagner-Jauregg had a hand in Adler's psychiatric education, yet in 1915 harshly had opposed any teaching appointment for him.[15] Adler was crushed by the unanimous faculty rejection, which effectively ended his hopes of ever becoming a professor in Vienna.

At the inauguration ceremony for Pötzl's new appointment as chief of the clinic, the hall was packed. Even the stairways were jammed with people wanting to hear Wagner-Jauregg at his departure and Pötzl's first major speech as chief. Viktor was in that crowd, as full of anticipation as anyone. As the platform party was entering the hall, Pötzl happened to spot Viktor in the crowd, broke protocol, and called out, "Frankl, come with me!" So Frankl, the young medical student, was ushered among the dignitaries into the hall and to a choice seat by fifty-year-old Pötzl himself.

A couple of years later at the Psychiatric Clinic, Frankl was the only intern allowed to do psychotherapy independently. Pötzl had instructed his assistant to allow this even though Viktor was uncertified for such practice. Viktor took advantage of his unique opportunity and did not disappoint Pötzl. These are his own words describing it. "At that time I tried to forget everything I had learned from Freud and Adler, and just listen to everything my patients told me. And sometimes to single out the self-curative mechanisms available to them. For example, I would ask: 'How is it possible that you overcame in just a week your intense fear of being away from home and in public places?' "

Then Viktor explained that such a patient would sometimes answer that he did exactly as Viktor had suggested, namely this: instead of being afraid of becoming anxious in a public place, he should *plan* to have the most fear possible when going out. In fact, Frankl urged, "go out and have not only fears but a stroke and heart attack as well!" Having taken this courageous, defiant, and rather humorous step, the phobia vanished and the patient enjoyed being out again.

This, Viktor said, is how logotherapy developed, particularly the intervention he later called "paradoxical intention"—whereby a person, instead of fighting an irrational fear, invites it, welcomes it, exaggerates it, deflating the anxiety by no longer resisting it. Thus, in Frankl's expression, while anxiety creates the symptoms over and over, paradoxical intention strangles them, over and over. Viktor discussed such interventions with Pötzl who, though somewhat Freudian himself, was impressed. The mutual respect between them grew. Viktor thought Pötzl an absolute genius, and the professor admired Viktor for his creativity and quickness.

In 1931, upon completion of his Psychiatric Clinic internship, Viktor started a residency at the private Maria Theresien-Schlössel Neurological Hospital on Hofzeile in District 19, a mental hospital nearly two miles north of the university and near what is today Kardinal-Innitzer-Platz. This hospital, set as it is among yards and gardens, also has the feeling of being a retreat from the city, even today. Much of Viktor's early life is still traceable to exact places, as the case is here. For more than two years he was under the supervision of Dr. Josef Gerstmann, head of the hospital. Gerstmann was well known for his work on disturbances in left-right spatial orientation. Viktor recalled a Gerstmann lecture in the former chapel of the old psychiatric institute. Though then used as a lecture hall, the stained-glass windows and a few other Catholic trappings had never been removed.

Gerstmann was interviewing a patient, and among the very first questions were some regarding the patient's orientation. "And where are you now?" Typically patients would look around and quite rationally reply, "In a chapel." But on one occasion Gerstmann used heavy Jewish jargon in asking the question. The patient looked around, hesitated a moment, and responded, "In a synagogue." Viktor thought that was very funny and quipped, "These patients were psychotic, but you can see they were not so crazy!"

DURING A DISCUSSION with Viktor and Elly in their home, Viktor revealed more about his early disenchantment with Freud's psychoanalysis. A particular incident is especially instructive. While still in high school, Viktor had gone to a Saturday evening lecture given by Paul Schilder, Freud's disciple. For the first couple of minutes many people laughed at Schilder's high-pitched voice and odd mannerisms, but then the audience fell silent, forgetting the voice as they were swept away by the lecture. Viktor described Schilder as "one of the best two or three orators I have ever heard in my life; the words he spoke were *druckreif*—ready for the printed page." Then Viktor launched into an impression of Schilder's case presentation, comical in voice and demeanor only.

> Schilder had a catatonic patient sitting down in the lecture hall, and he wanted to disclose a Freudian Oedipal situation by interviewing the patient in front of his students. So he stood up and approached her. "And have you fallen in love with your father?"
>
> A long silence followed, and the woman made no reply. [Viktor raised the volume of his imitation to a near shriek] "Were you attracted to your father? Have you fallen in love with your father?!" This time the woman answered with a sharp, unambiguous, "No!"
>
> Schilder then turned to his class and explained. "Ladies and gentlemen, thanks to Freud, now we know that—when she denies falling in love with her father—this is proof that she *has* fallen in love with him!"

I asked Viktor if this had impressed him. "Yes, I was very much impressed. But in a negative sense. I thought, now this has gone too far!" I urged Viktor on, "So even in your last year of high school you were becoming critical of psychoanalysis, even though generally you were taken in by it?" Viktor's reply stood: that he had been taken in by psychoanalysis, but that he also thought it was carrying things too far.

On a sad note, Viktor conveyed that Schilder, who did much to promote psychoanalysis in the United States, had emigrated to New York where, "rushing to the hospital to be with his wife who was delivering their baby, [he] was killed in an automobile accident" [1940].

As Viktor described the Schilder interview of the patient, it reminded me of Gordon Allport's encounter with Freud. Allport, of Harvard University and founder of personality psychology, also reopened the psychological study of religion. He was the one to introduce Frankl to American readers in 1959 and who arranged for Viktor's visiting professorship at Harvard in 1961. Allport and Viktor remained fast friends until Allport's death in 1967. The Frankls knew of this anecdote, in which Allport described how he managed to interview Freud in Vienna in 1919.

> With a callow forwardness characteristic of age twenty-two, I wrote to Freud that I was in Vienna and implied that no doubt he would like to make my acquaintance. I received a kind reply in his own handwriting inviting me to come to his office at a certain time. Soon after I had entered the famous red burlap room with pictures of dreams on the wall, he summoned me to his inner office. He did not speak to me but sat in expectant silence, for me to state my mission. I was not prepared for silence and had to think fast to find a suitable conversational gambit. I told him of an episode on the tram car on my way to his office. A small boy about four years of age had displayed a conspicuous dirt phobia. He kept saying to his mother, "I don't want to sit there . . . don't let that dirty man sit beside me." To him everything was *schmutzig*. His mother was a well-starched *Hausfrau*, so dominant and purposive looking that I thought the cause and effect apparent.
>
> When I finished my story Freud fixed his kindly therapeutic eyes upon me and said, "And was that little boy you?" Flabbergasted and feeling a bit guilty, I contrived to change the subject. While Freud's misunderstanding of my motivation was amusing, it also started a deep train of thought. . . .
>
> This experience taught me that depth psychology, for all its merits, may plunge too deep, and that psychologists would do well to give full recognition to manifest motives before probing the unconscious.[16]

AMID THE INTERACTIONS with the Frankls when I was with them in the summer of 1996, I asked about Pötzl. Viktor left his chair, which sat between his desk and the bay windows behind him, and went to fetch a photograph of Pötzl. After we looked at it, Viktor commenced an impersonation of Pötzl, complete with idiosyncratic mannerisms. Pötzl typically leaned against a wall or chalkboard as he lectured, and a particularly humorous incident occurred to Viktor.

Many years earlier in a classroom—actually in that former chapel of the old Psychiatric Clinic—Pötzl was sitting on a table in front of his students, reviewing a case history. He frequently interspersed remarks and went off on tangents as he lectured whenever something interesting occurred to him. Leafing through the psychiatric record, Pötzl described the patient in question and then came upon an illuminating anecdote. The patient, on an occasion in a public restaurant, had stood up, opened his trousers, and placed his naked genitals on the table in front of the other diners. Suddenly Pötzl jumped up from the table, faced the audience, and exclaimed: "Ladies and gentlemen! This certainly reminds you of these lines from the old German student song [here Pötzl lapsed into an exaggerated dialect]:

> Only would the finest man, and on occasion rare,
> Present in cordial greeting his genitalia bare."

Viktor could also do an impression of Adler that, like the others, was true to character—so others told me at least. Viktor launched his impersonation of Adler giving a lecture to the medical psychology group in Vienna, speaking slowly, softly, and ominously. "Here stands the neurotic. And here stands the task of his life. And between them is a compost heap, and this is the neurosis. And he uses his neurosis as an alibi—he cannot marry, he cannot be competent in his profession, he cannot lead a normal life. His inferiority feelings hinder him to behave like anyone else. [Then in a dramatic whisper] This is the neu-RO-zis." Ending the imitation, Viktor noted that such a style did not suit a scientific presentation but that "Adler had his followers, his community."

CHAPTER 4

Sifting, Settling, and Logotherapy, 1934–1937

AS HE COMPLETED his residency in neurology-psychiatry at the Schlössel in 1933, Viktor took up his new one at the Psychiatric Hospital of the City of Vienna, "Am Steinhof." That hospital is a story in itself.

The opening of Steinhof on October 8, 1907, had been a milestone in the treatment of mentally ill people as well as a triumph of modern architecture. The sprawling site on a hillside near the Vienna Woods in Penzing, District 14, had dozens of buildings integrated into the campus design—practically a state-of-the-art town, planned for thousands of patients. It would be half a century before the use of drugs would revolutionize the treatment of mental disorders, downsize, or even close such massive mental hospitals and leave many former patients to suffer homeless on the streets.

At the new Steinhof, patients were housed in twelve large buildings called pavilions, six for women and six for men. The architect was the celebrated Otto Wagner, a founder of the defiant *Jugendstil* movement in Germany and Austria, related to art nouveau in France and eventually to art deco in America. His Steinhof theater was striking. And on the highest point of the hospital campus was constructed St. Leopold's Church, legendary for its radical, stunning features, its use of marble and glass, metals and gold leaf, mosaic and lighting. From far away one can see the dome gleaming in the sunlight. Wagner designed it specifically for mental patients who were to be its unique congregation. It became popularly known as the Steinhof Church. Today the hospital is not on the typical tourist trails, but sightseers and architecture buffs from around the world still make their way to the church, especially in summer.

The building rests on the interface of psychiatry and religion, and in every detail it is considerate of mentally ill people. In Viktor's own view, the awe-inspiring building soothed and lifted the spirits of patients, even those severely troubled. The wooden pews have no sharp edges, each corner smoothly rounded to minimize injury upon bumping them. The mostly white, patterned tile floor slopes forward to drains so it can be hosed down after a mass should anyone have spit, vomited, or urinated on it. Even the feet of the pews are encased in sheet copper so the hosing does no harm to the hardwood. To the left of the soaring golden altar is a door leading to a washroom and toilet and to intervention rooms for psychiatrists and aides. Near the main church entrance is the font for holy water. It is of solid marble, matching the marble wall from which it protrudes with the cleanest of lines. The font was thoughtfully created so that dirt or bodily fluids, should they somehow get into the small marble basin, would immediately be drained away. From a little golden spigot about a foot above the basin, clean water trickles down into the font. In this way any person can receive fresh holy water without touching the pool or font. Viktor loved this building because of its kindly accommodation of its extraordinary congregation.

Elly had never been inside the Steinhof Church, but my description of its stained-glass windows by Kolo Moser (1868–1918) drew both Viktor and her into a lively conversation. Elly, raised and confirmed a Roman Catholic, recognized the themes in the windows. Viktor also knew of some of the Catholic works of mercy depicted in stained glass. This is understandable in light of Viktor's private faith, his long-standing interactions with theologians of various stripes, his lifetime in overwhelmingly Catholic Vienna, his careful considerations of psychology and religion, and his marriage to Elly.

On the campus and among the patient pavilions was the doctors' residence hall where Viktor had his own room. It was and remains a structure with a concrete foundation showing above ground, a decorative concrete façade around the first floor, and brown brick wrapping around the second and third floors. Its windows and roofline are white and ornamented. From the upper floors on a clear day Viktor could see the peaks of the Rax—his favorite Alpine range forty miles to the south where he was already climbing whenever he could make the trip. Of course it was impossible for him to see from anywhere at Steinhof all the way to the neighborhood of his family in Czerningasse. That was buried from view far on the opposite side of the city. Commuting from hospital to home was not feasible, and so he stayed at Steinhof where both accommodations and meals were provided to him without charge. But it would be a mistake to imagine that Viktor was putting his parents or their influence behind him. When it was first necessary for Viktor to stay overnight at the hospitals he was dreadfully homesick, although naturally this lessened after a while. Still, for a long time he persisted in spending weekends at home. Eventually just one overnight each month was workable. But Viktor did continue—even after finishing his medical education—to spend his March 26 birthdays with his parents in Czerningasse.

When Viktor first arrived at Steinhof, nightly homesickness was not his only struggle. The days were no fun, either. Among medical students there is a phenomenon known as "interns' syndrome"; they may imagine in themselves the same symptoms of illnesses they are treating in others. Something similar happens to many trainees in psychiatry and psychology, and Viktor experienced it himself. But another early and common occurrence affected Viktor most: an exaggerated and intensely personal sense of responsibility for whatever happened to his patients. Viktor, who was new in sharing institutional responsibility for the three-hundred-plus women in Pavilion 3, was distressed by his own nightmares regarding them. It was tough to separate himself from the unbroken routines of a large mental hospital, especially where he lived and worked virtually around-the-clock. Daytime encounters and nightmares fed on one another to produce Viktor's anxieties during his first weeks at Steinhof.

In Pavilion 3, Dr. Leopold Pawlicki was Viktor's supervisor. At the outset Pawlicki warned Viktor not to wear his dark-rimmed eyeglasses when entering the wards, since getting struck in the face by a patient was always a realistic possibility. Viktor remembered, "I followed this advice and, because I did not see well without my glasses, I was hit in the face the very first day. From then on I wore my glasses and thus could spot any woman who approached, ready to attack me. Thanks to my glasses, I could take to my heels in time."[1]

In the four years of administering Pavilion 3, Viktor estimated that as many as twelve hundred women, counting admissions and releases, were directly in his care. Most were depressed and at risk for suicide. In conditions of understaffing it is possible that Viktor had some kind of professional contact with twelve thousand disturbed women in the process of hospital admission and assessment. Viktor refined his very direct way of dealing with suicide.

How could I make any conclusions about a patient, except by considering her history? So I would ask the depressed patient, "Do you still have suicide ideas?" She might say no, but only in order to be discharged so that she actually could commit suicide. So I would ask, "Why not?" Then she was embarrassed, nervous, not able to answer, not looking at me, and offering no reason. On the other hand, the patient who was overcoming her suicide wishes would answer differently. To "Why not?" such a person would say something like this: "Oh doctor, as you told me yourself last week, I will recover. I am very religious and cannot think of anything like this. I have my home, my family, and I must care for them. And I have my lifework to fulfill, some writing to do." I knew that if there was meaning to their lives, these patients would become free from suicide.

Then later on, in the concentration camps, I found out that as long as prisoners had meaning—an orientation to the future, someone to love, something transcendent—they didn't commit suicide. *Under equal circumstances* they survived. Of course they could die in gas chambers or in other ways, but given equal circumstances the prisoners with a meaning were the ones who survived.

Upon admission to his pavilion and during their stays there, Viktor interviewed patients to review their condition and progress. The structure of a typical interview helped assess a patient's contact with reality, thought patterns, and behavior. Answers to questions could be unconventional and humorous. As part of an intelligence test, several lines of questioning helped determine a patient's reasoning capacity. One such question was, "What is the difference between a child and a dwarf?" The response that Viktor remembered best was, "Oh, a child is a child but a dwarf works in the mine."

Patients with very disturbed and dangerous behavior were placed into what was called a "net bed." It was simply a bed with a mesh tent over it to confine the patient in a safe way that also allowed some freedom to move and interact socially. One day a patient, upon being allowed to leave his net bed, approached Viktor in his bare feet, carrying his shoes. Viktor asked him, "Why are you carrying your shoes in your hands?" The patient answered, "Why not? After all, they are not very heavy." As Viktor often observed, even peculiar responses may have hidden wisdom.

Occasionally the psychiatrists had a roaring good time over the admissions forms completed by a certain police doctor (*Polizeiarzt*). It was his job to bring troubled and troublesome people to the hospital, fill out the forms, and sign the warrant with the reason for detaining the patient. Usually the reason was psychotic behavior that could be dangerous to the patient or others in the community. Here are Viktor's own words.

"There was from Brigittenau, Vienna's Twentieth District, a police doctor. And whenever he submitted an admissions declaration, all of us— six or seven doctors—assembled immediately to enjoy it! And for this reason: the police doctor—I can remember one occasion exactly—started a description of a patient with these words: *'obdachlos, bewusstlos, mosaisch'*— homeless, consciousless, Jewish. This was followed by the reason for the commitment: *'... wegen neuerlichen Leuchtgashahnaufdrehenwollens.' "*

Viktor burst into laughing so hard he could not continue the story. Elly and I were laughing, too, partly at Viktor's hysterics. Finally he calmed down enough to continue. The police doctor, after introducing the patient as homeless, unconscious, and Jewish, had invented an "official" diagnosis that strung together a series of German words in comical sequence. Viktor attempted a nearly impossible translation into English. *"Wegen neuerlichen Leuchtgashahnaufdrehenwollens"* meant that the hospital commitment was necessary "because of the-renewed-opening-the-gas-valve-intention." All of this effort and inventiveness could have been covered with one word: suicidal.

Despite the era at Steinhof and the seriousness of Freud's influence, Viktor nevertheless behaved toward patients in an encouraging, optimistic manner, frequently using humor to lighten their burdens. Indeed, humor became a key element in logotherapy. When I was Frankl's student in 1962–63, I was struck by this human way of dealing with troubled people. A few years later during my training as a psychologist, I was an intern in a large American mental hospital. Thanks to Frankl's influence I felt free to be myself with patients, even to kid with those I got to know. But this got me into a bit of trouble.

One day my supervisor sent for me and when I arrived, he closed his office door behind us and sat down. In a somber, even awkward way, he asked me, "Don, is something bothering you? Are you anxious about anything here at the hospital?" I had no idea what he was getting at and my internship experience was going very well as far as I knew. So I replied with my own question, "What do you mean?" Then he explained. "I have heard that sometimes you laugh with the patients, even kid around with them. That's why I'm asking if something is troubling you." My supervisor had interpreted my spontaneous manner with patients as a cover-up, perhaps a mask for some underlying anxiety, perhaps a disguise for some neurotic conflict in me.

I explained that I always joke with people I like, that it is part of my normal behavior when I am comfortable. Further, I said that I joked only with patients that I knew and who would also joke around with me. And I reminded my supervisor that my occasional joking in our staff meetings was apparently appreciated, and was no different. Tactless teasing can be hurtful, of course. And while clowning might be used to mask anxiety, must any use of humor *always* be such?

Viktor's resistance to unmasking everything helps us understand that there can be humor in good times and bad—even in crises and deep disturbance—humor which is "immediate, genuine, original" and helpful. Such an attitude stood in contrast to the Freudians, and even the Adlerians, who were determined to "unmask" psychological problems, to expose them as signs and symptoms of some underlying conflict or drive. Nothing, to them, was as it appeared. As Viktor put it:

> Everywhere, psychologism sees nothing but masks, insists that only neurotic motives lie behind these masks. Art, it asserts, is "in the final analysis nothing but" flight from life or from love. Religion is merely primitive man's fear of cosmic forces. All spiritual creations turn out to be "mere" sublimations of the libido or, as the case may be, compensations for inferiority feelings or means for achieving security. The great creators in the realm of the spirit are then dismissed as neurotics. After we have been put through such a course of "debunking" by psychologism we can with complete complacency say that Goethe or St. Augustine, for instance, was "really only" a neurotic. This point of view sees nothing for what it is; that is to say, it really sees nothing. Because something at one time was a mask, or somewhere was a means to an end, does that make it forever a mask, or nothing but a means to an end? Can there never be anything immediate, genuine, original?[2]

In the 1930s, Frankl was unique in his intentional use of humor with patients as a way to help them put some distance between themselves and their problems. The capacity to transcend through humor one's predicaments, drives, and limitations is a mark of humanness. And using defiant humor with certain types of psychological disorders, mainly phobias and anxiety, can bring enormous relief. Since Viktor's pioneering work with humor,[3] a great deal has been researched and published on the significance of humor in healing and psychological well-being.

Humor in the hospital was one way in which Viktor broke with conventions of the 1930s, and another was his informality with patients. Viennese society was exceptionally status-conscious. One's high position was treated with deference and denoted by titles, degrees obtained, and honors bestowed. Many of the old gravestones in Vienna's cemeteries display titles, degrees, and honors. Amid the bureaucracy and red tape, formalities still abound, though this continues to moderate. Back in my student days in Vienna some wives and even widows of physicians and professors demanded recognition by being addressed as *Frau Doktor*—even though they themselves had no doctorate or position of their own.

If somehow we could go back to the 1930s, when Viktor was at Steinhof, his demeanor toward his patients and their informality with him would seem peculiar indeed. For example, as a psychiatric resident he attended hospital social events with the women from his pavilion, itself not so notable. He had other ways to reduce the typical distance between doctor and patient. Once he had settled into Steinhof and was gaining professional confidence, Viktor enjoyed spontaneous rapport with patients as well as colleagues. With a knack for accepting his patients at face value, he respected what they had to say. No matter how disturbed, he insisted that there was always a residue in them of what is really human. Instead of attacking their illogical logic or trying to dispute their twisted perceptions of things, Viktor entered their world and communicated at their level. Because of this, patients came to trust and like him. Their interactions were increasingly marked by mutual respect, and this made his therapeutic impact on them more powerful, or at least more likely. One day Viktor described his attendance at a particular hospital dance for Pavilion 3. In the description one can see an example of his manner with patients.

"I was probably the only man in the world dancing the tango with a partner in a straitjacket. I was in my white medical coat, and she was in a straitjacket because she had been very aggressive and was hurting people.

But I danced with her, and this was bridging the gap between doctor and patient, normal and psychotic, you see. When we danced together she was very grateful."

My response to the anecdote was, "How great for the patient. Doctor and patient on the same level as human beings." Viktor was surprised when I asked him if he allowed patients to address him by his first name, and he responded instantly, "Of course. Why not?" Why *not?* For 1935, an interesting twist toward bridging the gap in a huge city mental hospital.

Another story from Steinhof illustrates Viktor's relationships with patients and their responsiveness to him. Identical Viennese twins had gone abroad to live. Both had gone over the edge emotionally and slid into paranoid disorders. Viktor described the situation.

> The twins were brought back to their native Vienna for hospitalization in my pavilion—one from Morocco, the other from Paris. Due partly to heredity, both were suffering from paranoid illness—at the same time but in different countries. One twin had the idea that she was Haile Selassie, then emperor of Ethiopia. The other claimed to be the second soul of Franklin Roosevelt.
>
> The two were fighting with one another and had to be separated into small private rooms. One day I was on duty and making rounds. I entered the room of one of the twins and said to her, "Now how is the second soul of Roosevelt today?" And she said, "Viktor, you are hurting my feelings. I am the one with the Haile Selassie. My sister is the one with the second soul of Roosevelt. Now her idea isn't bad, but mine is even better."

Viktor explained that this showed not only the woman's sense of her own disorder, but also her insight even into her paranoia. This story may illuminate what Viktor wrote shortly after Steinhof: "... even for the schizophrenic there remains a residue of freedom toward fate and toward the disease which man always possesses, no matter how ill he may be, in all situations and at every moment of life, to the very last."[4]

To make good on his resolve to forget what he had learned from Freud and Adler, Viktor worked at listening closely to his patients in order to learn from them. Doing so reminded him of a joke, so he told it.

An Austrian soldier in World War I is looking for a brothel. He comes into a little mostly Jewish town in Poland and sees there an old Jew—in a caftan and so on—crossing the street. The soldier is embarrassed to ask outright, so he asks, "Hello there! Where is the house of your rabbi?" The old man answers, pointing down the street, "Over there, in that house painted green."

"What?" the soldier yells, pretending shock. "Your fine rabbi lives in a brothel?" At that the old Jew rebukes the soldier, "Why do you speak such a scandal? How can you say such a thing about our famous rabbi! The brothel is that red house, over there."

"Thank you," says the soldier.

Viktor, after laughing again, said, "The nicest joke I ever heard. It is the same when I asked my patients, 'How have you overcome such a phobia in a few days?' Then they would tell me that they did exactly as I had recommended. I would ask next what it was that I had recommended. When they told me, I appreciated it—and this is how logotherapy started. Often I could not remember what I was telling my patients, but I did remember what they said to me! So I could say to them honestly, 'Thank you.' "

Viktor received another gift from his patients, albeit given inadvertently. It was his relative immunity to anti-Semitic insults. Later on in the concentration camps this helped him to react calmly when he was verbally abused, reducing the likelihood of a violent incident. Telling of this gift, Viktor put it this way.

"Again and again, when I made rounds at Steinhof, a patient in a net bed would see me and say, 'Jesus, Maria, and Joseph! Again this dirty Jewish swine is coming!' I heard this so many times that I developed an immunity to it. So later, whenever I was called a 'Jew-pig' or something like this, I would simply associate it—by thinking to myself, half-earnestly—that this is just another psychotic person. Therefore, long before Hitler came here, I was already used to hearing these things. And when later I had to wear the Jewish yellow star and people shouted anti-Semitic names at me, I had some immunity to it."

There were other memorable aspects of Viktor's Steinhof experience, though they may seem coincidental to his actual work. Once he entertained a distinguished visitor who had come to celebrate mass at the

Steinhof Church. It was Theodor Innitzer (1875–1955), who was for a time rector of the university and a federal minister before being named archbishop of Vienna and then cardinal in 1933. From the 1920s, Innitzer was to some degree trusted by Jews,[5] so his rather conciliatory encounter with Hitler in 1938 was surprising. Although the cardinal may have been naive about the Hitler threat, when he realized the danger he renounced any Nazi sympathies and did so publicly and courageously. Another act of courage was to turn his own home into a refuge for Jews. Despite these acts, however, Innitzer remained controversial.[6]

It may seem odd that a Jewish psychiatrist would welcome the assignment to host Innitzer at Steinhof even years before the Hitler controversy. But Viktor shared none of Freud's intolerance toward religion and was himself no longer an atheist. And already, in the private journey of his own faith, Viktor had a broad appreciation of religion and a particular admiration not only for his parents' practice but also for people of other faiths. He moved confidently among people of different religions. Given his slant toward faith, it was not out of character for him, even in his formative years at Steinhof, to entertain Cardinal Innitzer and recall the occasion with pleasure.

Viktor and Elly were always keenly interested when I returned to them from a Steinhof exploration. Among my visits there, in the summer of 1996 I ventured through the open doors into Pavilion 3. There was no one around to challenge my intrusion. I saw only two or three patients quietly walking about, and the offices on the ground floor where Viktor had worked for those four years were unoccupied. Though there were white iron bars on the first-floor windows, they did not look prisonlike. The sun shone brightly on the white woodwork of the offices and on a desk where sat a potted plant sprouting a brilliant red blossom. Pavilion 3 is an immense four-story structure that has on the ground level sheltered areas open to the outdoors. Above those are grand porches wrapping elegantly around the corners. Since 1930 the buildings have not changed much. The most striking difference in the place was the absence of hundreds of patients and the activity generated for them and by them. In summers in the 1990s I occasionally attended mass with patients at the Steinhof Church. While the church can seat up to eight hundred, on a particular Sunday there were just over a hundred there together with a few nurses and attendants.

FROM THE CHURCH on the hill and the cardinal's visit, we descend to an in-
glorious aspect of Viktor's Steinhof years. His behavior was, at times at
least, consistent with a nihilistic outlook. For not only did Viktor spend
many a Sunday at the city's vaudeville halls—a use of time over which he
became remorseful[7]—in his later adulthood he spoke regretfully also of
his promiscuity with nurses, willing though they were to fall for his ploys.
Viktor readily admitted, "I did not always live up to my principles." At the
time he also was searching for a true love, and there were three young
women for whom he had genuine affection and perhaps some hopes of a
lasting relationship.

One day, in an effort to gain more understanding of Viktor's loves and
marriage, I steered the conversation to Lola, his first real love in medical
school. I was surprised that he was surprised. "How do you know about
Lola?" "You told me," I replied. Then Viktor raised his voice in even
greater disbelief, "I gave you the name of *Lola?*" he asked. Apparently he
did not remember what he told his patients *or* his friends! "Yes," I said,
"when we were together with Elly here you told me about Lola." "And in
what year did I tell you about this?" "About three years ago, perhaps
1993," I reckoned. Viktor was becoming most curious. "Well then, what
did I *say* about her?" My honest response put him at ease: "Only that she
was your first long relationship, perhaps two years."

> Yes, right. I met Lola, perhaps in '24 or '25, in socialist youth
> circles. She was my first lasting girlfriend. Finally Lola became
> the love of the pathology professor, a colleague of mine. . . . At the
> time I needed a rucksack for an Alpine tour. He had two of them,
> so I gave him my love and took his rucksack in exchange. She was
> my first love. Elly and I once met this professor in Chicago years
> later.
>
> The second was about 1930, near my promotion to doctor of
> medicine, and this was Rosl. I had a short relationship with Rosl,
> whom I met on the street. She listened to some of my schemes,
> and I took her to a meeting of the socialist students—perhaps
> 1929—and told her I had been spokesman for the youth move-
> ment. And I danced with her and other socialist young people.
> Rosl was one of my great loves, a deep love, though later on she

married the prominent socialist architect who designed the Goethehof in Kaisermühlen, Elly's home district.

And my third real love was Tilly Grosser who became my first wife. I met her when she was the head nurse of the internal medicine department of the Rothschild Hospital.

Actually, Tilly was a skilled tailor and was never trained as a nurse. But in wartime it was not unusual for untrained people to do the work of a nurse. Viktor and Tilly met in 1940 when they were both at Rothschild Hospital—but that part of the story must wait.

"... Apart from them [Lola, Rosl, Tilly]," Viktor continued, "I was just interested sexually. At Steinhof I had relationships with nurses." But he did not justify his behavior.

There was an annual dating-mating ritual in which Viktor participated each February. *Fasching* in Vienna is party time—a festival of carnival dances, booze, and costume balls. "Each year at the Fasching ball, in the Sophia Hall, I would go to select girls for the coming year. Because the girls—who were looking for solid, reliable, halfway-intelligent guys, future medical doctors—would go to that ball. So each year there I caught two or three girls. This was about 1930, earlier and later." I inquired, "And other male students were doing the same thing at the ball?" Viktor showed his surprise at my question by shouting, "Certainly, certainly. Why not? What else?" Then in a quieter tone, "And once there was a girl, and it was difficult to catch her. And so I was dancing with her ..." Elly interrupted, "But Viktor, you have never learned dancing!"

"I never learned dancing, but I did dance! I took dancing lessons for one hour, but it was in vain. And guess who was my dancing teacher, who taught me privately for a bit of money? The chief orderly, the warden, of the Steinhof Hospital! I invited him to my room, gave him some schillings, but it was hopeless. At the balls I would dance spontaneously and people would say, 'And what new dance is this? What is it called?' I said, 'I can't remember.' Elly, have you not danced with me?"

Elly said, "Only with you, Viktor." Then he continued.

Anyway, this girl at the ball was hard to convince, to catch, so I asked her, "Are you interested in hearing a lecture at the adult education program? ... There is an excellent lecturer; you cannot imagine how interesting, how he holds your attention—so impressive that you have to hear him! I always listen to him, and I will accompany you if you will come with me to hear him." And she agreed. So we had a rendezvous at the very impressive *Festsaal*, the large hall at the corner of Blumauergasse and Zirkusgasse. We met and sat down at the end of the third or fourth row as the hall was filling up. And I said to her, "At any moment the speaker will appear." And then I left her, without saying a word, and went up to the stage and started my lecture. This is how I impressed the girls, playing such tricks.

Elly jumped in, "Like Viktor's hoax with the snake to get me to come up to his apartment when we first met. And the toothache hoax. Viktor, you were nothing but tricks!"

AS HIS STEINHOF years came to a close in 1937, Viktor was thirty-two and optimistic about his future. In the words of Professor Giselher Guttmann, professionally "Frankl was a rising star." Logotherapy was taking shape even though Viktor's earlier promiscuous lifestyle had not squared with the loftier logotherapeutic claim that sex and loyal love should be reconnected or with its stress upon personal responsibility. But by the time Viktor finished his residency there at Steinhof he was clearly stepping away from both nihilism and promiscuity, asserting "an unconditional faith in life's unconditional meaning."

In retrospect, however, Viktor did not contrive alibis to excuse his loose sexual conduct at Steinhof. He did not justify his behavior as a sexual neurosis, nor did he explain it away as surging libido in search of pleasure, nor did he excuse it as the outcome of unconscious conflict (Freud). And though he was in stature short and thin, at times sickly, and Jewish in an anti-Semitic city, he did not explain his promiscuity as an attempt to overcome his personal inadequacies (Adler). He told me that at Steinhof he had not yet found his true love, but this also was no excuse for his loose behavior. "There are terrible things that I have done, and I tranquilized my conscience; I must tell you about it in this context, so that you don't sanctificate me."

He had learned from his parents, and from Scheler, that sexual relations between human beings should be an expression of mutual devotion. Viktor himself said that only through love do we apprehend the uniqueness of the other person and thereby also discover ourselves, and that spirituality means that we can transcend commonplace conduct. Despite later critics who accused him of moralizing, Frankl insisted that we are by nature outfitted to manage instincts and passions. Since we are not mechanisms compelled to behave in particular ways, we do not *have to* hop from bed to bed. We are not "born to" philander. We are persons with wills and consciences, called upon by both nature and life circumstances to rise above appetites to callings, above drives to tasks, above impulse to loyalty, above desires to destinies. Bodily processes, social settings, personal histories and limitations—even all of these together—cannot determine what a person will make of life. Rather, these are the backdrop against which we face down what *appears* inevitable. Again, Frankl never claimed that our freedom to choose is unlimited, but he always said that it is far greater than we assume. We can act to change situations that are limiting, irritating, hurtful, wrong, even evil. And in circumstances where we have no say, where we are powerless against a truly inevitable fate, we still are free to change ourselves and our responses. This unflinching conviction—about human spirit, freedom, responsibility—is what Frankl made the cornerstone of logotherapy. And only when we fulfill our destinies, do our work, offer our love, make our sacrifices, and choose our attitudes do we find those meanings for which we long.

FOLLOWING HIS STEINHOF years, Viktor's sister Stella was living in Vienna with her husband Walter Bondy. Walter Frankl, Viktor's older brother, was also in the city, married to Else, and working on interior design. In Czerningasse, their parents were living a quiet life since Gabriel had become a "pensioner"—retired from public service on a very modest income. Viktor stayed in touch with his father and mother and went to see them as he could.

Viktor was very busy in his Steinhof years. The hospital schedule was demanding, but somehow he found time for more than just visiting family. There was the suicide prevention program in the city, he was crafting his logotherapy, writing, lecturing and traveling, discussing great ideas, swinging between and finally away from both Freud and Adler, climbing mountains, viewing vaudeville, and hoping that from among the girls he was chasing a true and lasting love would come. With such a full life it is unlikely that Viktor comprehended the implications of developments in

Germany, but Hitler's rise was watched from near and far with frenzy, hope, and apprehension.

The four years Viktor spent at Steinhof corresponded roughly to what Hitler scholar Alan Bullock called "the counterfeit peace."[8] The period 1933–37 in Germany began with Hitler becoming chancellor. By his "democratic" processes he ended democracy. Hitler's skills as opportunist and propagandist paid off handsomely and, once he assumed total power in 1933, he proceeded ruthlessly to neutralize or crush his opposition while posturing publicly as peaceful and sensible. In the same year the prison camp at Dachau was set up and it became a warning to those who might be tempted to resist Hitler.

In Germany official measures against the Jews, starting with bans on their businesses and professions, were deftly put into place as rapidly as Hitler dared. But he was cautious at first since the public needed to be educated regarding the Jewish menace before they would accept more radical measures. In Austria the Nazi party was growing rapidly.

Viktor started his private practice on Alser Strasse and his professional career was underway. That career was brimming with promise—except that it started just before the Nazi curtain fell on its opening scenes. Now we shall watch the horizon darken over several years and survey the events that eclipsed Steinhof's rising star.

CHAPTER 5

Everything Changes,
1937–1942

VIKTOR FRANKL NEVER served in the military for Austria or Germany. "For World War I, I was too young. For World War II, too Jewish."

During what should have been a banner year in his life, Viktor was in a stew. Attaining one's license to practice psychiatry in a dynamic city—the birthplace of psychotherapy where its founder was still living—would be cause, in good times, for high expectations. Professionally Viktor was all set with a first-class education, personal connections to pioneers in psychiatry, a sound reputation, plenty of energy and ideas for his logotherapy, and a close-knit family close by. But he was a Jew. He was in Vienna. And it was 1937.

By 1939, Vienna's centuries as an imperial center were long gone. Ever since 1918 the location of the belittled capital on the border between Western and Eastern Europe had made it increasingly vulnerable to political and military conflict. Now the Nazi steamroller was rumbling from the north. So the stew in which Viktor found himself was a weird blend of positive personal expectations and high anxiety over political developments. If you were a Jew or anyone else considered menacing to the Nazi regime, Vienna was a downright perilous place to be. Unknowingly, the city had contributed Hitler to Germany's army for World War I, a soldier bitterly resentful toward Vienna. Now, as the populace of the city watched Germany stagger back to its feet, they were divided in their opinions as Hitler fused together the Third Reich. While his next move might be to kidnap their republic, many an Austrian heart held the hope that Hitler would do exactly that and unite the two nations.

In 1937, Professor Freud—still godless, still a Jew, and still at Berggasse 19 with his family—was ill and darkly pessimistic. In the preceding year he had "celebrated" his eightieth birthday, and the flood of greetings from around the world did not cheer him greatly. No fewer than 191 writers and artists including Salvador Dali, Hermann Hesse, Aldous Huxley, James Joyce, Pablo Picasso, Franz Werfel, and Thornton Wilder signed a long birthday message written by Thomas Mann and Stefan Zweig. In his thank-you note to Zweig, Freud wrote, ". . . For although I have been exceptionally happy in my home, with my wife and children and in particular with one daughter who to a rare extent satisfies all the expectations of a father, I nevertheless cannot reconcile myself to the wretchedness and helplessness of an old age, and look forward with a kind of longing to the transition into non-existence."[1]

Freud was downcast not only because of age and illness. He was anxious about the well-being of his family and for the future of psychoanalysis under Hitler. It is impossible to imagine how such anxiety hangs over everything and how a deep foreboding spoils all but comradeship, love, and momentary pleasures. As Freud watched his lifework come under siege, he was powerless to do anything about it. More than fifty psychoanalysts had already fled Germany for safer shores. In May 1933 the SS had instigated public book burnings as crowds sang "patriotic" songs and listened to impassioned speeches. Anything on the petty SS blacklists was set afire—which included among many others the writings of Thomas Mann, Jack London, H. G. Wells, Marx and Kafka, Einstein and Freud.[2] Erich Kästner, author of that favorite Frankl story *Emil and the Detectives* and many other children's stories, stood watching in Berlin's Opera Place as his own writings were heaped onto the furious bonfire with the rest. A century earlier, Heinrich Heine had warned that where books are burned, the burning of human beings would follow.[3] Freud made this wry remark: "What progress we are making. In the Middle Ages they would have burnt me; nowadays they are content with burning my books."[4] But not for long.

Blinded in its own paranoia, the Third Reich took to preserving German culture by guarding it against the corrupting influence of Jews, whose contributions to the arts were enormous. How ironic. As the SS burned books they also prohibited any further writing by banned authors. In this way the Nazi regime arbitrarily ended freedom of expression, crushing writers, musicians, and artists. Imagine the effect on German culture and morale if the Reich had lasted—as the party line projected— for the next thousand years.

Both Freud's psychoanalysis and Adler's "socialist" psychology were

Viennese-Jewish inventions repugnant to Hitler. If Frankl had been well known or widely published at the time, surely his Viennese-Jewish logotherapy would have been panned and banned, too, especially for its stress on human freedom and individual responsibility. Freud's focus on sexuality and aggression, Adler's on individual social striving, and Frankl's on the personal quest for spiritual meaning—all of this was unsuitable stuff for the Nazi notion of the racially superior One *Volk* living subserviently under the One *Führer*. More palatable was the "analytical psychology" of the Swiss Protestant psychiatrist Carl Jung, though any endorsement of it by the Nazis required that they ignore Jung's immense debt to psychoanalysis.

In February 1934 a brief civil war broke out in Vienna, in which fascist and Nazi elements joined the Christian Socials against the Social Democrats. As the city was crumbling upon itself, the Austrian nation looked to Italy and the slippery Mussolini to shield it from Hitler. Of that February fighting in the streets of Vienna, Freud wrote:

> Our little bit of Civil War was not at all nice. You could not go out without your passport, electricity was cut off for a day, and the thought that the water supply might run out was very unpleasant. Now everything is calm, the calm of tension, you might say; just like waiting in a hotel room for the second shoe to be flung against the wall. It cannot go on like this; something is bound to happen. Whether the Nazis will come, or whether our own homemade Fascism will be ready in time, or whether Otto von Habsburg will step in, as people now think. . . . You are quite right in your expectation that we intend to stick it out here resignedly. For where should I go in my state of dependence and physical helplessness? And everywhere abroad is so inhospitable. Only if there really were a satrap of Hitler's ruling in Vienna I would no doubt have to go, no matter where.[5]

At about the time Freud wrote those words, Viktor was preparing to start his residency at Steinhof. That so much of life could go on as usual is a sign that many Jews in Vienna underestimated the danger Nazism posed to them. Nevertheless, early on and with Nazi encouragement, the emigration of thousands of Jews was underway. Though estimates vary, by late 1939 as many as 100,000 of Vienna's 175,000 Jews had emigrated here and there.[6] Some 66,000 stayed on in the city, including the Freuds and Frankls, hoping for the best and not wanting to believe the worst.

Among those departing Austria for keeps were Alfred Adler and family. In the late 1920s, Adler already had been lecturing occasionally at Columbia University in New York, and when the Social Democratic Party was suppressed in Austria in 1934 he became keenly fearful for himself, his family, and his lifework under Hitler. His guidance clinics were shut down and he turned his sights toward America as the best safe haven. Uprooting from Vienna, by 1935 Adler had made New York his permanent home, out of harm's way. His lecturing continued both locally and internationally— at least in politically hospitable territory such as Britain. But in May 1937 while on a lecture tour, Adler collapsed from a heart attack on Union Street in Aberdeen, Scotland. He died in a police ambulance at the age of sixty-seven. After Adler's death, his daughter Alexandra and son Kurt remained in New York and continued to practice there. Frankl learned of Adler's passing as he was finishing up at Steinhof.

It seems incongruous that Freud, fourteen years older, should outlive Adler. The two had hated one another for decades, and when Freud learned of Adler's death he had no kind word to say. Rather, Freud sarcastically summed up Adler's life and work: "For a Jewish boy from a Viennese suburb a death in Aberdeen, Scotland, is an unprecedented career and a proof of how far he had come. Truly, his contemporaries have richly rewarded him for his service in having contradicted psychoanalysis."[7] No love was lost where none existed.

TODAY ON ALSER Strasse, at number 32, there is a restaurant and an electronics shop on the street level. Above these, apartment 12 is the space that Viktor used for the start of his private practice in 1937—in the living room of Stella's apartment. As money was tight for all the Frankls, it is no surprise that they improvised in using one another's apartments for both housing and work. Brother Walter helped by designing a desk for Viktor— a creation that cleverly incorporated a few bookshelves on its front side, and Viktor was fond of it. This should have been a wonderful time for the senior Frankls too as their children settled into marriages and careers. They must have been especially proud of Viktor as he established his practice right in the university district, near the Psychiatric Clinic and only a block away from the General Hospital.

The Urania Theater was often the setting for public lectures as part of Vienna's extensive adult education program. Since 1910, the Urania with its distinctive observatory dome has stood prominently on the Ring at the Danube Canal, just where the Aspern Bridge crosses the canal into Leopoldstadt and the old Frankl neighborhood. Over the years the unique building has served variously as a cultural and learning center, an auditorium, and a movie house. It is still in use today.

On a particular occasion, a psychiatrist from the University Psychiatric Clinic was on the lecture schedule, but at the last moment he asked Frankl to stand in for him. "I'm just too busy this week to do the lecture at Urania. Would you do me the favor of lecturing in my place Friday evening? The Urania is even near your Czeringasse." Just before agreeing to take the assignment, Viktor asked what topic had been announced. It was "Anxiety as a Sign of Our Time."

As Viktor made his way to the Urania to speak, it was no ordinary Friday, that March 11, 1938. The streets of the city had been abuzz all day and the people flocking to the Ring were far more wound up than anxious. Among them were SS and SA personnel[8] and local Nazis organizing and agitating in their expectation that—at long last in the Austrian capital—they would have their day in the sun. In fact, they had essentially taken over the streets. People and buildings alike were decked out in swastikas. The event that was causing such a stir—and not just among the party faithful of Austrian Nazis—was the impending invasion of the country by German forces.

For months Hitler had been conniving to pull off the seizure of Austria, and now he was finalizing the plan. Kurt von Schuschnigg, chancellor of Austria, was still resisting the Nazis and had shrewdly scheduled a plebiscite for Sunday, believing that a public referendum would affirm Austria's independence. But under belligerent threats from Hitler it had been canceled. An ultimatum was phoned to Schuschnigg. The same Hitler who had left Vienna in 1913 as a draft-dodger was now adamant about his return—with his own mechanized military—to grab Austria as his first major international treasure for the Reich. And he would grab it one way or another.

That evening in Vienna, the Frankl story was placed at a curious intersection of the two events: one momentous—the imminent "homecoming" of Hitler; and one modest—a lecture by this young Jewish psychiatrist on the topic "Anxiety as a Sign of Our Time." Cutting through the Nazi mania on the Ring, Viktor arrived at the Urania with his lecture notes in his pocket. And while anxiety was no topic for the exhilarated mobs in the streets, it was most fitting for the Jews and other thoughtful people gathered inside the Urania.

Frankl started his lecture, but soon one of the auditorium doors was thrown open. In the doorway stood an SA official, having come in from the street in full uniform including brown shirt and high black boots. Viktor thought that the officer would force an end to the lecture at once and disperse the audience. "In a fraction of a second I told myself that there must be some way of stopping him, so that it will not be easy for him to carry out his intention. I must grab his attention so deeply that he will be nailed to his spot. At that moment I turned on the full capacity of my oratory. And he stood there listening for more than half an hour! He did not make a move to interrupt me. When I had finished and was going out of the Urania, in the streets must have been one hundred thousand people, many with torches. This was the coming of the Third Reich. . . . I dashed home and found my mother in bed crying. Chancellor Schuschnigg had just given his farewell speech and she was listening to very sad music on the radio."

At 7:50 P.M. that farewell message had been broadcast as Viktor lectured. The people gathered around their radio sets at home were variously stunned with fright or breathless with excitement. The fearful, among whom were most Jews of course, wisely remained in their homes. But thousands of citizens poured into the streets screaming, "Heil Hitler!" "Hang Schuschnigg!" "Kill the Jews!" "Heil Hitler!"

The next morning, Saturday, the German forces crossed the borders with their colossal war machinery, but there was no need for it. The Austrians who lined the streets were cheering. They reached out to touch the soldiers, not to strike them; they were throwing flowers, not grenades. Throughout the day the enthusiasm was so great that the troops were frequently delayed in streets clogged with admirers and blocked by their own broken-down tanks and trucks. Night fell and the "invasion" celebration continued.

Hitler had spent his day first flying to Munich, then traveling by car into Austria. On his way to Linz he made sentimental stops at boyhood places along the way. Then he settled into the Weinzinger Hotel in Linz, having seen for himself the tumultuous welcome of the very Austrians he had come to conquer. Here in the familiar surroundings of his obscure birth and childhood, Hitler was celebrity and hero.

It was past midnight in Vienna when the advance troops finally arrived. The mobs, already hoarse from shouting, mustered a raucous welcome. On Sunday morning, throngs were still waiting for Hitler, but he was in no hurry, visiting the cemetery of his family in Leonding. Later in the day he strutted at a reunion bash in his honor at the Linz hotel, which included people from his youth. Hitler enjoyed himself, but he was waiting for word that laws had been passed to legalize the annexation of Austria. Even Mussolini by then had pledged not to interfere with the German invasion. In the evening Hitler received from Vienna the news he wanted, and he was elated. Now the last obstacles to the peaceful takeover were removed, and what remained was the victory trip into the capital.

On Monday the journey from Linz to Vienna was slow due to exultant crowds and more mechanical breakdowns. Further, Hitler's henchmen were cautious about possible security breaches in the city. It was late in the afternoon before the convoy entered Vienna and by then Hitler was in a bad humor.[9] But the arrival became the public symbol of what would be known ever after as the *Anschluss*—the annexation of Austria. The Nazis put an even more positive spin on it by hailing the day as the longed-for union of the German-speaking nations. Those sentiments were splashed across a banner spanning the front of the famous Loos Haus across from the Hofburg palace: "The Same Blood Belongs to the Same Reich."

When Hitler finally appeared, the adulation of the crowd was good medicine for his foul mood. Standing erect in the front seat of his grand Mercedes convertible, he returned his Nazi salute to the throngs along the sidewalks. He was driven to the Ring and finally to the Imperial Hotel, which was now dressed up in swastikas. There he was ushered in on the red carpet and up to the royal suite. In front of this very hotel he had shoveled snow for a bit of money when he was a destitute would-be artist twenty-five years earlier. Now the imperial suite itself was his and he appeared on its balcony to appease the unruly crowd in the street below as they demanded a speech from him.[10]

The next day, Tuesday, March 15, Hitler left the hotel for the mass rally at the Heldenplatz, the "Place of Heroes" in front of the great Hofburg. There waiting for him was a sea of humankind, flowing from the palace over the broad lawns and roadways. As Hitler's magnificent vehicle came through the *Burgtor*—the arched gateway into the imperial plaza—the multitude cheered. Hitler ascended to the high portico of the Hofburg where the sight buoyed him up for his speech.

It was and is difficult to estimate the size of the crowd. Nazi propaganda chose certain photographs to maximize the impression. Hundreds of thousands had gathered, but there are documentary films in Vienna that show areas to the rear of the plaza that are not filled with people. But by any measure the gathering was enormous and the capstone of Hitler's return.

At once Vienna became the scene of concentrated violence against its Jewish citizens. By the time Hitler pulled out of the city that day, Jews were already being humiliated—including the aging Chief Rabbi Taglich—by being forced to scrub the sidewalks with tiny brushes in front of jeering audiences. Others were compelled under threat of violence to paint "JEWS" on the fronts of their dwellings and shops. A young girl was compelled in front of her parents' shop to bend and rise repeatedly, wearing a sign, "Do not buy from me. I am a Jewish sow."[11] The reign of terror was on. Here is one account.

> The horror of persecution of Jews and other "enemies" of the new regime emerged from reports of the British Legation. On 15 March the chargé d'affaires wrote: "Jewish cars and property have been seized and many Jewish houses searched. I hear that many Jews have been detained." Cars belonging to Legitimists and supporters of Schuschnigg had also been confiscated and many members of both groups as well as many socialists had been arrested; there were rumours of executions but he was unable to confirm this. A few days later he reported that the Jews were treated as they were in Germany and there were many stories of acts of brutality committed against them; arrests were said "to run in the thousands . . ."[12]

For Jews, socialists, and the supporters of Schuschnigg, staying off the streets that day was a very good idea. It became impossible even for average people to have a normal day. And in the epicenter of psychotherapy, even the significance of Freud and Adler dwindled in the whirlwind of public events. What did they matter compared to Hitler at the Heldenplatz? The relatively unknown Frankls were huddling cautiously at Czerningasse 6, since the streets of their neighborhood had turned treacherous. The very famous Freuds were nervously sticking to Berggasse 19, after quite a week of their own.

On the past Thursday an official from the American embassy had visited Freud, following the dispatch by President Roosevelt of his secretary of state to intervene diplomatically for Freud. The Nazis, afraid of an international outcry if anything happened to the ailing Freud, were prepared to grant protection and emigration to him and his family. On Friday evening Freud had listened to Schuschnigg's farewell speech on radio. The following day he penned two Latin words in his journal: *Finis Austriae.* Then on Tuesday, the very day of the Heldenplatz rally, Nazi hoodlums raided Freud's publishing house. Another group of brown-shirted storm troopers entered his home on Berggasse and searched it as the Freuds sat by watching. The troopers left with the family passports and six thousand schillings.

Even after this, Freud still hesitated about leaving Vienna—until March 22, that is. On that day the Gestapo showed up and searched the Freud apartment again. They apprehended Anna, Freud's much-loved daughter, and took her with them for questioning. So desperate was the situation that Freud had already provided Anna with drugs to use in case she was subjected to torture. Thanks to some strokes of luck and a bit of royal intervention at the Gestapo office by Princess Marie Bonaparte—a psychoanalyst herself and an intimate friend of the Freuds—Anna was released unharmed. But Freud had seen enough. Now the patriarch, weak as he was, started packing. Fortunately they had permits to go to England—the whole household of eighteen people, together with furnishings, books, and other possessions.[13] Trainloads of hapless people were departing Vienna, but not for safe refuge in exile. Jews and others who were problems to the regime were being loaded into boxcars for shipment to Dachau or Buchenwald. By the time Freud left by train for France and England on Saturday, June 4, thousands already had been deported from Vienna.

So the fates of the psychotherapeutic three were profoundly affected by Hitler. Only Frankl was left in Vienna. From natural causes Adler was dead, and for unnatural reasons Freud was in England. Psychoanalysis and individual psychology were suffering their Nazi fate, at least locally. As the Hitler vengeance was engulfing the Frankl family, so it also threatened to abort logotherapy and bury it with its founder. Unlike the work of Freud and Adler, logotherapy was unknown abroad and had no body of literature to prolong it.

After the *Anschluss,* the emigration process for Jews was slowed. Visas were hard to come by, and for the most part the nations of the world were not welcoming refugee Jews anyway. Although Viktor's name ended up on the visa waiting list at the American embassy, without the fame, connections, and good fortune of Freud, an escape for the Frankl family was now unlikely. However, there might still be some chance for Viktor or Stella to leave Austria as individuals.

BY 1938, FRANKL'S promising career was sidetracked by Nazi policy. All Jewish men had "Israel" added as a middle name on official documents, and Jewish women "Sarah." These identifiers helped the SS to keep tabs on the Jews and limit their activities and access. Some Jews kept tabs on other Jews, perhaps hoping for special privilege should the situation worsen as they assisted the SS in monitoring and enforcing constraints. Jewish children were shut out of public education and Jewish physicians lost their licenses for normal practice. Viktor had no choice but to move back to Czerningasse, there to both reside and work in the little flat where his old parents were still living. On the front of their building was the new mandatory blue sign for a *Judenbehandler:* Dr. Viktor Emil Israel Frankl, Jew-Caretaker for Neurology and Psychiatry. He was permitted to see Jewish patients only and his practice was shorn of its former respectability and affiliations.

It was not only Viktor who had to leave Alser Strasse and his practice. Stella had to give up her flat when the building was "Aryanized" along with housing all over the city. An Aryanized building was one purged, cleansed of its Jewish inhabitants. Their possessions were confiscated, including Viktor's custom-designed desk, the gift from Walter. "Aryanize" was a lovely label for the humiliating eviction of Jews from their own dwellings and businesses. As members of the superior Aryan race—non-Jewish Caucasians in Nazi doctrine—the new tenants took up the spaces under official policy. Stella's flat went to Oskar Helmer (1887–1963). Helmer became a socialist who was detained by the Gestapo repeatedly, and who after the Holocaust became Austria's minister of the interior. Helmer's postwar talk and behavior toward the Jews were mixed at best, and that he took possession of an Aryanized apartment added insult to injury.

In the fall of 1938, Hitler was continuing his bold adventures including a move into bordering Czechoslovakia. Such international exploits only inspired local Nazi fanatics and, on October 6 in Vienna, they set three synagogues ablaze. Within a month *Kristallnacht* erupted—the Night of Crystal—a poetic name for the broken glass littering the streets from two days of terror throughout Germany and Austria. It was a sensational escalation of anti-Semitic fanaticism, orchestrated from behind the scenes by the SS. Under orders, the police did nothing to stop the assaults on Jews and on their homes, businesses, and places of worship. The toll was enormous: over ninety dead, nearly two hundred synagogues damaged or demolished, thirty thousand wealthy Jews arrested, businesses ransacked, and insurance payments confiscated.[14] Thereafter yet more repressive steps were taken against the Jews. Public parks were put off limits and publications shut down. The intentions of the Reich became ever more transparent and terrifying. In Vienna, some Jews were beaten ruthlessly before being thrown aboard the Dachau-bound trains. SS men exploited women in daring disregard of the prohibition of sexual relations with Jews. Naturally, following *Kristallnacht* there was a new surge among Jews for emigration. In fact, Stella's husband, Walter Bondy, left in 1939 for Australia, hoping to start a business. Shortly after, Stella joined him there. Thus they escaped Vienna just in time and lived with their family in safety through and long past the Holocaust. Walter and Else Frankl also left Vienna and apparently found a measure of security in Italy. They belonged to a community of immigrants there who were supported and given at least some protection by the pope. But their safety was not assured as Nazis assumed more control.

Viktor also considered leaving and talked quietly with his close friend and colleague, Paul Polak, about going to England or America together. But months passed and no immigration visa became available to allow Viktor to go anywhere.

In September 1939 the Nazi regime brazenly invaded Poland and—because of a treaty—not even Russia interfered. But then Britain and France declared war on Germany. A week before the declaration of war, Freud died in his London home—in freedom, so to speak. To the end he had remained active, even offering interviews in English for British radio. He had suffered his cancer heroically, but with the assistance of his physician by mutual consent, Freud passed away quietly, and among the most famous of men. Peter Gay, Freud's biographer, notes the fortunate circumstance that Freud died before learning the fate of his sisters.[15] Adolfine died of starvation at Theresienstadt; the other three were murdered at Auschwitz.

Back in Vienna, despite the war, Frankl became chief of neurology at the Rothschild Hospital in 1940. Austria was fully part of the Third Reich, but Frankl's appointment as department head afforded him and his parents a degree of protection against Nazi measures being implemented. For practical reasons the Gestapo recognized that certain professionals were needed in particular roles, and Viktor hoped that he could continue to provide security for his mother and father as the deportations to concentration camps increased.

The Rothschild was a well-established Jewish hospital located on the Währinger Gürtel at Gentzgasse until 1960, when it was demolished. Today the hospital no longer exists in any form. But in its day the Rothschild played an important role in the city and for the thriving Jewish population.

Starting in 1938 the hospital's limits were stretched when it became the emergency treatment center for Jewish victims of violence in Vienna's streets. Following widespread eruptions of brutality the hallways and even the lawns of the Rothschild were filled with Jewish wounded.[16] By then Viktor had fixed his faith in life's ultimate meaning and had gained both bearing and footing as he took up his responsibilities at the Rothschild, which was already under the supervision of the Gestapo.

During this time Viktor began to collaborate with the fatherly Professor Otto Pötzl in some dangerous schemes to save Jewish mental patients from the SS euthanasia program—despite the fact that Pötzl was among many other decent people who had joined the National Socialists. There was an edge to be gained for the jobs and prosperity that the National Socialists presumably would bring to Germany and Austria. In any case, even after Pötzl became a party member he continued to receive Jewish patients illegally at his clinic and referred them to other Aryan physicians who provided treatment, also illegally. Viktor benefited enormously from Pötzl's power and connections in protecting Jewish patients. Pötzl even went to the Rothschild whenever Viktor called for him.

Pötzl was, in Viktor's enduring estimation, "no Nazi"—not in sympathy, not in behavior. In their repeated high-risk venture, Frankl and Pötzl were labeling Jewish patients with false diagnoses, using the categories of illness least questioned by Nazi authorities. Pötzl also helped protect psychotic Jewish patients who turned up at the University Psychiatric Clinic. From a certain time forward, whenever Pötzl had Jewish patients whose mental illness could be kept under control he referred them to the Jewish *Altersheim*—the "old folks' home" and hospital on Malzgasse. The referrals were made by telephone and Viktor was notified immediately to go to Malzgasse. There he certified officially that the patient was *not* psychotic, but rather suffering from aphasia or something else. Schizophrenia and other labels were avoided scrupulously since they might doom patients to euthanasia. It was Pötzl's willingness to risk his own neck by sabotaging the Nazi program to save Jewish lives that solidified Viktor's trust in his mentor.

Viktor described one of Pötzl's visits to the Rothschild. "Pötzl walked up and down the corridors with me, with the National Socialist pin in his lapel, enjoying the best of Jewish humor as he helped me with patients. In no way, *in no way whatsoever* was Pötzl anti-Semitic or a National Socialist in his heart."

The Steinhof Hospital also had come under SS supervision just three years after Viktor finished his residency, and a euthanasia program was underway there.[17] By the thousands, mentally ill and severely handicapped children and young people were killed in such "euthanasia sanitariums" in Austria.[18] Viktor recalled a very sad twist of fortune that he witnessed on a certain occasion.

> I remember having to pick up a Jewish man and woman who could no longer remain in the private care of a married couple. With me was a social worker from the Jewish Community Center. On the way back two taxis were ahead of us, each transporting a patient. At one point I noticed that one taxi drove in our direction toward the old folks' home, while the other made a left turn.
>
> "How come?" I asked the social worker.
>
> "Oh, yes," she said. "I forgot to tell you. The woman who was taken to the left is no longer Jewish. She converted some time ago, so we are not allowed to accept her at the [Jewish] home for the aged. Unfortunately, she must be taken to the Steinhof mental hospital."
>
> What a crossroad! Straight ahead the safety of the old folks' home, and to the left the road leads to Steinhof and on to the gas chamber! Who could have foreseen what would result from this

woman's decision, for whatever reason, to be converted. A shiver
ran down my spine when I realized what circumstances can turn
into a death sentence.[19]

The Jews in Vienna were soon required to wear the yellow Jewish
star—prominently pinned or sewn on their outer garments for identification. It was humiliating and invited taunts or worse from the Nazis and
their sympathizers. Jews were also banned from streetcars, but because of
Viktor's role as hospital department head he had a pass that admitted him
to the trams. However, Viktor recalled that the pass did not keep a conductor from harassing him.

"It could be dangerous to take the streetcar from Czerningasse to the
Rothschild. I had to wear the yellow star, of course. But I had a pass to ride.
Still one day the conductor refused to let me board. I told him that I was
the head of neurology at Rothschild Hospital. . . . The conductor said that
my pass was not valid on Sunday. But I told him that as head of the department, even on Sunday I had to go to the hospital if need be to do my
job. He said, 'You leave the car immediately or I will throw you out while
the tram is moving.' "

Another hassle occurred when a poster went up around the city announcing that men born between 1904 and 1906 must now register for
military service. Viktor did not do so, however, fearing a beating if he
showed the Jewish audacity to turn up at a Nazi recruiting office. But they
were keeping track and he was notified to report. When he got there, to
Viktor's surprise the military officer at the police station was a former
classmate from high school. Seeing this, he expected that they would exchange greetings in their old familiar way—*Grüss' Dich*—using the intimate pronoun. Instead, the officer addressed Viktor formally, *Grüss' Sie*.
Everything had changed between them. When Viktor explained the reason for not reporting—that he feared reprisals for doing so—his former
schoolmate slapped him with a heavy fine but let him go. Such damned-
if-you-do, damned-if-you-don't dealings went on almost constantly under
the Nazis. Flowing through the real dangers of the time were the petty an-
tics of Nazi bureaucrats. Much of the comedy was lost because of abuse
and violence, but there were lots of jokes going around—carefully told—
about Hitler, his henchmen, and the whole bizarre state of affairs.

While the development of logotherapy was stunted by the circumstances at the time, Viktor's approach was useful, even crucial, in his efforts

to survive and to shield his parents. Here is an incident described in his own words.

> One day I was called at seven in the morning. My mother went to the telephone and then told me, "Viktor, the Gestapo." I went to the phone. "We want you to report tomorrow morning at nine at room 208" or something like that. "Should I bring my toothbrush and so on?" "Yes." This was a sign that I might not come back, but be sent to a camp. I went there and I sat down and he started to interview me. "Do you know Herzog who is now a spy in Switzerland? Are you affiliated with him?" "No." Then he asked, "How come you have not yet been arrested?" "Because I hold this position at the Jewish hospital." "How come your father has not yet been arrested?" "He was for thirty-five years in government service as director of a ministry, now a pensioner." "And what is your medical specialty?"
>
> Then we discussed what is psychotherapy, what is psychoanalysis, and so on, even for two hours! Again and again another Gestapo official came in and I stood up respectfully. But each time he left, my interviewer became less aggressive, and we talked about how the psychoanalysts had emigrated and there was hardly anyone left in Vienna. Then he asked, "What about the fear of open spaces [the common agoraphobia], and how would a psychiatrist treat it?" He told me he has a friend who is suffering from it, and I told him about paradoxical intention. "Tell your friend that when his anxiety crops up, he should go for a walk and try to better his record by having five strokes, and if he dies what a nice funeral he will have—he will start smiling just as you are smiling, and he will have the victory over his anxiety by putting distance between it and himself, instead of trying to avoid it."

Viktor suspected that the officer himself was the patient. "And I gave him good logotherapy and it must have helped him. Otherwise I cannot explain why I was allowed to stay for another year in Vienna together with my parents. Perhaps as an honorarium, he saw to it that we might stay."

TO VIKTOR, PERSEVERING in Vienna with his parents was an obligation he took to heart. But as loving parents do, Gabriel and Elsa were more con-

cerned for their children than for themselves. They were relieved that
Stella was settled in Australia, though they missed her terribly. Missing
Walter too, at least they could hope that he and his wife were in a place of
safety. It was at this time, after years of waiting for an affidavit of financial support abroad, that Viktor finally received notice to come to the
American embassy to pick up a visa—his ticket to freedom and future.
And although his mother and father were growing old and were depending on Viktor in the menacing situation in Vienna, he recalled that they
were overjoyed when the visa notice came. They assumed, with high
hopes for him, that he would make the break for the United States—for
his own well-being and for the lifework he was yet to do. But instead of
being joyful over this stroke of good fortune, Viktor was conflicted.
Walking past *Stephansdom* (St. Stephen's Cathedral), the literal and symbolic center of Vienna, he heard organ music. Looking back on this, Viktor
explained that his privacy with regard to his faith has always kept him
from admitting that he prayed in the cathedral. Hence, the following
episode could also be understood by an atheist as serendipity.

Am I now allowed to leave my parents, to go somewhere to
develop my ideas? On the other hand, if I leave, within two weeks
they will be sent to a concentration camp. My parents were sure
that I would use this unique chance. I had talked about it again
and again. But on this day I went into St. Stephen's Cathedral to
sit down and think it over again. There was organ music, maybe
for one hour. But I could not decide anything. The situation
seemed unsolvable. What was my responsibility—to care for my
lifework or to care for my parents? In such a circumstance one
wishes for a hint from heaven.

So I went home and there was my father, and he had a broken
piece of stone, a remnant he had found in the ruins of the synagogue.[20] I found out that the chunk of stone was a piece of the Ten
Commandments. Aha, and on it was engraved a Hebrew letter.
And my father said, "Viktor, I know what part of the Ten
Commandments this piece belongs to, because this letter is part of
the abbreviation for only one of the commandments—*honor thy
father and thy mother and you will stay in the land.*" At that moment I told myself, this is the answer. I let the visa expire.

And at that time I didn't know Tilly.

TILLY GROSSER WAS Viktor's third real love, after he had gotten over Lola and Rosl. At thirty-five, Viktor was nearly twice Tilly's age when they met at the Rothschild and became friends. She was from a Jewish family in the city and was working at the nursing station of internal medicine for Professor Donath, who shared a hospital office with Viktor. Viktor first noticed Tilly for her beauty—like a Spanish dancer with very dark hair and dark, shining eyes, a straight nose—and her energetic manner, which was not overly feminine. But he became most enchanted by her disarming simplicity, about which she had no inferiority feelings.

> She was not primitive or silly but she did not grasp the importance of ideas or the quality of literary formulations. On the other hand, what she did understand was done with a naiveté that one could enjoy. It comes to mind, for instance, that once we strolled on a walkway across the Danube Canal, where the Gestapo office was. And it was windy weather, which is nothing unusual in Vienna. We were strolling there and I said we have a *Rückenwind*—a wind to our backs, a term I used only playfully. And she asked, "What then is the opposite, a *Bauchwind*—a belly wind—or what?" A good question, after all. Her naiveté was attractive; it was creative and one could laugh without apology. She did not go far in school and even her Aunt Hertha said Tilly did not have an academic way of thinking.

Also, whenever Tilly had a friend "there was such a solidarity between them that you would not want to become the enemy of either, see? Tilly would go through fire for a friend. But I loved her also for her understanding heart and her natural intuition." In time they both recognized that neither her attractiveness nor his intelligence or position drew them to each other. Rather, character was more important to them both.

In so ominous a time for Jews, Viktor remembered a severe scare for the family.

> Once Tilly and I were sitting in a small room in her mother's home, and it was night. And some Jewish policemen under the Nazis were going around Leopoldstadt with notices that people had to report the next morning at three o'clock with no more than

ten kilograms of baggage, bound for Poland or Auschwitz—it was
different places at different times. There was a great danger that
this might happen to Tilly's mother, who stayed in Vienna instead
of going to be with her husband in Porto Alegre, in Brazil, where
he had become a professor of English language. She did not want
to leave Tilly alone in Vienna. Tilly's brother also had emigrated,
to Switzerland. [Tilly's sister emigrated also, but her destination is
uncertain.]

Anyway, it was about nine in the evening and someone rang
the doorbell. Everybody was convinced it was a notice to come
with the luggage, and instead it was someone from the Jewish
Community Center giving her the message that she had to be, in
the morning at six o'clock, to join the young people who had to
bring the furniture from the apartments of Jews who had been
deported—the Nazis were taking everything. And Tilly's mother,
this cultivated lady, was happy to be told she must move furniture
because this secured her from being deported. After this notice arrived, Tilly said, with primitive Viennese slang expression, "Tell
me now, isn't God quite something?" Somewhere I have said that
this was the shortest beautiful definition of deity that I had ever
heard.

On an occasion at the hospital, Tilly told Viktor about her "subnormal
temperature" and at once he felt concern. So he told his colleague
Professor Donath about it, suggesting that he look at Tilly since she was
the daughter of Professor Grosser. Donath examined Tilly and later told
Viktor, "I can find nothing. But of course she is a very active girl, with a
lot of admirers. Perhaps there is too much nightlife and so on, with too
many friends, and she might be worn out."

Viktor recalled, "I had to listen to all of that! But then, a few weeks
later I announced to him that I am going to marry Tilly, and would he do
us the honor of being my best man. Then he may have regretted what he
said about her!"

One day Tilly was at home with Viktor in Czerningasse, and she was
preparing lunch for him and his parents. He recalled it vividly.

The telephone rang and I was called by the Jewish hospital to
an emergency. I had no time for coffee, so I swallowed a few cof-

fee beans—this was during war. I took a taxi[21] and rushed to the hospital. After two hours I returned to Czerningasse, rang our bell to indicate that I was home, and Tilly and my mother appeared at the top landing as I rushed up the stairs. I expected that Tilly would say that the lunch was cold or complain that she would have to fix it all over again. But she didn't mention anything and did not bombard me with questions about being late, and so on. Instead, she asked me how was the patient, and how did the surgery go, was I able to help him? It was at that moment that I decided to marry Tilly. . . .

There was a separate marriage office for Jews in the Zirkusgasse, but this office was closing permanently on the last day of 1941. So Tilly and I went there just in time and we were married. The other couple that married on the same day was my history professor from high school, Dr. John Edelmann, and his bride. I met him again in 1942 in the first concentration camp at Theresienstadt. So my history teacher was then *living* history: along with Tilly and me, the last Viennese Jews to marry under the Nazis, since the office there was shut down the day after our civil ceremony. . . .

Tilly and I also had a religious service at the Jewish Community Center, under the *chuppe*. After the ceremony we had our wedding photos taken and then walked through the streets, since Jews were forbidden to use taxis. . . .

Of course they didn't dare to make legislation to forbid Jewish couples to marry—not under the eyes of Britain or America and so on. But in fact, after the Jewish marriage office was shut down there was a notice sent around that if any Jewish couple ventured to apply for marriage at the regular government offices they would be sent immediately to the concentration camps. That [ostensibly] was the penalty for being a nuisance to the National Socialist officials.

And the same punishment was applied if someone became pregnant. Any Jewish woman who got pregnant would be sent immediately to the concentration camp. This resulted, of course, in a rash of abortions.

Tilly became pregnant and we had to have an abortion or be sent away. There was a sensitive woman, a novelist in Vienna, who was shocked that Tilly would be forced in the circumstances to undergo an abortion for her survival. This woman was struck severely, and it was moving to see her reaction. "How could you possibly agree to this? How could you accept this? Surely no child of love should ever be sacrificed!" Tilly and I took this from her, of course, because we had no choice and had to accept it.

Viktor and Tilly also had no choice but to move in with Viktor's parents in their tiny flat in Czerningasse, and there they lived childless. A third of a century later, in 1978, Viktor published *The Unheard Cry for Meaning*. Its dedication reads, simply: "To Harry or Marion, an unborn child."

CHAPTER 6

Life and Death at Theresienstadt, 1942–1944

EVEN IF THERE had been someplace for the Frankls to go, by 1941 there was virtually no way for the family to leave Austria. The city of science, songs, and dreams had become their cage. Of Vienna's prewar Jewish population only 20 percent was still there, and in a dramatic policy shift Eichmánn ended their emigration. Hitler's "final solution"—the extermination program—was implemented and applied to the Jews who remained in much of Europe. In fact many who had left Germany and Austria for other European nations ended up in concentration camps anyway when the Nazis occupied and extended the deportation program to those "safe" countries. This caused additional concern to the Frankls, for even though sister Stella was secure with her husband in faraway Australia, brother Walter and his wife Else were in Italy where the situation was much more shaky.

From Vienna the SS transports increased, headed for "the East." At that time the East meant something unsettling at best, but few imagined the extermination camps or believed the "rumors." Like most others, the Frankls expected to be resettled in Jewish ghettos and that life there would be tolerable. Ghettoizing meant massing and isolating the Jews in designated areas, typically near a city. Due to poverty the conditions were normally substandard, and with vast overcrowding the ghettos became slums. But since relatives and friends could still be with one another, this was better than being sent to a concentration camp.

However, the increasingly sinister impression created by the deportations made Vienna's Jews ever more apprehensive. Some non-Jews were so distressed by what was happening that they imperiled themselves to protect Jews and others from the SS. All Jews in occupied territory were compelled to wear identification on their outer garments, most commonly the yellow star with the word "Jew" appearing in the respective language of their country. Whether the sewn-on star, or a pin, tag, or armband, these made it possible for the SS to isolate Jews from other populations, and similar identification badges were developed for other "dangerous" elements—a purple triangle for Jehovah's Witnesses, a pink triangle for homosexuals, green for criminals, and so on.[1]

One of the people who was concerned about Nazi victims was a kindly old Aryan woman who lived in the second *Stiege*—the lower rent rear section—of the Frankl apartment building in Czerningasse. Toni Grumbach was her grandson, and Viktor recalled that the Frankl children were not close to Toni nor did they "take him so earnestly" in their youth. But in retrospect Viktor spoke gratefully of him. "I remember during the pogrom initiated by Goebbels that Toni came to our home just to tell me, 'Viktor you can come to me at any time and sleep in my flat. In that way maybe we can overcome these days of danger for Jewish people.'" Toni could provide secure shelter because he was in the SA—the nonmilitary *Sturmabteilung*—the Nazi Brownshirts.

So, in addition to family and Tilly, friends helped make life worthwhile for Viktor. Their stories illustrate what is best about human relationships. One such friend was Hubert Gsur, an Aryan. Although Viktor did not know it at the time, Gsur was an illegal communist and part of the resistance movement against the Nazis. In high-risk stakes, Gsur was also a member of the German armed forces, the *Wehrmacht*. The son of a forester and an uncomplicated man, by trade Gsur was a typewriter mechanic.

Even before Hitler, Viktor had become an avid mountain climber. Now the SS had petty regulations for everything, including rules to keep Jews from climbing. After a year away from the Schneeberg and Rax mountains south of Vienna, Viktor was having vivid dreams about them. He ached for a climb. But even in the mountains he did not dare be seen wearing his yellow star. Gsur understood Viktor's longing and made a dicey offer he could not refuse: that Gsur, in military uniform to deflect suspicion, would take Viktor, with yellow star hidden, for a climb. If the authorities discovered this escapade, both could be deported or executed. But they calculated the chances of being caught and off they went. Upon arriving at the foot of the Hohe Wand, Viktor convulsed with emotion as he kept on kissing the face of the rock in front of him.

Eventually the SS found out about some of Gsur's more subversive activities. He was arrested and imprisoned at Landesgericht, a few blocks from the General Hospital on Alser Strasse. At the time Viktor was drafting the manuscript for his first book, *The Doctor and the Soul,* pecking away at an old-fashioned typewriter loaded with paper and carbon sheets. Gsur's wife Erna smuggled into the prison one of the copies and Gsur, on death row, read it. After the war, those close to Hubert Gsur reported to Viktor that the manuscript had given him hope in his last days and courage to face his own death. The Gestapo executed Gsur by guillotine in the Landesgericht prison on December 5, 1944, for "crimes" against the Reich.

Much later, after Viktor had dedicated his first books to family members, he dedicated one to Gsur—*Die Existenzanalyse und die Probleme der Zeit,* 1947. Viktor did so because of Gsur's friendship, the tragic story, and the continuing friendship with his widow Erna.

IN DECEMBER 1941 the Japanese attacked Pearl Harbor and the United States was fully committed to the global war. This eased the fears of Jews and others regarding their plight and—more than ever—they saw the fall of Nazism as simply a matter of time. But months passed and, in September 1942, fate turned against the Frankl family. Viktor recounted the turning point.

> One day I was notified. Again, each week maybe one thousand or two thousand people were deported to some camp in the East, but nobody knew about Auschwitz. In fact we thought it was to Lithuania, or Czechoslovakia, or Poland or somewhere. I believed that as department chief, and as long as the Rothschild Hospital existed, I could stay in Vienna with my parents. Suddenly we were advised by a telephone call, "Tomorrow you have to be ready to be picked up by escorts who will take you to the *Sperlgymnasium.* So get ready with ten kilograms of baggage each." The next day we were ready with the baggage, but my father could not carry it, of course, so he had a round, ladies hatbox, and therein were the last things he had, including a very expensive cigar given to him by his former boss—he always kept it almost as something holy. Of course he was eighty-one or so and a little bit peculiar. He packed

a little bit of whiskey that we had preserved for years to someday celebrate Hitler's death—this also was in the hatbox.

That small bottle of whiskey bears witness to the hopes among the deportees: that they would survive Hitler in the ghettos, and after the war they would resettle and reestablish themselves. Few believed that anything as horrible as genocide could happen. Even the architects of the "final solution" were surprised early on at how readily their troops would carry out the gruesome work of genocide.

On the fateful day when the Frankls were to report for deportation, Viktor approached the owner of their building who lived one floor down. "A nice family—he was not Jewish and most of the residents in the building were Aryan. I told him that he could take from our flat whatever he wanted, to keep it for himself or if we survived he could give it back to us if he wished. So they took some things including my rope for mountain climbing, my fencing swords from '22 and '23, and a print by Egon Schiele, which I liked very much and had bought before Schiele was so well known. There were also a few books which a friend took over." As for family photographs, Stella had taken many of these to Australia where she kept them safe.

Young Jewish escorts arrived to lead the Frankl family—Viktor, his parents Gabriel and Elsa, his wife Tilly, and her mother Emma—from their homes to the same buildings in which the Frankls had attended high school. The school had become a main collection point for the Jews, though there were other facilities in the city for processing. This must have been on Tuesday or Wednesday, September 22 or 23, 1942. Viktor recalled that the family slept in the girls school for a night or two as they awaited transport. The building today bears a marker in memory of the thousands who were "processed" similarly in those years. Viktor was still lamenting as he described the events.

A terrible thing was done, there in the *Gymnasium* on Sperlgasse. Neither my father nor I even spoke of it. They shaved my head completely bald, but the terrible thing was that they took my father, old already, and shaved off his mustache, beard, and hair. It was such a degrading thing, as though he were a murderer on his way to prison. But apart from these sentiments, I could no

longer recognize my own father. His appearance was totally different, such as I had never seen in my whole life. He had been
bearded since he was himself in high school, and now I see him
for the first time without a beard. He could hide his feelings about
these experiences, but I felt so much pity. In his case a man like
him, serving the monarchy and the state for thirty-five years. A
man whose own father had been awarded a cross for seven years
as a soldier under Radetzky, and who also had a medal from the
pope and from the emperor for fighting in Italy.

At the school on Thursday the twenty-fourth the Jews were crammed
into open trucks, wearing their yellow stars and clutching their meager
belongings. It was a logistical feat to deport thirteen hundred people in
one transport, but the SS managed it efficiently enough. As if the women,
children, and men in their charge were refuse, the trucks moved along approximately two miles of city streets. On a typical deportation day onlookers jeered and shouted obscenities at the human cargo en route to
Aspang Station. Today one can visit the site of the station along Aspang
Strasse in District 3. A street sign denotes it as the Place of the Victims of
Deportation, and a low stone marker reads, "In the years 1939–1942 from
the former Aspang Station ten thousand Austrian Jews were transported to
the extermination camps and never came back. Never forget."

It was transport IV/11 out of Aspang Station that carried away the
Frankl family and their comrades. The train rumbled on through the
night heading northward toward Prague and to their destination,
Bauschowitz (in Czech, Bohušovice). Frankl's unique role as a psychiatrist
in the transport that day saved his family from the most offensive and dan-
gerously crowded "accommodations" on the train.

There were responsible, decent people—both Aryans and Jews—who
used their positions and connections to protect Nazi victims and minimize
their suffering. But the role of Dr. Emil Tuchmann, a Viennese Jewish
physician, is not entirely clear. He certainly had influence with the
Gestapo as arrangements for deportations were made, and he survived the
Holocaust in Vienna. When the Frankls were designated for deportation,
Viktor had Tuchmann to thank for the scheme that insulated the family
from the worst during transport.

A group of psychotic Jewish patients was to be deported the same day, and Tuchmann recommended Frankl to the Gestapo as the psychiatrist who should attend and help control these patients during the rail journey. One old passenger car on the train had separate compartments, each fitted with benches for a few travelers. Together with his mother and father, wife and mother-in-law, Viktor occupied one such compartment while the others were filled with psychotic individuals, locked in. An outdoor platform ran alongside the doors to the compartments.

"The Jewish functionaries who were making all the arrangements appointed me to be the medical caretaker for the whole wagon of psychiatric patients. So I fulfilled this by trying to do the best I could. I went from one compartment to the other, even while the train was moving, to look in on the other compartments to see if everyone was okay or if someone needed an injection or something."

When Viktor mentioned this, I commented, "You were making your rounds." He quipped, "Yes, but straight!"—referring to the narrow platform.

"Suddenly an SS man took his gun because he thought I was trying to flee, to escape. I did not think that I might be misunderstood in my intentions. So I shouted out, 'I am the psychiatrist in charge of this wagon of mental patients and I was just looking to see if everything is okay.' I could have been shot right off of the moving train!"

After a night on the rails, the thirteen hundred captives arrived at Bauschowitz, the nearest rail station to Theresienstadt. There the oldest and least able people were put onto open trucks and the rest set off on foot. They were headed for a unique Jewish ghetto created by the SS inside a former military garrison in Bohemia, in northwest Czechoslovakia. Theresienstadt—Terezín in Czech—was out in the boondocks an hour north of Prague. The Jews who had the "good fortune" to be sent to Theresienstadt were mostly well-known citizens, artists, musicians, intellectuals, professionals, and respected pensioners who were being "rewarded." They came mainly from Czechoslovakia, Austria, Denmark, Germany, and Holland. Theresienstadt was not simply a decent place in a relocation program—as the SS would have everyone believe—but an intersection in the persecution pogrom. Though it came to be known as "the gateway to Auschwitz," it had horrors enough of its own.

As they progressed along the roadway—electric power lines on the left and, in some stretches, trees lining the way—little could be seen ahead except for a church steeple and some low green hills. That was the first impression of Theresienstadt. Upon getting closer, the green hills turned out to be ramparts, the grassy slopes of the fortified walls of the town.

Built where the Elbe and Eger rivers meet, the huge fortress and a smaller garrison nearby were constructed in the decade starting 1780, right across the road between Prague, thirty-five miles to the south, and Dresden, about forty-five miles north through the mountains. The location was chosen to cut off Prussian invasions of Bohemia. Emperor Joseph II named the fort after his mother, Empress Maria Theresa.[2]

In 1941 the Nazi regime established a Jewish ghetto in the main garrison where the streets and structures were spread over 165 acres, a city in itself. Some of the barracks were the size of a town block, three stories high plus their immense attics. In transforming the town into the ghetto, the SS had displaced its 4,000 residents. When the Frankls arrived in September 1942 the deportations were peaking and there were already 53,000 Jews packed into the town previously inhabited by 4,000.[3] Other data are even more staggering. In the three and a half years that Theresienstadt served the Nazi purposes, 140,000 people were brought there. Of these, 90,000 were transported to Auschwitz-Birkenau, Treblinka, and other extermination camps where they died. Another 33,000 were killed or died from illness, exhaustion, and starvation right in Theresienstadt.[4] Fewer, perhaps far fewer, than 17,000 survived; they were mostly relatively healthy inmates who had arrived not long before the Russians liberated the ghetto in 1945.

For nearly an hour most of the thirteen hundred Viennese captives walked toward the Theresienstadt fort in what seemed an endless line. Viktor had a vivid memory of his father on this trek.

"When I was walking with my father to the concentration camp, he was in a cheerful mood and carrying his hatbox. In a way he was fatalistic, due to his religious orientation. He was not orthodox, but deeply pious. While he was walking with that hatbox, and to my right, I remember that he said to me spontaneously, *'Immer nur heiter, Gott hilft schon weiter'*—be ever cheerful, for God will help us.[5] He was truly pious and believed this, though it was also an admonition to himself to keep upright."

When the throng finally arrived inside the fortress walls they were shocked at the living conditions. The mumbled words of inmates matched those first impressions: "Welcome to Theresienstadt. Now you're in shit."

The arrivals spent their first nights in attics, sleeping body-to-body on straw-strewn floors.

The previous year the Prague Gestapo had taken over the "Small Fortress," about a mile away, for use as a police prison. Its name sounds too much like "dollhouse," a dreadful misnomer. Even "police prison" is a cultured label for what actually went on there. If the main ghetto was shit, the Small Fortress was hell. It was a large walled compound of many buildings, including a swimming pool for SS personnel—built by forced labor of prisoners—and a shooting range that was an oversized outdoor court for firing squad executions. The Small Fortress, like the ghetto itself, remains much as it was and can be visited today.

The victims at the "prison" were Jews and Aryans—not only Czechs, and not only from Theresienstadt. Frequently "citizens" of the ghetto were shuttled over to the Small Fortress for punishment, including long incarceration in dank basement cells or for torture and execution. They were selected on trumped-up charges or for resistance to authority or for something trivial. A malicious official might take pleasure in shipping someone to the Small Fortress knowing that there some methodical sadists, for pleasures of their own, might maim or kill ruthlessly. As always there were acts of human kindness coming from unlikely people even in those perilous circumstances. But if good people, even those in official roles, became too kindhearted they could meet the same fate as the doomed victims.

Not long after Viktor arrived at Theresienstadt, an SS man selected him for a trip to the Small Fortress, perhaps as an example, though the real reason was never clear. The incident was terrifying. Yet having entered "The Gate of Hell" to the Small Fortress, Frankl came back through it alive. He recalled a kindly warning.

In advance, a friend of mine from the Twentieth District in Vienna—a very honest man and one who loved me—tried to do his best to protect me from the worst. He said, "Should you ever be ordered by the SS to join a group going to the Small Fortress, I implore you at the first chance to behave as if you are fainting and fall on the ground. Do not let yourself be taken to this Fortress." And I was too proud—it's ridiculous—I was just too proud to faint, to fake fainting. . . . So I was selected by an SS man for espe-

cially hard, let's say, "entertainment." I was taken to the Small
Fortress and was there about three hours. He sadistically forced
me to do totally senseless work. It was raining and I had to bring
a bucket with water, running. And I had to take this bucket and to
splash the water on a compost heap taller than I, but it was too
heavy for me. I could not reach the top, and I was very hungry. So
he took the bucket and showed me how to do it. Then he ordered
me to do it again. Of course I could not. And thereupon I got an
uppercut from him. I was stunned and thrown through the air
into a puddle and mud. My glasses fell off and were broken as far
as I can remember it.

I was brought back to the ghetto with thirty-two injuries.
Tilly saw me on the street in Theresienstadt and said, "Viktor, for
heaven's sake! What have they done to you!"

With her good sense and nursing skills, Tilly led Viktor back to the
barracks and there cleaned and bandaged his wounds. She stayed with him
for the rest of the day.

That evening, when I had recovered somewhat, she wanted to
divert my attention from my misery. So she took me to another
barracks where a jazz band, known in Prague, was playing—without official permission. They played a tune that was the unofficial
national anthem of the Jews in Theresienstadt, *"Bei mir bist du
schön"* [To me, you are beautiful].[6]
The contrast between the indescribable tortures of the morning and the jazz in the evening was typical of our existence—with
all its contradictions of beauty and hideousness, humanity and in-
humanity.[7]

The clever SS drove a wedge between reality and impression when
they duped an inspection team from the International Red Cross. In June
1944 the official visitors, invited with Hitler's consent, came to see his
"gift to the Jews." They were given exceptional treatment: plays and concerts, visits to parks and shops all vastly upgraded just for the occasion. The
"beautification program" had turned the place into something presenta-
ble on the surface, a "model ghetto" for the world to see. Hitler had a
sound film produced—now well known in Europe—showing a soccer

game, artistic events, and happy citizens thriving in their special, fine-looking place. It was a grand scam with the title, "The Führer Gives a City to the Jews."

ALTHOUGH THERESIENSTADT WAS presented to the outside world as a self-governing Jewish settlement, the Jewish administrative structures were given only carefully measured authority. There was never any question about who was really in charge, and the SS recruited some Jews to serve as their functionaries and agents—the Capos. But there were many upright Jews in places of leadership whose courage and wisdom were devoted to minimizing cruelty under the circumstances.

One of these was Jakob Edelstein of Prague, "elder of the Jews,"[8] with whom Viktor was acquainted. He also knew Rabbi Leo Baeck of Berlin. Both Edelstein and Baeck were respected leaders in the ghetto community. A much more controversial leader was Benjamin Murmelstein, a rabbi from Vienna. In their various positions these and other leaders were forced to work with the SS, which highlighted the touchy matter of collaboration. In one sense all of them "cooperated" with the SS out of necessity—there was no other way in the circumstances to have any positive influence over what happened to the Jews in the ghetto. Of the leaders, Murmelstein was the most suspected and least trusted, however.[9] He survived the Holocaust and lived until 1989.

Jakob Edelstein was deported with his family to Auschwitz where Eichmann himself may have given the order for their extermination. Edelstein watched while the SS shot his wife, son, and mother-in-law before he was murdered in the same fashion.[10]

Rabbi Leo Baeck may have been the most revered of all the Jewish leaders. To say he was in an awkward spot is understatement gone wild. Some survivors of the Holocaust were critical of him because Baeck may have known at the time about the real destinies of the transports to the East—the deathcamps—but did not tell others. In Baeck's defense, his behavior was judged prudent of him since the transportees could never have endured if they had known that they were headed to almost certain death.[11] Baeck himself narrowly escaped execution thanks to the liberation of Theresienstadt by the Russians in the nick of time, May 8, 1945. Baeck settled in London, taught there and in the United States, and died in 1956. He became a very-well-known Jewish liberal thinker and author.

Baeck was in large measure responsible for the ongoing intellectual life of Theresienstadt while he was there. When I questioned Viktor about Baeck, he immediately retrieved a photograph of him from an adjoining room. Until I saw that photo I had not realized that Baeck was already in his seventies when he came to Theresienstadt. Viktor admired Baeck very much and, later in his life, dedicated a book to him in 1977 simply this way: In Memoriam: Leo Baeck.[12]

Viktor took up the story.

Baeck was highly regarded in Theresienstadt even by the SS. The SS would have let him emigrate to Britain as a special case, but he refused this to stay with his people, the Berlin Jews. So Baeck came with them to Theresienstadt and there he was declared one of the *Prominenten*—a few highly honored Jewish leaders. As such he could have his own apartment and so on. But he never gave up his humility or his dignity. He was culturally-minded and took care that there were always cultural events going on. The attic of one of the barracks was used for lectures, more or less illegal ones. I attended a lecture given by him, and he also attended my lecture there for a small group. . . . But since it was Baeck these did not need to be hidden so much. If he announced something, the SS hardly objected because he was respected so highly—almost like a saint. This was partly because they knew he had refused emigration to stay with his people.

As I write I have in front of me a photocopy of an original announcement of Viktor's lectures in Theresienstadt. Baeck had invited Viktor to offer the series, part of Baeck's attempt to keep minds stimulated and spirits alive in the ghetto. Viktor's topics drew upon his education and experience in Vienna, of course.

1. Sleep and sleep disturbances

2. How can I keep my nerves healthy?

3. "Life weariness" [suicide] and life courage in Theresienstadt

4. Body and soul

5. Psychology of Alpinism [mountain climbing]

6. Rax and Schneeberg [Austrian mountains]

7. Medical ministry

8. Social psychotherapy

9. The problem of existence in psychotherapy

10. Of peculiar people and curious facts (Experiences of a neurologist)

A sentence, handwritten by Viktor, appears in the announcement next to the topics: "There is nothing in the world that can so much enable a person to overcome outer difficulties and inner troubles as the awareness of having a mission in life." When he wrote that, Viktor did not know that the worst lay ahead for him and his family or that this notion would be put to the extreme test.

Once I learned about Viktor's lectures and his acquaintance with ghetto leaders, I wondered if he had himself been among the official *Prominenten* of Theresienstadt. But he told me, "No, never. That was a small group of the most venerated and influential people." We talked further about other honorable people, rabbis, whom he had known in the camps and back home. There were also bad characters who assisted the SS in their malicious undertakings. In Vienna there had been a rabbi who was feared by many Jews and suspected of giving tips to the Gestapo. The bragging of this rabbi was also no secret—particularly the boast that he could easily deny a wish or need to anyone. Viktor remembered a particular line from this crass rabbi: "I wouldn't even hesitate to give a *lady* a kick in the ass."

SOON AFTER ARRIVING in the ghetto Viktor ran into John Edelmann. Edelmann, we may remember, had been Viktor's high school history teacher and the one who was married the same day as Viktor and Tilly. So here, of all places, the two couples shared in history once more. Following their first anxious nights in the Theresienstadt commotion, the Frankls had been separated by their housing assignments. There were barracks for old people, for women, and for men, and the young were placed in "children's homes" right in the town. The women—Tilly, her mother, and Viktor's mother—were assigned to female barracks, probably along street L2 in-

cluding the Hamburg Barracks, C-III. Viktor's living and working a sign-
ments placed him in the building known as *Geniekaserne (Kaserne* means
barracks), indicated by #19 on present-day visitor maps of Theresienstadt.
Spouses and families saw one another at least in daytime.

Medical doctors were given assignments, and Viktor was appointed to
a "ministry" subdepartment—the *Krankenbetreuung*—where he was in
charge of looking after a particular group of sick people. In addition he
had a less defined but more specialized role in "psychohygiene" as section
chief for psychological support services. He lived together with five or six
other physicians in two rooms of the *Geniekaserne*, which also had an infirmary and accommodations for old people. Under the windows where
the doctors lived was a coal cellar, and on delivery days they were shaken
awake very early by the roar of coal going down the chute.

By a cooperative arrangement among themselves, the physician-
roommates stayed out of their rooms for designated hours so that each in
turn could be alone there with his wife. The doctors were from various
countries and one couple was elderly. That husband offered their privacy
hours to Viktor, who was delighted to have twice as much time there alone
with Tilly. It was about the only place where they could be together undisturbed. But it would be a mistake to suppose that conjugal visits with
spouses and intermittent contact with kin could be called family life. The
ghetto conditions took a devastating toll on couples and families. The social structures that enhance family life were absent or corrupted. Even so,
the situation also bred loyalty among families and friends.

Thankfully the oppression in Theresienstadt could be forgotten now
and then through music, art, reading, lectures, and drama. Humor played
no small part in relieving the stress of the situation. Long before coming
to the ghetto Viktor had recognized the restorative value of humor, so he
was not surprised that in Theresienstadt spells of laughter gave a spiritual
lift to people.

In the ghetto were a number of Jewish physicians from Prague who
had been students of Professor Pötzl at Charles University. Viktor recalled
the immense pleasure of the Theresienstadt doctors in swapping stories
about Pötzl and his idiosyncrasies.

"One night we psychiatrists had to be ready to assist with a transport
just in case someone was psychotic or something like that. It was midnight
and we were waiting several hours, and so we started exchanging memories of Pötzl. While we sat there we had a contest imitating him, each one

of the assistants doing it in his own style. Then I did my imitation and won the contest!" Viktor started laughing as he described the situation and could not resist getting to his feet, going to the doorway of his study, and launching yet again his infamous imitation in which Pötzl describes the patient putting his genitals on a plate in a restaurant. One can imagine the doctors, tired and waiting in the ghetto darkness, giving Frankl the award for that one.

THE HEALTH OF Viktor's aging father deteriorated rapidly. Less than six months after their arrival in Theresienstadt, Gabriel was placed in the infirmary in the same barracks where Viktor lived and worked. Difficulty in breathing and sensations of suffocation made Gabriel anxious, at times desperate. As a physician, Viktor recognized the life-threatening signs and later described the situation.

> Among the few things I was able to smuggle into Theresienstadt was a vial of morphine. When my father was dying from pulmonary edema and struggling for air as he neared death, I injected him with the morphine to ease his suffering. He was then 81 years old and starving. Nevertheless, it took a second pneumonia to bring about his death.
> I asked him: "Do you still have pain?"
> "No."
> "Do you have any wish?"
> "No."
> "Do you want to tell me anything?"
> "No."
> I kissed him, and left. I knew I would not see him alive again. But I had the most wonderful feeling one can imagine. I had done what I could. I had stayed in Vienna because of my parents, and now I had accompanied father to the threshold and had spared him the unnecessary agony of death.
> When mother was in mourning, the Czech Rabbi Ferda, who had known father, visited her in the camp. I was present when Ferda, comforting mother, told her that father had been a "Zaddik"—a just man. This confirmed my conviction that justice was one of my father's chief characteristics. And his sense of jus-

tice must have been rooted in a faith in divine justice. Otherwise I cannot imagine how or why he would have formulated the adage that I heard from him so often: "To God's will, I hold still."[13]

Ever after the time of his father's death, Viktor determined to kiss his mother twice whenever he saw her: once upon meeting her and again as they said goodbye. He wanted to be certain that they always parted with this expression of affection, not knowing if they would see one another again.

THERE WAS SOME mail service in and out of Theresienstadt. Families back home sent packages, many of which got through to their loved ones in the ghetto, and prisoners succeeded in sending some mail to friends and family at home. Viktor related the popular story about an agreement made by a Jewish couple in World War I to disguise the messages in their notes to one another, assuming that everything would be read by military censors. It was dangerous to write honestly "where one is in an evil situation, hungry and in danger of being shot by the enemy and heaven knows what else."

So a woman had told her man, "You just write to me that life here is just wonderful, quiet, and I see no enemy and the food is excellent, and so forth. And then you sign the note, *'Moische Punkt Verkehrt'*"—in Yiddish jargon as if a name, Moses Dot Reverse. This means that everything described in the note is, in fact, just the opposite. Viktor noted that the real humor and irony are in the dialect. In fact, the expression became a favorite one used in the Frankl family. For example, someone who did not like the Frankls might say, "I am so happy to see you all again!" and among themselves the Frankls might think or say, *Moische Punkt Verkehrt.*

In the Frankl archives is a postcard written to Tilly's aunt, Frau Hertha Weiser in Vienna. Its return address is "Dr. Viktor Frankl, Theresienstadt, EIIIa," and the postage stamp bearing Hitler's image was canceled April 21, 1943. On the card Viktor typed, probably at the infirmary office, acknowledgments of cards and packages received. He also wrote that everyone was in good health, thanks to heaven, and that "our Papa on February 13, almost 82, passed away gently." The card is signed by Viktor and by Tilly.

The Frankls at Theresienstadt also received a postal card from Walter in Italy, written in a community of fifty to a hundred refugees sustained by the pope. It was in a little mountain village where they could move about freely as long as they did not leave the village. The card seemed to carry good news. Viktor remembered that from this card, or perhaps from somewhere else, they learned that Walter, the designer-painter-artist, had been asked by his comrades to create a message of thanksgiving to the pope. He did the message in calligraphy and then illuminated it with a small drawing of the village. Later on, as Viktor eventually learned, that community of Jewish refugees was discovered by the SS when the Nazis occupied northern Italy. They were deported and Walter and Else ended up somewhere near Auschwitz, as the story goes, working in a mine of some sort. It is all but certain that they perished there. The postcard from Italy turned out to be the last direct message from Walter and Else, and the parents, Gabriel and Elsa Frankl, did not live to learn of their fate.

VIKTOR HAD WORK to do at Theresienstadt. And to his psychohygiene responsibilities he brought his experience in Vienna and his own logotherapeutic approach to suicide risks. He organized suicide intervention teams in the ghetto and recalled their task.

> For instance, when there was the announcement of the arrival of a transport of a thousand people or so, I ordered a couple of assistants to go to the Bauschowitz station to care for them.... Because for the first nights these people were accommodated in the large attics of the barracks and had to sleep on straw—so different from their hopes. Some were immediately in despair.... After all, the old people had been promised good homes for aging people in a nice place, and they need not work and so on. We eased the shock and told them that after some nights they would have a place.... Many of the people had been learning English, hoping to get a visa to the United States and so forth. So I arranged that these people would be visited by volunteers three times each week for half an hour and engaged in English conversation, to keep up their hoping for the future—that the war would end and that Hitler would be gone so they could emigrate then.

When I was with Viktor and Elly, discussing this, I read to them from a book on the history of Theresienstadt.

Some doctors, however, had become quite sensitive to the psychological toll that the stresses of life in Theresienstadt were placing on its residents and wanted to do something about the situation. One such doctor was Karel Fleischman [sic], a Czech who was a close associate of medical director Munk. . . . Another of these doctors was a Viennese named Victor Frankl.

Frankl, who has become the best known of all Theresienstadt's survivors, was working simply as a young general practitioner in a clinic, where one of his surviving nurses remembers him as good-natured, helpful, and intelligent. In her words, "Such a good man."

Fleischmann, who was not a psychiatrist—his prewar specialty had been dermatology—apparently sensed the capacities which Frankl would soon demonstrate and asked him to organize a special unit to help new arrivals overcome the shock of Theresienstadt life. The group, which called itself the *Stosstruppe* or Assault Squad, included many nonmedical personnel. According to Frankl, one of its more influential and important members was Regina Jonas, the camp's only woman rabbi.

The Stosstruppe centered much of its attention on the most vulnerable, such as epileptics, neurotics, the physically sick, and the elderly. Stosstruppe members sought to engage the minds of such people in constructive ways. For example, a despondent philologist who had specialized in English was comforted in English by a group member having some familiarity with that language. The latter would ask his patient to explain some of the language's peculiarities.

The Stosstruppe's success led Frankl to set up a suicide intelligence service whereby any expression of a suicidal idea or intention would be immediately reported to him. He would then contact the would-be suicide and seek to dissuade him/her. He based his approach on Nietzsche's dictum that "He who has a 'Why' to live can endure any 'How.' " Thus in talking with two men who said they wanted to kill themselves since they could expect nothing from life, Frankl told them that life nevertheless expected something from them. His efforts are a major reason for a steep drop in the suicide rate after the first year.[14]

The translation "assault squad," though the idea of an attack by a raiding party is conveyed by the German *Stosstruppe*, is unfortunate. While there were violent attacks at Theresienstadt, particularly in the Small Fortress, the work of Viktor's "squads" was emergency interventions to prevent suicide; hence they were suicide response teams. Viktor knew well both Erich Munk, the medical director, and his assistant, Karl Fleischmann.[15] Fleischmann, Viktor recalled, had a spinal malformation, and it was he who advocated for the suicide response teams. Munk gave them official sanction. But when I mentioned the name of Regina Jonas, Viktor burst into joyful emotion.

> *Jaaaaaa!* The first woman rabbi! I not only knew her, but when I made her acquaintance I immediately invited her to assist us. . . . She was very gifted and I remember that when I invited her to give to my staff, as it were, a lecture, she spoke on growing old—she was an excellent preacher also. She reminded us of the story about Israel wandering in the wilderness for forty years. First Moses went up to the Sinai to receive the Ten Commandments. When he went down, there was dancing around the golden calf and he was so angry that he took the stone tablets and shattered them. And then he went up again to receive new tablets. During the forty years of wandering the tablets of the Ten Commandments—the broken ones—were carried together with the new ones in the Ark of the Covenant. And this she used to show that people who are very old and useless, as it were, retain their human dignity up to the end. That human dignity is not lost in spite of uselessness.

Elly and I both responded to the word-picture and story. I said further, "So the broken tablet is carried as if it were just as good as the whole tablet." Viktor affirmed, "Exactly. The broken one received the same reverence." Still moved, he turned toward me, "I am grateful to you that you have squeezed out from me this memory." I thanked him again for the story, which can be an encouragement to others in the human experience of uselessness, whether due to the ravages of aging or to other limitations. Elly wished, "This story should be much more known in the world."

We were having our discussions in the bright and airy study that Viktor used for more than fifty years. On the wall near Viktor's desk is a painting of Theresienstadt by the Czech artist Professor Otto Ungar from Brünn, the capital of Moravia, that is of particular relevance to the story at this point. Viktor told us about it.

> I met Ungar in Theresienstadt. There the Gestapo and SS had pampered him because each of them wanted Ungar to paint their wives or girlfriends, you see. So Ungar got bread and some privileges. And then they accused him of making paintings to use as anti-Nazi propaganda. He was put in the Small Fortress—a full-fledged evil concentration camp—with his wife and little daughter. But they survived. It was his wife who rescued this painting, which had been buried underground. There was an exhibition in Brünn after the war and I visited with Ungar's daughter and widow and she gave it to me as a souvenir . . . since I was the only survivor of her husband whom she knew . . . he died a few weeks after liberation, of tuberculosis.
>
> Here in the picture you can see the fortress wall, and the bridge across the channel. And here in the foreground are ten or so coffins, outside the walls of the fortress, and this place was used for the ceremonies for burials. And these coffins were used again—recycled—and the bodies cremated. And in one of these very coffins painted by Dr. Ungar I said goodbye to the body of my father. . . .
>
> In the 1950s I smuggled the painting through the Iron Curtain to Vienna.

The death of one friend may bring to mind another friend. This time the conversation turned to Freddy, the brother of Paul Polak, Viktor's close friend. While the Frankls were in the concentration camps, Freddy happened to be on a streetcar in Vienna where he sat next to a young lady. They conversed and seemed to like one another, so Freddy invited her to go with him to a movie. There, as they were chatting, he rather casually criticized Hitler and his book, *Mein Kampf.* This unguarded moment turned out to be lethal for him. During the movie the young woman simply got up and left Freddy in the theater, with no explanation.

Four days later he was arrested and taken to the infamous Landesgericht prison near the General Hospital. There, despite the efforts of a lawyer, he was guillotined December 5, 1944. When Paul Polak went to visit his brother Freddy in the prison that very day, he learned of his execution. Paul talked with the executioner himself who said that Freddy was steadfast and strong even to the last moment.

The father of Paul and Freddy was a Jew. As for the religious identification of the sons, the Nazi rule of thumb—which determined life or death—was that if one had been baptized lying down (as a Christian infant) it was valid; but if one had been baptized standing up (as an adult) it counted for nothing. More Nazi logic.

AS ALWAYS, I reported to Viktor and Elly on my visits to the places they told me about. Thus I told the Frankls about my visit to Prague where I had spent time in the synagogues and the Old Jewish Cemetery. There I had seen the grave of Rabbi Löw, and in the old synagogue his chair from 1600. I also thanked Viktor for the maps he had drawn before my trip to Theresienstadt. Despite his virtual blindness, he had made the maps with his ever-handy Flair felt-tip pens on scrap paper, the only kind of paper he used even for his lecture notes. Thanks to these rough maps, in Theresienstadt I had been able to find some of the buildings he had described for me, particularly his own barracks E-IIIa, the church, and other buildings around the town square.

I was surprised that Jan Hus is still memorialized in Theresienstadt. Hus was the Czech-born Christian preacher who led the reform movement in his homeland partly against indulgences that made the church and clergy rich on the backs of the poor. Even through the Hitler years a statue of Hus stood undisturbed in the small park across from what is now the Theresienstadt museum. How great the irony of the statue: Hus was burned alive at the stake by other Christians in Constance, Germany, July 6, 1415, following a trial for heresy.

In some mysterious way, on my visits there I had soaked up some of Theresienstadt by lingering in its museum, poking into unguarded buildings, and walking its dilapidated streets in the dark. In a conversation with Viktor about this he called it the *Spiritus loci,* saying that perhaps I had picked up the spirit of the place even fifty years later as I walked there—some streets now paved, others still the very old cobblestones—once in summer sunshine and on beautiful, warm evenings, and again on a bitter cold winter night, eerie as it was with not another soul in sight. Always I was struck by the stars that looked down on the surrounding hills and upon Theresienstadt—the same stars that had witnessed the goings-on in the ghetto and Small Fortress, in those years when all the gods kept silent.

In Chicago in April 2000, I had another contact with Theresienstadt. On a break from writing, my wife and I went to see *Brundibar* staged by Lively Arts of Chicago and the Lookingglass Theatre Company. This is the musical, sung for us in English, that was performed fifty-five times by and for the prisoners in Theresienstadt, and once for the Red Cross inspection team. Its cast were children, its plot the eternal struggle of good over evil, its ending a song of victory. The promotional ad for the performance had read in part: "A children's opera in two acts performed by thousands of children in the Terezin concentration camp before they perished."

At the end of the performance we in the audience had an opportunity to interact with Ella Weissberger, the survivor who as a little girl actually played the part of Cat in *Brundibar* at Theresienstadt. She told us that for the closing song of the opera, even visiting SS and Gestapo officials removed their hats.

Were they thinking about good and evil? Were they thinking of their own children back home?

CHAPTER 7

The Crucible of Auschwitz and Dachau, 1944–1945

IT IS 1944 and they are still at it. The Nazi SS are moving their prey around like pawns. Trains and trucks rumble onward day and night. The transport system is complex and effective if erratic. The same human freight is shipped and reshipped, loaded and unloaded, mostly on one-way trips to destinations in a colossal network of ghettos and camps that blankets much of Europe. By now there is even a rail spur between the Bauschowitz station and Theresienstadt, built by forced labor of course, so that the thousands of victims can be moved in and out more efficiently.

Because Viktor's father died there, he was the only one of the extended Frankl family at Theresienstadt who was never loaded into another transport. Ultimately Tilly would be in at least three camps. Elsa and Emma, mothers of Viktor and Tilly, would be in two. Brother Walter and his wife Else would outlast their hidden community in Italy only to be sent to some subcamp(s) of Auschwitz. Viktor was to survive four different camps, three in the final six months of the war.

In addition to the fixed sites of the Nazi system—ghettos, camps, and centers—the mobile killing squads (*Einsatzgruppen*) in Eastern Europe were carrying out massacres of men, women, and children and then moving on for more. Late in the war the forced processions of prisoners, rightly called death marches, snaked along miles of roadways, leaving behind their own enormous trails of corpses. Even on a gigantic wall map it would be virtually impossible to put all the names of the Nazi-created ghettos, forced labor camps, transit camps, internment camps, deathcamps, marches, euthanasia centers, and killing sites for such ventures as the *Erntefest*—code name "Harvest Festival" for the massacres in Poland. The place names alone would be in the thousands, and site markers in the tens of thousands. The map would be littered with labels on top of one another, spreading over Germany, Austria, Czechoslovakia, France, Poland, Croatia, Serbia, Albania, Greece, Romania, Hungary, the Baltic states, Holland, Belgium, Luxembourg, and occupied regions of Italy and the former Soviet Union.¹ It took such a network to lodge millions of prisoners—Jews, Roma (Gypsies), Poles, resisters, mental defectives, criminals, homosexuals, Jehovah's Witnesses, etc.—and exterminate them. This was industrial-scale killing not possible prior to the twentieth century. Within such incomprehensible data lies the plight of the Frankl family.

An agonizing development for them was the transport of Emma Grosser, Tilly's mother, from Theresienstadt after a year and a half there. She was herded onto a train with hundreds of others, all uninformed as to their destination. We know now that the transport left Theresienstadt on Tuesday, May 16, 1944, and went directly to Auschwitz.² Emmy, as she was known to her family, was only forty-nine.

The rest of the Frankl family presumed they would be transferred shortly after Emmy, but there was an unexpected lull in transports. Then suddenly a new series of transports was announced. It was Viktor's hunch that the Gestapo had ordered replacements for the labor force, prisoners "from whom they could squeeze out some physical energy for work. And so Murmelstein and his staff had to make the lists."

In October, Viktor was listed for transport. Naturally the deportees wished to believe the official line that they were headed for another ghetto where things would be "even better." There was also that pervasive optimism that something big must be happening in the war, something that finally would bring its end. Nevertheless, Viktor was among those who regarded every transport as portentous. In his later years, as he lectured and wrote, Viktor referred to these transports as headed for Auschwitz but he did so based on his subsequent knowledge, using prolepsis as a literary device. But back then prisoners had no truthful information in advance.

It was possible to volunteer for a particular transport out of Theresienstadt, which some inmates did in order to stay with their relatives. When Tilly heard that Viktor was to be transported, she volunteered to go with him despite the fact that to do so was hazardous—such volunteering provoked violence from the SS when they viewed it as a brash request. Furthermore, Tilly's job in a munitions plant, where they split minerals for ammunition and optics, exempted her from the transports. The SS might interpret her request as an attempt to shirk her work. Viktor implored her *not* to volunteer since the transport might well be heading for something worse. But in what Viktor viewed as Tilly's solidarity with him, she defied his wishes, took her chances in volunteering, and was admitted to the same transport. Tilly's loyalty to Viktor sealed her fate. He was thirty-nine and she almost twenty-four.

For undisclosed reasons Viktor's mother was not listed for the same transport, though at sixty-five Elsa was at the cutoff age for deportation. The damnable task of creating the lists, each a thousand names or more, was forced by the SS on Jewish functionaries. Many years later Viktor recalled his hopefulness that his mother would survive by remaining in Theresienstadt. That she was not listed for transport seemed a good sign. And of course he was hoping that somehow Tilly and he might endure the war, which clearly could not go on much longer.

On the day of their transport, Viktor and Tilly helped others get ready. Tilly was particularly effective in reducing departure chaos by organizing the handling of prisoners' belongings. Both of them helped avert panic by calming their comrades, which in turn lessened the likelihood of violent reprisals from the SS.

We know "passenger" numbers from written records: Tilly Frankl, 1069; her mother Emmy Grosser, 1070; Elsa Frankl, 1073.[3] Again, perhaps due to his role, Viktor's name is not on the same list—was he 1071? The date of the death of his father Gabriel (1072) is listed.

The poignancy of the parting of Viktor and his mother shows their anxiety. They were keenly aware that this farewell might be the final one. It was likely Thursday, October 19, 1944, the day the transport took Tilly and him away. At the moment of their parting, Viktor asked his mother to give him her blessing. Never could he forget how she cried out from the depths of her spirit to him, "Yes! Yes! I bless you!"

That was the last blessing she ever offered in Viktor's presence. Unknown to him at the time, Elsa was to be deported from Theresienstadt only four days later. In another cruel irony, her transport to Auschwitz was one of the very last from the ghetto. Viktor knew nothing of his mother's fate until after the war. From the moment of their farewell in October 1944, Viktor kept himself going partly with the dream that one day he would find his mother alive and be reunited with her—in the concentration camps she was never far from his mind. "I thought, what would be appropriate if I should find her again in Vienna? I imagined only one thing: the old gesture one uses when approaching a queen, to kiss the hem of her coat! What else could be appropriate in the unique moment, in the most moving moment of my life? This is an almost ridiculous dream of mine, which I had for years."

AS THE 250-MILE rail journey progressed from Theresienstadt, Viktor, Tilly and their companions became aware that their transport was headed in the direction of Auschwitz (Oswiecim, just north of the Czech–Polish border). Auschwitz was the largest extermination system established by the Nazis—hence its hideous fame. It is estimated that well over a million victims were killed there. It was not just one camp, but an array of scores of subcamps in addition to the primary ones, Auschwitz I, II, and III. Auschwitz I, originally a Polish military compound, was taken over by the Nazis as a penal complex for political prisoners. Because many of its barracks were brick, the site has remained intact and now is the principal museum of Auschwitz. The former crematoria may be visited as well as the venues of brutal incarcerations and exterminations by the SS using gallows, firing squads at the Black Wall, gas chambers, and basement torture cells—all of this starkly documented. For the Frankl story it is not necessary to sort out the complex operations of the Auschwitz system, but rather to identify the one camp to which they were sent from Theresienstadt.

Auschwitz II is also known as Auschwitz-Birkenau or simply Birkenau, which is the German name for the nearby Polish town, Brzezinka. This now-infamous camp is less than two miles from Auschwitz I and out in open fields. It is correct to say that the Frankls were taken to Auschwitz, but Birkenau was the actual Auschwitz camp of their experience.

Birkenau was immense. Its 425 acres and 300 buildings housed up to 100,000 prisoners by the time Viktor and Tilly arrived there, though these figures fail to convey the impression of the camp.[4] Viewed today from the guard tower above the Death Gate through which the transport trains entered for unloading and selection, chimneys and footings of destroyed barracks stretch nearly as far as the eye can see. They stand in stark contrast to the new museums of the Holocaust that are more typically stunning in their architecture, lighting, and creative displays—much like art museums—where one may browse in air-conditioned souvenir shops. That kind of memorial is controversial and chilling in its own way.[5] But Birkenau has been left to decay and is uniquely unnerving. Except for identifying signs and photo kiosks, there is little that is museum-like at Birkenau.

Viktor remembered well that he was in one of the wooden barracks of the so-called "family camp"—one group of structures among the many. He guessed that the name came from an earlier Nazi scheme for the buildings, and we know that there was a Romani section called the "Gypsie family camp" at Birkenau until 1944.[6] Originally the huge frame buildings were horse stables, something a visitor can readily imagine upon seeing them. At least one of the "family camp barracks" is still standing.

The situation was desperate at Birkenau, which was infested with rats and rampant with disease. Water was inadequate and sanitation amounted to rude latrines—hundreds of holes in long, poured-concrete benches. From the former guard tower one can see at the farther reaches of the camp the gas chambers and crematoria, where Holocaust killing reached its most appalling proportions. And from up close one readily sees in the ruins of the gas chambers the stairs that descended to the basement changing rooms and "shower rooms." Outside, alongside the foundations, are the openings into which the Zyklon B gas pellets were dropped for extermination of as many as one thousand prisoners in one session.

Today one can walk about on the very railroad siding where new arrivals were unloaded, including Viktor and Tilly. This is where Dr. Josef Mengele, the Angel of Death, made many of his villainous selections with the wave of his finger, consigning most prisoners to immediate death. Photographs show exactly how the selections were carried out at the spot. It was nearby that Tilly and Viktor had their last minutes together. He recalled it this way.

It was a moment full of irony because we knew that no one would give a damn for our lives and that everything would be robbed from us. So we just laughed, and with the greatest pleasure Tilly showed me that she had destroyed her gilded watch or clock by stomping on it. We also had a bit of powdered sugar, and she threw this away too as an SS man and two Capos arrived with bags, ordering us to give up all our jewelry—to throw everything we had into the bags. . . . As we were parting we looked at one another with detachment because emotions cannot cope with such a situation. And we took our golden marriage rings and threw them away. At such a moment you either defy the situation or die—you defy even with just a smile at each other in a climate of love in such a circumstance. And I told her to stay alive at any cost, "Do you understand what I mean, at any cost?"—anticipating that by granting sexual favors to SS men she might save her life.... I didn't want her to feel in the least inhibited by thinking that "I cannot do this to Viktor." So without saying anything more than necessary, she understood it. And I thank heaven that I was up to the situation enough to tell her this at the last moment, so that for my sake she would not carry the load of this....[7]

Another treasure lost on arrival at Birkenau was the necklace ornament Viktor had given Tilly shortly before they married. It was a tiny globe which could be spun around. On it the oceans were painted blue, and these words were on the charm: "The whole world turns on love." Viktor said, "She liked it very much and was enthusiastic. It was not so valuable in financial terms, but it was unusual for a Jew at the time to buy something like this." Also among the small but cherished pieces with which Viktor parted at the selection was the pin signifying him as an alpine guide.[8]

A year after the first selection at Birkenau, Viktor wrote about it.[9] Across the years, understandably, he wondered if the SS man doing the selection that day had been Mengele himself—with that casual wave of his finger to the left or right. In any case, an SS man directed Viktor and he joined some colleagues whom he recognized in the line to the right. In fact, he may have slipped into that line behind the SS man's back—a courageous or foolhardy impulse, but one that may have saved his life.

At some point Viktor had to strip and to surrender all of his clothing, keeping only his belt and eyeglasses. So the coat, in whose lining he had sewn the notes for his book *The Doctor and the Soul,* was also taken.

Thus I had to overcome the loss of my spiritual child, as it were, and had to face the question of whether this loss did not make my life void of meaning. An answer to this question was given to me soon. In exchange for my clothes I was given the rags of an inmate who had already been sent to the gas chamber; in a pocket I found a single page torn from a Hebrew prayer book. It contained the main Jewish prayer *Shema Yisrael,* i.e., the command "Love thy God with all thy heart, and with all thy soul, and with all thy might," or, as one could interpret it as well, the command to say "yes" to life despite whatever one has to face, be it suffering or even dying. A life, I told myself, whose meaning stands or falls on whether one can publish a manuscript would, ultimately, not be worth living. Thus in that single page which replaced the many pages of my manuscript I saw a symbolic call henceforth to live my thoughts instead of merely putting them on paper.[10]

On Monday, October 23, 1944, the situation at Birkenau could hardly have been more bizarre. It was Tilly's birthday and they had been separated since the selection. After his liberation Viktor wrote about that night.

> I shall never forget how I awoke from the deep sleep of exhaustion on my second night in Auschwitz—roused by music. The senior warden of the hut had some kind of celebration going on in his room, which was near the entrance of the hut. Tipsy voices bawled some hackneyed tunes. Suddenly there was a silence and into the night a violin sang a desperately sad tango, an unusual tune not spoiled by frequent playing. The violin wept and a part of me wept with it, for on that same day someone had a twenty-fourth birthday. That someone lay in another part of the Auschwitz camp, possibly only a few hundred or thousand yards away, and yet completely out of reach. That someone was my wife.[11]

At Birkenau, Viktor and Tilly had been separated only since the first selection a day or two earlier.

In one of our relatively recent conversations, Viktor talked about other details of his brief stay at Birkenau.

> Let me pick up one aspect of the selection at Auschwitz. Even several transports per day might arrive, with perhaps a thousand people in each one. And then they had to line up, single file, and I also. Mengele stood there [Viktor demonstrated the movement of Mengele's finger to the right or left to direct prisoners one-by-one.] Ninety percent of them went to the left—old people,

women, children, mothers, sick people—and were marched immediately to the gas chambers. They didn't even stay overnight.
What for? . . . Instinctively I stretched myself to stand erect, to
look good. Now some were sent to other concentration camps as I
was. After three nights some hundreds of workers were selected
and sent to Bavaria. During those three days we had to march
again in front of Mengele because he was especially interested in
people who were wearing trusses for some abdominal problem
and he was doing experiments. He was particularly interested in
twins.

So we were distributed to other camps. For instance, if Bergen-
Belsen needed five hundred female workers for a factory, they
would just call Mengele to say they needed so many people. My
own transfer was caused when we had to build a concentration
camp in the Dachau system, a subcamp—the same subcamp in
which I was confined later on.

Viktor actually endured four selections at Birkenau, any one of which
could have led to his death. The first was on arrival when he and Tilly
were separated. The next was done by Mengele in his search for twins and
people with certain ailments, when Viktor was apparently of no interest
for medical experimentation. In a third selection he narrowly missed being sent off with a group of prisoners to an undeclared destination, possibly to their deaths. Viktor was convinced that the same petty criminal
from the neighboring district in Vienna who had taken him back to
Theresienstadt after his beating in the Small Fortress this time saved his
life for the second time.[12] The scoundrel, a Jewish Capo for the SS, saw
Viktor near the end of the line of a hundred or so and created a scene that
took him out of that formation and replaced him with another prisoner. It
was one more twist of fate. In a conversation I had with Viktor he became
philosophical: "I have a version of this story in my concentration camp
book where I said you could not do anything because you never knew
which was the better option, you see? So you left everything to fate . . . absolutely nothing was rational. Let go. Let go." That attitude applied to situations that were unmistakably beyond one's control and to those in which
even some room for decision led to utterly unknowable outcomes.

The fourth selection in the three or four days Viktor spent at Birkenau
was the one that identified him for labor in the Dachau system. "Suddenly

we had to leave the large barracks where more than a thousand stayed, formerly a horse stable—I know you have a picture of the *Stockbetten* [the "beds" stacked in large tiers, nine men in each bunk]. Immediately some hundreds of us were selected and sent to a workers' camp . . ."

FOLLOWING THE THREE nights at Birkenau, Viktor was on another Nazi transport. The cattle car carrying him and his comrades was part of a train that pulled out of Birkenau and headed south through the Czech countryside. The captives did not know any more than before what to expect—a work-camp at best, or another deathcamp perhaps. All they knew were the rumors about the worst concentration camps, so during the journey their fears grew as the train's direction eventually suggested the possibility of Mauthausen as a destination—Austria's main camp and one of the most atrocious and brutal anywhere. Located about eighty-five miles west of Vienna and near Linz, it had sixty subcamps. At its central facility many of the seventy thousand who died were literally worked to death in its quarry, shot, or gassed.

To their surprise, after the first two hundred miles out of Auschwitz the train made a long stop in a great metropolis, and it was an emotionally powerful stop for Viktor. Imagine his racing heart as the train entered the outskirts of Vienna and then pulled into North Station, of all places. The station still stands in Leopoldstadt, right between the traffic circle at the end of Prater Strasse and the entrance to the Prater Park where Viktor had spent so much of his childhood and youth. How crazy indeed was the whole set of circumstances, which he described in writing.

> With the majority of prisoners, the primitive life and the effort of having to concentrate on just saving one's skin led to a total disregard of anything not serving that purpose, and explained the prisoners' complete lack of sentiment. This was brought home to me on my transfer from Auschwitz to a camp affiliated with Dachau. The train which carried us—about two thousand prisoners—passed through Vienna. At about midnight we passed one of the Viennese railway stations. The track was going to lead us past the street where I was born, past the house where I had lived many years of my life, in fact, until I was taken prisoner.
>
> There were fifty of us in the prison car, which had two small, barred peepholes. There was only enough room for one group to

squat on the floor, while the others, who had to stand up for hours, crowded round the peepholes. Standing on tiptoe and looking past the others' heads through the bars of the window, I caught an eerie glimpse of my native town. We all felt more dead than alive, since we thought that our transport was heading for the camp at Mauthausen and that we had only one or two weeks to live. I had a distinct feeling that I saw the streets, the squares and the houses of my childhood with the eyes of a dead man who had come back from another world and was looking down on a ghostly city.

After hours of delay the train left the station. And there was the street—my street! The young lads who had a number of years of camp life behind them and for whom such a journey was a great event stared attentively through the peephole. I began to beg them, to entreat them, to let me stand in front for one moment only. I tried to explain how much a look through that window meant to me just then. My request was refused with rudeness and cynicism: "You lived here all those years? Well, then you have seen quite enough already!"[13]

The rail journey west from Vienna shows us how relative the causes for joy may be. Just past the town of St. Valentin, Austria, the rail splits to the right heading north to Mauthausen across a Danube River bridge. Otherwise, at that point trains continue west toward Linz. Through those peepholes the most-traveled captives were watching their route carefully. When the train did not turn off but continued west, they were thrilled— as Viktor put it—to be heading "only" for Dachau. After the three hundred miles from Vienna in that cattle car, with not enough room for everyone to sit on the urine-soaked straw, they arrived at camp Kaufering III, their new place. They laughed and joked when they were told that there was no "chimney" and no gas at the camp. Even after standing in the wet, freezing cold all night as a kind of punishment on their arrival, they were still relieved and pleased.[14]

Each morning about five o'clock we had to line up at the *Appellplatz* [literally the "roll call place"] before our work. We would get some hot black water they called coffee. Then we marched out, but often only to the nearby railway station where we were taken in special trucks ten kilometers or so to the work site. And there, most of the time, I had to carry and lay down steel rails for the trains and these were very heavy—we used something like giant scissors to lift them, and just two people had to carry each long rail. And we may have had 850 calories per day to do this work. Many people died in Kaufering, even some friends I had before the camp—themselves doctors.

Once I had to carry some people to Landsberg, a few kilometers from Kaufering, close to where the woods are. These people were dying and a medical doctor was with them. I carried them in a kind of vehicle together with two or three others. The designation was a reconvalescent camp.... I also remember a medical doctor who was walking behind me to Landsberg who said to me, "Frankl, I see from how you are proceeding that you have a way of conserving your energy when you are not using it to do something, like an Alpine climbing guide." My body condition was such that I did not look like a climbing guide, but he could tell anyway because I used the minimum of energy.

I asked Viktor if there was any music or any cultural life of any kind at Kaufering III to help people forget their circumstances, at least for a few moments. My question was naive but he answered it in this way.

The SS did have some prisoners working for them, for their own private interests and these prisoners were privileged. There was a man—Reynolds was his name—one of the strong, privileged people who had their own barracks. He allowed me in the evenings, for ten minutes each time, to come where he was and to stretch on the ground in his barracks, where they had heat. And we conversed for these minutes and he allowed me to get warm. In America I met him again, together with his son, at a conference where I told my audience about our common experience at Kaufering.

At another Kaufering work site Viktor was assigned a job by himself, but under supervision of course.

I was given a crowbar for digging a tunnel under a road in the Bavarian woods. And I alone had to dig out the stones, for several weeks. An SS man criticized me for the little amount of stones I got out during an hour or so. And I said, "If you were in my place to do brain surgery as I used to do, you would be equally as helpless as I am digging this tunnel . . ."

[On another occasion] I remember I was working on a street and there was an SS man watching me. For a moment I stopped shoveling and in those few seconds the SS man threw a small stone at me. It was so humiliating that he didn't find me worthy to command, only to treat like an animal. It was at the same place, it now comes to mind, that I had secretions from my nose which I did not sneeze out, but swallowed because I thought there might me a few calories in it which must be stored. I meant this. As a medical doctor I thought that this should not be spit out. I have never told this to anyone.

I recounted to Viktor my visits to the United States Holocaust Museum, where *Man's Search for Meaning* was selling in its bookstore, and to the National Archives in Washington and College Park, Maryland, where "after-action reports" on American military engagements are stored. There I had gone through hundreds of photos of Kaufering, since the camps there were liberated by American troops. The photos of Kaufering camps washed away at least some of my naiveté. Though they were not technically extermination camps, the photographs make clear that mistreatment, malnutrition, filth, and disease were rampant. There were heaps of naked and emaciated corpses on the muddy ground. I described to Viktor the photos of the "barracks"—underground buildings with the sloping roofs above ground and small doorways under the peaks. Immediately Viktor took up the conversation.

Half-underground. I remember sleeping in my clothes and an overcoat because of freezing. I did not undress at Kaufering. In the winter we had to sleep on the cold ground with shoes on, too, on the loose earth that was the floor of the barracks. I remember how I enjoyed a small dosage of warmth. I had no time to go to the latrine, so I used to urinate in my clothing and enjoyed the warmth after working in the freezing air. Even in the so-called soup line I enjoyed urinating, even for a few moments, like sipping a hot tea [Viktor snickers at the irony].

We can see that life at Kaufering III was reduced to subhuman conditions and that any pleasure was relative and fleeting. Daydreams and night dreams could transport prisoners away from their real circumstances for brief moments. In conditions of bare survival the fantasies of their waking and sleeping hours had little if any sexual content. Viktor repeatedly said that sex vanished from prisoners' dreams and sexual activity ceased amid physical and emotional exhaustion. When I asked him what dreams did consist of he immediately asserted that they were mainly about food— also the favorite topic of prisoners' conversations. His own good dreams drifted now and then to a warm bath and to that special sweet treat *Schaumschnitten*, which had so delighted him through the Vienna years.

In 1996 I found—for the first time and never since—*Schaumschnitten*. I was showing an American friend around the old Frankl neighborhood in Leopoldstadt. We were walking down Karmeliter Gasse on the way to Viktor's old high school, and there in the window of a pastry shop was a *Schaumschnitte*—only one piece left. We bought it and shared it, eating with our fingers. It was exactly as Viktor had described it repeatedly: delicious and delicate, and very sticky with sugar and egg white. When I told Viktor about our luck in finding *Schaumschnitten* that day, he was charmed. He said again how that pastry broke into his dreams at Kaufering. Then I smiled, "So Viktor: in the hierarchy of human desires *Schaumschnitte* ranks higher than sex." He smiled in return but did not openly agree.

In the camps there were also dreams of a frightening sort, of course. Viktor recalled being awakened abruptly one night in the hut by a comrade who was thrashing about and moaning from a nightmare. A normal instinct might be to wake the sufferer, but Viktor did not do so since the reality of which he would become conscious was probably worse than the nightmare.[15] Even more starkly terrifying were the hallucinations of delirium, frequently brought on by starvation and dehydration, head injuries, circulatory problems, infections, and raging fevers.

We have already noted how relative joy can be. This was brought home to me again one day when we were talking about Kaufering. Viktor told us that as humiliating as it had been to wear the yellow star, those times seemed not so bad. In fact, he said, in conversations with his fellow inmates they would reflect aloud—joking in a way but absolutely in earnest—on what good times those were when all they had to put up with was wearing the yellow star. "It seemed ridiculous that we had complained. There in the concentration camps we reminded one another what beautiful times they were when we wore the yellow star—nice times— and *we meant it*—and when we had to tolerate being called 'Israel' and so forth. In the camps what I would have given to be called or to call myself Israel *ten times*! You see how relative it is."

Aware that rumors flourished in the camps, I asked Viktor if actual news reports reached Kaufering and if these heightened prisoners' expectations that the war would soon be over. He replied that after so many disappointed hopes a pessimism set in: that even if liberation came in three or four months, they nevertheless could perish in the camps since each day more comrades were dying. "In my concentration camp book, where I wrote about once again not being home in time for Christmas, I quoted the Psalms that the heart that is disappointed becomes ill. And so after these disappointments the mortality increased."[16]

Because of his training, Viktor readily recognized in his fellow prisoners the despair that typically led to giving up the fight for survival. While Viktor's optimism and good sense—together with the twists of fate, of course—protected him in many dire situations, at Kaufering his own spiritual resources were depleted. At this time a comrade by the name of Benscher—who survived to become a Munich television actor—saw that Viktor was sinking into a dangerous malaise. He talked with Viktor, urging him to shake his dark mood. In a natural way Benscher challenged Viktor to rally his last bits of resistance. In retrospect Viktor believed that Benscher had saved his life.[17]

A TRANSFER LOG shows that it was on Monday, March 5, 1945, that Viktor was moved from Kaufering III to Türkheim, another camp in the Dachau system. What Viktor thought astounding about his listing in that document is the identification of him as *Arzt*—physician—for the very first time since that title was taken away back in Vienna, when he was dubbed a "Jew-Caretaker."

Türkheim was to be Viktor's fourth concentration camp and his transfer was a muddle of possibilities and hazards. "The chief doctor of Kaufering, a Hungarian who liked me, one day let me know there is tomorrow a transport for a new camp and if I wish he could put me on the list of one or two hundred people as a medical doctor for the new camp. But he said he did not advise me to do so, that would be taking a chance, and I understood that it might even be to a gas oven or something. But I told myself, 'I prefer to die in a camp in which I have a chance to work as a doctor, because it would be a meaningful death rather than a meaningless suffering.' So I said yes—not knowing, because there were also transports going from Kaufering back to Auschwitz."

The decision to go to Türkheim became yet another life-saving twist, as it was a kind of "rest camp" for sick prisoners. So Viktor left Kaufering behind, where the famine was so severe that cannibalism may have broken out shortly after.[18] Had he remained at Kaufering it is almost certain that he would have perished there.

That is not to say that Türkheim was any paradise. In addition to starvation, filth, brutality, freezing, and potentially lethal forced labor, Türkheim was also ravaged by typhus. That made the "rest camp" a dangerous place even for those who, like Viktor, were brought there as physicians to help with the situation. Almost inevitably he came down with typhus and a raging fever. Thankfully, as a prisoner-physician, he knew the danger of slipping into delirium, stupor, and finally to death during the night hours. Many typhus fatalities came about in this way. So he forced himself to stay awake and described it in an indirect way when he wrote *The Doctor and the Soul* a few months later.

> [In the barracks at Türkheim] lay several dozen men down with typhus. All were delirious except one who made an effort to avert the nocturnal deliria by fighting back sleep at night. He profited by the excitement and mental stimulus induced by the fever, however, to reconstruct the unpublished manuscript of a scientific work he had written, which had been taken away from him in the concentration camp. In the course of sixteen feverish nights he had recovered the whole book—jotting down, in the dark, stenographic cue words on tiny scraps of paper.[19]

During his nearly seven weeks at Türkheim the war in Europe actually was caving in on the Nazis. The camp staff knew this and opportunistic guards became kinder and friendlier to the prisoners. Viktor recalled that "shortly before the end of the war things were a bit different, changing at Türkheim. The people in charge thought that they might have to defend themselves in a couple of months, that they would need friends. So in the last weeks, in addition to my work as a doctor, I was ordered to take over the barracks for those who were not working due to medical reasons."

There was one SS man, the camp commander, whom the prisoners regarded as a genuine human being, even as a kind of protector. They did not interpret his kindness as an effort to save his own skin when the war ended. Viktor remembered this SS man as follows.

> When we arrived in Türkheim [this SS commander] started shouting, "This is a scandal how you have been treated! Clothed with blankets and smelling—how you have been treated at Kaufering!" This was the SS man Hoffmann, and years after the liberation I organized in Landsberg a reunion [of survivors], and wanted to invite him also. But to my dismay I heard that he had died shortly before, and that up to his death was suffering severely from self-reproaches [for his role in the war]. This I learned from a Catholic priest who knew Hoffmann and wrote a letter to me. This Hoffmann was a decent man, almost like nobody else.

Shortly after the liberation Viktor wrote the following about Hoffmann.

> An interesting incident with reference to this SS commander is in regard to the attitude toward him of some of his Jewish prisoners. At the end of the war when the American troops liberated the prisoners from our camp, three young Hungarian Jews hid this commander in the Bavarian woods. Then they went to the commandant of the American Forces who was very eager to capture this SS commander and they said they would tell him where he was but only under certain conditions: the American commander must promise that absolutely no harm would come to this man. After a while, the American officer finally promised these young Jews that the SS commander, when taken into captivity, would be kept safe from harm. Not only did the American officer keep his promise but, as a matter of fact, the former SS commander of this concentration camp was in a sense restored to his command, for he supervised the collection of clothing among the nearby Bavarian villages, and its distribution to all of us who at that time still wore the clothes we had inherited from other in-

mates of Camp Auschwitz who were not as fortunate as we, having been sent to the gas chamber immediately upon their arrival at the railway station.[20]

Hoffmann illustrates Viktor's relentless contention that good, decent people are found in all groups—even *occasionally* among the SS. In 1945, Viktor wrote: "Human kindness can be found in all groups, even those which as a whole it would be easy to condemn. The boundaries between groups overlapped and we must not try to simplify matters by saying that these men were angels and those were devils."[21]

At Türkheim conditions improved rapidly—and for Viktor in the nick of time. Aspirin helped to curb his temperature of 104. He continued to work but rested better and took nourishment. He survived his typhus as others did, even without antibiotics. In the final weeks his weight increased to eighty-three pounds at the time of liberation. But his medical report indicates that Viktor had irregular heart rhythms and quite probably a damaged heart muscle, edema from hunger, and frostbite on three fingers. "My blood was sent to the large Dachau camp to check for typhus transmitted by lice in clothing and rat fleas, which for the malnourished and elderly could be fatal. This typhus is not to be confused with typhoid fever, the intestinal infection." Viktor added in his typical manner, "Thanks to heaven I survived it"—as if to remind himself and us that we have no sovereignty over our lives and circumstances. This was a major motif of his life: we may act upon situations to change them and we must do so; but there are also circumstances where we must resign ourselves to fate or Providence—then we must let go. With his logotherapy he was always pushing the line separating the two, so that he and we would not make the mistake of resigning too soon.

APRIL 1945 WAS a month for the history books. In its first days, as Viktor was regaining some strength at Türkheim, the Allies were storming the last strongholds of the Nazi forces. On the twelfth, American President Franklin Roosevelt died unexpectedly from a massive cerebral hemorrhage at the age of sixty-three. The nation and much of the world were stunned, particularly amid the escalating expectation of war's end. The very next day the Russian army seized Vienna and took prisoner thousands of German soldiers there. They also shut down the rail routes out of the

city. Of all places, Leopoldstadt—the former Jewish district and Frankl
neighborhood—saw the final terrifying street battles which brought down
the German forces.[22]

The wretched inmates at Türkheim and in camps throughout the
crumbling Reich—at least the inmates with enough strength left to hope
and to cope with the news reports—wondered about the day of their liberation, and if it would come in time. For reasonably healthy survivors it
did, and Viktor wrote about it after he reached Vienna again. He recounted
the last week of April when the International Red Cross entered the camp,
followed by a last-ditch effort by the SS to clear the camp. In those last
hours Viktor and some comrades were distressed when they were left out
of a group boarding a truck—everyone believed that the truck was heading to freedom. Later he learned that those prisoners, on the very threshold of liberty, had been burned to death in a hut not far away as the SS got
in their last licks.[23] Thus Viktor's long list of narrow escapes grew longer.
Finally, on Friday, April 27—just two weeks after the Allies had taken
Vienna—an American military unit from Texas rolled through the
Türkheim camp, ending the terror for those who were still in that place.
Viktor Frankl was among them. The prisoners celebrated as their strength
allowed and raided the storage rooms for clothing to improve upon the
filthy rags they had worn through the winter to keep from freezing. Viktor
picked up a necktie, perhaps as mere "souvenir" or as a small sign of his
hopefulness. And though the tie hosted clusters of lice eggs, he took it and
cleaned it and kept it.

In Milan the next day, the decaying body of Benito Mussolini, Italy's
fascist "Il Duce," whom the Nazis had tried to save, was hung by its heels
in public, its head riddled by gunfire. That was Saturday. On Monday following, with Russian forces subduing Berlin, Adolf Hitler blew out his
own brains with a revolver. He and his mistress, Eva Braun, died together
in the Berlin bunker. Of the thousands of decisions Hitler had made as
führer, his last was to entomb himself in the very bunker that had been
constructed so that no harm would come to him.

In *Man's Search for Meaning*, Viktor described how he walked for
miles through open country shortly after his liberation from Türkheim. In
poetic language he described the flowering field and the songs of larks.
Alone and looking up at the sky, he sank to his knees in the meadow. "At
that moment there was very little I knew of myself or of the world—I
had but one sentence in my mind—always the same: 'I called to the Lord

from my narrow prison and He answered me in the freedom of space.' How long I knelt there and repeated this sentence from memory I can no longer recall. But I know that on that day, in that hour, my new life started. Step for step I progressed, until I again became a human being."[24]

Something else happened on that same walk in the fields. It was mysterious, and Viktor was ambivalent in describing it. He recognized that nothing profound may have taken place and that his interpretation may have been wishful, even silly, given his heightened emotional state in those hours.

Someone came from the opposite direction, a foreign worker—Greek or Italian or Dutch, I don't know—someone Hitler had driven into the Reich. And he was playing with something in his hand and I asked him what it was. And I noticed that it was the same globe with the same inscription, "The whole world turns on love." And I offered him any price to buy it, and he sold it to me and I treasured it and was looking forward eagerly to the moment when I would meet Tilly again, because I didn't doubt that she was alive if I was alive even at my age. I was so happy, because I thought that Tilly might be thinking that I would buy her another one of these. It was nonsense I suppose, but it was a recurring theme. For all prisoners who survived the Reich, with poisoned memories in tow, there began the long road back to becoming human beings again.

CHAPTER 8

Something Waits for You,
1945–1946

AFTER THE DEATHCAMPS, survivors never returned to life as it had been. How could they? Even—or especially—those few who went back "home" found that too much had been destroyed, their loved ones gone. And, no matter where they went, some memories were too vile to be borne even in freedom.

AT THE END of the war the borders between Germany and Austria were reestablished and the victorious Allies divided Germany into zones of occupation by American, British, French, and Soviet forces. Southern Germany, which included Munich, was designated an American zone while eastern Austria, including Vienna, came under the Soviets. The division of Berlin—set squarely in the Soviet zone of Germany—into sectors for Allied occupation was the blatant and symbolic example of slicing up territory, and it became a tragedy of errors during the Cold War. Vienna was actually carved up in the same way, but the agreements that assured Austria's neutrality averted its becoming another Berlin.

For a period the borders between American-occupied southern Germany and Soviet-occupied eastern Austria were closed. So although Viktor was determined to return to Vienna, he could not do so right away. Instead he was assigned by the Americans to work as a physician in the hospital in Bad Wörishofen, near Türkheim, which had been taken over to care for the war's displaced persons—"DPs." Viktor worked at the hospital for about two months but learned nothing about the fates of his loved ones. During this time some of the same daydreams and hopes that Viktor had used to fend off despair in the camps kept him going.

Since midcentury, research in cognitive psychology and cognitive-behavioral psychotherapy has verified the power of mental attitude, of re-framing and restructuring experiences; logotherapy no longer stands alone in urging what Viktor called acts of self-transcendence. Although natural disasters certainly are not controlled by cognitive strategies, and human evil in the world is not eliminated by acts of individual self-transcendence, the human spirit is still potent in the face of adversity. Having something to live for, to look forward to, helps one to cope with the odds. This is why Viktor was relentless in his focus on the importance of meaning in life. In circumstances of adversity, his perspective was that meaning is *necessary but not sufficient for* survival. As we see in his own concrete experiences, there are also crucial factors such as luck, twists of fate or Providence, and impinging elements over which we have no control whatsoever.

At the DP hospital Viktor met a nurse from Munich who helped him edge toward Vienna. Her family offered him a place to live in their home, so he left Bad Wörishofen for Munich without talking to his supervisor. A carbon copy of a letter from Viktor to American Captain Schepeler sur-vives, and in it he explains his departure and his determination to find out about his mother and wife. Viktor assures Schepeler that Dr. Heumann, Viktor's medical colleague, knows everything necessary and that the work can be covered. Viktor leaves open the possibility of his return, but repeats that his leaving is a matter of conscience with regard to his family.

Viktor stayed with the nurse's family at Zaubzerstrasse 36[1] in Munich from late June until mid-August. During those six weeks he toiled over his manuscript—the mission that kept him going amid all the uncertainty. In Germany, information about his mother and Tilly was hard to find, so he kept an eye open for a first chance to reenter Austria. In a Munich cinema he saw graphic war footage in newsreels and documentary films. He was shaken to see the conditions in other concentration camps at the time of Allied takeover. The scale of terror and death was brought home to him when he saw a newsreel on the gas chambers of extermination centers. This struck him to the core and raised his anxieties about his mother and about Tilly. He had to find out about them.

At this time Radio Munich (6870th District Information Services Control Command, U.S. Army) employed Viktor to do radio talks on psy-chological problems in reconstruction. So in a way his concentration camp fantasies about writing and public speaking were finding an actual outlet even during his short stay in Munich. Just before Viktor left for Vienna, Field Horine, chief editor at Radio Munich, wrote two bilingual letters of recommendation for him dated August 13, 1945. One letter is a general reference that applauds Viktor's caliber and qualifications. The other is an appeal "to whom it may concern" for help. It states that Frankl is on his way to Vienna but wishes to return to Munich if possible. "We should like very much to employ him in Radio Munich, a Station of the Military Government, and would appreciate any assistance which could be rendered him in securing transportation to Munich." Apparently Viktor was keeping his options open, not knowing what he would find in Vienna.

But on his last day in Munich, Viktor learned of his mother's fate, and it was the worst news. She had been killed upon her arrival at Birkenau—coming there directly from Theresienstadt four days after Viktor. At the selection she had been sent to the right-hand line and directed without delay to the gas chambers. According to Viktor, in a single session a thousand prisoners stripped—women, men, and children together—and were herded into the "shower room." Typically it took up to seventeen minutes for the victims to die from Zyklon B gas.

When he thought about the newsreel and the likely manner of his mother's death, Viktor hit one of his lowest points, even contemplating suicide. As the shock of the news diminished, he was heartbroken to think that he would never see his mother again, never have that chance to kiss the hem of her coat. Though he never got over the manner of her death, the last blessing she gave him at Theresienstadt would remain with him always.

ON AUGUST 15, Viktor left Munich for Vienna. The three-hundred-mile drive was arduous in an open troop transport truck with perhaps thirty passengers. Viktor remembered that among his travel companions that day was the antifascist and resistance fighter Rosa Jochmann, after whom a Vienna street is named. He described their crossing the national borders as "half-illegal"—perhaps due to tensions between American and Russian occupations—but there was no problem in doing so.

In the late afternoon or early evening they arrived finally at Rathausplatz, the open square right in front of Vienna city hall. The surroundings were recognizable of course, but the city seemed to be tottering in the wake of recent bombings. Many landmarks had been hit including, as Viktor would soon see for himself, the city centerpieces: the opera house, the Ferris wheel, even the great St. Stephen's Cathedral. Probably a third of Vienna's residential buildings had taken bombs and many had been rendered uninhabitable. But Viktor was intent on the people significant to him as he made his emotional reentry to the city.

He was traveling light. In his pack were the following: the necktie from Türkheim; the notes on his book and bits of its manuscript; the reference letters from Radio Munich; some other correspondence; the page from the Hebrew prayer book found in the coat pocket at Auschwitz; and the little charm of blue and gold, "The whole world turns on love." From his former life in Vienna he retained only one tangible thing: the wire-framed eyeglasses, still bent out of shape from being hurled into the mud when he was beaten at the Small Fortress. Among intangible remnants were his passions, ideas, and stubborn will. At least in some residual form these were still alive in him.

In his first moments after jumping from the truck at Rathausplatz, he inquired what he might do. He was advised to go to the Jewish *Altersheim*—the old folks' home and hospital on Malzgasse. He knew it well—the same facility in Leopoldstadt where he and Pötzl had sent Jewish mental patients. So Viktor made his way on foot to Malzgasse—there were no taxis and the bombing had knocked out telephones and most tram lines. But at the *Altersheim* he was welcomed, given food, and offered a place to sleep. He remembered very well spending that first night in a dormitory room with thirty others. He was restless. Thousands of bedbugs infested the place and he had to share his bunk with many of them. Though he was used to worse, he sought other accommodations the next day. But the city was infested with fleas, and finding a place free of dirt, bugs, and vermin was a challenge immediately after the war. (Viktor continued throughout his life to shake out his clean socks and shoes before putting them on, as if to dislodge cockroaches that might be hiding therein; this was not compulsive behavior but something he did with a half-smile—rather like celebrating an old habit and the fact that the need for it was gone.)

To anyone who had known the city before Hitler, the absence of Jews was conspicuous. Not many had survived in the city and very few were returning from the camps. Consistent with the situation there was more news for Viktor of a very bad sort. That first morning, either from a nurse at the *Altersheim* or from Dr. Tuchmann—or both—Viktor learned that Tilly had died at the women's camp at Bergen-Belsen. So in the space of a few days, two of Viktor's deep-seated hopes were dashed and anxieties fulfilled. Neither his mother nor his wife had survived the camps. Later on, a friend of Tilly told Viktor that near the end Tilly had felt all but certain that Viktor would not survive the camps, since he was older and more frail than she. An irony is that Viktor was optimistic for Tilly because of her youth and good health—he had survived and he believed her chances of doing so were even better.

In time Viktor found out still more about Tilly's demise. At some point after they had been separated in the Birkenau selection, she was transported to Bergen-Belsen, perhaps spending time in other camps en route. Bergen-Belsen was a large camp system centered thirty miles north of Hannover in northern Germany. By the end of the war the main camp at Bergen-Belsen had eight sections, two for women, plus an array of subcamps. Anne Frank, the most famous victim of the Holocaust, perished there as well.[2]

When British troops arrived to liberate the camps on April 15, 1945, they found 60,000 prisoners still alive at Bergen-Belsen, but the site was littered with thousands of unburied corpses. Tilly Grosser Frankl was among the living—barely. Many of the prisoners were too wasted away to recover, and another 10,000 to 20,000 died from malnutrition and disease *after* the liberation. Tilly was among them, succumbing at the Hohne camp near Belsen, without strength to take up the newfound freedom for which she had longed. It simply came too late.

The British liberators burned Bergen-Belsen to the ground to rid its turf of lice and deadly filth. In doing so they contained the scourge of typhus in that place.

ELLY AND I were listening to Viktor as he recalled his return after the war, disclosing many details we had never heard before. Though he was coping with the deaths of his mother and wife, nevertheless he had to do something about his situation after that first night at the *Altersheim.*

The next day I went to Dr. Tuchmann in the next block. He was the communicating officer, as it were, and of Polish-Jewish origin. He was also a general practitioner and throughout the war was liaison between the Jewish community and the Gestapo. He was suspected at the time, but I do not wish to make any reproaches of him. . . . He tried to do the best he could. . . . After the war he was a prominent Jew, and toward me he was very cordial and tears came from his eyes when I told him that my mother had been killed in the gas chamber. . . . [Tuchmann] said immediately that something must be done for me. He owned a car for official business, an open car, and he said, "Come with me!" And the first drive we did was from Leopoldstadt into the First District to the Ministry of Social Affairs—the same department where my father worked for thirty-five years. There Tuchmann handed me over to Dr. Bruno Pittermann, whom I knew from the times around 1924—because then and later I was the spokesman for the socialist high school student organization. So I was very familiar with Pittermann. . . . And he provided me with a very old Remington typing machine so that I could work on my manuscript. . . . Once I knew that my family was gone, except for my sister in Australia, this was the only thing I wanted to do before dying, spontaneously or from one cause or another. Beyond that I didn't want to exist. But I decided not to commit suicide—at least not before I had reconstructed my first book, *The Doctor and the Soul*. I wanted to rewrite it and this became my habilitation to become a *Dozent*[5]. . . . You see, I was emptied out [exhausted] and had no plans beyond this.

If you wish, Don, I can show you the pension [guest house] where I stayed the first two weeks. . . . The Pension Auer is in Lazarettgasse, just around the corner from bookseller Maudrich. I was there for about two weeks. . . .

Pittermann—first the typewriter—and then he found me a place to live, a rental apartment. And he installed me as the manager of this whole apartment.[4] He freed one room for me—this very room, with boarded-up windows and no light. . . .

The man who had owned the apartment was now a refugee because he had been an SS doctor; and he had Aryanized the apartment and took it over. He was a dentist, and this was his office and waiting room and so on. . . . This SS man had driven away the Jews, so when the Russians came he fled to the west . . . and he took everything from this apartment with him. . . . And refugees came here to avoid the bombing.

This was flat 14 on the third floor at Mariannengasse 1, to be Viktor's permanent home. Its setting was right between the vast General Hospital across Spitalgasse and the Poliklinik just down the street. I learned from Hermi Ecker, the resident housekeeper in the apartment house during the war and ever since, that it had taken no direct bombing hits, though other buildings along the same street had been demolished. The Poliklinik across the street was damaged also, though its main structures had remained intact.

Tuchmann and Pittermann were a great help to Viktor upon his return. And, once the loss of his family was known for certain, Viktor went to look up other people, particularly his friends Polak and Pötzl. He went to the home of Paul and Otti Polak on that first or second day. Under his load of grief and lost hopes, Viktor desperately needed someone to whom he could pour out his heart. After a brief reunion, the two men went out on the apartment balcony, which overlooked some gardens below. There Viktor opened up to Paul about the appalling deaths of his parents and Tilly. The gatekeepers of his emotions abandoned their watch and the torrent broke loose. Viktor the stoic sobbed and sobbed in the presence of his friend. When he calmed, he turned and said, "Paul, I need to tell you some things, and I know that if anyone can understand me it will be you. When all of these things happen to someone, when a person is tested this way, it must be for something—it must have some meaning. I have a sense—which is nearly impossible for me to describe—that there is a task waiting for me, that now something is expected or required of me. I feel strongly that I am destined for something, to do something."

His beliefs regarding the unconditional meaningfulness of life and the necessity of some cause or love beyond oneself were passing further from theory toward the farthest reaches of personal conviction. Why he was permitted to survive at all puzzled him, but he set himself to make the most of his remaining days, however few or many they might be.

Unlike Polak, Otto Pötzl was a broken man when Viktor found him, and there was little he could offer his old mentor. Just the day before, Pötzl had been fired as chief of the University Psychiatric Clinic because of his former affiliation with the National Socialists. For Viktor to find Pötzl in that situation added to his disappointments. Nevertheless, Pötzl, then sixty-eight, remained active in practice, research, and publishing for many years.

For whatever reasons, it was some time before Viktor went to the apartment building in Leopoldstadt where he had grown up. Of course he knew that someone else would be living in the flat, but he wanted to find

Toni Grumbach, who had sheltered him during the early Hitler years. So Viktor went to Czerningasse and found Toni's grandmother still living there. He wanted to be sure that Toni was well and offer him any help if he were in need now. But the old woman, after living through such an era, was suspicious of anyone who came inquiring after Toni. So she gave Viktor no information about her grandson and it was not until sometime later that he found Toni.

The return to Czerningasse put Viktor into a swirl of emotions since so many memories and associations were anchored there. But there was one bad recollection that stirred up in him a desire for revenge against a man who was formerly a neighbor. Revenge was utterly unlike Viktor, but he described the incident.

> From the first day I said that I cannot resist to take revenge on one man—a man who in Czerningasse had insulted my mother. And I went to his grandmother and asked, "Where is your grandson?" She told me he was still there but he had lost in the war one leg—amputated, you see. And after awhile the grandson came in and I told him, "My name is Dr. Frankl, and you are the one who insulted my mother. And from that time on she suffered arrhythmia of the heart because she was so upset. And you caused this," I said quietly to him. He shrugged his shoulders and I said no more. But then when I left, I embraced his grandmother and said good-bye. But I was not able to give a handshake to him or say good-bye to him. That was all that was left of my intention to take revenge. And then it was over, it was done. Such things remain in our minds.

I said, "But Viktor, he had not insulted you. If he had insulted you, you probably would have forgotten it." Viktor replied, "Of course. But this was my mother, and he not only had insulted her but also had started this heart trouble. But then a few years later she entered the gas chamber of Auschwitz and it was all the same." Viktor, ending a powerful series of recollections, took the words of the American news anchorman he admired greatly. "As Walter Cronkite always said, 'And that's the way it is.' "

By the end of September it is clear that Viktor was not only writing but making a professional reentry. A Vienna councilman for culture wrote a letter to the police requesting travel documents so that Viktor could go

to Switzerland for a psychology conference.⁵ Carl Jung and Medard Boss
were on the program, though even there Viktor did not meet Jung personally.

At about the same time, though Viktor thought that violence against
him had ended with the war, he was assaulted on the street.

> I had an experience with American soldiers in August '45.
> The transportation was very poor in Vienna, and only a few lines
> of the streetcars were operating. And I was down Alser Strasse and
> near the Ring, when suddenly out from the doorway of a building
> jumped two American soldiers. They asked me how they could get
> to Döbling or some outer district, and I told them in a friendly
> way in English, "Use that tram, but hurry because it is the last one
> of the night"—what we called "the last blue" at the time. And
> just before they ran across the street to get the tram, each of them
> gave me an uppercut so that I tumbled down to the ground.

Elly tried to soften the story, perhaps out of consideration for my na-
tionality. "But what can we say? We could ask twenty Americans to give us
some food or something and they would do it." But Viktor saw in the incident just one more illustration of the point he argued all his life: "It de-
pends on who it is! Decent and indecent people cut across every nation."

In time Viktor recovered a few belongings from before the deportations. The neighbor in the Czerningasse apartment building returned to
him the Schiele print—the one Viktor bought when he was a medical student and which hangs in the Frankl flat to this day; his twenty-meter rope
for rock-climbing; the fencing foils from his schoolboy days; some pencils
and other small items of his father's; and a few books. From Paul Polak,
Viktor recovered a copy of the original manuscript of *The Doctor and the
Soul* from before the war, which he used in rewriting the book. And from
a neighbor or friend Viktor was happy to have again his hand-sized porcelain bust of Savonarola. The face of the Christian reformer, who had opposed the pope and corrupt clergy, bears a visage of suffering—Viktor had
been moved by this image and had brought it before Hitler. Another link
to his former life was returned to Viktor, and this one he treasured greatly:
his father's phylacteries—the Jewish straps with the little leather boxes
containing Holy Writ. Stella in Australia kept family photos safe during

the Holocaust and gave many of these to Viktor when it was over. Only these things were left from Viktor's former life, and none of it was of much value except to him.

By the end of 1945, Viktor finished revising and expanding his manuscript. He took a copy to the university for his habilitation and another to his publisher. Having done this, he experienced great relief since so many attempts to write the book had been aborted during the Hitler years. When it finally appeared in bookshops with the title *Ärztliche Seelsorge* ("medical ministry," hence the later English title, *The Doctor and the Soul*), the first edition sold out in a few days since Vienna was starved in body and in mind as well—what Viktor called "an intellectual vacuum." In its two hundred pages he addressed directly some of the most insistent questions of the day, such as what to make of suffering, of life such as it was, and why to go on living it. He had added, following the section on "the meaning of death," a few pages on the "psychology of the concentration camp." It was that brief section that led Viktor's friends to pressure him to write more about it.

Immediately after writing that book, and in response to his friends, Viktor rerecruited secretaries to take dictation. In the nine days they worked together the German manuscript of *Man's Search for Meaning* was completed. He went to his publisher and offered the manuscript on condition that the little book be published anonymously. Again under pressure from friends, Viktor relented on this condition and, while his name did not appear on the cover, it did on the first page.

It was published early in 1946 in a run of only three thousand copies, but the publisher's expectations were high and almost immediately a second run produced a few thousand more. The second printing did not sell well, however. So the publisher offered Viktor copies at a low price, and he took a hundred of them. The publisher ultimately discarded much of the second printing for lack of sales.

Franz Deuticke was also the first publisher of Sigmund Freud. One day I talked with Deuticke [about the failure of my new book] and he said, "Wait a minute!" He went to his archives and took out some files and said, "This cornerstone of psychoanalysis, *The Interpretation of Dreams*, was published in 1900." He had printed it in 1,000 copies, first edition. One hundred copies were reserved for reviews, so 900 copies were for sale. Guess when the 900 copies were sold out? *Ten years later!* At first no commercial success, but people liked it and made jokes about it.

Freud's first book remains in print in multiple languages a century later. Deuticke's anecdote, told perhaps to encourage Viktor, turned out to be a prophetic prelude to *Man's Search for Meaning*.

VIKTOR'S FIRST TWO books were the products of his revising and writing between his August 1945 return to the city and January of 1946. By then he had followed the strong urging of Bruno Pittermann to look into a couple of positions in neurology-psychiatry.

It was Pittermann who sent me to the First District to the office of the administration of hospital affairs . . . though I had no interest in getting a job then. I was not even thinking about that. But Pittermann insisted that I sign a blank paper, and he will take care of the rest to find me a position. Then I was invited by an official of the hospital affairs bureau, and he said yes, that Bruno Pittermann had told them they should offer me a position. And they had two possibilities: either that I take over as director of the four-thousand-bed Steinhof mental hospital of the city . . . or, another position which was still open was the head of the department of neurology at the Poliklinik Hospital. And I said, "Sir, I was for four years a resident in psychiatry at Steinhof and this would be a task that would interest me, to put my stamp on this institution, to bring a new spirit to it." But he said, "This will not be possible—putting your stamp on it is out of the question. You will not be able to bring any new spirit there." Then I remembered that my director at Steinhof was almost never seen by us because he was forever waiting in the anteroom of the mayor's office; he was always trying to get the city to increase the payment for even one patient from one schilling and twelve groschen to one schilling and fourteen groschen.

I asked Viktor if I understood this correctly. "You are saying that Steinhof was so big, and there was so much red tape, that you could not influence the system?" He said this was exactly the case and continued describing his meeting.

"So I said to the official, 'Okay, then, for heaven's sake, let it be the neurological department of the Poliklinik.' The man who had been in charge of the department had fled because he was SS, and so the position had become vacant. So I took it over and when I started, there was a woman doctor who was assistant to the former chief. But my first-assistant was Dr. Schober."

In February 1946, Viktor started at the Poliklinik on Mariannengasse ("Poli-" is from the Greek word *polis*, for city). The Poliklinik was and remained a small hospital for people of the city, including its poor—hence it might be understood also as the "people's hospital." It was only a couple of minutes' walk down the street from the apartment where Viktor had settled. It was a most convenient arrangement and the beginning of a quarter of a century for Frankl as *Vorstand* or chief of the Poliklinik department of neurology. Vienna was filled with bureaucrats and even the medical community was layered in ranks and appellations, so as department chief Frankl was called "primarius." For him to be addressed as "Herr Dr. Primarius" was not unusual; the title of "professor" had not yet been added.

ELLY AND I talked with Viktor about the period in his life shortly before they met. The Türkheim liberation came up again and Viktor recalled the soldiers from Texas, some of whom were from the city of Austin. Viktor brought forward a cherished memory of a later trip to Texas when he was invited to stop by to meet the mayor of Austin. To Viktor's surprise, the mayor presented him with a medal signifying that he had just become an honorary citizen of Austin. This was Viktor's response to the mayor.

"It really is not appropriate that you make me an honorary citizen. It would be more fitting if I make you an honorary logotherapist. Had not so many young soldiers from Texas, among them several from your city, risked and even sacrificed their lives, there would be no Frankl and no logotherapy today. You see, it was your Texas soldiers who liberated me and many others from the camp at Türkheim."[6] The mayor had been visibly moved.

The conversation about Texas led to another human connection to the liberation. Dallas had hosted the Tenth World Congress of Logotherapy in

1995. Viktor reminded us that he had been unable to attend the congress, but that his granddaughter and grandson, Katja and Alexander, were there to represent him. "There was exhibited the uniform of the soldier who was the second to enter and free us at the Türkheim concentration camp. His son and widow were there, and she had loaned his uniform to the congress to be exhibited for the duration. And when I learned this over the telephone I asked Katja and Alexander together to place a rose from me on that uniform."[7]

IN THE OPEN time between our conversation sessions I continued to explore the places of Viktor's life and, as usual, reported to Viktor and Elly on what I had found and photographed. In one case I had taken a ride on the giant Ferris wheel—the *Riesenrad*—in the Prater in order to get a view of the neighborhood of the Frankl family in the decades before Hitler. From the top I could see the position of the North Station railroad tracks in relation to the end of Czerningasse. Viktor immediately cited the passage in *Man's Search for Meaning* where he described looking down and into his street from the train that was taking him and his fellow prisoners to Dachau.[8] Then I told him that I gone even farther than the Ferris wheel to catch the view that he had described. Hearing this, Viktor and Elly were fascinated since what I had done was really not permitted and perhaps a bit risky. I found the best vantage point by going up to the elevated tracks at North Station and, between trains, walking southward on the tracks quite a distance beyond the loading platform. From there I caught virtually the same view from the tracks into Czerningasse, though some new apartment buildings were there. Passersby who saw me with my camera seemed to be trying to guess why I was taking pictures *there*.

Earlier, Viktor had offered to take me to the Pension Auer—Elly also was willing to do so. It was the guest house where he had stayed for those first two weeks after his return to Vienna. But instead he—the cartoonist-cartographer—started drawing a map and diagram of the Auer, still there with the same name after half a century. He explained the inner courtyard as he remembered it. "If you enter, there you go down—subterranean— and here is a garden. And you can see from the garden the small windows. There are one or maybe two rooms to rent, with windows opening to the garden, and in that room I was spending fourteen days . . . a small room, you see, half-underground, where I was asking myself for what I should continue to live at all."

I told Viktor and Elly I could find it alone, and I did. Armed with his instructions and the diagram, I entered the Auer. No one was around, so I ventured into the courtyard and found it just as Viktor had described it, except that now "garden" was too kindly a word for the overgrown outdoor space. But the small windows of the basement rooms were still there, and I poked my way around, taking some photographs. I even ventured into the basement area where Viktor's room had been. When I returned to the Frankls and told what I had found, Viktor was very pleased with my exploration and also, I think, with his ability to recall the place precisely.

An automobile journey with a friend in 1996 involved exploration on a wider scale. We went to the venues of the two Dachau camps, and Viktor had briefed us on what to look for on the trip. Again, as it turned out, his memory was extraordinary, though there was little at Kaufering and Türkheim to compare with the preserved sites of Auschwitz-Birkenau and the main camp at Dachau. There were no buildings left—no traces of those mostly-underground barracks with roofs sloping to ground level on both sides that characterized Kaufering III and Türkheim. There were no actual museums, and at the sites we found mostly fields and woods and residential areas, beautiful now but eerie to us. We also saw markers and reminders, and many a burial place (KZ-Friedhof), some with massive gravestones now obscured among the trees. Among some houses we found an open space where an old aerial view of Kaufering III was posted alongside some concrete slabs, presumably where buildings stood. That aerial view looks sickeningly like other camps, with row on row of barracks surrounding the *Appellplatz* where Viktor and comrades had stood for roll calls.

(Back home I had learned that Kaufering had fifteen subsidiary camps of its own, eleven for men and four for women. The central administration was located about four miles north of Landsberg, in whose prison Hitler did time before his rise to power.)

After the long day, my friend and I looked for a place to stay and ended up at Hotel Rid, directly across the road from the Kaufering railroad station. At the hotel we neither saw nor heard any other guests and, given our objectives, it seemed a sinister night. If that train station could talk. . . .

In 1999, three years after this visit to Kaufering, its town council named a street at the southern rotary Viktor-Frankl-Strasse. The announcement said simply that Frankl's name stands to represent the great sorrow of the fields of Kaufering and what had happened there.

Upon leaving Hotel Rid the next morning we took up scouting the area, and our first destination was the hospital in Bad Wörishofen where Viktor had worked immediately after liberation. It was not difficult to find what had become the Hotel Sonnenhof or to imagine its older sections as the former hospital. Then on to nearby Türkheim.

We found the city hall (*Rathaus*) in this attractive town, where I hoped to get our bearings. My companion found a spot to sit in the sun and I went inside. No one was about until I happened on the mayor's office. It was fairly early on a July Monday, and when I knocked on the door my expectations were exceeded by far. The mayor himself, Dr. Klaus Bühler, came to the door, and he seemed surprised that anyone would knock there. When I explained that I was writing a book about Viktor Frankl, he brightened to a warm welcome. From his cabinets he took a copy of *Für die Vergessenen*[9] (For the Forgotten), flipped through its pages with me and made a gift of it. Then he opened a map of Türkheim, marking out Viktor-Frankl-Weg—yet another street (way) named after Viktor. I met my traveling companion at the car and we drove off with the help of the map.

We found the road near the Türkheim train station where Martinstrasse and Martinring meet. Viktor-Frankl-Weg headed into a tunnel formed by overarching trees. We passed a few residences and then the pavement ended and a dirt road continued into open fields of corn and hay. At 99 Viktor-Frankl-Weg stood a memorial building, round and domed, with one room. Engraved on the interior walls in poetic German were the words, "Let this marker be dedicated to devout atonement, so that we may walk anew in justice." Outside and to the left above the doorway, a Jewish Star of David, and on the right a Christian cross.

It was at this very spot on April 27, 1985, on the fortieth anniversary of the Türkheim liberation, that Viktor addressed a large gathering. Now, a decade later, the place was peaceful, shaded and cooled by large trees. Not far away was a plaque that referred to these Dachau camps as "cold crematoria" because of the thousands who died there from freezing, starvation, and illness. It was at curbside, along this road now bearing Viktor's name, that he once took on the duty of a pastor. "On the first day of liberation at Türkheim I had to say a few words, because there was no priest, no rabbi—there was nothing available—when we buried someone who had died the preceding night in one of the barracks. . . . We dug out a grave for him and put the body therein. And, before we closed it by shoveling again, I thought something should be done in a religious sense. And so I said one of the few Hebrew texts I had memorized and also the prayer for the dead [the mourners' Kaddish]. And then it was closed. That was all that we could do."

NOW WE CLOSE Part I and leave Viktor in Vienna at the end of 1945 as he is trying to resettle. He is writing and looking into the positions that Pittermann is advocating for him. Though Viktor has found some of his friends, he is lonely without family, and so he is mulling over the possibility of emigration to Australia to be near Stella and to make a fresh start of some kind. Part II, to which we now turn, tells of Elly, a child and young woman who lives on the other side of the Danube. At this point in the story, Viktor and Elly have absolutely no knowledge of one another. So Viktor will be absent from Part II, except where he sits in during my interviews with Elly. Following the two chapters about Elly—which comprise Part II—Part III will tell about their meeting and about their life together across the years.

PART TWO

Elly Schwindt

1925–1946

CHAPTER 9

Child Across the Danube, 1925–1937

ON THE WALL of my study hangs a large map of Vienna and its environs. North to south the map represents thirteen miles, and west to east twenty, so it takes in the suburbs, surrounding towns, and large portions of the vast Vienna Woods. In order to trace the lives of the Frankls, I have put marker pins at key spots on the map. A dozen pins or "map flags" denote Viktor's places—mostly of his childhood, education and medical training, and one for the family cemetery plot. Elly's four pins indicate her home and schools, the house of her Tante (Aunt) Mitzi, and the family gravesite in a different cemetery. No pin on the map marks any spot farther than six miles from St. Stephen's at the center of the city. Thus the Frankl story is virtually surrounded by a circle twelve miles across and centered at the cathedral.[1]

In the center of the wall map I have positioned the boundaries of a much smaller area of Vienna, creating a map-within-the-map. This denotes a sector approximately 3.1 miles by 4.3 miles, and ten of the sixteen pins are within these boundaries. Whether on an expansive wall map or on one as simple as the one in this book, a particular distinguishing feature of Vienna gives us the setting for Elly Schwindt, the "child across the Danube."

There are actually four waterways (see Vienna map) that bear the Danube name: the surging Danube River itself (Donau); the New Danube (Neue Donau), running alongside; and the Old Danube (Alte Donau) in Kaisermühlen; and the Danube Canal (Donaukanal) that runs from the river into the city and then back into the river far to the south, creating the "island" on which Leopoldstadt is located. Although the Danube River is now the object of environmental cleanup, it probably was never as beautiful or blue as poets and musicians would have us believe. But it is majestic and, in a way, beautiful. Entering the city from the north, it flows toward the southeast in a wide expanse that appears as two channels (Danube and New Danube), separated by the recreational Danube Island, which stretches for twenty-five miles. The effect of the river is to cut off the smaller northeastern regions of Vienna from the sprawling metropolis. The city is united now by a series of modern and heavily traveled bridges.

On square maps, the section at the upper right that is cut off by the river typically appears as a triangle. Inside that triangle is Kaisermühlen, a small neighborhood near the waterways. The Danube runs along one side, and the Alte Donau curves around the other, creating a massive "island" for the Danube Park, the imposing UNO City—since 1979 accommodating several United Nations agencies, and Kaisermühlen. Extensive development of the area has changed the aspect of Kaisermühlen since 1925 when it was lush and tranquil.

The Alte Donau and its islands, the Grosse Gänsehäufel and the Kleine Gänsehäufel, are summer vacation spots known mostly to locals. But one tourist guide now describes them together as "by far the most attractive stretch of the river, whose weeping willows and rowing clubs resemble the Thames at Eton."[2] An electric or rowboat rental permits one to see the area, to imagine a simpler time when luxuriant woodland surrounded the trademark waters, and to sense Kaisermühlen's rural texture and isolation from the city. In fact, in 1925 it was a thinly settled residential area, mainly of working-class Catholic families. The parish church, *Herz Jesu* (Heart of Jesus) at Schüttauplatz, is very near the Gänsehäufel islands. And Schüttaustrasse 64 is the apartment building in which Elly was born. The windows of the family flat looked over *Herz Jesu* and the waters beyond it.

Though the birthplaces of Elly Schwindt and Viktor Frankl are only a couple of miles apart, the worlds they entered as infants were very different, both in time and place. Viktor was born nearly a decade before World War I started; Elly seven years after it ended. His childhood was in the Jewish bustle of Leopoldstadt, near the commercial and intellectual ferment of the central city. Her childhood, which began two decades later than Viktor's, was in the more sheltered and slower paced Kaisermühlen.

ELLY'S MOTHER WAS Hermine Prihoda, born December 12, 1900, in Leopoldstadt. The parents of Hermine—Elly's maternal grandparents—

had been born in Czechoslovakia: Johann Prihoda, July 22, 1875, and Maria Tuma, November 29, 1868. Johann and Maria came from Prague and settled in Kaisermühlen, where they remained for the rest of their lives. Maria died in 1922, before Elly was born, but Johann lived a full life. He was a successful photographer and his studio was in the attic of the building at Schüttaustrasse 64, above the family flat. The building is still standing, at the corner of Schüttaustrasse and Moissigasse.

Though Elly never knew her grandma Prihoda, she learned later that Maria had been a frugal woman who, with five daughters, was saving money so that each girl might someday have a house. But the money she saved across the years was lost in the economic depression of the 1920s and nothing was left. One character among the Prihodas made the family name famous. Vasa Prihoda was an eminent violinist who played concerts not only in his native Prague and Czechoslovakia but also in many foreign countries. Audio recordings of his playing are still marketed today. It was said by concertgoers that Vasa could play compositions faster than anyone else in the world.

All five daughters of Johann and Maria Prihoda were born and raised in Kaisermühlen. Hermine at age twenty-five would become the mother of Elly, and her four younger sisters were to be Elly's Tante Tilde (born 1902), Tante Mitzi (1909), and twin aunts Grete and Gusti (1910). All five lived out their lives in Vienna. Among the four aunts, the one-of-a-kind Tante Mitzi played the most significant role in Elly's story.

Elly's ancestors on her father's side are attached to a legend that goes back centuries to a band of rogues in the Salzburg region who stole from the rich and gave to the poor. When I told Elly that this sounded like the legend of Robin Hood, she said perhaps so. Then Viktor quipped, "And the legend of Karl Marx also."

Elly's paternal grandfather was Richard Schwindl, born September 21, 1862, in Laxenburg, a small town about six miles south of Vienna. He fell in love with Leopoldine Michtner, also Austrian through-and-through and born in Laxenburg May 11, 1867. She came into a family fortune and, after they were married, Richard and Leopoldine practically owned much of Laxenburg. They had four sons: Karl (1895–1972); Richard (born 1897, wounded in World War I, who lived with this mother thereafter); Robert (1898–1973); and Leo, who was born October 30, 1900, and would one day become the father of Elly. Little Leo and his siblings lacked nothing, but their privileged lifestyle was not to last.

As Viktor and I listened to Elly, she spontaneously traced her father's origins.

> I don't know how many houses Leopoldine had. She and her husband had four sons, but he died fairly young and she remarried. And her second husband, whose name was Schulz, took all her money and sold everything and put it into a business. Then he lost it all and died at a young age . . . so she came to Vienna with her four boys—my father the youngest—and she started doing laundry for a living in Leopoldstadt.

It is not surprising, given their family heritage and the region in which they lived, that all four of Elly's grandparents were Roman Catholic. Austria has remained overwhelmingly Catholic, largely unaffected by the Protestant Reformation that swept through Germany and other parts of Europe centuries earlier.

Leo Schwindl and Hermine Prihoda were married April 18, 1922, in a Catholic ceremony at *Herz Jesu* in Kaisermühlen. They created their household in a small flat on the third floor at Schüttaustrasse 64—apartment 22, which is still there today with the same door and number plate. Leo worked as a clerk in a shop in the First District, the old inner city. The shop was a supplier to tailors, carrying textiles and everything else they needed in their trade. At the time, in the absence of mass-produced, ready-made clothing, people relied on local tailors for made-to-order garments—at least those people who could afford new things.

Leo and Hermine had three children, each born in their little apartment 22. Kurt arrived August 12, 1922, but he lived only a few weeks. In September the young parents suffered the ordeal of burying their tiny firstborn. A year later, on August 22, 1923, Hermine gave birth to another boy. They named him Alfons, but called him simply "Ali." Occasionally they used the childish "Alala" or even Ali Baba from the *Arabian Nights* story, "Ali Baba and the Forty Thieves." When Ali was just over two the family was awaiting their next child, and she arrived November 6, 1925. Her name was a respectable Eleonore Katharina Schwindl. To make that manageable in daily life, family and friends at once started to call her Elly—in her early years spelled Elli, and when Anglicized, Ellie. But in her adult life, "Elly" is the form she normally uses.

As in various cultures today, it was not unusual in Vienna at the time

for babies to sleep with their parents. For the Schwindls this sleeping
arrangement was not merely custom, but an arrangement required by the
cramped space they shared. As children grew older in small apartments,
sons might share beds with each other or their fathers, and daughters with
each other or their mothers.

About the only times frisky little Elly was really quiet were during
sleep and when ill. In fact, during her first several years she was often ill
with childhood ailments. Thankfully their physician came to the flat
whenever they summoned him. "We had a Jewish family doctor in
Kaisermühlen, and his name was Leopold Frucht. He came over, though
we could not pay him. He never asked for a schilling—on the contrary, he
always brought me chocolate or an apple or something. So I was always
happy to be ill, because I knew the doctor is coming and will bring something. . . . It seems like we experienced the best of Jewish people and the
worst, but not much in between."

Viktor, listening in, mumbled to me, "I would never venture to ask her
on which side I am located."

By the time she started school, Elly was what we call—ever since
Thomas Edison—"a live wire." She was into everything, and as she advanced through school she became more healthy and robust. Not as close
to her mother and much quicker temperamentally, Elly adored her father.
He was an unassuming man, yet rooted in principles that he simply would
not compromise. Like his own mother, Leo had come from wealth and
ended up poor, but never lost his self-respect even through the eleven years
of his unemployment that began in 1927. Consequently, during most of
the first decade of Elly's life her father worked at odd jobs to keep his family afloat. Many of those jobs were menial labor such as cleaning public
buildings and doing yard work, and everyone in the family pitched in to
earn their livelihood. "For hours each day," Elly recalled, "I was cleaning
in private homes. Each day my mother, my father, Ali and I went at three
in the morning to clean apartments and shops to get some money." Leo
Schwindl was one among hundreds of thousands of unemployed in the
desperate conditions between the world wars. Leo finally found full-time
work again in 1938, shortly after Hitler swooped in on Austria. Nevertheless, in their extended family Leo was one of the most apprehensive
about the Nazi regime and the real substance of Hitler's aims.

Elly's father had been born Leo Schwindl, but he had the family name
legally changed to Schwindt in 1934. The main reason was that *Schwindl*

is pronounced the same as the German *Schwindel,* which means cheating or lying, like the English "swindle." So with the change—simply crossing the name's final letter—the Schwindts diminished a negative undertone, which they did not merit even if bandits do lurk somewhere in the family tree.

As Elly was telling her story, Viktor turned to me with a sly grin and said, "In contrast to my wife, who changed from Schwindl to Schwindt, I never changed from Frankl to Frank." To me, that was funny. It seemed even funnier when Elly just ignored it and continued thumbing through pictures and documents.

Another time when Elly was digging through old photographs of her swimming, her first communion, and so on, I was passing them along for Viktor to see as he was able—by then his vision was so poor that we described the key photos to him. An exchange erupted between Viktor and Elly that might have frightened any stranger listening in. But I was so accustomed to their prickly banter that I laughed aloud—just the reaction that the two of them preferred. Viktor said to Elly, with a twist of rebuke in the tone, "Elly, to me you have never showed these pictures." Elly replied definitively, "You have never been interested in these." Viktor, raising his voice even more, came back, "What can I say? How can I be interested in pictures I have never seen!" Elly just ignored him again but let me laugh. Then we continued browsing through photographs in which all three of us were genuinely interested.

When I asked Elly about her earliest memories—an Adlerian question—it did not take her long to fetch one. As a very little girl she had gone to Tante Mitzi to ask, in her own distinctive and childish *Wienerisch,* for a treat to settle her hunger. No one outside the family could have understood Elly's slurred plea for *Ganslschmalzbrot*—bread spread with goose fat. Elly remembered that she often asked Tante Mitzi for two pieces—one for Ali, too. Elly as a girl in that time and place was already conditioned to be of service to men, even to boys. Helly Fischer (later Helly Puhm), Elly's closest girlhood friend, recalled that Elly was nearly always second to her brother, that Ali was the one preferred socially. Elly picked up on the observation.

> You see, he was a boy, and at that time the boy was much more important than a girl. . . . Even when it came to food, the largest plate always was for the boy. . . . So I stood always behind Ali—ex-

cept with my father and my grandmother. They loved me as if they could not love me higher. But other people saw Ali first. When he was twelve and had his confirmation, the Jewish Uncle Roman came over for Ali in an elegant car—with flowers—that he had rented. And Alfons was dressed very nicely. I quite remember that Alfons was sitting in this wonderful car with Uncle Roman and Tante Mitzi, and I was in the house behind the door watching this, and I was crying and thinking, "Never will this happen to me. No one will do this with me." At that time I was very much hurt by this, but if I now think it over, I am so happy that all this happened to Ali.

Indeed there never was a confirmation celebration for Elly. Her parents and grandma Schwindt, who gladly would have made a fuss for her, were too poor at the time and Uncle Roman did not step in. As for other church observances the Schwindts went to mass on the Christian holidays, but from the twenties on they worked on Sundays and did not attend regularly.

One thing that enchanted Viktor and Elly especially was the business card of her grandfather: Johann Prihoda—Artist, Photographer, and Fire Chief. When Elly handed it to me, Viktor laughed enthusiastically, "Isn't it *unique?*" Apparently Johann had been a private volunteer firefighter. His photography studio was for portraits and not for fires, of course, so it was a favorite and safe place for little Elly to play. She described her grandpa as a funny guy—and Elly always liked funny, unique characters.

ELLY DID NOT know much about her father's youth, but she speculated that he must have been playful, perhaps even a rascal as she was. She thought so because he enjoyed her mischief and clowning so much. "But Ali was embarrassed by me among his friends. . . . He was somewhat closer to my mother, and my father was extremely proud of him because he was good—for his goodness. But I was always the rascal." Evidently, as a girl Elly specialized in shenanigans. "I was always a devil, a witch. . . . After school I was waiting only to wrestle with the boys, and Ali was ashamed [Elly giggled here] . . . he never did this. He was not so physical." When I challenged Elly that the English words "witch" and "devil" might be too strong, she left that to me but persisted in characterizing herself as a mischievous girl and a real cutup.

After listening quietly to most of the conversation between Elly and me, Viktor at this point injected, "But when she married me she began to become a witch!" But Elly corrected him, "I have been a witch before I married you, Viktor!" He insisted, "But now she is a *complete* witch." Elly enjoyed this, giggled, and agreed, "Now a total, complete witch!"

Once when Elly's father was cleaning a cinema, he picked up some small advertising leaflets left behind by moviegoers. On them was a photo of actress Greta Garbo, and he brought these home for Elly and Ali—a simple favor. Elly took some of them and wrote the name Schwindt on them, then dropped them into the collection box at Heart of Jesus Church. When the priest found them, he scolded Ali for the prank. When Elly told Ali that she had done it, he unleashed his displeasure on her.

When Elly and Ali were barely four and six, there was a special day when Schwindt family portraits were to be taken. The day before the scheduled sitting, Elly and Ali got to playing barber with a pair of scissors. Each hacked away at the hair of the other. Alfons chopped off the sides and left Elly's hair long on the top of her head. When Elly took her turn with the scissors, she clipped Ali's top short but left alone the long hair at the sides. In this way they rendered one another unfit for portraiture. So their mother hustled them off to a real barber for repairs. But they had done so much damage that, to even out their hair, he had to trim it down to almost nothing. In the portrait their mother Hermine poses in the center, flanked by three of her sisters; cousin Kurt wears a full head of hair, but Elly and Ali are shaved nearly bald. To Elly it was a comical picture—she appears as the smallest child and not only looks like the imp she was, but also like a boy who might jump out of formation in a split second. But she looks also like the kind of kid we'd like to chase around the house, or to hide from and then jump out and hug (see photograph).

As Elly approached school age, Tante Berta, wife of Uncle Robert, was well aware that the Schwindts were living on a shoestring. Though she could be harsh with the children, Berta nevertheless wanted to help the family with their situation so she found a place for them to live in Grafenwörth, a small town in a farming area thirty miles northwest of Vienna. They had to pay the rent, but part of the arrangement was Leo's employment at the *Spezerei & Delikatessenhandlung*—the local market. Elly's mother also helped there. The whole venture was a hard-times ex-

periment. Ali remained in school back in Kaisermühlen, living with Tante
Mitzi in the Schüttaustrasse flat. Uncle Roman, Mitzi's long-term partner,
helped the family by paying the rent there.

In the yard behind the Grafenwörth deli, Elly was permitted to keep
a dog and a cat and, with her affinity for animals, it was a wonderful time
for her. The deli building was also an ideal site for some of Elly's mischief,
which made the place all the more fun.

With an inventiveness beyond her age, Elly climbed up onto a low part
of the roof, out of sight to passersby. There she crouched down and low-
ered to the sidewalk a small, empty money-pouch on the end of a string.
The pouch lay on the walkway in front of the store, the thin string virtually invisible. Just as a passerby stooped to pick up the pouch, Elly jerked
it up and away. This trick amused her enormously. Elly remembered how
much she enjoyed watching as people, after first spotting the pouch, would
look around with a false nonchalance and—as soon as the coast was
clear—dive for the pouch. But Elly was quicker than her prey, who then
had to slither away in an even tougher act: false nonchalance layered with
embarrassment.

"Being in Grafenwörth," said the grown-up Elly, "was like vacation,
there in the countryside. There was a girl, the daughter of a real farmer,
and they had horses and cows and pigs and dogs . . . and I enjoyed it immensely . . ."

"There is nothing like comradeship," Viktor chuckled, and Elly instead of laughing agreed, "Yes I was so happy. And at their place I had a
baby calf, and I loved it. I was there with my family for eight months at
one stretch and I am sure if my father had kept this shop I would have
been very happy being a kind of farmer. But he had to give this up, so we
moved again back to Vienna, to our old place in Schüttaustrasse on the
fourth floor. . . . But I have no wish to go back to any of these places—I
have no idea how they look now. You see, my father died and my mother
died . . ." Viktor offered a suggestion to explain this in English. "The
memories are sacred and she wants to preserve them. . . . They do not need
to be covered with new and meaningless impressions." Elly affirmed his
formulation and said, "Yes, the memories are left as they were, and not
disturbed."

Little schoolgirl Elly was a handful, and her teachers sometimes did
not know what to do. "They couldn't do anything with me. Sometimes I
was in the closet [toilet] and I was singing! They no longer could handle

me and they called my home to ask for help." She was not only a toilet singer but a classroom chatterbox. And she slurred her rapid speech with a kind of lisp from which she suffered, "but not always." Apparently this was another game that emerged from a minor flaw in her speech pattern, of which she made the most. "And all my friends in school [Elly started laughing here] spoke the same way to have fun, and I encouraged them because it irritated our teacher . . ."

Viktor raised a disastrous possibility. "What if they had remained speaking that way, and you got over it!" Elly let that bit of bait go and persevered, "You see, it must have been a terrible time for my teachers!" Viktor, not one to be left out again, added, "And for my marriage also!" Whenever Elly chose to ignore Viktor's input, her timing was as good as his. (I wish these printed pages could convey the comedy in our conversations. Laughter was the spiritual tonic that kept us going day after day. Following a long session, often we were paradoxically tired and buoyed up for more the next day.)

Because a zest for life was so apparent in Elly as a seventy year old, she was convincing when she shared that in her early years she could hardly contain her exuberance. "I was in school and one day ran over to my father with my mouth closed with tape [*Leukoplast*, a sticky bandage] because I had been talking so much in class." The teacher literally had taped Elly's mouth shut to keep her quiet, and decades later Elly delighted in telling about it. As we joined her laughter, I asked Viktor if he had ever thought of using tape when Elly gets cranky. He replied, "What I am using is earplugs. When I fly to the United States they always give me earplugs." Elly and I laughed even more, and Viktor beamed his pleasure.

On a serious note, I asked Elly the exact location of the Grafenwörth store and school. She said they were very near one another, and that the church and their house were close by as well. Viktor saw that I was fishing for places again, which I did often to get a sense of a story's setting, and he was aware of my ever-handy camera. So he offered some unsolicited advice which doomed the serious note I had introduced. "You see, it doesn't make sense that you include in your book an illustration or photograph of a church or building in this story. Just take a photograph of bandage—we have here some *Leukoplast*." I said to Elly facetiously, "Listen to him." He took *that* seriously and stressed his point the more. "You see, this could have happened at any place, but it could not have happened without *Leukoplast!*" By then Elly and I were laughing and I managed to convey a restatement of the absurdity, "Elly, Elly, he says it doesn't matter *where* this happened. The place doesn't matter—you can talk too much *wherever* you go and the important thing is this tape!" Viktor just could not resist having the final word: "You have to stick to the essentials."

Regarding the lean years and how her family got through them, Elly reflected this way.

> We had enough to live on, but I think it was in '28 that the depression started here in Vienna. My father was unemployed and there was no welfare from the government. Not a schilling. But he was like me and remained a happy man. He was still the same person and never lost his dignity. We even went to the opera, my father and me—on foot all the way from Kaisermühlen [more than three miles each way]. We went ten hours before the opera started to get tickets for standing room. And it was so cold outside, and my mother put on me very warm things. That was fine when we walked, but standing at the opera—my goodness. . . . The cheapest tickets were for the upper level where it was very hot! With no money for the checkroom we had to keep our coats. . . . But my father loved to go to the opera; he loved music, and I also. We had a wonderful time.

Except once. Elly, in the first row of the standing area inside the elegant State Opera House, vomited. Her donation to the atmosphere ended up on the clothing of someone nearby who, according to Elly, was so intent upon the music that he didn't even notice—at first. Because they had no money whatsoever for cleaning the man's clothing, she and her father sneaked out of the opera and headed directly home.

THOUGH ELLY HAD started school in the Grafenwörth elementary school [*Volksschule*] at age five, she did not finish the first grade there. "So I had to do it again in Vienna, but I was young and not too healthy. I went for four years to the *Volksschule*, then for four years to the *Hauptschule* in the same building at Schüttauplatz 22." While Elly was too active outside of school to ever become studious, her classmate said that "it didn't matter if Elly skipped school anyway because she already knew everything—she was very smart."

As for Ali and school, he was not much interested in academic subjects. His interests and abilities were in things mechanical and practical, and he liked to work with his hands. Elly remembered, "Even when he was younger, when he had to write an essay he came to me and asked me to write for him and he would give me ten groschen. School was not his thing." In after-school activities Ali and Elly were sometimes comrades, especially along the Old Danube. "We had a pair of rails—rails that you strap on your shoes for ice skating. We had only one pair, and Ali and I were not willing to give to the other one. So we went together on the ice; and he used one rail and I used one. . . . Always one—we never skated with both rails. But we enjoyed it immensely." Through the summers the two were in the water whenever possible, sometimes from early morning until late afternoon. It's a wonder they didn't develop gills.

so that i could meet and talk with her best childhood friend and school-mate, Elly arranged a session with Helene Fischer Puhm. They first met as preschoolers, then attended the same schools only one grade apart. The Fischers lived just a couple of doors away from the Schwindts, in another building, since replaced. School for Elly and Helly was only a two-minute walk from their homes.

"Helly and I were both fun-loving, and seemingly we both existed only for making trouble and having fun." Helly was a bit better off, since her father's unemployment lasted only half a year or so. But the Fischer apartment was even smaller than the Schwindt flat, so Helly, with her parents and brother Ferdinand, made do with very little space. As we chatted about the economic conditions during their girlhoods, Helly remembered Elly at age ten washing clothes and sewing to help her family while other girls were playing. These two chums, now decades later, laughed as they cued each other's recollections of happy times despite the circumstances. They recalled also that they were "always swimming"—even at the *Dianabad*, a large public indoor pool. To keep their mothers in the dark about their swimming plans, Elly and Helly had to wear their woolen swimsuits under their clothing, and that got very warm. After the indoor winter swims their wet hair froze on the way home.

Elly's father was an excellent source for play ideas, as when he brought home from work heaps of mismatched and leftover buttons. Elly & Helly, Inc. made a great sport of dropping the buttons from several floors up to watch them bounce on the street below, making a snapping sound and scaring pedestrians. When button bombing got old, they turned to dropping little water-bags. But the day of reckoning for this misconduct arrived when the building manager reported it to the girls' parents. After a bit of time the two girls took revenge by peeing anonymously in a hallway of the manager's building. So Helly was no angel either in the stories she and Elly were swapping. Elly ventured some responsibility, however. "Maybe Helly was an angel until I made her into a witch! . . . If I think back now on this time, I ask what happened to me that I enjoyed all this so much?" But when Helly told us that as a five year old she picked up smoldering cigarette butts flicked from the streetcars and smoked them, Elly reassured us, "Now this I have never done."

One day three girls—Helly, Elly, and their friend Judith—skipped school and headed by streetcar to a hospital across town. Judith had fallen for a physician who was working in that hospital and Elly explained that "she wished only to see this doctor. So she said we both had to go with her to the hospital, and go into the emergency room and tell them we had pain here and there—just so she can see this doctor. But Helly told Judith, 'But my underwear is not clean, so we must change in case I have to be examined.' So they went to the ladies room and changed underwear with one another." But then Helly panicked and took off, wearing the good underwear, and Judith was left behind with Elly. So Elly went in as the sick one. It turned out that the doctor was not even on duty that day, so all the effort was wasted.

Ali and Ferdy—the brothers of Elly and Helly—were the same age, in school together, and the best of friends. In that time one might expect the boys to be more physical and puckish, but in the case of these four the stereotypes broke down. The boys were quieter and tamer, and the girls were the rambunctious ones. So the two boys had much in common with one another but not with their sisters. Except, that is, when it came to water sports.

Elly became a well-built and resilient swimmer, naturally athletic, a fearless flirt, and what in former times we called a tomboy. (When Elly described how she would tussle with the boys in school, Viktor chimed in, "She still does this, but now with me.") But brother Ali was a gentler, quieter sort, and not flirtatious. Though he may not have been a versatile athlete, he took bicycling seriously and was also a superior swimmer. When Ali and Elly had to work in summer, they often swam in the evening even

after dark, or at five in the morning before the sun came up. Elly was well
aware of her brother's Olympic potential, and Alfons even had a swimming coach with hopes that high for him. After a busy day and hours in
the water, the two famished youngsters devoured dumplings prepared by
their mother, often with plum pudding. Elly could put away eight or nine
of them and Alfons up to fifteen—another record of sorts.

In Elly's childhood home the Schwindts never had butter, the high-
priced spread. Instead they were accustomed to *Schmalz* (lard), which they
ate on bread and used for cooking. So Elly had to get her butter by devious
means. "I must have been twelve or thirteen when I first tasted butter—
butter that Helly and I had stolen! . . . Tante Mitzi used her cellar like a re-
frigerator, and she had butter there. We saw this and opened it and ate
some and wrapped it again carefully. My goodness, it was excellent."
Viktor mused, "It tasted even better than paid-for butter! But Elly, you
have never told me this." As for *Schlag,*—the pure whipped cream heaped
upon Viennese pastry to this day—that was something Elly did not taste
until after the war, when she was twenty.

Although Elly outgrew her frequent childhood illnesses, Helly continued to be afflicted with this or that into early adolescence. Once, after
she was admitted to the Augarten Children's Hospital, Helly's parents
were alarmed to hear their physician say that she was so seriously ill that
she might have only six months to live. Helly was less alarmed and saw an
opportunity. "Mama, I want a goulash and a beer." A friend advised
Helly's mother to give those to her, since if she did not and Helly died, she
would feel awful.

Looking back at photos of Helly and her, and of their friends and families, Elly said yet again how happy they were. With her solid family, her
penchant for fun and the funny, her physical endurance, and her optimism
even in the face of adversity, Elly felt she had been as happy as a child
could be. In her maturity she was still saying of their hardships, "But this
was the situation for thousands of people here."

Fortunately there were good-hearted people with the ability and
means to help those trapped in the economic crunch. One such person became very close to the Schwindts and was kind to them continuously for
many years. Roman Wilkoschevsky was a Jew from Russia living in
Vienna. He was the Uncle Roman we have already met, though actually
he was not an uncle to Elly and Ali. Uncle Roman and Tante Mitzi lived

together as partners for twenty years, yet never married. Elly always called him Uncle Roman and fondly remembered him as a generous, good man. "And I loved him, very much."

There was an occasion when Elly took Viktor and me on a walk in the area of her childhood. Except for the incongruous new bell tower, Elly said the Heart of Jesus Church was much the same. Between the church and their apartment building she paused at a flower bed still in the same spot after sixty years. From it she used to take flowers each year for Mother's Day. Since brother Alfons would not pick them himself, Elly would filch two flowers for mama, one for Alfons to give.

Their mother kept among her treasures two cards, one each from Elly and Ali when they were eleven and nine. The children had created their greetings from paper and string, using colored pencils and scissors. Each card has a handwritten message and some copied poetic lines, dated 12 May 1935. The messages are floridly sentimental and would be more touching had they not been part of a socially ritualized convention in the public schools. In fact, the cards had been done in class. Here is Ali's message:

> Mother eye—your rays I wish to see shining forever, because they glow, because they paint, purest love, angel-fair.

The flower that accompanied each greeting had been stolen by the little girl Elly, poor and enterprising, from the very Heart of Jesus.

I WAS WORKING in my study in Chicago one summer day when Elly and Viktor phoned from Vienna. They had been out walking and had seen an ice truck drive by, probably carrying bagged ice for picnics, pubs, and cocktail parties. That had prompted in Elly another very early memory. Viktor was enchanted with the story and told Elly they should phone immediately to tell me about it.

As a little girl Elly had to have her tonsils removed. Her father carried her from Kaisermühlen to Leopoldstadt and the Barmherzigen Brüder (Brothers of Charity) Hospital, right in the old Frankl neighborhood. The distance was two and a half miles each way, but since there was no charge at the time for medical care at that hospital, they went there. "And they took out my tonsils. Immediately after surgery my father put me on his shoulders, and I was bleeding. I remember that his hair was red with my blood."

Viktor, from another telephone in their home, injected the story of his own tonsillectomy at the age of six, but its telling was not to upstage Elly at all. He said that after his tonsillectomy his father took him immediately to an ice cream shop—a smart thing to do since the cold ice in the throat causes blood vessels to constrict and bleeding to diminish. Viktor's point was the touching difference in Elly's case: her father had no money for ice cream. Elly continued, as if grateful for the gift of memory.

"Someone told my father to buy ice cream for me, and I saw my father look at his money but he had only three groschen—not enough. As we went over the bridge to our street, an ice truck was delivering blocks of ice for refrigerators—then called iceboxes. The iceman was cutting blocks to carry on his shoulders, and small pieces of ice were falling. And my father picked up a small piece and gave it to me, and I was—oh—it was so good! Since that time—you wouldn't believe it—forever after I was so happy when I was on the street and saw an ice truck. Always I ran behind to get a small piece of ice. I can still see my father's hand with three groschen— three pennies."

I said, "Elly, that is a wonderful story. It is as if you were conditioned from that one incident to enjoy chips of ice ever after." Viktor agreed, "Exactly." With its tenderness and simplicity, Viktor treasured this story from Elly's childhood. I think it was for him a favorite new glimpse into the sources of her strength and character: the admiring devotion of a humble man to his impish little daughter, and the utter trust she placed in him as she rode on his shoulders homeward—bleeding, yet because of him without a care.

CHAPTER 10

Everything Changes
1937–1946

BY 1937, ELLY was no longer a little girl riding on papa's shoulders. The in-nocence of her childhood had been pushed aside by the passage of time and the troubles of the day: economic distress, political tensions, social in-stability, the fear of war. The incongruous assessments of Hitler's rise as threat or promise divided the people. Austria was still officially independ-ent of Germany's Third Reich, but nothing was certain.

There was Leopoldstadt, teeming with Jews of diverse persuasions and origins and bustling with commercial competition. There was Kaisermühlen, seemingly far removed from the ferment of the city. But if Kaisermühlen seemed more out of reach, its isolation was superficial. The surrounding wa-ters and the bridges that spanned them, the woods, and even the sense of community in Kaisermühlen could not shield it from its larger context. It was no safe, suburban neighborhood.

For the 1873 World's Fair in Vienna, the great Rotunda had been built as its focal point. It was a cavernous and ornate exposition center designed to be a permanent major facility of the city. It stood monumental across from the Prater and for more than six decades hosted major public events and exhibitions. Visitors took the elevator to the observation deck for strik-ing views of the city and its surroundings. From there it was easy to scan the Danube waterways to the east and spot the forests of Kaisermühlen. Elly went to the Rotunda many times but not for its exhibits. Rather, she was assisting her papa as he cleaned its large toilet rooms and other inte-rior spaces. In the time and circumstances, children pitched in to help their parents make a go of it.

But on November 17, 1937, the Rotunda caught fire. Word of the dis-aster spread quickly and the inferno could be seen from miles away. Elly, who had just turned twelve, watched the smoke filling the sky and became very anxious.

Elly showed Viktor and me a photo of the Rotunda ablaze and said, "When the fire was burning I watched it from the dam in Kaisermühlen, and I was crying because on that day my father was cleaning and I was afraid that he was working in that building."[1] Thankfully no harm had come to Leo Schwindt, though the Rotunda disintegrated to smoldering ash.

Following the Rotunda disaster, Viktor conveyed that there was a popular sarcastic jab at Adolf Hitler, though it was carefully whispered only among trusted friends: "The Rotunda burns to the ground and this guy lives on." Not only did Hitler live on, but in a few months he would take Austria into the Reich. What lay ahead for Vienna would make the Rotunda calamity look like a family picnic in the Prater.

For all of Kaisermühlen's former natural serenity, it took its share of the city's growing violence. Even in the brief civil war of February 1934 between the Social Democrats and various fascist and Nazi elements, Schüttaustrasse had seen vicious street fighting. The Schwindts were unharmed, but the combat shook the neighborhood. The well-known Goethehof—the large housing complex built in 1928 just down the street—was badly shot up; its face was shelled and mortar fire blasted its main-floor coffee shop and some of the balconies.

At the time of the *Anschluss*, Elly was an impressionable youth and had by then picked up some of the anxieties and attitudes of the adults around her. As a seventy year old she spouted about the *Anschluss* and gave a clue to her outlook back then. "I get furious even now when someone says the whole of Vienna was in the Heldenplatz when Hitler came. It's a lie! I know it exactly because when Hitler was coming I was in school. School was let off and we had to go together with our teacher to wherever Hitler was and had to stay there! We *had* to go. And I myself saw Hitler on the balcony of the Imperial Hotel—with my whole school class."

As I listened to Elly and Helly Puhm recall the coming of Hitler to Vienna, Helly said that her own father had been there for Hitler's historic—or histrionic—speech at the Heldenplatz. He came home a troubled man, saying that nothing good was happening, that it would end in war. But some friends of the Puhm family disagreed. One couple in particular seemed to be thrilled with Hitler; the future was bright because he would bring security and prosperity to the Reich and they all would reap the benefits. That kind of assessment was not universal but it was wide-spread. The irony in this case is that the husband conveying it was himself a Jew.

For whatever reasons, Elly's father sensed how ominous were the times, and his distrust of Hitler went deep. His own brothers—Elly's uncles Karl and Robert—had married Jewish women, which was in itself not unusual. Uncle Robert came by to visit the family and was enthusiastic about Hitler. Elly was present when "Robert said to my father, 'Leo, this is the start of a wonderful time—everything will get better now!' And my father told him, 'Robert! Are you *crazy?* You are saying *this,* and you have a Jewish wife? Are you nuts?'"

On one of the days immediately following the *Anschluss,* after Hitler had left Vienna, Elly witnessed Jews being humiliated in the street. She even recognized a couple of the victims as Jews who had treated her family badly, and she watched as they were forced to scrub the sidewalk with toothbrushes in front of sneering onlookers. When Elly went home she told her father, "Papa, you have no idea what I have just seen"—and she described it. In doing so she snickered a bit, thinking that her father would accept this from her. But with no warning he sent a stinging slap to her face. "I was shocked. And he stood there looking at me. It was the only time in my whole life he struck me. I took some hits from my brother, of course, but never—before or since—from my father or from my mother. Not ever."

As she recounted that incident, Elly was visibly moved. To her father it did not seem to matter whether she had understood what was happening in the streets or whether she simply did not take it seriously. And apparently it made no difference to him that Elly was only twelve. That he hit her, and in that way, went straight to her heart. A face is the central physical feature of personhood, and hers had taken a blow from one who loved her most. It was her face that had delighted her papa always, and so often he had kissed it in crib and carriage. It was the face that had made him laugh whenever a crafty smile or an impish grimace came over it. At first Elly was stunned by the slap, and then realized that she had done something terrible in her father's eyes.

Leo Schwindt may have wondered himself what he had done to his dear Elly, but we shall see that he lived long enough to find reassurance. He lived until 1975 and knew the grown-up Elly had become a decent and fair-minded woman whose values appeared to be as high and go as deep as his own. And she married a good Jewish man whom she loved with all her heart.

How cruel it seems that young Elly had to see her father assaulted in hatred, and right in the bungalow of Tante Mitzi at Laberlweg 11. This is her recollection. "You see, when Hitler came, Tante Mitzi was living with Uncle Roman, and he was Jewish. And a man came into their home and said to Uncle Roman, 'You Jewish pig' or something like this. And my father before my eyes stood up and shouted at the man. Then the man hit my father. This I saw with my own eyes."

Viktor got to know the Schwindts after the war, of course, and as he listened to Elly talk about her father, he said, "Though he was a simple man in some ways, he was one with unique character strength not to fall prey to slogans or ideology—confronted with so many situations and occasions that favored anti-Semitism, so many seductions for that. He was faithful to his principles."

"If my father had joined the Nazi Party," Elly surmised, "his life could have become immediately an easy one, but he never gave in. But two brothers of my father married Jewish women, and one of these aunts urged my brother and me, 'You must join the National Socialist Party, and when you get the uniforms you must come each day to me and you have to walk with me in the neighborhood so that everyone will see it.' " Viktor clarified it, "This was so that everyone who saw it would know that they were affiliated with the Nazi Party." Elly went on, "But my father said absolutely we cannot do it, and so we borrowed some uniforms for a day and went to the aunts and later returned the uniforms. . . . Imagine! The two Jewish women in our family urged us to join the Nazi Party!" Viktor noted that it was opportunistic to urge such a thing, and Elly agreed that her aunts did so for pragmatic reasons, not ideological ones. "It is interesting," said Elly of her Jewish aunts, "that they were not harmed during the Hitler time. Both uncles stayed here in Vienna and kept their beautiful apartments—through the whole time."

How is it possible to understand the twists of Nazi ideology and how they played out in people's lives? In a telephone conversation Elly tried to explain the situation. Because her uncles Karl and Robert were married to Jewish women they were judged unworthy to serve in the German military; hence they were never drafted. So in this case Aryan men avoided *Wehrmacht* combat duty thanks to their Jewish wives. That's not all. The two Jewish wives, Elly's Tante Berta and Tante Martha, were never deported to

concentration camps because they were married to Aryan men—men who
were not only safe but successful. That's not all. If a Jewish man were married to an Aryan woman, that afforded no protection from deportation.

As the Nazi noose tightened around the Jews remaining in Vienna,
Uncle Roman decided to flee the Reich while there was still time. He
chose Holland as his safe haven for the duration of the war. But then the
Germans occupied Holland and the Nazi net dropped over the Jews and
others who were there even as refugees. The last communication from
Roman to Kaisermühlen was a postcard he wrote to Alfons from Antwerp.
Later the family learned that the SS deported Uncle Roman to Auschwitz,
and there he died. Roman had loved the Schwindts in Kaisermühlen for
more than twenty years, and they loved him in turn as long. One wonders
how many Jews, in the time of their great desolation, were mourned not
only by their kin and kind but also by others at home—the way Roman
Wilkoschevsky was mourned in Kaisermühlen. There, no one had doubted
his intention to return to Mitzi after the war.

Tante Mitzi eventually married a policeman and, according to Elly,
the man was just the opposite of Uncle Roman. He was a heavy drinker
and Mitzi worked for him and did everything she could. "I don't know
what kind of marriage this was . . . and after a few years they got divorced
when she was relatively young. All these years since she has lived alone"
in her little bungalow on Laberlweg.

In her advancing years the family urged Tante Mitzi to move to the
flat on Schüttaustrasse where Leo and Hermine were still living. She
wanted to give her little house, which remains today, to Elly. But by then
Elly was exceedingly busy with Viktor and their work and had no time for
maintenance of another place, let alone one with a garden. Elly simply
said, "I had no time for it," and Viktor expanded playfully, "No time to
care for the cherries on the tree."

AGGRESSION IN THE war was not only between military adversaries.
Soldiers on both the Nazi and Allied sides of the conflict perpetrated in-
human acts on innocent civilians. Elly remembered too vividly the occupation of Kaisermühlen by Russian forces.

> In 1945 a friend of mine was living in a building nearby, and
> a Russian soldier tried to rape her. She jumped out a window to

her death—she preferred to be dead. . . . And in our own apartment they even tried to rape my mother. . . . They took her, in
front of me, and I was standing next to three soldiers and crying.
Thanks to heaven nothing happened, but it could have very easily.
Rape was incessant. From room to room they took whatever they
found, or whoever. But the soldiers never looked at me, even
though I was grown up. I would dress, you see, like a terrible dirty
person who didn't wash, in my old boots and a coat from my
brother. I even put more dirt on my face and so on, so no soldier
ever tried to rape me. But I would say that most of my friends
were raped. It went on day after day, day after day, day after
day. . . . We had at the General Hospital a center for treating vene-
real diseases, and thousands of women came—including many
nuns—who had been raped. When I met the first American soldier, I thought I could respect him. But he was arrogant and he
never paid any attention and looked away. They were not very
friendly. You could have everything from American soldiers, but
first you had to go to bed.

Despite the terror of the rapes, Elly still hoped that someday she
would have a real romance. Of course she saw boys socially in the neighborhood and on the way to school. By 1940, before the worst of combat and
bombings hit Vienna, Elly had completed her eight years at the
Schüttauplatz schools and, at the urging of her principal, continued her
education. Elly remembered, "In District 6, in the Loquaiplatz, was a
school where I could go for two years and get my junior *Matura* [diploma].
Each day I took the streetcar from Schüttaustrasse across the two bridges
to school. I did well except in mathematics—I made it, but I hated it.
Thanks to heaven, next to me was sitting a girl who was an excellent
mathematician and she helped me a lot. After these two years in
Loquaiplatz [1941–42], I went to the same school as Helly for one year—
the *Haushaltungs Schule,* the girls' homemaking school in Brückengasse."
Elly's report cards in her final years of public school show unexcused absences. This suggests that she didn't always have good reasons for missing
school. While not confessing too much to Viktor and me, Elly admitted
some truancy and chuckled.

It was during the war years that Elly's former flirting with boys
evolved into some serious attention to—even intentions toward—young

men. She was not at all eager for marriage, but there was some leeway for romance. "Each morning I went from Kaisermühlen to Loquaiplatz to school by streetcar. And I noticed one day at 7:15 a wonderful looking young man was sitting in the streetcar. So I went each day half an hour early so that I could be on the same tram as this young man. One day I just missed the tram and I was running after it—at that time the streetcars were open and I wanted to jump on. But I fell down and was lying like a frog in the street, and he was looking at me and laughing! From that moment on I never saw this man again. I never talked with him but I was fascinated by him, and I ruined the whole thing."

After that one-sided and ill-fated infatuation, Elly found her first real love. Half a century later Elly spoke of that love with feeling, and of its loss with sadness. Her friend was a young man she had met in Kaisermühlen. "He was a student of pharmacy and I fell in love with him. We thought we would marry after the war. Of course he was in the military and, after half a year, he was dead—killed in action. He was very, very warm, intelligent—a wonderful young man. And I'm sure if he had lived we would have married and it would have been an excellent marriage. But that was not to be."

It is remarkable among the tragedies of war that life goes on and that even romance finds ways to flourish. At the time Elly lost her Kaisermühlen friend, the neighborhood was taking aerial hits as the bombardments of Vienna intensified. Terrified families huddled in basements along Elly's street.

After the bombings we went outside, and then we saw buildings bombed, and people died in the cellars. So we had to dig out the bodies. And each day we would say, "Thanks, dear Lord, that we survived, that our mother survived." But who knows, tomorrow it may be over for me. And after the bombing we were hungry, so what did I do? I went to the Old Danube to pick out the dead fish that were floating on the water—we cooked it and survived. I also was running on the street under airplane machine gun fire, going to steal some rice and then running back again. On the street next to me were dead people ... we had to step around and even over bodies to walk ... but somehow I survived and brought rice to my mother. ... Even Tante Mitzi's house was bombed, and I went over there in the night to find her. But she was not under the rubble. She lost everything but she was okay, hiding in the basement of the Goethehof.... When the bombing began it was terrible and I thought I would not survive it.... Shortly before the war ended, the Russians flew very close to the ground shooting, and whatever was on the streets was killed.

ONE DAY AS Elly and I were looking through photographs from her youth, one of them cued a bicycle story. As she began to tell about it, Elly giggled. Alfons taught her to ride his bicycle, but with mixed results. It was March and the Alte Donau was still frozen over. As Elly pedaled, Alfons walked just behind her to steady the bike. At some point she glanced backward and got nervous when she saw him a distance behind her. She panicked and headed, out of control, straight for the Old Danube. There the bike broke through the ice and Elly got soaked in the bitter-cold water. "Alfons came running, and he didn't look at me of course. He only was interested in what happened to his bicycle! He just shouted at me, 'You dummy!' "

After all, to Ali bicycling was serious business, not just fun. In 1940 his father was drafted into the *Wehrmacht* and assigned for training to the boot camp in Reichenau, a mostly sleepy village in the valley beneath the Rax mountains south of Vienna. Alfons, wishing to see his dad and lacking money for public transportation, bicycled the forty miles from Vienna to Reichenau. After visiting with his father there, he pedaled the forty-mile return. He did this more than once while his father was in training. There are photographs of Ali in the Reichenau area, one of him standing on a bridge over the Schwarza River. When I asked Elly how Alfons could have ridden so far—and on a relatively primitive bicycle by today's standards—her reply was instantaneous and simple: "He wanted to see his father."

Leo Schwindt was fighting somewhere on the Russian front when, in 1941, Alfons was drafted. The Nazis were calling up every suitable man, increasingly from the younger and older ends of the age range. Ali's best friend, Ferdy Fischer, served in the German marines. He survived sea battles and ended up a prisoner of war under American forces in southern Germany. Ferdy eventually returned to Vienna and lived a full life. But the story of Alfons took a much sadder turn.

At call-up, Alfons received orders to go for his army training to Nicholsburg (the Czech Mikolov), an old fortress town just inside the

Czech border, not far north of Vienna and on the road to Brünn. Elly and her mother had received a letter from Alfons and learned of his desperate situation and dark mood. So sixteen-year-old Elly packed coal and bread for Ali and took a train from Vienna to Nicholsburg where she found him. When Elly described that moment to Viktor and me, she broke down sobbing. In conversations with the Frankls I had seen Elly's tears now and again, but never an outpouring like this. As if heartbroken anew by the recollection, she wept and wept. When the wave of grief finally subsided, Elly said, "He was sitting there in a small room, like a frightened girl, and he was cold and hungry and crying. He *hated* Hitler and said, 'I should take my life.' And I had to say to him, 'Ali, don't do it!' . . . He was like my mother and at times could not fend for himself."

Another memory followed immediately. During his military training Alfons had returned once to Vienna to see his family. When he had to leave again, Elly went to see him off at North Station in Leopoldstadt. At the time Alfons had no idea where he would be sent for battle. "He went up the stairs to his train, and there I saw him for the last time. Anyone who says now that all German soldiers were murderers, *it is a lie.* When I think of my father and my brother, it's like the people who say that are killing *me.* It's a lie." I mused, "The world may look on all of them as criminals, but many were victims of Nazism," and Elly said instantly, "*Genau, genau* [exactly]."

At this Viktor added, "It is easy—as I am always saying—for people who had the good fortune to emigrate to reproach those who remained here, 'Why didn't you at least join the resistance movement?' That is easy to say from a distance." "Yes, that is so easy to say," Elly earnestly agreed. Balancing his remarks, Viktor explained, "It is good when people are admired for joining the resistance and putting their neck on the line—this is true heroism. *However,* heroism cannot be demanded of anyone except oneself, as admirable as it may be." This, one of Viktor's lifelong motifs, insists that one has only to ask oneself what he or she might have done in exactly the same circumstances.

Viktor and I were listening closely to Elly as she asserted yet again that her story is nothing special, that most people living at the time had similar tales to tell. When I said that this fact does not diminish the suffering of one person in one story, that the suffering of one may be suffering on a vast scale, Viktor agreed, "Each person must carry his own cross." In her resiliency Elly replied, "But when I look back I always see the good things. . . . For me it's natural. If you are a cheerful person you do not think only on the bad things, but on the good things." I said, "Elly, I think you became a strong person, both physically and emotionally, partly because of the way your parents cared for you. When you were a small child you didn't have to worry whether someone loved you—you knew it, and that made you free." "Yes. As I told you, I was the happiest person."

Elly's mother also was required to work as part of the war effort. As the conflict staggered toward its end in Europe, she was working in a paprika plant, producing artificial pepper. The plant was on the Venediger Au, in Leopoldstadt. "It was forced labor, but she was paid for it. When she came home she was sneezing from the work. . . . And father was in Russia and lost his teeth from vitamin deficiencies there. . . . From Russia he came to Hamburg where the bombing was terrible. Dresden also was full of refugees, children and women, and the bombing was terrible. They said that thousands of people were killed by the Allies in a few minutes—civilians, children and women. This was not fair. It was not necessary."

In the turmoil immediately after the war there was virtually no communication between the war fronts and the families back home. Thankfully Elly's father returned safely, but only after some very long months with no news of him. As they had not known where Leo was until he came home in 1946, so they still knew nothing about Alfons. Elly did check with the International Red Cross from time to time but they had no information about her brother. It was not unusual, however, for soldiers to return many months, even years, after the war. Some married and settled in foreign lands before eventually contacting their kin.

THIS IS HOW Elly in 1943 became part of the staff at the Poliklinik in Mariannengasse. Shortly after she completed her courses in the homemaking or domestic science program at Loquaiplatz and got her junior *Matura,* she received an official letter. It notified her that she must report for a physical exam to determine if she was fit for service in *Flak*—as an antiaircraft gunner. She was only seventeen, but more personnel were needed as the German war effort stumbled.

Oh my goodness, in two weeks I must go for this examination, and what should I do? Both my father and brother were away in the war . . . and my mother was obliged all day here in Vienna;

and I thought, "No I cannot leave my mother alone, and second, I am not interested in serving in the German army . . ." But in a hospital, even if you are doing only cleaning, you can be excused from the military. My mother didn't even know that I was going from hospital to hospital to find such work. I started early in the morning and kept looking even until late in the day, but no one was willing to take me.

But then here at the Poliklinik Hospital they took me as a volunteer in the dental department, and I was very pleased. I was trained as a dental assistant, first in x-ray and later on as a surgery assistant. . . . We had very bad cancers of the jaw, and children with deformities. The clinic was run by Catholic nuns and I became very close friends with many of them.

I quite remember the first surgery. It was a jaw surgery on a baby with a deformation, and we started early. There was the first cut and a nurse—a Catholic nun—was behind me, and in case I fainted she could take over the work. She said that each time someone sees this for the first time she will faint. But I was stronger and did not faint. To tell you the truth, the first cut is terrible, but after this, when everything is open, it is okay. And after they started surgery they started telling jokes and laughing, and I was not expecting *that*. It was not understandable to me.

Viktor and I had been listening quietly, but Elly's reference to her first surgery brought him out. He remembered the first operation he observed in medical school, when the surgeon—while he was operating—talked about where he had gone the day before in his automobile. That surprised Viktor in a way similar to Elly's first exposure to a surgical team.

I enjoyed my work as a dental assistant. It was a wonderful situation of teamwork, and when I started there no one asked about Hitler Youth or who was a Nazi. I found out that my boss was a Nazi who was a well-known doctor and people were coming to him; and one dental technician was a Nazi. But we were all working together and laughing—and everyone knew that we were friends with these two guys and it was no problem. What was important at that time was survival and that our loved ones were okay. I was a happy person then, even when I was working in the

Poliklinik. You see, we had Hollanders there and one Russian who were brought from their homelands to do forced labor. Two of them had been medical students in Amsterdam and so they got to work in a hospital—which was better than nothing. They lived in the Poliklinik and officially were not allowed to leave the area. But even at that we took the chance and went out sometimes. They became my closest friends.

At seven in the morning the boss was standing at the front door in his uniform with a stick [somewhat playfully] to see who is coming late to work. And clever as I was, when I saw him and was late, I went through the window into the kitchen.

Among Elly's photographs are several of her and the Hollanders on outings to the woods or mountains. Any excursion was strictly forbidden, but in the photos they seem to have no anxiety. In fact, they appear to be enjoying themselves enormously, clowning and laughing genially.

The boss saw me many times with the Hollanders even though it was strictly forbidden for us to be with them. And after bombardment, as we were all cleaning up debris at the Poliklinik, he would come and give cigarettes to them and to us, to every-one—even to the prisoners of war. He was still a human being. . . . At other times he had sugar or something and gave it to all of us, everybody.

Viktor agreed, "Real human beings cannot fully deny their own humanness, even in such extreme situations—it breaks out, breaks through. To look at human beings with one eye only leads to viewing noncriminal people with a criminal eye."

Something about the new generations occurred to Elly. "I think, in everything I have been telling you, that young people should know this. You cannot say, 'We are good and they are bad'—it's not true." Viktor could not leave that alone. "There are only two 'races' of people—the decent and the not-decent. And the border between them cuts across all nations, religions, races. There is no nation free of the possibility to degenerate into holocausts. *No nation* should pride itself [on goodness] and look down on Germany and Austria and say they fell prey to racism.

Each nation is capable of holocaust, given the 'right' circumstances and the 'right' führer."

As a young girl Elly had wanted to become a dentist, but after working for a while at the Poliklinik she gave up this wish since she had no money for dental school. Her pay was too little to live on, so she learned a skill on the side to earn additional money. At night she created mesh bags with rough twine for ladies to use in shopping. Packaging was practically unknown at the time, so little was wrapped, and whatever could be purchased was carried in one's own shopping bag.

> This work was good for income but bad for my fingers—they were always bloody and it was painful work. Each morning I had to clean my hands for surgery. And when the streetcars were not running after bombing, I had to walk to the Poliklinik from Kaisermühlen. . . . But it was dangerous to walk across the bridge over the Danube. I was the only one there and—oh my goodness!—they started bombing the bridge to destroy it. There were Russian machine guns shooting anyone, and I lay down and they didn't see me. But the bombs were falling here and there.

Walking across the Reichsbrücke was about the only way Elly could get from Kaisermühlen to the Poliklinik. Other bridges had been taken out by bombs, and this one was badly damaged. Along with other people she had to walk its span on the footpath, jumping over large holes that opened to the Danube waters below in which floated war debris and sometimes the carcasses of horses and other animals. Once Elly also saw the corpses of three human infants float by in the remains of a small boat. Casualties sometimes clogged the streets after bombing and strafing, but no stream carried them away. Starving people cut chunks of flesh from dead horses to take home and cook. Elly herself did this for her own famished family, telling them she got the meat at the Poliklinik. But sometimes Elly could not, or dared not, leave the Poliklinik because of air raids. At these times the staff moved patients to the basement for safety, and then back to their wards at night. There were even night surgeries performed in the cellar. Then Elly stayed over with the nuns, in their quarters near the chapel. But she always worried about her mother and Tante Mitzi at home, and was joyful on returning there to find them alive and well.

I remember Elly saying on another occasion, "What hurt me most after bombing was the death of little children, with their mothers surviving. . . . Once I was walking in Leopoldstadt after bombings, and there on
the sidewalk they had lined up the bodies of twelve or fifteen small children, probably from a kindergarten. As their mothers arrived there they
grabbed and held the bodies of their little children, and it tore my heart
to see this." After saying that Elly simply sat for awhile with no further
words.

WHEN ELLY FIRST came to the Poliklinik she knew nothing of Freud and
psychoanalysis nor of Adler and individual psychology. Even Adler's stint
at the Poliklinik as a medical student many years earlier had mostly been
forgotten there. But in the dental department Elly met Professor Hans
Pichler. He was an eminent oral surgeon, retired after being head of the
department at the university hospital where he had trained the surgeon
who was now Elly's boss. Pichler was Elly's first link to Freud, and the connection was a human one, not academic. From 1923 on, Freud had relied
on Pichler as his primary surgeon in the battle against cancer of the jaw
and palate. In the decade following 1929, Pichler performed twenty operations on Freud, including the final one in London after Freud had settled
there.[2]

At the Poliklinik, Elly met not only renowned physicians but many interesting patients. For example, she remembered the visit of a kindly
woman. "There was in the waiting room a very simple lady, dressed like a
farmer's wife, and waiting for her turn. This was the sister of Adolf Hitler,
Paula Wolf—it must have been 1944. . . . The Poliklinik accepted people
who could not pay anything, and—imagine!—this lady was sitting among
the other poor people waiting. And after her turn she asked what we
needed, and we told her we were hungry. The next time she came with
bags of bread and sugar and lard and so on."

At another time, Elly said, a man came to the Poliklinik in a large gray
business suit. "My boss asked me to take x-rays of his teeth. Afterward I
had to label the x-rays, so I asked his name. I found out it was General
Erwin Rommel. In his civilian clothes no one recognized him as the Nazi
field marshal . . . and he seemed shy when he came in." Part of Rommel's
personal security lay in his anonymity. Historically this incident is entirely
believable since "the Desert Fox," between his legendary military cam-

paigns in North Africa and elsewhere, used to retreat for rest to his favorite towns near Vienna.

With Elly's physical strength and her fantasy of having a chance to sacrifice herself by killing Hitler in bed, one dreads the thought—or savors the image—of what she might have done with scalpel or x-rays if Hitler himself had ever turned up for a dental exam. At the time Elly was still unaware of what was happening to brother Ali and Uncle Roman. Nevertheless, in her later years Elly looked back on her youthful violent fantasies and doubted that she ever could have killed anyone.

WHEN FRANZ VESELY, son-in-law of the Frankls, suggested that I go to the archives in Vienna to view documentary films of the war in the city, Viktor and Elly thought that an excellent idea. So Franz arranged this for me and I watched many hours of videotape. Some footage was in full color—for example Hitler in Munich among the reds in flags and banners. The colors jolted my senses after having seen for years only black-and-white films. Somehow the moderation of black-and-white seemed well suited to Vienna's dismal days.

After viewing the tapes I had a new awareness of things that had happened half a century earlier in the streets where I often walked. Late in the war I had been a little boy living safely in faraway America, and now as a man I watched carefree Viennese youngsters chatting and shopping and joking and smoking. Their distance from the awful events of the city was great also. But the Frankl story had drawn me into connections and impressions at least. I thought about what they had said so often in my hearing: that the new generations should learn about and sense the former times; that to do so would deepen their empathies, enrich their grasp of how evil may triumph, and perhaps move them to join that race of human beings who are decent and kind—and watchful.

SHORTLY AFTER THE war the situation regarding food and supplies actually deteriorated. During the war people could obtain minimal food at least, using ration cards. But at war's end chaos set in and infrastructures crumbled. Viktor and Elly described taking a few things—such as a spare shirt—and going two hours outside the city to swap them for some potatoes. These errands Elly clearly remembered.

So I went with my mother, Tante Mitzi, and another lady with a small cart. We walked a couple of hours and then went from house to house to trade our possessions for a pound of potatoes. "No, no," they would say, "but if you have gold—we are interested only in gold." But gold we didn't have, so we left with nothing. But then we saw a field full of potatoes, so Tante Mitzi and I went in and dug out potatoes. After we left there with our cart, five policemen came with bayonets and arrested us. They brought us to the police station and we were in prison for six or seven hours, and my mother was crying. But I was laughing because the policemen were so ridiculous. One of them asked me what is your profession, and I told him a surgical nurse, which was not true. But he wrote down something that I was in charge of operations—he must have been stupid. And they put Tante Mitzi and me in a separate room! You won't believe it, but after these hours Tante Mitzi and I stole again a few of the same potatoes from the police station!

Elly continued, "On the way home we had to urinate, so we went under a bridge and made our business. Afterwards we saw that we had urinated on a heap of live grenades! It was dangerous, but we were laughing." To Viktor this was a new story and worth a good laugh in retrospect. He was surprised though when Elly told us that she had told the whole escapade—stealing, jail, grenades—to her boss. Apparently he enjoyed it and afterwards sometimes jokingly called Elly the Poliklinik's "ex-convict."

One day when we were walking past the Poliklinik, Elly pointed out the wall along Mariannengasse. In 1945 she and her colleagues had done heavy repair work there that ordinarily would be done by building contractors. After the bombings—once the staff agreed to keep the Poliklinik operating—everyone including nuns, professors, and janitors pitched in. No work was beneath them. There are photographs of Elly and others in surgical gowns, and other pictures show them in crude coveralls. The crew formed lines to pass along heavy stone blocks from the piles of rubble and then refit them into the wall of the building. So Elly learned to do the work of a surgical assistant and of a stonemason, as the situation required.

———

BACK AT THE Frankl flat we had a discussion one afternoon about anti-Semitism, and I prodded Elly to say more about her experience. "Don, you ask me these questions but otherwise I do not think much about those times. Back then I met marvelous people, the most marvelous people." Viktor inserted, "Those who said 'Yes' to life in spite of everything." I asked Elly about Jews that she knew as a girl. "But, you see, I was brought up not to differentiate between Jewish people and others, so I did not really know who was Jewish, and I cannot tell you. This started when Hitler came, but before then I didn't know. . . . I'm sure that I, as a little girl, met many Jewish people who were friends of my father. . . . As I told you, my father was brought up in Leopoldstadt, which was full of Jewish people, and they came sometimes over to Kaisermühlen. . . . He was often surrounded by Jewish Austrians and refugees from other countries."

Later on and inevitably Elly became aware that the distinctions between Aryans and Jews were of ultimate importance to the Nazis, but it was too late for her to become anti-Semitic—thanks to her father and mother and their circle of friends; thanks to her experience with Jewish aunts Berta and Martha, and to that splendid Uncle Roman. And how could Elly forget Leopold Frucht?—the doctor who tended her in illness and need, whose only fee was to *give* an apple or piece of candy, and medicine, too.

It seemed a natural place to ask Elly about the most significant influences, the most important people in her life, not only her immediate family. "The mother of my father was very close to me and told me things that happened to her when she was young. She taught me not to give up, whatever happens in life. Never give in, and be yourself no matter what happens. . . . You see, I told you that she was extremely wealthy and overnight she became extremely poor. But she behaved as the same person—she never was crying about it or saying, 'Oh, I was rich and now I am so poor.' This was something that molded me and showed me the way—even in the worst times—not to give in. And in a way she was a funny person, too. She could laugh like me, like a little girl. She was playful and I would say that she is the one who influenced me the most."

"She must have loved you to influence you that much," I prodded. "Yes. She was such a poor person; she cleaned leather gloves to earn some money, and I quite remember that she was saving ten groschen each week so she could buy me for Christmas something that I liked. But imagine saving this each week until Christmas. She always brought something really great to me."

Elly spoke of another person who was important to her along the way. Carola von Kolbliz was a unique teacher in the domestic science program at Loquaiplatz. This lady from nobility was very dignified, though not elegant, as Elly described her. She also was a model for Elly, and often they both stayed after school just to talk with one another—Elly admired her very much.

Another woman from nobility in another country became a model for Elly. But as in the case of her teacher, it was not nobility that mattered but rather her humility and humanness. Perhaps the key was that these women spent their time with her.

Countess Ostrovsky—when I met her she was an older lady, perhaps seventy-five or so, and I was only fourteen. She was the wife of the cultural attaché from Poland. . . . In the house of Tante Mitzi on Laberlweg, I met her—seemingly she and Uncle Roman must have known each other. She was the lady who gave me the Siamese cat. She went away on a trip with her husband and asked me to take care of her cat for a few days—but then the cat never would return to Mrs. Ostrovsky. It would not even eat except in my presence. So she told me, "You have to keep this cat." So during the whole war I was not eating much, and if I got a hundred grams of meat I gave it to the cat! It was wonderful, the cat. I loved her . . . but I had to share everything! In the war I was not allowed to take her into the cellar during bombing, but sometimes I smuggled her in. And after the war I had nothing to eat, and a butcher told me to give the cat to him—at least in his house she would have food. I had to give him the cat . . . and it was very hard. But it's strange that for the whole war I had a Siamese cat!

Attached as Elly was to animals, there was no time or wish to play with dolls. Instead she actually put a dog or cat, or both—live animals, not stuffed toys—into a doll carriage and went about the streets of Kaisermühlen pushing them. Viktor added one word to her story, "Proudly." And he could not withhold another clarification. In German the "th" in first syllable of *Katholik* (Catholic) is pronounced hard, as a "t." Viktor said, "The animal was not a *Katholik* but a cat." I asked, "But was the cat Catholic?" Viktor answered, "It was a holy cat." But Elly had the final word this time: "No. It was Siamese."

Then she turned serious again, saying that Countess Ostrovsky had been like a mother to her. She enjoyed Elly's spontaneity, liveliness, and openness. The countess even laughed when Elly stole apples to ease her hunger. But when it came to more weighty offenses, Mrs. Ostrovsky "showed me the way: like my grandmother, she told me never do anything against my conscience or just to get money. Never do this! You see it would have been easy for me, when the Americans came in, to have a friend and in this way to get food and clothing and money, and many have done this. They were called 'Chocolate Girls'—the ones who went to bed with the soldiers for food and money and so on. But Mrs. Ostrovsky taught me that I should never do this. . . . She was a devout Catholic.

"These three ladies have been my greatest influences, those who molded my life," said Elly, and Viktor restated it, "Molded her character." "All of them loved me just the way I was. They never tried to change me, and in a way all three enjoyed me and what a rascal I have been . . . and they told me that when they were young they were like me."

The afternoon had become evening and I was leaving the Frankls' place. I stuffed my backpack with recorder, camera, papers, and books, and Elly walked with me to the door. She was still caught up with our conversation and said again how blessed she had been by so many people who showed her the way. Especially by those who never told her what she ought to do, but who rather showed it by living before her eyes with integrity, kindness, and courage.

PART THREE

Viktor and Elly

Together

1946–1997

CHAPTER 11

Someone Waits for You, 1946–1947

THOUGH THE SITUATION in Vienna after the war is beyond the power of words to convey, those who were there understand the destruction and demoralization of the city. Structures and infrastructure had collapsed. The delivery of services and energy and the flow of supplies and food were truncated. The odors of war were thick in the air and the dust sent whirling by bombardments settled deep upon heaps of debris. Under the debris carcasses decayed. Eight thousand buildings were destroyed, 40,000 damaged, leaving 270,000 people homeless.[1] The Central Cemetery had taken five hundred bomb hits and, to this day, in the Jewish section, gravestones are heaped one upon another as though they are rubbish. The road back to a civilized way of life in Vienna stretched farther than any eye could see.

Now, with no more German Reich and Vienna under occupation, of course people were no longer required to carry the *Ahnenpass* as proof of their Aryan origins. But now citizens were required to have a different local passport issued by the Allies. Elly kept hers and, like all others, it has on its front cover the words "Identity Card" in German, English, French, and Russian. Inside is Elly's photograph and signature, personal identifying information handwritten in German and in Russian, and more than a dozen official rubber stampings in official purple ink. As citizens moved about Vienna their identity cards were demanded at "border crossings" between city zones. The center was an international zone, in which the four major powers shared control. In practical terms it meant that each power had its headquarters there, typically in a principal hotel. Patrols went about in multinational military vehicles. A jeep would carry four soldiers on patrol duty, one from each of the occupying forces, typically having no common language among them.

During the Allied occupation the Russians controlled various sectors, among them Leopoldstadt and the regions beyond the Danube including Kaisermühlen. The university district and large areas to the north and west of the inner city were under the Americans. British and French troops occupied areas mostly to the west and south. There is a motion picture made entirely on location in the city in 1948, *The Third Man*, and it gives a visual impression. The film's musical soundtrack—which became an international sensation—has a story which connects the film to Elly and Viktor personally.

Anton Karas was born in Vienna in 1906, so he was virtually the same age as Viktor. Both survived the two world wars, and Karas lived in the city until his death in 1985. After World War II, Karas played the zither—a laptop stringed instrument—in Vienna's wine-garden restaurants (the *Heurigen*). By all accounts Toni Karas was a humble man, even self-effacing, and he was Elly's great uncle on her mother's side—the Prihoda line where he was not the only musical genius.

In October 1948 a welcome party was put on for the film crew just arriving to make *The Third Man*, based on a story by Graham Greene. For the reception Toni Karas had been invited to provide background music. Among those dining, drinking, and listening was British filmmaker Carol Reed, director of the project. After hearing Toni play, Reed sought him out and asked if he would compose a theme for the film. Toni was a self-made musician with no experience to suggest that he could take on a film score. But on the spot he improvised and created a melody that Reed seized upon as the very thing he wanted. That simple but haunting tune catapulted Toni to worldwide fame and helped push the film to its international success. This unknown and untrained player with his zither did the entire musical soundtrack for the film—no other musicians or instruments were used. Roger Ebert, film critic of the *Chicago Sun-Times*, wrote that the film "reflects the optimism of Americans and the bone-weariness of Europe after the war" and praises it as one of the greatest films of all time. Interestingly for our story, he begins his review of the film this way: "Has there ever been a film where the music more perfectly suited the action? . . . The score is performed on a zither by Anton Karas. . . . The sound is jaunty but without joy, like whistling in the dark. It sets the tone; the action begins like an undergraduate lark and then reveals its vicious undertones." Ebert writes further: "Vienna in *The Third Man* is a more particular place than almost any other location in the history of the movies; the action fits the city like a hand slipping on a glove."[2] The British Film Institute named it the best British film of the twentieth century. Viewing it offers a grim glimpse of postwar Vienna, where crooks and con men would even resort to murder as they worked the black market. The film shows the actual debris and darkness of the city in 1948.[3]

While Elly and Viktor talked about Toni Karas, Viktor started whistling the entire "Third Man Theme." Viktor and Elly remarked that Toni traveled to many countries to play that theme, even for British and Japanese royalty. With his sudden fame Toni stopped composing but, according to Viktor, he remained the same humble man he had been before.

IN THE FRANKL archives in Vienna is a document dated March 31, 1946, just five days after Viktor's forty-first birthday and only a week or two before he met Elly for the first time. The typewritten poetic lines in German are on a Poliklinik prescription form, printed at the top with "Primarius Dr. Viktor Frankl." Scribbled revisions are scattered on the page. Viktor's disposition at the time is revealed also in an English translation:[4]

> *While I was still waiting*
> *for my Spring to come,*
> *This heart grew heavier*
> *with every March.*
> *Impatience asked: When will*
> *Spring come at last for me?*
>
> *But now when more composed I am,*
> *and now when more forlorn I am,*
> *I smile at every Spring that's gone.*
> *I know that none has bloomed for me!*
> *Another blooms, to fade again?*
> *For itself!*

On the day they met for the first time, Elly Schwindt had been working at the Poliklinik for nearly three years and Viktor Frankl for only two months. But as chief of neurology he was already exercising medical and administrative powers. His birthday had been a quiet one since he had no family left in Vienna. And he still had received no official confirmation that his wife Tilly had perished at Bergen-Belsen.

Most of the workers at the Poliklinik were unaware of Frankl's personal life. If they knew at all about his first two books, just published, they were saying little. However, word passed among aides and nurses that the new chief of neurology was a difficult man. Nonetheless, as a bright and able psychiatrist surely he would become successful, even prominent, which would make him quite a catch in a city with a serious shortage of men. Among the veterans who had survived the war and returned, many were disabled and destitute. The prevailing fancy for many young women was to have a family and be provided for by a good husband.

Elly Schwindt, by 1946 and even without formal training, had become so competent as an operating room assistant that the oral surgeons often asked for her. And she looked quite the part in her starched white gown with the bulging side pockets. With this she wore the only footwear she owned—gigantic admiral's boots built for soldiers. Commuting to the Poliklinik from Kaisermühlen each day, sometimes she had to walk and stomped the whole distance in those boots. But she was happy and not thinking of marriage anytime soon. She was only twenty.

Even in a relatively small hospital, during the ten weeks that their employment had overlapped at the Poliklinik, it is not surprising that Primarius Frankl and Elly Schwindt had not met, since neurology and dentistry were not closely tied. Also, in the medical pecking order of the day, Frankl—as both psychiatrist and department chief—was far above the girl who had become a wartime dental aide. He knew nothing of her.

Elly, however, was forewarned directly about the tough new head of neurology. On this particular morning in the dental department, an acute jaw surgery was completed but no bed was available for the patient's recuperation. The lack of a bed in the dental department was not unusual, and departments often accommodated patients from other sections. Although the staff thought there might be a spare bed in neurology, no one was willing to deal with Frankl.

While her colleagues wrangled about approaching Frankl, Elly, though she did not know the Primarius, spoke up. "I'll talk to him. I'll find him right now and ask if we can use a bed in his department." "Well, it's your neck, not ours."

Off she went, paying no mind to the warning. At that moment Frankl was leading his medical rounds, interacting with his colleagues and students as they moved along. Elly tracked them down, meeting them on a semisubterranean level of the hospital where their footsteps and chatter bounced off the high ceiling and the hard sterile surfaces. She approached the group in a natural manner and courteously interrupted its obvious leader. "Herr Primarius, excuse me. I am from the dental department and we have no bed for a patient just out of surgery. Is it possible to use a bed in your department for two or three days, four at the most?"

He looked at her intensely and faltered. His associates stood by, awkward but deferential. For a moment it seemed that he had missed her question, and the situation struck her as odd. She thought, "He is strange, maybe a little crazy even. Not like his reputation. What is wrong with him anyway?" Rounds had come to a halt, but Frankl collected himself and replied to Elly, "Yes, of course. I'll arrange for the bed immediately."

"Thank you, Herr Primarius, very much," said Elly as she turned and started to climb the three flights of stairs back to her department. There she announced, "We can have a bed in neurology. One is available now and we can move the patient anytime."

"What? Frankl approved the bed?" Elly's colleagues were disbelieving. "Did he shout at you? What did you say to him? Was he angry about it?" "Not at all," Elly said. "I met him on rounds and just asked for the bed. He said he would arrange it right away. He was rather friendly about it. Quite a nice guy actually." Her coworkers still could not believe it. "Are we talking about the same doctor?"

What Elly had not heard after she left the small group to complete their rounds was Frankl's question to Walter Schober, his first-assistant: "Did you see those eyes?" "Yes, I suppose so. But why do you ask?" Schober had replied. Frankl had been entranced by the young woman from dental, and he would later call it "love at first eyesight." Elly was not struck, though she did think Frankl a decent man even if a little odd.

A couple of days later, perhaps by coincidence, they met just outside the *Kassa*—the cashier's or business office at the Poliklinik. There Frankl said to the young aide, "Good to see you again, sister. Look, I have a terrible toothache," pressing on his cheek as if to relieve pain with the pressure of a fingertip. Elly responded by suggesting the obvious, "But you know you can come up to our department anytime you want to and one of the doctors can take a look at you." "But this is no help to me, what you are asking me to do—" Frankl replied. "I also have a terrible fear of dentists. All my life I have been this way. You would have to catch me with a

lasso and drag me upstairs! That is the only way. Otherwise there is no possibility to get me there." After chatting a bit more they parted. Elly enjoyed the encounter and was amused. But she felt no romantic spark, not
right away.

A day or so after this, Elly in her playful manner fashioned a lasso
from strips of gauze bandage. She took it to the bottom floor where Frankl
had his office. Upon entering she lifted the lasso into the air, swinging it
back and forth in front of him. She motioned as if to put the noose around
his neck. "Okay, okay. I'll come with you," Frankl yielded. They climbed
the three flights to the dental department and on the way Viktor made his
first confession of trickery to Elly. "Sister, I must tell you now that I never
had a toothache at all and I am not afraid of dentists. I just needed an excuse to see you again."

Elly was delighted—with both the confession and the hoax itself. It's
a good thing, she thought, that he doesn't know how many pranks she has
played in her own life or what an imp she could be! They entered the vast
oral surgery together, a room lined with operating stations. The dental
chairs were arranged in a row, as working spaces might be arranged today
in a large hair salon, with no partitions between them. So the two found a
corner and sat down to talk. They chatted good-naturedly for quite a while
before Viktor ventured an invitation.

"You see, Elly, I live just half a block away—my place is here in
Mariannengasse. Why don't you come home with me for a visit? In my
room I have something that will certainly interest you. I have killed the
most poisonous snake in all of Austria. Actually I killed it with an ice pick
and decapitated it with an ax, then brought it back from the mountains to
Vienna in my rucksack. Now I have preserved it in formaldehyde and have
it in a jar. Wouldn't you like to see it?" Elly thought, "This is funny, but
why not? It might be quite interesting." So she agreed and after work they
walked together down Mariannengasse to number 1, then up to the third
floor where Frankl was living. As she accompanied him into the flat she
encountered many other people who were living there in a most peculiar
arrangement due to the war.

The flat was comprised of several large rooms, though only Viktor's
had windows on two sides plus bay windows at the corner. Still living there
was a motley assortment of mostly unrelated people. Though Frankl had
the responsibility for managing the rental spaces, he did not mix much
with his inherited housemates. They were not friendly to him anyway,

probably resenting the physician who, at least from their perspective, was privileged in having work, a room to call his own, and young women flirting with him. Frankl never told his housemates about the concentration camps. Why would he? These people were preoccupied with their own situations and would not have believed that the worst of these cramped conditions were to him almost a paradise. With each passing month more of the residents were moving on or finding new housing of their own.

When Elly entered Viktor's room for the first time she saw only the following: a simple single bed under the window on the wall to the west, a small cooking stove on the floor, a large dining table, and a little cabinet. On the table sat the old typewriter given to Viktor by Bruno Pittermann. Alongside was the bottled snake in all of its gory glory, so at least the snake story he had used to lure Elly was true enough.

In the days that followed the friendship warmed. They spent more and more time together. Elly continued her daily commuting between Kaisermühlen and the Poliklinik on electric streetcars, now back in service. Viktor knew that she walked the last block just below his windows along Spitalgasse early each morning. Often Elly had to be dressed and washed for surgery by 7:30. One morning as she glanced upward to his third-floor flat, she saw hanging from a window opening the lasso she had made. She was charmed and laughed.

Viktor wondered if Elly discerned the longings beneath his abrupt manner and professional crust. Would she ever understand his determination to live without revenge? Most of all, would she ever find it in her vibrant young heart to love him? In placid moments Viktor turned over these questions in his mind. Amid the distractions of his work at the Poliklinik, Viktor hardly dared to hope that Elly might herself be heaven's way of smiling on him.

When Elly made her first visits to Viktor's place, girls from the Poliklinik and others were dropping by to see him. It was their way of letting him know that they were quite available, and he had done little to discourage their visits. So there were ample opportunities for Viktor to resume the promiscuous life he had led before he had met Tilly, but he did not. The young women came by less and less as they realized that Viktor was interested only in Elly. Apart from the silly behavior of the girls, most people kept their distance from Viktor—perhaps because of his abrupt manner, his medical position, or perhaps because they knew he was a Jew who had suffered devastating losses in the concentration camps. It was

Elly who spoke to him openly, directly. Since she made no effort to impress him, he was the more impressed.

Elly felt for Viktor. She even pitied him sitting there in his one shabby jacket—the one issued to him from the storeroom at the Türkheim camp on his release. It was the "sport coat" he wore with his only necktie, itself the one that had been laden with lice eggs when he had found it. As their friendship grew, Viktor started speaking his heart to her. Elly could hardly believe the things Viktor told her about: the conditions in the concentration camps; what he himself had witnessed and endured; the monstrous manner of the deaths of his mother and wife. She noticed the careful, feeling words he used when he spoke of his godly parents, and her heart went out to him even as she became more fascinated with him. Though Viktor was old enough to be her father, she thought him handsome and admired his maturity and wisdom. They shared outlooks and values—a crucial factor in relationships that endure.

Viktor told Elly about his first days back in Vienna, less than a year earlier, and particularly how he had looked up his old colleague and friend, Paul Polak. How he had sobbed on Paul's shoulder as he released his grief over the loss of his family. Elly learned about the close calls and how improbable Viktor's survival had been. Bit by bit she became aware of the questions that dogged him, even in his dreams. For what purpose had he been spared so undeservingly? For what cause did some mysterious grace offer to him the life denied to most prisoners, even to selfless victims far more virtuous than he? What could he possibly do to justify in some measure the time he was being granted?

Elly, naive and trusting at the time, had no notion of what these questions would come to mean for her, how they would change her life forever. All she knew was that she began to love Viktor in his struggle, and because of it. And her listening and spontaneous responses made her like an angel unaware for Viktor. He in turn became more hopeful and more open with her, and she noticed that his sense of humor was emerging. Slowly but surely he was becoming more playful and free with his quick wit. But most of all Elly marveled at the absence of bitterness and vengeance in Viktor. Decades later she still recalled that this is what stirred her first affection for him.

In their early courtship, while Elly was still living with her family, she was involved in an accident on the Reichsbrücke, which she crossed daily on her commute. At midbridge a drunk driver crashed his automobile into the streetcar in which she was riding just behind its operator. There were very few cars in Vienna at the time, but the driver in this case was a son of one of the city's wealthiest citizens. In the crash three automobile passengers were killed and Elly was thrown against the streetcar interior. She had no visible injuries but she did not feel right and immediately went back to her family in Kaisermühlen. At home Elly became aware of pain in her head and of an inability to grasp things with her hands. Thinking she would be better off near the Poliklinik and Viktor, in the evening she took a streetcar to Mariannengasse. By this time she was carrying a key to Viktor's flat, where she admitted herself quietly. Viktor was asleep and, while she was arranging a makeshift bed for herself on the floor, she passed out. Near dawn she awoke and got up, and for the first time Viktor became aware of her presence in the doorway. From his bed he asked, "Elly, what are you doing? What has happened that you are here?" "I have been here for hours," she told him. "I was in an accident yesterday and I came here last evening, but I think I have been unconscious for a long time."

Viktor was concerned and got dressed at once. They walked across Mariannengasse together and he admitted her to Poliklinik neurology for observation. Viktor later described this playfully as "moving Elly from the apartment to the department." She was given a bed in a room with five other female patients. Next to Elly were ladies who had already become acquainted with one another as ward patients do. Soon they included Elly in conversations, but they had no notion about her relationship to Primarius Frankl. Before Frankl and his associates were due on rounds, the ladies in the room began fussing with their hair and layering their faces with lipstick and rouge. As this expectant preparation was underway one of the ladies spoke to the others as if she were making a newsworthy announcement: "Do you know why I am in here in the hospital?" Elly offered a guess, "Not exactly, but because you are ill of course."

"No," the patient said as she continued to preen herself. "I am here because I want to marry Viktor Frankl." Elly said nothing, but inside she was laughing over the absurdity of the moment. She thought how much she and Viktor would enjoy this incident later on!

When the physicians finally arrived, Frankl had with him none other than the brain pathologist Otto Pötzl, his great mentor. Because Viktor was already in love with Elly, it was difficult for him to be objective about her condition, and Pötzl was the finest neurological consultant he knew. The VIP attention to Elly by two doctors made quite an impression on the ladies in the room. Elly had suffered dizzy spells immediately after the accident and for a longer time she dropped things occasionally. Eventually she regained her ability to grasp and hold with her hands, and in a few weeks she was back to work with no lasting effects of her injury.

IN THE SUMMER of 1993, among our earliest conversations, Viktor and Elly were reminiscing about their meeting and courtship. I asked if Elly had known much about Viktor as a popular author and lecturer in the city when they met. "Nothing. I didn't know anything about this." So I asked, "Elly, how then did you learn about this guy you were getting involved with?" Viktor ventured the first answer, "She needed a bed. She needed not my bed, but a bed *from* me!" Elly agreed with his main point, "I was asking for the bed, and that was it. For me it was over. Seemingly he was interested, but for me it was over—I had got the bed. At first I never thought about Viktor Frankl." Then Viktor guessed, "Everybody had warned her about approaching me because I am not easy to get along with." Halfway asking, halfway saying, I injected, "This is a tough boss." Elly went on, "*Ja, ja. Ja, ja.* And it was a few days later we met in the Poliklinik."

"She was nurse and I was . . ."—Viktor started, but Elly interrupted him. "I was no nurse. Please Viktor. I hate to be called a nurse—I was never trained as a nurse." But Viktor was not deterred. "You assisted in surgery." I attempted to clarify by saying, "Elly, you did the work of a nurse." "Yes, I did the work of a nurse, but I was never trained, so it is not correct to call me a nurse." "But you wore a white coat," Viktor insisted. Elly was adamant, "But a white coat is no nurse!" Then she changed the subject.

They told me more about the lasso hanging from the window above Spitalgasse, that in fact it was hanging there day after day where Elly could see it each morning. Suddenly Viktor injected a joke into the flow of the conversation.

"An Austrian soldier in the First World War was in a little Jewish town in Poland and needed a repair on his watch. So he went to a shop where

watches were on display in the window. He entered and asked the proprietor about service for his watch. 'But I am no watchmaker,' the shopkeeper
replied. 'So then what is your profession?' the soldier asked. 'I do circum-
cisions on little boys, here in the back room.' The puzzled soldier asked,
'Then why do you have all those watches hanging in your window?' The
shopkeeper answered with a question: 'What else should I be hanging up
in my window?' "

Immediately Viktor added this line: "So if not the lasso, what else
should I have been hanging out the window?"

We liked the joke and laughed even more at Viktor's application to our
conversation. Turning serious again, Elly continued. "So here we were, in
this very room. Right there on the table was that snake in a bottle. I think
it was here that our first mutual interest started." "In snakes,—" Viktor
quipped, "it was the snake that attracted her. Who else?" Elly smiled, "*Ja,
ja*. And when Viktor opened that little cabinet and—oh my goodness—it
was dirty and looked terrible. It was full of old bottles of whiskies and
cough medicines and so on."

"I gave the whiskey to others and kept the collection of cough syrups,"
Viktor explained. "I would use a little cough syrup to take the edge off my
hunger now and then." "But inside the cabinet was a mess," Elly remembered. The bottles were dirty and stuck to the shelf. Only some paper and
a pencil, maybe a book—everything in this little cabinet was dirty and
sticky. I thought it was terrible." But Viktor defended the thing in a serious manner, "Everything I owned was in this room, and most of it in that
small cabinet."

During her hospital lunch breaks, Elly walked almost daily all the way
to the Jewish *Altersheim* and hospital on Malzgasse to pick up sacks of
food for Viktor. Foodstuffs were provided there to the small remnant of the
Jewish community—the few thousand still in Vienna. Provisions were
hard to come by, even for those with means, and the black market for virtually anything was thriving. An honest family as poor as Elly's struggled
against the odds from one meal to the next to have anything at all on the
table.

One day upon entering Viktor's room, Elly saw that he had been sipping cough syrup again from bottles left by a former tenant of the flat. He
did this more out of craving something sweet than because of hunger. She
chided him for it, but he shrugged, "Calories are calories." Those words he

had said repeatedly in the starvation conditions of the camps, as he swallowed his own saliva and phlegm rather than spitting out what might contain a few calories.

After a pause the discussion returned to nutrition in the postwar situation and Elly elaborated. "My family was so poor, and I was so hungry. You have no idea how hungry I was. Sometimes we had *nothing* to eat. If we had some lard to spread on a crust of bread we were happy beyond words. . . . When I brought food to Viktor from the Jewish hospital, I was too hesitant to say to him, 'Look, I'm hungry. Can I have something to eat, too?' He didn't even think I might be hungry. When he was eating I hoped that something would be left for me, but I never told him. When he finished we put the food there, on the coal oven in the next room. When I was leaving he would pull the doors closed, and then I would stuff the leftovers into my mouth and gobble them down as I walked out."

"I didn't *know* that she was hungry! I found it out only later. I would have given her anything. The food was even more than I needed." "Because I was too silly to ask him! I brought food to him for weeks and yes—I was stealing the leftovers." Viktor couldn't resist saying, "After all, calories are calories."

When I appealed to Viktor and Elly to say more about their early poverty, he again referred to his one old jacket and necktie from the Türkheim camp. Also the girls' shoes he wore on his small feet—the only footwear he had after the war. With a sudden and insistent emotion, Viktor said, "But you see, I felt very rich." Then a pause.

Elly expanded on the peculiar thought. "We were so happy. We had almost nothing, but you have no idea how happy we were." We talked about how peculiar such happiness sounds in more affluent places and times, and I told the Frankls about the visit of a young physician to a lunchroom where my parents worked. I was only a boy at the time, but I remember it distinctly.

On the wall of the dining area there was a painting of an old man at a crude table who had laid down his spectacles and book. His hands were folded in a prayer of thanksgiving alongside a simple crust of bread and bowl of soup. The young physician looked at the picture and snapped, quite sincerely, "Now who could be thankful for an existence like that?"

"Exactly," Viktor and Elly chimed in. "People today cannot understand how happy we were with almost nothing!" The Frankls and I talked

about the evidence now coming from research in social psychology regarding our capacity to adapt to having more, or less. Certainly poverty
gnaws at persons and families and societies. But when we have enough for
living, having more and more does not bring greater happiness. We adapt
to what we have and only want more. The lessons of simplicity are lost on
many people, but it is possible to find contentment with less and less. We
can adapt either way.[5]

On another day during that same stay in Vienna, Viktor and Elly took
me around the city to see this and that. During the last taxi ride of the
day they showed a new burst of enthusiasm about our final stop: the
Poliklinik. With camera still strapped to one hand and microphone in the
other, I followed the Frankls into the front entrance, past the Poliklinik
doorman who responded when Viktor explained our mission. "Okay, fine,
Herr Professor. Please go in as you wish." As we ascended the stairs
Elly explained that the interior had changed little in fifty years, though
some spaces had been assigned to different functions. Then down into
the semisubterranean level we went, to the very spot where they had
met for the first time in April 1946. The surroundings were unchanged,
even the tiled floor. It surprised me when Viktor and Elly started to reen-
act their first meeting. I halted them so I could ready my camera and
recorder.

There I was, witnessing as two mature people—eighty-eight and
sixty-seven—acted out on the very spot, using the same German sentences, their first encounter nearly fifty years earlier. "Herr Primarius, excuse me. I am from the dental department and we have no bed . . ."—the
opening of a conversation that had altered the courses of their lives forever. What is now called in psychology a "flashbulb memory" had blitzed
into their brains the exquisite details because of that meeting's significance for them.

Some years after this reenactment and a few weeks after Viktor's
death, Elly and I were sitting together at his desk. She shared with me a
treasure that she had discovered only the evening before among papers
Viktor had saved since 1945. On flimsy blue paper now yellow with age at
its fringes, she had written one sentence to him. Both the note paper and
the envelope bore Elly Schwindt's initials, "E. S." On the envelope the
penned words: "Herrn Primarius Dr. V. Frankl." And on the inside, written in her own hand:

28.IV.46
Nicht Mitleid sondern Liebe ist's.
Elly

In English:

28 April 46
It is not pity but love.
Elly

At the time, as Viktor said many times thereafter, he could not believe that such a young girl could really love him—"I had nothing and could offer her nothing." What Elly had expressed reassured Viktor, since the Jews who survived the Holocaust and returned were pitied by many. Elly recalled that the Viennese survivor and author Hans Weigel portrayed this situation in his *Unfinished Symphony.*

Upon reading her own short note to Viktor again after fifty-one years, Elly was surprised that she had written of her affection so soon after she met Viktor—in the same month. While she never "fell for" Viktor as he did for her, it was not very long after their meeting that their friendship became romance. And Viktor kept the note "throughout decades" as he would have said.

As Elly was fitting to words her memories of those wonderful days, I mused aloud on what that little note must have meant to Viktor when he opened it and read it the first time. How he must have thrilled to think that, after all, she had found it in her vibrant young heart to love him. All Elly said to me in response was, "I don't know." But her eyes welled up. In Viktor's absence that day, which still seemed so discordant, Elly also placed in front of me on his desk a copy of the 1946 first edition in German of *The Doctor and the Soul.* Inside on the title page Viktor had inscribed the book to her:

"Wer das Tiefste gedacht, liebt das Lebendigste" (Hölderlin)
In Erinnerung an den Stadtpark am 6. Mai .46
DrV Frankl

The second line is transparent: "On our first visit to the Stadtpark on the 6th of May '46." But the translation of Hölderlin's poetic line is difficult. Viktor, in one of our earlier conversations, had offered this rough translation: "Who thinks most deeply loves what is most lively." He explained further the sense that he took from it. "The one who is caught deep in his own thoughts is the one who is drawn most to what is full of life, to the most spontaneous expressions of our human experience." Viktor repeatedly used the Hölderlin words, even in his last year, when he spoke of Elly and what she meant to him.

On another occasion the following interchange helped me understand why the Hölderlin line was so important to them. I pressed them to explain the poet's words for their journey. Viktor hesitated a moment, so Elly responded first. "Without me he would get lost in his own world, in his own thoughts. I am down-to-earth, and he needs this. If I died today, in about three days he would die also—he would be so lost by himself." Viktor simply grinned and said calmly, "I would be co-dying." As usual, he seemed pleased when Elly and I laughed at the way he expressed his agreement with her.

At least two more things about that book inscription are curious. He scrawled his signature "DrVFrankl" as he would on a prescription—just as American physicians sign and add MD after their names. How strange that he would sign a love note in this way. But one time when Viktor was inscribing a book to me, instinctively he signed with that DrVFrankl scrawl. Immediately he apologized, "*Ach*. I should have signed it 'Viktor' but now it is too late." DrVFrankl was simply his habitual way of signing.

More worth noting is the date of that Stadtpark inscription. This is the same park, incidentally, where little boy Viktor had often met his father after work for their happy walks back home to Czerningasse. The date of the inscription to Elly is 6 May '46. This means that Viktor penned Hölderlin's words to Elly within a month of their meeting. And only one week after he had received Elly's little note, "It is not sympathy but love."

How could Viktor have known—from the time of his youth counseling centers in Vienna, to his suicide prevention work at Theresienstadt, to keeping himself alive at Kaufering by imagining seeing his wife and mother again—how could he have known the significance of his counsel to himself and others, "Someone waits for you." The fulfillment of this hope was tied earlier to Tilly, to his mother, brother Walter, and to other friends who might possibly have survived. But not one of them was waiting for him—not parents, wife, brother, or mother-in-law—though they remained profoundly present with him. Somehow he had retained or was given an enduring sense of a benevolent Providence in spite of all that had happened. Even though some critics discredit Viktor's interpretation of his Holocaust experience and his "unconditional faith in life's unconditional meaning," the conviction that "someone waits for you" found an enigmatic fulfillment in Elly. She was a gift he did not expect, nor could she possibly have been waiting for someone who, as far as she knew, did not exist. Yet in a mysterious way it may be said that Elly was waiting for him, even if not in the way we normally understand human waiting.

IN 1946, ELLY moved in with Viktor. At the time, doing this before marriage was frowned upon. Though Viktor knew by various reports that Tilly was dead, he still lacked *official* notification from the International Red Cross, and so on this technicality was not permitted to remarry.

Although Elly's family was certainly open to Christian-Jewish inter-marriage, Viktor could only speculate about what his parents may have thought of his marriage to Elly. He recalled that his father and mother never objected to his non-Jewish girlfriends, but recognized that marriage is another matter. Nonetheless, Viktor felt certain that even if his parents had objected on religious grounds to this marriage, once they had met and known Elly they would have welcomed her to the family. And in the circumstances they would have understood the obstacle to official marriage as Viktor was forced to wait for word from the Red Cross. For Elly, marrying a Jew "was absolutely no problem." With her upbringing and the many Jews among her friends and relatives by marriage, to Elly it was simply the person that mattered. Elly told about the pessimism of one of her Jewish aunts toward Frankl, however. "Tante Berta went each day to my grandmother and she often said, 'You will see, a Jewish gentleman will never marry a poor Christian girl. It never will happen.' My grandmother was very unhappy about this, and she said to Berta, 'You are right. She is a poor girl—you are absolutely right. But what she can make with her hands and her brains is more important than to have money. Those she can keep her whole life, but money she can lose. But what Elly does possess, Viktor will get a very rich girl in a way.' Seemingly it was important for Jewish people to marry someone wealthy. You do not marry a poor girl, and a poor Christian girl even less."

In the other room Viktor was watching the evening news on television but listening with one ear to Elly and me. From there he shouted into the conversation, "If she is a *Christian* girl she must be *very* rich!" I added, "So the benefits have to be worth it?" We all laughed, and then Elly continued. "Berta bombarded my grandmother about this, but grandmother believed in me as she did even when I was a little girl."

In the religious communities it was another matter. Among orthodox Catholics and Jews this relationship was neither blessed nor acknowledged. Elly, under the strict Catholic practice of the day, was a sinner on two counts: first, she was living with a man and having a sexual relationship without marriage; second, the man she eventually "married" was a Jew. And in the exacting Jewish perspective the marriage of Viktor and Elly could not be recognized.

In July 1947, Elly was four months pregnant when Viktor finally received official confirmation of Tilly's death. A couple of days later Viktor and Elly were married in the simplest of civil ceremonies at the Ninth District offices on Währinger Strasse—the same building where Viktor had once done suicide prevention work among Viennese youth and which remains the district headquarters to this day.

They walked to Währinger Strasse in their best clothes, carrying their birth certificates, and entered a small assembly room. A couple of photographs of the ceremony show Viktor and Elly sitting in front of a table and before a robed civil official. Witnesses are Elly's parents, an aunt of the deceased Tilly accompanied by a friend, and grandmother Schwindt who loved Elly deeply—Elly remembered that her grandma was very proud of her marriage to Viktor. For the ceremony Elly held some flowers from Viktor and wore a "wedding dress." Her mother, grandmother, and Elly herself had saved their ration coupons for a long time so that Elly could have a better dress for this great day. "It was a terrible dress, but in my eyes it was beautiful. And I was so happy. I also saved a pair of stockings, which were very old and nothing but runs. My shoes had no heels." Viktor wore his one jacket and necktie.

"And after the wedding we went back to Mariannengasse," Elly remembered. They had printed a simple announcement of their marriage, and to their intimate circle they had sent this special invitation: "Dr. Viktor Frankl and wife request the honor of your presence at a reception Friday, the 18th of July [1947], at 6 P.M. in their home, Mariannengasse 1. Casual dress. Beverages and ice cream provided." Elly's closing comments were, "My father brought a bucket with terrible ice cream made with water and sugar and colors. And that's it. No honeymoon. Nothing more."

The couple continued to live in one room after their wedding. They took over a second room at Mariannengasse in time for the birth of their only child, a daughter, December 14. Gabriele would be known thereafter among family and friends as Gaby. It was a joyful time for the humble household.

With continued urging from sister Stella in Australia, Viktor and Elly contemplated emigrating. In fact, they had visas and affidavits all in order and could have uprooted and moved with little Gaby to Australia. But because of Elly and Gaby and the expansion of his work, the future looked brighter to Viktor. Together they were still attached to Vienna as he continued to emerge from the shadows of his darkest years. He was taking heart more and more. Wherever they might live, Elly and little Gaby were the clearest signs that spring might yet come for him.

THE YEAR 1947, seemingly as much a springtime as Viktor could hope for, was darkened in the Schwindt family when their most dreaded news arrived. A young soldier-comrade of Elly's brother Alfons returned to Vienna, bringing to Leo Schwindt the story of Alfons' death. This comrade had actually witnessed the killing. The Russians had taken as prisoners of war a group of German soldiers. Alfons and his comrade were among them, held captive in the region of Budweis, Czechoslovakia. Five days *after* the armistice, Alfons and his comrade were expecting their release and return home. In his native goodness and naiveté, Alfons had put an unloaded handgun in his rucksack. It was to be only a souvenir of combat, but when the Russian soldiers searched the pack and found the gun, one of them shot Alfons to death on the spot at point-blank range. The death of Ali at age twenty-one was another pointless and appalling waste. So the gloom that befell so many families settled also on the Schwindt household. The news was so horrible that Leo did not even tell his wife for fear that she would not be able to bear it. Elly, then just over twenty herself, joined in keeping the news from her mother. So Hermine Schwindt lived the rest of her days in hopes of seeing Ali again. He was the apple of her eye.

CHAPTER 12

Controversy, Conflict, and Criticism

A CHARACTERIZATION OF Frankl by his friend Robin Goodenough goes like this: he was a great person at whose heels puppies were nipping constantly. Although this reference was to people who hounded Viktor for petty reasons and/or with petty criticism, Frankl survived personal foes more portentous.

Viktor and Elly actually warned me that if I wrote their story frankly and honestly I should be prepared for criticism also, even of a spiteful sort. At first I wondered if they were exaggerating the threat to me and even to themselves, but my naiveté was dealt a blow during one of my winter stays in Vienna.

Viktor had been interviewed for television and, quite predictably, had restated some of his insistent themes. Typically his public denunciations of collective guilt were followed by a spate of letters from grateful listeners as well as a few critical, insulting, or threatening messages. During the night after this interview someone gained access to the Mariannengasse building. In the morning Elly found on their front door a swastika, smeared in feces. Elly put on rubber gloves, then cleaned and disinfected the door. When I arrived the Frankls were still dumbfounded that such a thing had happened. "We haven't seen anything quite like this since 1945," they said. Still Viktor was quick to point out that the swastika incident was both cowardly and—by Holocaust standards at least—trivial.

Since no one has ever been apprehended it is not known if attempts to intimidate the Frankls over the years were the work of an organized group of extremists, a couple of political cranks, malicious pranksters, or folks who were simply unhinged. In any case, what follows is not intended to implicate anyone in committing spiteful acts against the Frankls. Certainly all decent people, including most of Viktor's detractors, would join in condemning malevolent behavior.

Controversy and conflict per se were nothing new to Viktor. After all, he had watched Freud and Adler and their disciples, had seen medical faculty scrambling over one another for recognition, had grown up among the factions of the Jewish community, and had witnessed constant political scraps in the wider city. By the time the Holocaust was over he had seen up close how far human hatred and conflict can go.

Even though Viktor fully expected that fair-minded critics would take on logotherapy even as he had taken on psychoanalysis, surprises lay ahead for him both professionally and personally. To the criticism of his ideas he responded with reasoned if impassioned defense, sometimes in writing, though he loved the rough-and-tumble of face-to-face debate on a level field. Toward those who attacked him personally, even to the point of slander, he preferred to maintain a stoic silence. And in the face of bizarre acts—such as the always-anonymous death threats by mail and telephone—he simply stayed his course. The Frankls reported those incidents to authorities but refused police protection when it was offered.

Without spending time with the Frankls in Vienna, one might never know about the nature and weight of controversy since most of it was local—only occasionally did it turn up beyond Austria's borders. What follows is my own overview of the controversies, not that of the Frankls. They never organized or presented the issues in this way; in fact, Viktor discounted some of the factors I identify as significant for him personally or professionally. Though controversy was not perpetual—it seemed to occur in cycles—and though it was not stable in its intensity, it was significant enough to merit its own chapter here.

This also marks a temporary departure from the predominant storytelling style. Though anecdotes are used to illuminate what follows, identifying seven areas of controversy is my own way of summarizing what I learned about them. In the next chapter, on mountaineering, we shall return to the storytelling style but in a more topical and less chronological structure.

ONCE MARRIED TO Viktor, Elly learned a lot in a hurry—including lessons about controversy. By 1949 even little Gaby was picking up on it. After all, the family flat was becoming the nerve center of logotherapy, and each day Gaby overheard her parents deliberating—sometimes arguing—about mail, phone calls, and visitors as the line between a private family life and a public vocation blurred ever more. How much Gaby had taken in is illustrated by something that happened in the early 1950s. Viktor had to go to London on a business trip and Gaby, then only five or so, went along to see him off at the Vienna airport. Her caution to her father was precocious. "Please, papa. Speak loudly and clearly, and take care that your airplane will not be shot by your enemies, the psychoanalysts."

1. Opposition from the Freudians

As we have seen, it was in high school that Viktor first became disillusioned with psychoanalysis. In his maturity, Frankl's ultimate critique of psychoanalytic doctrine was scathing. It is criminal, he would say, to pursue "hidden motives" that may not exist at all or, if they do, may have nothing to do with a patient's suffering. For example, it is disgraceful when a psychotherapist convinces a vulnerable patient that his "real" problem is his hatred of his father or sexual attraction to his mother when these are purely the therapist's own inventions. For Frankl such psychologizing went far beyond ethical boundaries. In addition, the lucrative practice of psychoanalysis—up to five appointments each week for each patient, sometimes for years and at top dollar—was challenged by logotherapy's straightforward and much briefer approach. Frankl also was challenging the need for prolonged and intimate dependency of patients on their analysts. The development of logotherapy as a corrective or alternative brought down the Freudian fire. Nevertheless, even with his rejection of psychoanalysis, Frankl maintained to his last day an immense respect for Sigmund Freud as a person and creative genius.[1]

Frankl was never as critical of individual psychology, but still his differences were enough to alienate Alfred Adler. To some, nonetheless, Adler's expulsion of Frankl was unwarranted and Frankl remained in good relationships with many Adlerians across the years. Viktor's own view of the early years was that "I had no enemies other than the Freudians."

2. Resistance in the Psychiatric/Academic Establishment

In Vienna's neurological-psychiatric establishment, where the Freudians did not predominate, Frankl still encountered resistance from some colleagues. Within the university the contributions of Freud and Adler were often denounced as unscientific. In Freud's case, his ideas—especially about sex—had offended even intellectuals in still-Victorian Vienna. Other objections to Freud related to his personal style, heady ambition, intransigence, widespread recognition, and his Jewish roots. In Frankl's case—except for offensive ideas—the same factors may have hurt him academically. Though logotherapy generally was not disparaged as unscientific, certainly professional jealousy was a factor in holding Frankl back, though he discounted it.

A central figure in postwar Viennese medicine was Professor Hans Hoff (1897–1969). Hoff was successor to Pötzl, following the brief term of Otto Kauders, as head of the University Psychiatric Clinic. Hoff had been born a Jew and escaped the Holocaust by living first in the Middle East and then the United States. He had kept in contact with Pötzl and others in Vienna and returned in 1949.

Advancing readily to full professor and chief of psychiatry, Hoff became a singular power in the medical school and in neurology particularly. He gained a solid reputation and had patients coming for treatment from the Middle East, America, and elsewhere. With influence on the Viennese press, seemingly Hoff prevented the name Frankl from appearing in a particular paper. A friend of Viktor who was in the inner circle at the Psychiatric Clinic reported that it was protocol in staff meetings to laugh whenever the name Frankl came up. In fact, despite Hoff's expansion of his psychiatric empire, there was never a place in it for Frankl. Even though Hoff launched new departments continually—a new department every month, rumor had it—he planted his own crew as administrators. For example, Hans Strotzka, a respected and open-minded psychoanalyst with a research bent, became head of a novel department of psychosomatic medicine. Another innovative unit was for child and youth psychiatry, and Hoff placed Walter Spiel as its chief. Spiel was son of Oskar Spiel, one of Adler's closest and most effective disciples.[2] Although Hoff was always socially friendly to Frankl, he may have been the only one to oppose Frankl's promotion to full professor—even though the university rector was pushing for Viktor's advancement.

However, Frankl felt that Hoff had never been unkind toward him and insisted that Hoff was no enemy in any scientific sense either. With his focus in neurology, Hoff had little interest in psychotherapy and did not strive to understand it, even though psychiatry and neurology still were joined at the hip.

Giselher Guttmann, head of the psychology department at the University of Vienna, shares with me the view that ultimately it was to Frankl's advantage *not* to be promoted to full professor—he was advanced only as far as associate professor—and *not* to become administrator of the huge Steinhof Hospital. A full professorship would have laid on Frankl the burdens of university affairs and time-consuming faculty meetings in addition to regular teaching. As for Steinhof, its sheer size and the complexity of its affairs would have consumed him. Even a Hoff clinic might not have worked for Frankl's creative bent and independent streak. But the small Poliklinik department suited him: it was completely independent of the university and beyond Hoff's administrative province. Consequently Viktor found time to write and lecture, develop and practice his ideas, and to go abroad to sow the seeds of logotherapy.

Viktor believed that psychoanalysis never would have reached its pinnacle if Freud had become full professor. Perhaps the university inadvertently blessed the work of both Freud and Frankl by placing a ceiling on their academic advancement.

3. Anti-Semitism

The price that anti-Semitism exacted from the Frankl family has been covered in detail, but here the matter is raised again in the post-Holocaust context. For a brief time after the war some doors were opened in Vienna, especially to remaining or returning Jewish professionals, even as former Nazis lost their positions. But the advantages faded and it is safe to assume that Frankl's Jewish identity over time and in certain circles actually held him back—everyone knows that anti-Semitism did not die with Hitler. It has remained alive in many places, certainly in Austria and Germany, though public manifestations are prohibited by law and even casual public statements are derided, at least in the open. Despite this, Viktor gave little credence to anti-Semitism as a factor in his personal experience in the postwar years.

4. Criticism of Frankl's Personal Style

Frankl has been criticized for his personal style. He could be demanding, impatient, too quick and tart in debate, and overpowering in public and private discourse. At times he sounded boastful, self-congratulatory. Often Frankl presented his ideas with a finality that led some people to regard him as dogmatic and authoritarian.

Even though he knew he could be a difficult person to get along with, Frankl remained adamant about his ideas, and Rollo May, the well-known American existentialist, at first accused logotherapy of bordering on authoritarianism.[3] Rabbi Reuven Bulka, editor of the *Journal of Psychology and Judaism*, responded to May's claim and gives insight into the matter in his own book, *The Quest for Ultimate Meaning*.[4] What is not known is that May and Frankl, at the 1990 conference on the Evolution of Psychotherapy in Anaheim, California, met in a restaurant for a conversation of several hours. In that dialogue May confessed that for years he had underrated and misunderstood Frankl and logotherapy. This was late in the careers of both men. May died in 1994, Frankl three years later.

On the issue of therapists pushing their own values onto their patients, James DuBois, professor of health care ethics at St. Louis University and secretary of the Association for Moral Education, has written about the position Frankl took in 1945—that the therapist must never take over the patient's responsibility but rather lead the patient to experience the "depth of his own responsibility." DuBois writes, "The very same ideas are emphasized also in *Man's Search for Ultimate Meaning* (Frankl 1997, pp. 120–21), precisely because Frankl both heard this accusation repeatedly and insisted that it in fact contradicted logotherapy's deep concern to foster responsibility alongside of freedom."[5]

Irvin Yalom, a well-known author whose work includes evaluations of group therapy, the encounter movement, and existential psychology, also commented on Frankl's personal style. "His arguments are often appeals to emotion; he persuades, makes *ex cathedra* proclamations, and is often repetitive and strident." Yet Yalom as a mature scholar looks beyond those personal objections to the substance of logotherapy and Frankl's contributions. He notes that Frankl's style may help explain why "he has not gained the recognition he deserves from the academic community."[6]

In his humanness, Frankl was paradoxically dogmatic and open, strident and gracious. Giselher Guttmann said that Frankl could be "an angel, a miracle of tolerance" but that he could also from time to time send an arrow at his opponents. And Frankl was capable of banishing someone who, in his view, undermined logotherapy.

In addition to the imperial style of Freud's Vienna—versus the more democratic style of Jung's Zurich, for example—there is another perspective on the personal style of Freud which may be quite instructive in understanding Frankl. That Freud was a creative genius is not questioned, and his profound impact on Western culture is established. While Frankl has nowhere near the fame or influence of Freud, I found no one who denied Frankl's creative genius—even his critics seem to grant him that. It is with regard to the personal behavioral styles of extraordinarily creative people that the work of Howard Gardner of Harvard University is so helpful—particularly through what he calls the "anatomy of creativity."

Gardner studied people who have had a major impact on their own fields and on society: in the arts and literature, Picasso, Stravinsky, T. S. Eliot, and Martha Graham; in science and human relations, Einstein, Gandhi, and Freud. He discerns in these people patterns of personality, motivation, and social relations. They are absorbed in their creative work and—by increasing degrees of difficulty—disregard others, are difficult toward others, or are frankly sadistic. Freud is in the middle group on the dimension of interpersonal difficulty. Self-promotion is another characteristic of extraordinarily creative people, since they need to call attention to their work. Of the seven creative geniuses in his study, Gardner ranks Freud the most extraordinarily self-promoting.[7]

Freud's interpersonal difficulties and his self-promotion may be viewed in the context of extraordinary creativity. This is so for Frankl also—even though his detractors paint Frankl's self-promotion as a character flaw. The point here is not to excuse Freud or Frankl from responsibility for their behavior, but simply to point out some of the quirks that seem to characterize exceptionally creative people. We may be dismayed by the behavior of a particular genius without recognizing the patterns of behavior that may be "normal" for people with extraordinary, creative gifts.

Most of us may never meet a real genius. If perchance we get to know one, it is likely that we will face some difficulty in relating to her or him.

Gardner, by his biographical research, attempts to understand factors that are common among extraordinarily creative people. Frankl fits the paradoxes that Gardner identifies. Viktor could be variously, even simultaneously, strident and tolerant, self-promoting and self-effacing, harsh and humanly tender.

In the midst of his creative outpouring in 1957, Viktor scribbled some lines on a scrap of paper which he dropped into his personal folder for that year. They show an awareness of his personal struggle. The words in German are poetic, but difficult to translate.

> Gott, Du hast mich mit Geist geschlagen;
> So hilf mir nun, das Leben tragen!
> *God, You have stricken me with mind;*
> *So help me now to bear this life!*

5. Jewish Opposition

While the resistance of psychoanalysts to Frankl from the start is understandable, the tensions that developed later between him and the Jewish community are more difficult to comprehend. It is ironic that one who endured so much evil from anti-Semitism would in time be alienated by some of his fellow Jews. In 1980, Rabbi Reuven Bulka wrote:

> The best way to describe the relationship between Frankl and the Jewish community is to call it "paradoxical." This, to be sure, comes without any "intention."
>
> If one compares the number of invitations Frankl receives to address universities and religious groups, the ratio leans astronomically away from exposure to Jewish organizations.
>
> On the other hand—and this may surprise even Frankl himself—his books, especially *Man's Search for Meaning*, have formed the basis for an untold number of sermons by rabbis in their synagogues and perhaps rank among the most popular books being circulated within the religious environment of *yeshivot* (schools for intensive Jewish learning).[8]

On this positive side of the paradox was Leo Baeck, the famous and widely influential rabbi who lived in London for some years after surviving Theresienstadt. It was Baeck who had arranged Frankl's lectures in the ghetto. Years later, in communications with Frankl regarding the *Encyclopedia of Psychotherapy* (then in preparation) Baeck commented that "logotherapy is *the* Jewish psychotherapy"; Frankl thought this "understandable in view of the fact that he [Baeck] once translated 'torah' as 'life task.' "⁹ Another positive example is that for decades following the war, Viktor had many Jewish friends in Vienna as well as abroad. He and Elly entertained many of them in their home. And at first Viktor was well-connected and respected in the city's *Kultusgemeinde*—the council or organizational nerve center of the then-small Jewish community.

But the rising resistance of local Jews to Frankl came from a mix of political, ethnic, religious, and interpersonal factors. One point of contention later on was his marriage to Elly. In postwar conditions and with Viktor's horrendous Holocaust experience, his marriage to a Catholic woman had been accepted—at least tolerated if not approved—by Viktor's Jewish comrades. In such desperate circumstances the usual barriers between groups seemed rather irrelevant. Over time, however, and at a distance from the war and Holocaust, some in a new generation of Jews saw the Frankl interfaith marriage as less forgivable.

A more central issue was Frankl's stand against collective guilt, which he had taken publicly right after his liberation from the Türkheim camp. Apparently this was tolerated at first, but by 1970 Viktor's relationships among Viennese Jews were frayed, though the conflict over collective guilt generated more heat than light. Frankl absolutely refused to participate in efforts to blame by association or to take revenge for the Holocaust in any way—he was downright defiant about it. He would have no part in answering hate with more hate, and his tilt toward reconciliation grated on those who were politically or personally motivated to avenge the Holocaust. For Frankl, guilt was a matter of individual responsibility. It is wrong—he insisted from the start—to ascribe Holocaust wickedness to people who could not be personally responsible.

But once Viktor's foes took out after him, of course they focused on "evidence" to make a case against him. For example, his ongoing close relationships with onetime National Socialist Party members Otto Pötzl and Martin Heidegger were used to suggest Viktor's "Nazi sympathies."

There is a telling incident that took place in New York which illustrates how resistance to Frankl had spread to certain Jewish elements on the United States East Coast. At the Institute of Adult Jewish Studies at Congregation B'nai Jeshurun on Eighty-eighth Street, New York, the roster for the 1978 lecture series, preceding or following Frankl, included Shimon Peres of Israel's Knesset; Jewish Holocaust thinkers and leaders Irving Greenberg and Elie Wiesel; Sammy Davis, Jr.; and President Gerald Ford. Frankl's lecture was on November 13, moderated by the congregation's rabbi, William Berkowitz.

To an overflow audience in the temple Frankl talked about his camp experiences and again took a stand against collective guilt. Part of the audience grew angrier as Frankl described the kindness of some Viennese people during the Hitler time, even some who had become members of the Nazi Party. At his mention of Bruno Kreisky hundreds of enraged Jews stood up, shouting him down in threatening tones, shaking their fists and handbags. They booed and called Viktor a "Nazi pig." Kreisky had been born a Jew and survived the Holocaust by living in Sweden. He had returned to Vienna and became socialist chancellor of Austria in 1970. But Kreisky was controversial and distrusted or even reviled by some Jews— even in New York.[10]

Rabbi Berkowitz intervened and reminded the audience that they were guests in his house and must behave accordingly. He invited those who could not listen to leave, and a large number did. But of the three thousand in the original audience the vast majority remained, listened, and interacted respectfully for the balance of the hour. The press gave gentle coverage of the event, noting the controversy, but Viktor had been seared by the heat of the reaction. Elly said that in that situation, for the first time she had thought that Viktor could be killed by the mob surging toward the platform.

Elie Wiesel, the prominent author and Nobel Prize winner who survived the Holocaust, has devoted himself to keeping the Holocaust in memory and preventing further genocide in the world. When I wrote to him about collective guilt, he replied with a short note pointing out that he had written already on the matter; he added simply, "I never met Viktor Frankl. But I am glad that you are writing about him." Later on I discovered an extraordinary event that had taken place earlier, in January 2000. Professor Wiesel had been a guest of the German Parliament and he spoke there as a Jew of course. He acknowledged that many others were Nazi victims also—"As I like to put it: not all victims were Jewish but all Jews were victims." The speech deserves a full reading, but here is one paragraph from his address to the *Bundestag*.[11]

> I feel compelled to tell you what I repeat everywhere I go, not only here: I do not believe in collective guilt; only the guilty and their accomplices are guilty, but surely not those who were not yet born, surely not their children. The children of killers are not killers, but children. And your children, many of them are so good. I know some of them; a few have been my students. They are so marvelous, so highly motivated, and at the same time tormented, understandably so. They somehow feel guilty, although they should not feel guilty at all. And what they are doing to somehow redeem your country, your people, is extraordinary. Whatever touches the spirit is of concern to them. They go to Israel to build, and they help in any cause that deals with violation of human rights because they feel, your children feel that it is important not to forget this dark period.[12]

Viktor Frankl, had he lived to hear this speech, would have been gratified that another famous survivor was taking this public stand—one that he had taken in the heat of Holocaust ashes in 1945 and for which he had been reproached for decades.

Frankl was a psychiatrist, not a political scientist, theologian, legislator, lawyer, or juror, but he did not disparage the pursuit of justice among nations and courts for the Holocaust. What Frankl detested was not restitution but retribution. In fact, he believed that the apprehension and prosecution of war criminals was important. Viktor and Elly regarded the Nazi-hunting efforts of Simon Wiesenthal as rightful, since they believed his motivation was to bring criminals to justice and not to exact revenge.[13] Viktor believed that government efforts to compensate Holocaust victims were one way to acknowledge national and corporate responsibility—a way for a nation to repudiate its past atrocities and injustices.[14] Finnish scholar Risto Nurmela points out that Frankl did distinguish between collective guilt and collective responsibility.[15] Viktor was put off, however, by exploitation of the Holocaust for financial gain and was critical of the repetition of horror stories to pressure governments as though money per se could actually compensate. In fact, Viktor thought that constant rehashing of atrocities might inadvertently elicit responses in the general public that would prolong racism rather than subdue or end it. Thus he appears to have grasped the subtleties, complexities, and risks of hammering on the Holocaust.

The Frankls' relationships in international ecumenical circles also played into some Jewish displeasure. As the Frankls logged millions of air miles, Viktor was embraced increasingly by religious thinkers and leaders in other faiths. Millions of non-Jewish laypeople latched onto logotherapy, even across cultures. In *Man's Search for Meaning* he never used the word Jew, which certainly raised Jewish eyebrows. Viktor knew, however, even in the camps that Jews were not the only Nazi victims, and throughout his life he refused to reinforce the identity of Jew-as-victim. He shunned the victim image and the sympathies generated by accentuating it. He would not exploit the fact that he had suffered for being a Jew. For him, being Jewish had other, resonant meanings reaching back to his earliest memories.

Viktor bore his experience and memories stoically, though poignant reminders often summoned his deep feelings and moved him to tears— mostly in private, but even in interviews. Throughout the decades following the Holocaust he was gallant—or stubborn—in his determination to rise above himself, to somehow transcend his circumstances and recollections and to live free of vengeance. His boisterous spirit, humor, defiance, irreverence—all these were signs of the self-transcendence he practiced, saying "yes to life in spite of it all." He really did believe in the triumphant power of the human spirit, for himself and for others.

There are those who speak and write as though no human reconciliation is possible or that the only credible stance among Holocaust survivors is atheism and nihilism. Over against that Frankl claimed that he saw faith hanging on among his fellow prisoners. Now, decades later, other survivors continue to reflect, to change in perspective, even to move away from revenge they felt earlier. Thousands of testimonies of ordinary people who survived the Holocaust have been videotaped by Spielberg's Shoah Foundation and by other independent researchers. In New York's Holocaust Memorial in Battery Park, in Washington's United States Holocaust Memorial, in the Holocaust Exhibition at the Imperial War Museum, London, at the Memorial and Museum at Auschwitz, and at many other places visitors may watch and hear the reflections and confessions of survivors. The many I have watched comprise only a sample, and I know that the vignettes have been selected by researchers, curators, and technicians. But I was struck by how many times I heard the sentiments of Viktor Frankl, even virtually the same words. There are descriptions of horrific events and dreadful losses, and of the struggle for faith stretching across five decades of remembering and coping. How little I heard of revenge, or of the nihilism and atheism that seem to pervade the words of some intellectuals and academics. At the Yad Vashem Holocaust Memorial in Jerusalem there was a haunting recorded theme that those who perished "died hallowing the name of God." In London, I found myself jotting down words from various testimonies. One Jewish lady, flooding with emotion, said, "In every nation there are good people. It is true that the Germans killed my family. But it was also a German who saved my life." A shaken Jewish man explained, "I prayed to God to save my family but they were killed by the Nazis. I still believe in God, but I no longer believe in all the prayers."

During Viktor's final years, leaders high in the government of Iran were negotiating with him to come for a lecture tour. He and Elly tentatively accepted the invitation and Elly even started to scout for appropriate attire out of respect for their potential hosts in Iran. Viktor's already frail health suddenly declined further, making the journey impossible. He never traveled long distances again. But I can imagine not only Viktor's readiness to enter an Arab and Islamic culture with his message of meaning, but that he would have been warmly received there. I can also imagine outrage from extremists on various fringes.

For all of that Viktor maintained his respect and openness to those whose experiences in the Holocaust or elsewhere had robbed them of faith. He applied his conviction that we cannot judge another person without asking what we would have done in exactly the same circumstances. For Viktor this meant that heroism cannot be demanded of another person and that forgiveness cannot be demanded of those who suffered the Holocaust. Each person, on the other hand, may be as heroic or forgiving as they choose to be.

6. Criticism of Frankl's "Use" of the Holocaust

Another criticism of Frankl is that he misrepresented his Holocaust experience in *Man's Search for Meaning*—that he exaggerated or embellished it in an effort to promote himself. There are at least two different explanations offered for the "misrepresentation." First, that Frankl was simply naive—that his tendency to look at the good in people meant that somehow he did not fully comprehend the evil of the Holocaust. This, the critics say, also helps to explain why he was altogether too ready to reconcile after the war. Or, second, that since he was in the "milder" concentration camps he did not really suffer so much. Frankl's most extreme detractors—and they are very few—accuse him of having an opportunistic streak that led him to "use the Holocaust" to present himself as a hero and to make more insistent certain themes in his logotherapy. In its wildest form the accusation is that Frankl embellished his Holocaust experience to gain fame, when actually he was an unscrupulous schemer and Nazi sympathizer or even collaborator.

For justification of various claims the severest critics advance a couple of main lines of reasoning. One is Frankl's inconsistent use of the names of concentration camps, done to mislead readers into believing that he had been in harsher circumstances than he had. Further, his pretending to be an observer of Holocaust carnage also shows this self-serving tendency. Another line is that he claimed—as part of his logotherapy—that surviving adversity, even Holocaust adversity, is simply a matter of having the correct mental attitude.

Since part one of *Man's Search for Meaning*—abbreviated now as MSFM—is essentially Frankl's account of his concentration camp experiences *and* observations, it will be useful to take a closer look at it in light of these and other criticisms.

It is important to recognize from the outset that Frankl never set out to chronicle the concentration camps he was in, nor to write Holocaust history. He does mention Auschwitz in MSFM a number of times, though he was there only about three days—and we know now that he was referring to Auschwitz-Birkenau (see chapter 6 in this book). In spoken and written word Viktor was not precise about the four camps of his experience. But the names Theresienstadt, Kaufering, and Türkheim were—and still are—practically unknown to the general public. Even Birkenau is not nearly as well known as Auschwitz. So when he referred occasionally—in speeches or writings—to the three years he spent in Auschwitz and Dachau, for example, he used these names as the ones his audience likely would recognize; in every instance his point *in context* was something other than naming or chronicling the camps.[16] In fact, in the first paragraph of MSFM Frankl mentioned "a concentration camp"; then in the paragraph following immediately he declared that what he reports "did not take place in the large and famous camps but in the small ones where the real extermination took place . . ."[17] Later he described the long transfer via Vienna to "a camp affiliated with Dachau"[18]—we know now that it was Kaufering III.

Frankl—and logotherapy—have been accused also of the notion that surviving any adversity, including the Holocaust, is simply a matter of having a positive mental attitude. This is a bizarre claim. Of course Frankl wrote and talked about spiritual resources and their role in behavior and survival, and he did lay stress on the importance of the last human freedom—the freedom to choose one's attitude toward an unavoidable fate. He also claimed consistently that an orientation to the future increases one's resistance and makes suffering more bearable. He even claimed that people who did not seize upon reasons to survive and gave up hope were more likely to die. But Frankl never alleged that mental attitude is all that mattered or that by some courageous act of sheer willpower one could survive the camps. Meaning and purpose are necessary but *never sufficient* conditions for survival, he said.[19]

A careful reading of MSFM will reveal how many elements Viktor identified as playing a role in his own survival—elements that had little or nothing to do with maintaining the proper mental attitude. The Capo who saved him from death repeatedly. The capricious selections at Auschwitz and the narrow chances of surviving them. Medical doctors who helped him and prodded him when he was on death's doorstep. His own medical knowledge, which gave him a clear advantage in avoiding fatal responses to symptoms of illness.

Viktor's life was saved once when he bit his lip so he did not laugh in a precarious moment. A fire alarm saved him on another occasion. Because he was sick he was spared at least once. He narrowly avoided death by volunteering to go to another camp. He knew the tricks of getting into formation at roll call—to stand straight, look smart, and ruddy up his cheeks by scraping them with broken glass. Once he hid and avoided death. His fellow prisoners and captors alike found Viktor interesting to talk with, which meant that some simply liked him and protected him. He pilfered potatoes to postpone starvation. He avoided delirium by forcing himself to stay awake in fever. In addition to all this—and more—he also did whatever he could to keep his mental attitude up, including improvising prayers.

Given his identification of so many factors playing into his survival, it

is clear that what he was saying is: *all other things being equal,* the attitude
one took and the meaning one found could make the difference between
life and death. In last-ditch efforts to survive and while one was still co-
herent, "luck" was crucial. But so was some cause held in mind—a loved
one waiting, or some task beckoning—and clutched at even for a moment
longer against the odds. Yet, as Viktor made clear, it took more than meaning to survive—it was never a simple matter of mental attitude. There
were still "millions who had to die in spite of their vision of meaning and
purpose. Their belief could not save their lives . . ."[20]

A key cognitive strategy Viktor did use to keep himself going in the
camps was to imagine himself an observer. At other times he seized on
various fantasies to fight off ultimate despair. He envisioned meeting his
mother once more. He hoped to find Tilly alive after all. He wanted to
climb mountains again, and to taste *Schaumschnitten.* He ached to take up
his work where he had left off and lecture in a warm, packed auditorium—in this way his own ambition held him back from a final despon-
dency. As an ordinary mortal he also lingered on the merely imagined
sensations of what a warm bath would be like, someday.

In the situations where Frankl challenged his victim-comrades, they
were the ones with some good chance of surviving the immediate crisis.
He did not challenge those who no longer had the resources to respond
somehow. If anyone had reproached a victim for giving up, Viktor would
have launched his lifelong adamant rebuke: heroism can be demanded
only of oneself, not of another; and whoever would judge another person
must ask himself what he would have done in exactly the same circumstances. It is unthinkable that Viktor would reproach those who died in the
camps as deficient in mental attitude or inferior in spirituality. *On the contrary,* ambitious rascals were more likely to survive while others perished.
"We who have come back," he wrote, "by the aid of many lucky chances
or miracles—whatever one may choose to call them—we know: the best
of us did not return."[21]

Viktor knew about Janusz Korczak, the Polish doctor who ran an or-
phanage in Warsaw. Korczak is not well known, though he is memorialized in a moving sculpture at Yad Vashem in Jerusalem. In 1942 his
orphans were being deported to the Treblinka deathcamp and Korczak
was given the chance to remain behind. He spurned that chance and
boarded the deportation train, carrying two small orphans in his arms and
telling them funny stories. He was killed in solidarity with the orphans he

loved. In this case, Viktor pointed out, this great man did not live because of the meaning of his life—he died because of it. Other real heroes, Viktor added, were killed in the camps for defending a fellow prisoner, or for taking a place in line to spare another inmate, or for refusing to follow an SS order to harm another person, or for giving up a last scrap of bread to a starving child. "The best of us did not return."

After Viktor's death I sat down for a fresh reading of MSFM and was ambushed by surprises. Two key elements may account for it. First, in preparation for writing this story I had become aware of a few people's criticism of *Man's Search for Meaning.* Second, and more significant, by the time of the rereading I was outfitted with new and detailed information about the four camps. Having listened to Viktor and having visited the sites of the camps, I had gained novel insights into MSFM. With a high degree of confidence I was able to place nearly every anecdote into one of the four camps. While it is not necessary to do that—a book like MSFM may be more powerful without dissection—it does show the internal consistency and integrity of what Viktor was doing as he wrote it.

A reader who wishes to see MSFM with new eyes can read it in the light of the chapters here on Theresienstadt and Auschwitz-Dachau. You may be able to place most of the incidents where they happened. Further, you may have an "Aha!" experience when you realize how Viktor drew upon his experiences and observations in the camps. For example, I found a few implicit references to Theresienstadt but no explicit ones. In an offhand comment Viktor told me that 95 percent of MSFM is *not* about Theresienstadt. There are a number of explicit references to Auschwitz. To Kaufering there are both implicit and explicit references, and to Türkheim only implicit ones.

Since MSFM is not Holocaust documentary history, what is it? By its own definition it is an autobiographical fragment, constructed around a prisoner-psychiatrist's observations of three phases of prisoner reaction— shock, apathy, and the psychological bends that set in upon release after the depersonalization of the camps.[22] For the first phase—shock—Viktor drew most heavily on Auschwitz and some on Theresienstadt. This makes sense, since at Auschwitz-Birkenau he underwent and witnessed debilitating shock concentrated in approximately three days; earlier at Theresienstadt he was in charge of a program over a period of many months aimed at assisting prisoners in shock upon their arrival there. For phase two—apathy—naturally Viktor drew mostly upon Kaufering since conditions there were the most appalling imaginable: rampant starvation, abuse, and disease, impossible forced labor, heaps of naked and emaciated bodies between the huts. He did not tap Theresienstadt to illustrate apathy, since the conditions there were less reprehensible, and he was not at Auschwitz long enough either to experience himself or to observe the more flagrant slide into apathy. For phase three—disillusionment on release and the psychological bends—of course Viktor draws upon Türkheim from which he was liberated, and finally upon the weeks that followed as he and his surviving comrades struggled back to becoming fully human again.

Consequently, it is clear that Frankl's intention, far from trying to chronicle the Holocaust in MSFM, was instead to "squeeze out some meaning"—as he put it—from his own experience, something that might encourage others. This he wrote explicitly in 1983 in a preface to a new English edition of MSFM:[23]

> I had wanted simply to convey to the reader by way of a concrete example that life holds a potential meaning under any conditions, even the most miserable ones. And I thought that if the point were demonstrated in a situation as extreme as that in a concentration camp, my book might gain a hearing. I therefore felt responsible for writing down what I had gone through, for I thought it might be helpful to people who are prone to despair.

In the twelve years I have been professor of psychology, I have required my students to read MSFM. Out of hundreds of papers written in response to the book, virtually all have described its positive effect; many report the dramatic impact of the book and its role in provoking a new, more hopeful outlook on the world and on their own lives and responsibilities. Several of my students pulled back from contemplating suicide. One with a terminal illness took heart that his life, which was to end so early, could still be filled with meaning as he tried to help others in their need. Such was Frankl's "use" of the Holocaust.

7. Tensions over Psychology and Religion

Frankl has been criticized from many sides on matters of faith and religion. Here is a sampler. He was too Jewish; he was not Jewish enough. He was too religious; he was not religious enough. He was too open; he was not open enough. He was too close to people of faiths outside of his own and too often spoke in their religious venues. Logotherapy is too religious in nature; in fact it is like a religion itself, since Frankl even said that logotherapy is "education to responsibility." Frankl was himself personally religious though he denied it all the while. Frankl was really a preacher in a doctor's smock.

Despite these claims, Frankl insisted that psychotherapy and religion were distinct domains and he wanted to keep the lines between them clear, even though they overlap in actual experience. He simplified the distinction this way: the aim of psychotherapy is healing and the aim of religion is salvation—though some Greek root words for healing and saving *(therapeuo* for example) are the same and generally mean "to make whole." Still, Frankl wanted to make both psychotherapists and religionists aware and respectful of the differences in their roles and aims.

What muddied the distinctions in the minds of people was Frankl's view that psychotherapy and religion have some similar and interrelated effects. He held that psychotherapy helps people to open up to new possibilities, including in religious and spiritual domains. But he made it clear that if people opened up to faith in the process of psychotherapy, it should happen only as a side effect. Psychotherapists have no business promoting a particular religion to patients who have come to them for help. On the other hand, Frankl observed that religious faith may boost personal well-being. It is well known now that practicing one's faith may have powerful positive consequences. Therefore a strong faith may be a valuable asset in finding wholeness. Frankl insisted that religion is not interested simply in psychological health and personal satisfaction. It has moral dimensions and ultimate concerns.[24]

Why then did religious scholars and practicing clergy of various denominations take to Frankl? Apparently they found logotherapy compatible with their understanding of human nature and need—its "concept of man" simply fit. Anyone who reviews a comprehensive bibliography on logotherapy will see how it has bridged the gap between religion and psychology, between believer and agnostic, even between Eastern and Western worlds. Frankl's own writings often settle at the very frontier between religion and psychology[25]—but it was a frontier he wanted to keep in place.

A look back at the founders of psychotherapy, particularly Freud and

Jung, may be helpful in understanding why Frankl was novel regarding psychotherapy and religion.

Freud was a Jewish atheist—he kept his ethnic identity as a Jew but did not practice Jewish religion. In fact he identified himself as "a completely Godless Jew."[26] He regarded religion as a crutch—an infantile projection issuing from our neurotic needs; we create God in our own image to help us cope. His well-known attack on religion is *The Future of an Illusion* (1927); in the final creative writing of his life, Freud continued his quarrel in *Moses and Monotheism* (1939), a book that seemed outrageous to many scholars and observant Jews.[27] Though Freud's disparagement of religion was relentless, psychoanalysis became foundational in the Protestant pastoral care movement in the twentieth century. It is less ironic that many orthodox psychoanalysts have been nonobservant Jews. Still, even Freud was surprised at the wide acceptance of psychoanalysis among Jews, given his stance on religion.

Carl Jung had quite a different take on religion, or at least on religious experience. He was the son of a Protestant pastor and grew up in a parsonage. Jung was fascinated with religious phenomena and delved into their existence both in the human unconscious and in cultural symbols that he believed were universal. Dabbling in séances and the occult, Jung presaged the development of New Age themes. Jung was clearly more interested in unconscious experience than in religion per se. Practicing believers take a pummeling from Freud's psychology *against* religion, but many religious people embrace Jung as a champion of psychology *and* religion.[28]

Erich Fromm (1900–80) was a Marxist atheist and a Freudian whose writings became immensely popular starting in the 1950s.[29] Fromm was critical of both Freud and Jung for their views of religion and the unconscious.[30] Fromm characterizes the Jungian unconscious as the best that is in us and the Freudian unconscious as the worst that is in us—but he thought that both Freud and Jung had missed the point. For Fromm the unconscious is simultaneously the best and worst of us: it is neither "a God whom we must worship nor a dragon we must slay."

From Frankl's point of view both Freud and Jung were reductionists, treating truly human phenomena—including religion and faith—as unconscious processes, as drives. For Jung, religion emerges from universal unconscious archetypes and therefore is just as deterministic as other drives. Hence, religiousness is instinctual, not existential. In Frankl's

(TOP) Walter, Viktor, and Stella Frankl, c. 1910 [FRANKL ARCHIVES]

(BOTTOM) Elsa and Gabriel Frankl with their children, Stella, Walter, and Viktor, c. 1925

[FRANKL ARCHIVES]

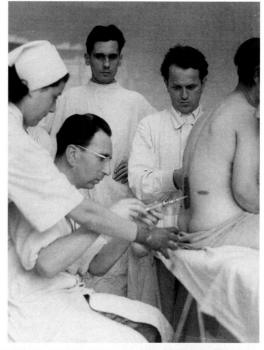

(RIGHT) Viktor as a young physician, with Paul Polak (tall) looking on [FRANKL ARCHIVES]

(BELOW) Best friends (left to right) Erna Gsur, Paul Polak, Otti Polak, Tilly and Viktor Frankl, and Hubert Gsur, near the time of the Frankl wedding, 1941 [FRANKL ARCHIVES]

(TOP) Hermine Prihoda and Leo Schwindt wedding photo, April 22, 1922 [FRANKL ARCHIVES]

(LEFT) Elly Schwindt (smallest child) and brother Alfons (lower right) on their "bad hair day" (Chapter 9). First row: cousin Kurt and Aunt Tilde; row behind Elly: Aunt Mitzi, Hermine (mother of Elly and Ali), and Aunt Grete [FRANKL ARCHIVES]

(BOTTOM) Ali and Elly Schwindt on the Old Danube at Kaisermühlen, c. 1939 [FRANKL ARCHIVES]

(RIGHT) Elly Schwindt (right) with her friends Gerti and Alexey, helping to repair bomb damage at the Poliklinik, 1944 [FRANKL ARCHIVES]

(MIDDLE) Interior of barracks at Kaufering in 1945, similar to the one in which Viktor nearly died [UNITED STATES NATIONAL ARCHIVES]

(BOTTOM) Conditions at the Kaufering concentration camp upon liberation, 1945. Half-underground barracks visible at top [UNITED STATES NATIONAL ARCHIVES]

(LEFT) Elly at the Poliklinik about the time she met Viktor (1946)—one of Viktor's favorite photographs of her
[FRANKL ARCHIVES]

(BOTTOM) The wedding of Viktor and Elly, July 18, 1947. Next to Viktor, his "best person," Grete Weiser (aunt of deceased Tilly Frankl); next to Elly, Grete Krotschak, her "best person"
[FRANKL ARCHIVES]

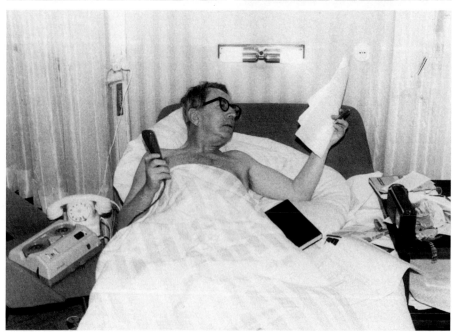

(TOP LEFT) Viktor, Elly, and daughter Gaby climbing in the Dolomites [FRANKL ARCHIVES]

(TOP RIGHT) Franz Vesely with Gaby Frankl on the Hohe Wand [FRANKL ARCHIVES]

(BOTTOM) Viktor dictating correspondence on a typical morning [FRANKL ARCHIVES]

(TOP) (Left to right) Norma Tweedie, Viktor Frankl, Elly Frankl, and Don Tweedie clowning at the Tweedie ranch in California [FRANKL ARCHIVES]

(BOTTOM) Pope Paul VI with Elly and Viktor in Rome, 1970 [FRANKL ARCHIVES]

(TOP) Elly and Viktor in the mountains [FRANKL
ARCHIVES]

(LEFT) Alexander and Katja Vesely, the Frankls'
grandchildren [FRANKL ARCHIVES]

(BOTTOM) The Frankl family in 1996, standing be-
hind Viktor's desk: (left to right) Franz and Gaby
Vesely, Viktor, Katja, Elly, and Alexander [AUTHOR'S
PHOTO]

words, "What sort of religion would that be—a religion to which I am driven, driven just as I am to sex? As for myself, I would not give a damn for a religiousness that I owed to some 'religious drive.' Genuine religiousness has not the character of driven-ness but rather that of deciding-ness."[31]

To Jung, the divine Self was a central and universal archetype. For Frankl, there is no divine Self—rather a human being whose spirit is by nature set to seek something other than self, something outside, something greater. So we arrive again at the key element in logotherapy that sets it apart from all other major schools of psychotherapy: its centering in transcendence. Self-transcendence is what makes human beings unique— the ability to rise above oneself and one's circumstances, to direct intention and devotion to things other than oneself. Fitting closely into this is the possibility—though there are no rational proofs for or against the existence of God—of a transcendent Divine Being existing independently of humans. If such a Being exists, it is possible for that Being to summon us, and it is possible for us to respond by transcending ourselves through trust in that Being.

In its focus on self-transcendence and on the possibility of relating to a transcendent Being, logotherapy has been reproached and rejected especially by people who are secular, or atheistic, or nihilistic in orientation. These days, however, the arrogance of many scholars and academics against religion is diminishing amid the rediscovery of spirituality, and the Freudian influence in psychotherapy is fading. But Frankl came too early to be embraced in academic and psychotherapeutic circles for his stress upon spirituality and values. Yalom asserts that logotherapy "like most contributions to existential therapy, can find no home in the 'better' academic neighborhoods. Logotherapy belongs neither to psychoanalytically oriented schools, nor to formal psychiatry, nor to religious studies, nor to behaviorally oriented academic psychology, nor even to the 'pop' personal growth movement."[32] And while Yalom concludes that Frankl's approach is fundamentally religious, he does not seem to identify that as a factor in academia's resistance to logotherapy or, for that matter, in Frankl's tremendous appeal to a wide audience of "the people in the street."

For further insights into Viktor's stance on religion and faith, I have included in chapter 15 a report of a question-answer period with Frankl and an audience. There a "person in the street" asks Frankl to explain what he means by statements he makes about religion and faith. Frankl remained clear that genuine religious experience can neither be "driven by an instinct" nor "pushed by a psychiatrist."

IN THE FRANKL home one evening we were chatting about the political controversies into which Viktor had been drawn, the things of which he had been accused, the way he had been treated by a few adversaries. Elly and I could have gone on about these things, but Viktor stopped us. I did not have my audio recorder with me, but here is the gist of what he said. Would it be better to try to please everyone and say nothing important and worthwhile? Should I keep silent about my deepest convictions just to acquire some shallow approval? And what is most important after all, appearance or substance? Look at the mail, which nobody knows about: for every reproach hundreds of thank-you notes from people who are nobody in the eyes of the world. This is what is important, that people find meaning in their lives no matter what the world throws at them. It really doesn't matter a damn that a few people have called me this or that or have said one thing or another against me— even one letter from someone who has overcome despair cancels all of that.[33]

On another occasion in a different year, a roomful of Frankl family and friends had gathered and the mood was jovial. We sat relaxing, chatting, and laughing. Somehow even in the light mood of the hour the matter of controversy turned up, and as usual Viktor became the center of attention. Perhaps to reassure everyone with regard to controversy, a person remarked that sometimes we can't win, no matter what. I tossed in a memory from my youth—that of a favorite Hank Williams country & western song that I still like very much: "No matter how I struggle and strive, I'll never get out of this world alive." The Austrians had never heard of it, but they liked it, too. Then, having found the context for a joke, Viktor took over. "Wait-a-minute-wait-a-minute!" It was a favorite Jewish joke about how the *goyim*, the Gentiles, have it better.

"An old Jewish man who had emigrated to Berlin is walking in the famous park there. Then a bird overhead lets its droppings go and they land right on the old man's hat. He takes off his hat, looks at it, and says, 'For the *goyim* they are singing.' "

The place broke into a roar. Even Elly was laughing, though she had heard the joke a hundred times. I was sitting next to her and, settling down to a reflective smile, Elly turned to me and said, "If we couldn't laugh, what would have become of us?"

CHAPTER 13

Mountains and Horizons

VIENNA STILL BUTTONS up on Sundays. Most stores are closed and the city sleeps in. Even if not well attended, masses are celebrated in churches all over the city. Commerce is at a standstill, and one can find parking on the street. Along with other retail shops, even grocery stores are shuttered in the early afternoon on Saturday and do not reopen until Monday morning. This may be a nuisance to foreign visitors, but a city at rest one day each week can grow on you.

For a particular weekend during one of my stays in Vienna I was unprepared. Typically I had at least one meal each day at my room, but by habit I had bought no food on Saturday morning. So on Sunday I hopped the empty tram for a quiet ride to the nearest railroad station (Westbahnhof). There the food shops are open every day. As I got off an escalator I stopped to ask an old Austrian a question, and that led to a genial conversation. He was interested in where I was from and what I was doing in Vienna. So I told him I was working on a book and perhaps he had heard the name Viktor Frankl?

"Aber natürlich! Der Bergsteiger!" the old gent snapped. "But of course! The mountain climber!" The next day I told Viktor about this encounter and he liked it very much—the idea that someone on the street would know of him in that way. After logotherapy, alpine climbing was Viktor's second personal obsession. And it was not simply hiking in the hills, but rock climbing—up sheer mountain walls or jagged formations with chasms below. Scaling the heights was a channel for Viktor's almost superhuman energy and the challenge of it thrilled him. He got tired *from* climbing but never *of* it. It made him taut and cleared his head. In this life-and-death contest with nature his concentration was so intense that he entered heart and soul into another world, a different mode. Elsewhere his

mind was nearly always racing; on the face of a mountain everything dropped from his consciousness except the climb. The break from his daily work was total.

Viktor first climbed when he was nineteen and for the next sixty years he did so whenever he could. His last climb was at the age of eighty, still *leading*, and he quit then only because of failing eyesight. Though he never complained about giving up climbing—but then he never complained about anything truly significant—it must have been a terrible loss for him.

From the start the whole mountaineering enterprise seems paradoxical since as a child he had been rather frail and as a lad always asthenic, even spindly. In spite of that he pushed back the limits by taking up and excelling at this dangerous, demanding sport. Viktor's father loved to walk in the Vienna Woods and when it was feasible he even hiked in the Salzkammergut—the legendary lake district near Salzburg—where mountains soar from water's edge to sky, some peaks reaching nearly ten thousand feet. Gabriel Frankl hiked only on established paths, some of which were challenging all the same. Viktor recalled one incident from the mountains of the Salzkammergut.

> Once at the Schafberg there was a way up where the last quarter of an hour or so it was possible only for someone absolutely free of dizziness, vertigo. And my father described that he was there on a narrow way, close to the wall and with an abyss below him. And at that moment someone came from the opposite direction. And they had to find a way to get around each other. . . . It was at a place where only one person could go, one step at a time. I passed this trail also once and I was reminded of this. But my father did no rock climbing—only hiking on these trails.

Viktor did his first serious rock climbing with a friend in their last year of high school. The friend took him to a quarry as a rope helper and there Viktor got his first taste of the teamwork required in mountaineering. He loved the challenge immediately and never worried about the risks. By the time he was in medical school Viktor was heading south to the Rax Mountains, an easy round trip from the city. Perhaps he felt no fear but others worried about him, as this recollection shows.

I recall that one time I went to the Rax Mountains and made
a climbing tour—a not-too-easy one—and then I could not reach
the bus on time to get back to the railway station. So I missed the
train that I typically used for coming back. It must have been two
or three hours that I did not get home. Then I thought, after having a meal with my rope comrades, that my mother might worry
about me. So I gave her a telephone call, and—I will never forget—just as soon as she heard my voice, even before greeting me,
she sighed, *"Gott sei dank!"* [Thanks to God!]. She was so happy
that I was still alive and that no accident had happened.

In 1939, with the coming of Nazi rule and the imposition of the yellow star for identification, Jews were forbidden to climb in the mountains.
So Viktor entered what he called a time of forced abstinence, except in his
dreams. In recalling this, Viktor shouted defiantly about his wonderful
dreams. "I was enjoying dreaming of climbing. It was such passionate
dreaming, as one has only with regard to sexual or emotional things—
most intimately involved, and then waking up."

A most passionate and memorable moment for Viktor was when his
friend Hubert Gsur invited him to go to the Rax for a climb. "Viktor, you
take off the yellow star and we will go climbing." Gsur wore his
Wehrmacht uniform to deflect any attention from Viktor.

It was only the second time I hid the star—the first time was
when I went into St. Stephen's Cathedral to ask what I should do
about the visa to emigrate and my responsibility to my parents. So
I went south to the Hohe Wand with him. And when I came to the
foot of the wall, where the first rock is, I could not resist spontaneously the most intensive outburst, and I kissed the rock. It occurs to me right now that only one other time would I describe
such a fervent expression from the depth of the heart. That was
my mother when I asked her to bless me as we parted in the concentration camp. She did bless me from the very depths of her
spirit. One might say that the emotions were hot.

The fervent feeling that Viktor attempted to describe came over him
in some measure even far from home. In the 1970s when Viktor and Elly

were in California for his spring lectures, a local radio station played a song well known in Austria. It was about how people enjoy the glorious mountains. When Viktor heard on the air in San Diego *"Herrliche Berge,"* he wept. As he told about that powerful, sudden nostalgia, he spontaneously started singing and humming the whole song.

After they had married, Viktor always wanted Elly to go climbing with him. "I was an official climbing guide, in the Donauland Alpine Club. Elly was my student. . . . Later on we went nearly every weekend in summer except when we were away from Austria." Reflecting on it, Elly said, "When we married, I thought that if I go with him he will not go on the hardest climbs and this would restrain him a little. But I didn't like it." Viktor appended, almost under his breath, "She didn't like me at all." Elly ignored that and continued, "But when I got to the top it was a wonderful feeling. I was so proud that I did it. But when I started, I hated it."

Before they had their first automobile, on each trip to the mountains they had to take the train from Vienna to Reichenau and then a bus to the base of the *Seilbahn*, the funicular railway that runs up to the Hotel Bergstation on the Rax plateau. Both rail and hotel are still operating. For many years the Frankls had their own room at the hotel and always had the key. They left their climbing gear and other things there. Elly cleaned the room and windows, and they had to pay only for the nights they actually used the room. Earlier they also stayed on occasion in the Ottohaus, farther up on the plateau. One time on the way to the Ottohaus, Elly was walking roughly sixty feet behind Viktor. A man and woman were sitting together on a bench by the path, resting. Viktor had passed them already and as Elly walked by she overheard the man say, "That guy looks just like Professor Frankl—even the glasses he is wearing. But of course it is not possible in such dumpy old clothes." When Elly told me this story I said to Viktor, "That is what you said when you first saw old Freud at the Schottentor." He had never thought of the parallel but agreed that the impressions were similar. Elly added, "But we enjoyed it immensely to be dressed up in that way, there up in the mountains."

Viktor explained the irony that sometimes people on the Rax did not believe that it was he, and at other times climbers missed him when he was *not* there. "On a favorite trail on the Preiner Wand—and on each technical climbing path—there is in a crevice a *Steigbuch*, a trail book to sign each time you go through because it is important if someone does not return to the alpine hut, and for a search. Usually climbers sign with the date. Once when I opened the book—because I liked to read who was there recently, writing about a beautiful day and so on—there was an entry, 'How come that Viktor Frankl has not signed in a whole year, and it is August?' "

Another mountain experience, this one at the Hochkönig near Salzburg, had stuck in the Frankls' memories. It was not long after their marriage, so they were approximately forty-two and twenty-one. "At nearly twenty-five hundred meters we had to cross a small glacier, and Elly kindly carried the rucksack. And when we crossed the glacier, some younger people passed us. I was without a burden, so in front of them I shouted out to Elly, 'Do you have with you this or that, my lovely child?' In this way they believed that I am the father and she is the daughter, and this saved me some embarrassment."

While it may appear that Viktor was taking advantage of Elly, between them it was not a point of tension. Elly explained that actually she insisted on carrying the heavier packs because she was strong and robust, and she worried about Viktor's weak legs and ankles. After a while the daughter act became a kind of joke, since Elly felt that Viktor never put her down, never diminished her but rather respected and admired her.

In the Italian Dolomites, Viktor recalled, "Because I wanted to climb a famous vertical wall I hired a professional guide, and in the morning Elly wanted to go with us to the foot of the wall. The guide persuaded Elly, 'Why don't you come up with us!' And finally she said, 'Oh for heaven's sake, okay.' And the entrance of the climb was very steep, with little holds only, and she started complaining and shouting, 'I'm an idiot. Why did I come here? Why did I join these guys at all!' She was reproaching *herself*."

Elly and I laughed (at her expense) but Viktor continued, "Wait-a-minute-wait-a-minute. Another climber heard Elly shouting this and told others about the Frankls climbing. Later a man in charge of an alpine hut in the Rax heard a version of this story—and with him I was often climbing, using him as a guide. And he was being interviewed by a radio station. They asked him about any recollections of Viktor Frankl, the alpine guide. He said, 'Oh yes,'—and the guy was shouting into the microphone—'yes, you see once Frau Frankl was shouting at Viktor Frankl, "You idiot! You idiot! You have forced me to join you!" ' " Elly swore she never shouted that at Viktor, but only at herself. Viktor absolutely agreed, but broke into laughter, "Now out to one hundred thousand people it was told that Elly shouted at me, 'You idiot! You got me into this situation!' " The two Frankls utterly relished this story.

I asked Viktor if he ever had to overcome acrophobia, the irrational fear of heights, and he said no. But he understood other specific phobias. Once on a delay between planes at the Athens airport he and Elly got stuck in an elevator between floors. It was only for ten minutes or so and they were banging on the door. "Then I understood my patients who were suffering from claustrophobia. Also, though I have never cared for soccer as a typical Austrian boy, Hans Weigel, the novelist and one of our best friends, invited me to watch a soccer game at the Prater Stadium. We were in the middle of a bench [bleachers] and everything was overcrowded. And then I understood my patients who were suffering, not from claustrophobia, but from agoraphobia. I became so anxious. I thought, if something happens, how will I get out? It was terrible at that time. Since then, of course, the stadium has been improved to reduce the crowding."

But Elly did experience fright in rock climbing. "One time Viktor was the guide ahead of me on the wall of the mountain. I was in the middle of the rope, and a man was below me on the rope. I became so frightened that I froze to the spot and could not move. I thought, I cannot do it. Maybe for half an hour or so. And the man below me was speaking to me kindly and softly, but Viktor was laughing and laughing. And then Rudy, our companion, came up to me and slapped me to bring me to my senses. And I was filled with anger at him. But then I was able to continue climbing and it was no problem. Viktor also knew it would be no problem, so he was laughing. But I didn't know this."

Viktor remembered that Elly often complained about things on the Rax, but she defended this by saying, "I was *forced* to go!" Viktor added, "I helped you with self-actualization." To that Elly replied, "I don't give a damn for self-actualization. You can keep it for yourself!"

The Frankls' son-in-law, Franz Vesely, told me, "No one can understand Viktor who does not know how much climbing meant to him. He was obsessed with it." It was to the Rax that Viktor went to contemplate and to weigh options that he faced after the war. "I was addicted. . . . Every important decision I have made was on the plateau of the Rax. But when I reached the wall, from that moment, by life danger, you will not find me thinking of anything but the climbing. So by life danger I was prohibited from thinking about my next book or anything else."

One day the Frankls were showing me old photos of rock climbing, and there was one from between the wars. Viktor is with his friend and dentist Ludwig Werber. Even with his limited eyesight, when Viktor saw the photo he remembered it and said, "I look like some character from a Dostoyevsky novel."

When Viktor was sixty his family took some color home movies of him climbing a near-vertical wall. While the film projection probably increased the impression of speed, nevertheless I was amazed at how Viktor ascended the rock—no pausing, as if choreographed, or like a cat creeping steadily up a tree. Climbers rely mostly on their legs for upward lift, but Viktor always had relatively weak, thin legs. A famous mountaineer, Ignaz Gruber, once observed Viktor on a climb and noted his peculiar technique, which relied more on upper-body strength. This *Bergführer* had led a Himalayan expedition and said that there were things to learn from Viktor, whose unique climbing style compensated for his weak lower body. The *Klettertechnik* that Viktor used was both thought-out and refined, but also natural for him. When I was talking with Giselher Guttmann about Viktor's climbing, he said that some have a certain gift for graceful motion and that Viktor was one of these, a kind of "climbing artist" with fluid, rhythmic motions. To this Viktor replied, "But this is understandable because I fell in love with the walls, the rocks. I *loved* them. I was related to the rocks, and perhaps now you can understand the story when I kissed the wall." Elly said, "But Guttmann himself was like a cat"—moving up the walls gracefully and with his own rhythm.

There was a small hut at the foot of the Rax climbing walls where Viktor and Elly went many times, since the proprietor was their rope comrade. As the one in charge of the hut, though, he had to serve the meal, and the Frankls not only waited tables for him but helped clean up after the guests. Elly washed dishes and Viktor cleared the tables, bringing trays of beer mugs and tableware to the kitchen. In this way the owner would be free to leave earlier for a climb. After Viktor's death, Elly remembered those times and said that Viktor *had* to do such things. "He needed to be connected to ordinary people in ordinary places. I was not always so happy to go to the Rax in summer because I liked to swim. . . . On some very hot days I would have preferred to go swimming, but he needed this—the fresh air and good sleeping. In his pocket he always had scraps of paper and a pen with him. Never in his life did he have a notebook or anything—only scraps of paper, and whenever an idea came he scribbled it down."

"What a character he was," I said, but Elly was not sure. "You see I cannot say he was a character, because if you are together with such a man—for me it was natural because I never knew anything else. What else? . . . Don, many people will be surprised with your book because so many things will be new to them. They will see Viktor in a completely different way. . . . In my eyes Viktor and Martin Heidegger were alike in their simplicity and greatness. . . . The few people who knew Viktor and experienced him will be able to imagine that what you write is true. All his friends on the mountains, they know him and they will believe your book. He was the happiest man when he was in the mountains and surrounded by ordinary people who didn't even know who he was except a funny guy. These people will understand your book. . . . We were laughing so much, and if I was silly Viktor would be laughing about me and about himself, too. Oh he could laugh!"

IN VIENNA I had the chance to talk long with two of Viktor's former "rope comrades"—*Seilkameraden*—climbing partners who shared responsibility for one another's safety: university professor Giselher Guttmann and Viennese neurologist Gustav Baumhackl.

Guttmann's father had been a climber and had around the house ropes, hammers, and other climbing paraphernalia, though the family was glad Giselher had not taken up the dangerous sport. Eventually, however, they had Viktor to blame and Giselher had him to thank for his climbing obsession. At the age of nearly forty Guttmann went on his first climb with Viktor, who had invited and encouraged him—they addressed one another formally, of course, as Herr Professor and Herr Doktor. Before long Guttmann was surpassing Frankl with ascents even at the *sixth level* of difficulty—severe and very dangerous climbs. Guttmann was strong and wiry, well suited to the sport, and he loved it. For a couple of decades he climbed vigorously and many times on tamer ventures with Viktor and Elly. He became their intimate friend, and Gisi—their familiar, affectionate name for him—was always kind to Viktor and Elly.

When I had asked Giselher if he liked climbing the first time or if it took a while, he said, "About three seconds." Although he went rapidly from one level of difficulty to the next, he still enjoyed the weekends on the Rax plateau and climbing with the Frankls. Gisi explained that he was a sound sleeper in the mountains, except for one night at the Hotel Bergstation, right at the top of the cable rail car and on the Rax plateau. Gaby Frankl remembered that night also and augmented the details. This is mainly Guttmann's recollection.

We all love Viktor, but it is true that at times he could become very angry and sharp. And if he got angry you could hear it for a mile, but this you know. Once we were at the Bergstation and we needed to get a good night of sleep before our climb the next day. And I woke up to *loud* shouting, and it was Viktor. The next day I asked him about it and he said, 'There was such incredible noise downstairs and they didn't stop singing.' But when he shouted they stopped. I would not compare Viktor too much in this way, but the Buddhist monks—and also in Judo—do not get angry easily. But if you get them to a certain point they become shouting monks and then return quickly to quiet again.

Gaby recalled that many tourists were in the restaurant below the rooms at the Bergstation that night. Most of these were not climbers but had simply taken the rail car to the top to have a Saturday evening of fun. In fact, the television was blaring, the drinking was heavy, and the crowd became boisterous and even obnoxious with shouting and laughing. But the booming voice of Viktor Frankl cut through the inebriation and frightened the revelers into immediate silence. The party ended. The serious climbers were grateful and fell asleep.

Gustav Baumhackl was another *Seilkamerad* of Viktor and Elly, both of whom described him as "a wonderful person, full of goodness and humor. And we have had many wonderful days with him climbing."

Baumhackl, after retiring from both mountaineering and the practice of neurology, welcomed my visit to his home on Erzbischofgasse in District 13. Among books and contemporary furnishings, he struck me as a lonely man. Later I learned from the Frankls that he had lost his wife only the year before. They said that Gustl, using that intimate diminutive form of his first name, had been devoted to her throughout her illness and dementia, when she did not even recognize him.

Incidentally, even as "Baumhackl" in Austrian German means "little tree ax,"—the final "l" a diminutive—so the Frankls called Gustav Baumhackl "Gustl." And on occasion someone from Viktor's boyhood addressed him as "Vikerl," even in his adulthood.

Back in their mountaineering days Viktor and Gustl had actually gone to level six on the Preiner Wand, the most challenging and risky of their climbs. But more typically they climbed the Rax with Elly and enjoyed it each time. Dr. Baumhackl had memories he cherished.

"There is a very cold stream that runs between the Rax and Schneeberg. The water was icy, and Viktor and I would go naked into this stream two or three times and back out at once. We thought we would die from the cold. But then we were completely refreshed, like newborn, and ready to go down from our climb.... Actually the water we drink in Vienna comes also from the Rax.... To climb together, to be on the same rope, bound us together literally and emotionally."

Gustav Baumhackl took it as a very tough question when I asked him *why* he climbed. It was difficult to explain, he said. "I climbed because I loved it—it is like falling in love. Who can explain it? . . . I liked just hiking also, but Viktor loved only the climbing."

Our conversation drifted away from mountaineering. Baumhackl told me that in his own medical practice after the war he had two patients who had been with Viktor in the concentration camps. From time to time each of them would talk about those terrible times, and each told how Viktor Frankl was always trying to find ways to help them and other prisoners in the camps—that even then he was the same man. Baumhackl finished the anecdote simply by saying, "Viktor practiced what he preached."

When I was leaving Baumhackl's home, he walked with me through his small front yard, as neatly tended as his apartment. He pointed out the green garden hose lying on the grass and told me that whenever he waters his lawn he thinks of Viktor Frankl. When I told this story to Viktor, he interrupted me with a guess, "Why? Perhaps because I urinated on the Rax?" I said, "No, not that." "But I *did* urinate on the Rax." "I'm sure that you did, and that he did also," I agreed, "but he was not speaking of this."

In fact, Baumhackl's story had to do with being a rope comrade of the Frankls. When climbing, one person would brace himself in a surefooted place and slowly let out rope as his partner climbed on ahead, just in case the partner were to slip or fall. The climber below, who secures the rope, would watch carefully and whenever necessary whip the rope gently around some obstacle so that it would remain free. If this rope got caught on the edge of some rock, it could be deadly. Keeping the rope free and snug was important so that no sudden yank would throw a climber off balance.

Whenever Baumhackl watered his lawn he would whip the hose in a circular motion to get it around or over an obstacle. And every time he did this he thought of Viktor, his lifetime *Seilkamerad*. As I departed, Dr. Baumhackl told me that he visits each year at the Frankl home, in a way to renew the rope comradeship, but that he should go there more often.

The next day I called Dr. Baumhackl to thank him and he responded, "How kind of you. I did not tell you very much; I should have talked more with you." At the Frankl place I told Elly and Viktor about my hours with their dear friend "Gustl."

They remembered what a gentleman Gustl was, even on the Rax. "Gustl was first in our group of friends to get a car, and it was loud and stinking," Elly recalled, and this was a cue for Viktor. "Once we had to drive two hours from the Rax back to Vienna, and it was raining. The windshield was broken and Gustl was wearing not driving glasses but diving goggles. The car had been waiting on the ground and a falling rock had broken the windshield." Apparently they rode home soaked by a driving rain with Baumhackl at the wheel of their craft. Elly asked, "Viktor, do you remember what he was eating? He put together dark bread, gray bread, and white bread—he put these into a sandwich." From the Frankls I learned that at Christmastime, Baumhackl brought flowers to their home—something he had done for nearly five decades and never, ever missed. I was impressed to learn this, but I told the Frankls I was not surprised. Gustav Baumhackl had said to me, simply, "I love them." Instantly Viktor responded, "We love him also."

Where does such love come from? Only from mountaineering? I was granted more insight into the Frankl-Baumhackl bond when Baumhackl told me that he had been a Nazi. He broke down sobbing when he said it, as if he carried titanic regret for having joined, though he was innocent of any crime, or violence, or even ill-intent. He then explained to me that as a former party member he had no work after the war. A friend urged him to see Viktor Frankl at the Poliklinik, who might have a position for him.

When I reminded Viktor that he and Baumhackl had met in that way, he said, "I did not bestow on him any formal duty, but only allowed him to see patients and sent some patients to him." "So you trusted him and befriended him," I observed. "Certainly. Why should I not have done so?" But I insisted, "No one else was trusting him—that is his point, Viktor." "Then that is *their* problem, not mine." I was persistent, "But Viktor, you cannot take away from Baumhackl his gratitude to you. . . . These were his own words to me: 'It was Viktor Frankl who gave me a little bit of friendship when there was almost none, and I will never forget this. He had just come back from the concentration camps.'" Viktor remained defiant: "So what."

The affection between these *Seilkameraden* was astounding, and as fixed as the mountains where it was forged. This was Viktor's way of putting it: "You see, on the ropes each climber is co-responsible, interdependent, and this remains for life."

But before these two ever went to the Rax together, the Jewish neurologist—who in the deathcamps had been dehumanized and barely escaped the fate of his own loved ones—gave his friendship to an Aryan colleague. And the only retrospective explanation from the poor Jew for the trust and friendship he gave was, "Why should I *not* have done so?"

TWO BOOKS ARE relevant to the story here. One is a photo-essay by Karl Lukan, published in 1978, about the Schneeberg and Rax Alps. The text is in German and the color and black-and-white photographs and maps give an overview of the region where the Frankls climbed most often. There is a brief section of text about "the doctor who belonged to the Rax. . . . And this is University Professor Dr. Dr. Viktor E. Frankl . . . founder of logotherapy . . . and first recognized by 'papa Freud' in 1924."[1] The passage conveys Viktor's understanding of mountaineering as an active sport: it forces one to overcome by getting the last out of oneself in life-threatening situations. And rope-comradeship is the all-important relational aspect of climbing. When Frankl returned from an exhausting lecture tour in the United States, his comrades watched out for him. A simple worker who was Viktor's *Seilkamerad* was heard to say, "We must be a little bit more concerned about the doctor. . . . It is a pity he is so out of shape."

The second book is an intensely personal one, written by Viktor. Christian Handl is an alpine photographer who picked up on Viktor's public talks and writings on alpinism. Viktor remembered an earlier version of the essay that Handl eventually published in the book together with his photographs. "I gave it first as a keynote lecture on the one hundredth anniversary of the famous alpine club at the Imperial Palace. And afterward I learned that a group of forty people, members of the club, had said, 'If this guy Frankl gives a keynote lecture we will leave the hall.' You see, the alpine club had a long tradition of anti-Semitism and for a long time had no Jewish members. . . . But when I gave the lecture nobody left the hall."

For the little book, Handl assembled some of his own stunning photographs of the Rax and persuaded Viktor to prepare the German text for this photo-essay of forty-seven pages, published in 1991. A translation of its title could be *The Mountain Experience and the Path to Meaning.*[2] In the foreword Handl explains that the book builds a bridge between nature and the mountain experience on one side and the human search for meaning on the other. Handl finds his own life-meaning in experiencing and photographing nature and mountaineering. For him the mountain adventure is new every day and—happily—it is removed from the pursuit of money and success.

There is only one man, Handl concludes, who can write about this topic because he has contemplated both the meaning question and mountain experience: Viktor Frankl. His books, confesses Handl, have "struck chords inside of me again and again."

The text of the book is vintage Viktor. He writes of his patients and their fears, asking, "Must one put up with everything? Can one not be stronger than his fears?" Then his favorite theme, the defiant power of the human spirit, is used to illuminate the challenge of climbing and of facing one's fears. In mountaineering one competes only with oneself and with nature, not against other athletes. And its demands may amount to "good stress."

Viktor cites Hans Selye, sometimes referred to as "Dr. Stress." Born in Vienna less than two years after Viktor, he was educated at Prague's Charles University and at other great schools abroad. Selye ended up in Canada where he pioneered physiological research on animal stress and then applied it to humans. Borrowing the concept of stress from physics and engineering (how much weight can a bridge take before it collapses?), he demonstrated the corrupting influence of extreme and prolonged stress on humans—how it lowers the defenses and depletes the resources of the organism.[3] He dedicated his landmark book "to those who are not afraid to enjoy the stress of a full life, nor so naive as to think that they can do so without intellectual effort." This may seem paradoxical, but Selye understood very well the importance of some stress to give life its spark, texture, color. Life without some stress and challenge is boring and unsatisfying. So he coined the term "eustress"—meaning the good kind of stress—and that is precisely the conclusion that Viktor draws as he turns to contemporary society and youth in his essay on climbing.

On one of his favorite themes, Viktor assails the notion that humans fundamentally seek to satisfy all needs and wishes, to avoid tension and seek pleasure. Certainly too much demand, too much stress, may evoke illness, but the tendency in society now is to avoid stress as far as possible. So the education of our young people is reluctant to challenge them for fear of creating tension.

But human beings *need* tension. It is the spice of life. And wholesome tension is set up in a kind of polar field, with the human person on one side and some goal or task on the other. Viktor writes that we should listen to him, the old neurologist. Nothing will help one overcome difficulties as much as a meaning, or something that waits for one to fulfill. He cites the international literature on prison camp survival—that the chances improve when one is oriented to the future, to some task to fulfill in freedom.

It is the pointlessness of living that affects so many young people today. Biologically underchallenged, we invent jogging and other sports to compensate. Viktor wrote elsewhere that the very absence of tension in our lives is related to the loss of meaning.[4] The "existential vacuum"—the sense of emptiness, the frustration of the will to meaning—occurs when life seems to be at its best, when there is little tension and abundant pleasure. In the mountains one does not choose the path of least resistance, but the most difficult route that one can safely handle. Even the rankings of "degrees of difficulty" arose from pushing back the borders of human possibility further and further. The horizon recedes as we approach it, and pressing toward it ever more gives life its zip and zest. When one reads about "flow" in the writings of Mihaly Csikszentmihalyi, his description of optimal experience dovetails with what Viktor described of his mountain experience.[5] Even when Viktor was too old to climb, to watch him lecture was to see "flow" in action—it is simply the way Viktor lived and worked. Once he decided something was meaningful and important, he held nothing back but threw all his strength at it. As Viktor pointed out in his lectures, the lesson from physiology is that an organ that has no demand placed upon it will atrophy. So it is with the human spirit.

Near the end of his mountain essay, Viktor becomes even more personal. "When we 'old folks' who have crossed the threshold into our ninth decade look back upon the experiences that the mountains and precipices and ridges have given us, a feeling of sadness may pass over our hearts. However, there exist some consoling words from a poet: 'No power on earth can take away what we have experienced.' "[6] This was one of the motifs of Viktor's life and outlook, which he expressed this way in another place: "In the past, nothing is irretrievably and irrevocably lost, but everything is permanently stored. Usually, to be sure, people see only the stubblefield of transitoriness—they do not see the full granaries into which they have brought the harvest of their lives: the deeds done, the works created, the loves loved, the sufferings courageously gone through."[7]

The final words of Viktor's mountain essay are these:[8]

In St. Ulrich in the Grödner Valley I once bought a plaque that expressed much more beautifully all that I have been saying:

Radiant days—
Do not weep
That they are gone
But smile
That they have been.

CHAPTER 14

Life at Home

IT IS IMPOSSIBLE to separate the home life of Viktor and Elly from their involvement with the wide world beyond Vienna. They were constantly on the move—from one lecture venue to another, one city to another, one continent to another. When they returned to Mariannengasse from globe-trotting there was no chance to disengage from the wider world—not even for one day. Rather, what awaited them was unpacking; ongoing local obligations; and the tall stacks of mail to be opened, read, discussed, and replied to; plus other messages, phone calls, and drop-in visitors. As soon as the correspondence was under control—if it ever was—they were packing again and heading for the airport.

Nevertheless, for the sake of the story, this chapter will look into their daily life between trips abroad. For somehow their stamina was renewed at base camp: Vienna; it was there that they had their small family and friends.

Viktor and Elly derived and rendered a camaraderie among their intimate friendships that was vital for them. Their get-togethers were marked as much by lofty conversation as by earthbound humor. Mutual encouragement was continuous, and in times of particular need they looked after one another. There was an uncommon closeness in the dire postwar situation; caught in the same predicament, people understood one another.

Before the work of logotherapy really got going, Viktor and Elly remembered, they had time for new friendships and they introduced each other to people who had been close to them before they married. For example, when Viktor introduced Elly to Erna Gsur—widow of Hubert whom the SS had executed nearby—the two women became devoted friends. There was Hertha Weiser, aunt of Tilly Frankl, and she became ever closer to Viktor and Elly, prolonging the bonds with Tilly's family.

The two women—Erna and Hertha—were often together with the Frankls in their home. Years later, when Erna was confined due to advancing age and illness, Viktor and Elly visited her very often.

Viktor met Elly's friends and family, and he became especially fond of her father, Leo Schwindt. Leo helped gather pieces of furniture for the Mariannengasse flat, actually delivering some of them with a wheelbarrow. Leo also helped install glass in the window frames that had been boarded up ever since the bombings. Viktor admired Leo very much for his humility, his kindness, and for the way he had stuck to his steadfast convictions right through the Nazi era.

Memory also tied the Frankls to Vienna. Naturally their preferences for particular places varied. Elly's happiest associations were with the waters of Kaisermühlen. Viktor was drawn back to the park and playgrounds of the Prater—but Elly had no nostalgia for that. "I hated the Prater, my whole life. Even in former times when Viktor wanted to go to the Prater, I hated it."

Newlyweds Viktor and Elly moved on from their old neighborhoods to put down new roots in Mariannengasse. As they settled more and more into their apartment, many things were changing for them. Soon, because of their work, they had to ration the time they could spend with friends. The former energy available for social life was drained away by the increasing stream of visitors from near and far, official and informal. Entertaining overnight guests became virtually impossible and the battle to preserve a measure of privacy was a losing one. Denied an ordinary life, Elly craved more than ever something she had wanted since childhood: a room of her own.

We remember that Elly, her brother Ali, and their parents had lived in a couple of rooms in their cramped apartment in Kaisermühlen, and when she finally moved in with Viktor there were still more than a dozen unrelated people living in the flat. As those tenants moved away, Viktor and Elly took over more of the apartment and Elly's dream came true. The rooms of the flat were spacious, airy, and—once the glass was replaced in the windows—flooded with daylight. Elly claimed a smaller room, ideally placed with access to the hallway and to Viktor's study. From there she could assist him readily but also could close the doors for privacy or move about the flat even while Viktor was shut in his study with callers and patients.

During a rambling conversation with the Frankls about their roots in

Vienna and their travels around the world, I told them about Carl Jung's attachment to his home. For Jung it was his family in Küsnacht, on Lake Zurich in Switzerland. He described it this way: "Particularly at this time, when I was working on the fantasies, I needed a point of support in 'this world.' It was most essential for me to have a normal life in the real world as a counterpoise to that strange inner world. My family and my profession remained the base to which I could always return, assuring me that I was an actually existing, ordinary person."[1]

As it turned out, Viktor and Elly could feel at home anywhere in the world. What made that possible were the excursions to the mountains, the familiarity of their place in Mariannengasse, and their small family.

THE TENSIONS BETWEEN the demands of their work and family life are signified by the Frankls' decision to have no more children after Gaby. As Viktor's work engulfed Elly she began to use a joking characterization that was shared later by the expanding family: "The meaning of logotherapy is work." From the time of Gaby's birth to her starting school, Elly fought off the encroaching demands of Viktor's work in order to care for Gaby and their household. This minimized Viktor's domestic chores and allowed him to focus on his work. Anyway, the parental roles were largely defined by the traditions of the day—in some ways a good thing since Viktor was so impractical in child care. He never changed a diaper or fed his little daughter, though there exists a humorous photograph of Viktor standing outdoors in the sunlight, holding a bottle up to the mouth of baby Gaby.

Still Gaby was the delight of both her papa and mama. They regretted then and later that they could not give Gaby as much of their time as she deserved. In looking back Elly said this one day: "Sometimes I think— and I became a mother in relatively young years—that two years after Gaby's birth I was involved in too much work with Viktor, but I tried to be a good mother and a good wife. Later when Gaby was in a kindergarten people told me that an only child needs to be with other children. . . . Viktor urged that we should send Gaby also to summer camp for two weeks. He said that she needs something like this, that it would be good for her. . . . Sometimes I think I have taken away from Gaby, but I always tried to do my best for her." Gaby did regret that she had been an only child but never felt cheated of parental attention. In fact, she believed that she had more contact with her parents than many other children had with theirs, for whenever her papa was not traveling he was available to her virtually always. As for storytelling, no one could match her papa. She was delighted with his clever myths and legends and he with her quick understanding and wide-eyed responses.

When he finished his work at the Poliklinik, on most days Viktor came home for lunch and a nap before tackling the work on his desk. Recalling this pattern, Gaby said that he was always ready for a chat with her, or just to have some fun, or even to argue. "You know how immediate and boundless his rapport was when he was with somebody." And even in the mornings, papa was just down the street at his office. So, for example, when Gaby received her good report cards from school, she would run over to the Poliklinik and up the stairs to Viktor's new office, certain that she would be welcomed by his staff and ushered in—after a few minutes at most if her father was attending to a patient.

Gaby remembers with particular fondness summer weekend outings when she was a little girl. Many of these were to the Rax Mountains, but not all. A favorite place for Gaby was Gänsehäufel—the swimming resort in the Old Danube in Kaisermühlen, right where her mother had grown up. The Frankls went there occasionally with Paul and Otti Polak. In advance, Viktor would phone to reserve a *Kabine* so they would not be faced with the blue flag that signified the resort was full. Lunch would be schnitzel and potato salad, packed ahead of time. (Viktor hated to see perfectly good potato salad—a favorite—packed up so tightly for a picnic across town.) The three Frankls would hop the "C" tram all the way to Gänsehäufel. But once there Viktor was typically more interested in discussing than in eating or swimming. He and Paul would spread their towels on the grass, as if setting up a symposium. There they would sit or lie down and carry on their intensive dialogues while the other family members enjoyed the water and surroundings.

Once again Elly was reminiscing as Viktor listened in. Her conversation was animated when she turned to Viktor's swimming ineptitude. Then he confessed it himself. "I am a very poor swimmer. Whenever I tried to swim I was always gladly surprised when I moved *forward*. Once I went to the Gänsehäufel myself, and there was a marker at fifty meters for swimming training. I wanted to conquer my poor swimming style, and so I had the ambition that I would like to swim—at any price—one kilometer without stopping. And after two hours I was having heart palpitations, but I insisted I must be stronger than that." Elly challenged, "But Viktor, how can you do such a silly thing?" He admitted that, on that occasion, he had been foolish indeed.

There was another simple family diversion, out in the open near the *Konzerthaus* in the city. The space was used in winter for skating and in summer for wrestling "performances." The wrestlers in the Heumarkt ring drew crowds of fans to jeer the bad guys and cheer the good guys. The Frankls enjoyed the spectacle, and sometimes they were accompanied by Willibald Sluga, a big man and a criminal psychiatrist who knew well the manner and language of the streets. On one occasion Elly made the mistake of cheering for the wrong wrestler, and the crowd surrounding the Frankls became edgy. But Big Willi Sluga knew how to settle them down. Viktor and Elly loved to laugh about the cries of that audience against her.

As we saw in the prologue, Viktor liked to get autographs of people he admired, and once—right in a local café—he spotted the wrestler Schurl Blemenschütz. He requested and obtained the man's autograph. Later, when Viktor and Elly were often in the United States, he was captivated by the *Muppet Show* on television and by Captain Kangaroo, whose autograph he cherished. When these shows came on, Viktor would drop whatever he was doing to watch. He even learned certain songs—such as "Java" or "Popcorn"—and did his own renderings and impressions. In fact, Viktor, with his rather large trunk and spindly legs, liked the image of himself as Kermit the Frog, and his large-framed sister Stella became Big Bird. The entire Frankl family enjoyed these caricatures, but no one was more enchanted with them than Viktor. Over the years Elly collected little decorative frogs fashioned out of pewter, porcelain, or whatever. She had a cabinetful on display in her room.

STEPPING BACK TO the time of Gaby's birth, sometime during the 1947 Christmas season Professor and Frau Pötzl dropped by for a holiday visit with Viktor and Elly and to celebrate the arrival of baby Gaby. Although Viktor already had a hundred hilarious stories to tell about his mentor Pötzl, he was ever ready to add another. No one knew what the absent-minded old genius would do next. It could be unnerving to be with Pötzl socially until one got to know him. His attention jumped from one thing to another and, smack in the middle of a conversation, his whole demeanor would change abruptly and he would shift to a completely unconnected topic.

Elly recalled that Pötzl "was very often in this apartment together with his wife. I was at that time very young and he was a famous man, of course. When I greeted him, '*Grüss Gott, Herr Professor*,' he smiled and shouted, '*Grüss Gott!*'—and it was over in one second." Pötzl's smile vanished instantaneously. "Even in a fraction of a second," Viktor stressed. "He was so mentally absent that, when Elly addressed him, in a split second his mind was sticking to something else!"

An example of Pötzl's absentmindedness occurred on this holiday visit, about a month after Gaby was born. Among the various residents still sharing the flat with the Frankls was a five-year-old. As they started describing this incident, Viktor and Elly were so enthusiastic that they competed in telling the story simultaneously. "Pötzl took off his coat and suddenly there came out from the kitchen this little five-year-old girl. When Pötzl saw her he said, 'Ah, look at the little Gaby. How grown up she is!' " Viktor and Elly were in stitches, partly over my disbelief that Pötzl could be that far out. Viktor continued, "So I said, 'But excuse me, Herr Professor. This is the daughter of our neighbor.' " Then Pötzl recovered a bit, "Oh, I see. Yes, I myself thought she was too big for her age." This is the same Pötzl whose successor at the Psychiatric Clinic, Hans Hoff, said at the time of Pötzl's death, "I know of no other person who had a more profound knowledge of the functions of the cerebrum than Pötzl."[2] Brilliance and wisdom resided in Pötzl right alongside his eccentricities and idiosyncrasies, which the Frankls and others found immensely winsome.

It was all but impossible to interrupt the Frankls when they were swapping Pötzl stories. It was Elly's turn and her story was about Frau Pötzl. The incident is difficult to translate across cultures, but it was not unusual in 1950s Vienna for a woman of means to boast about her furs by saying such things as, "Isn't my new raccoon marvelous?" or "I have bought me a fox." Elly told this story about Frau Pötzl.

"She was a very beautiful woman. Beautiful. But she was also spacey. And once I was going to the center of the city from here, and the bus was crowded. I stood there with many, many people. And suddenly someone shouted at me, 'Frau Frankl, where are you going?' 'I am going to the city.' 'What are you doing in the city?' 'I have something to buy.' And suddenly," Elly continued, "she shouted out, 'Don't buy a horse!' "

Certain that I had missed something, I pressed, "What? A horse?" Viktor seized at my skepticism, "What she meant as she was shouting over the heads of thirty people was, 'Look here, I have this horsehide coat, and it has no fur!' " Viktor and Elly were having a roaring good time and I was swept into their great pleasure. Viktor continued with yet another story.

"Once I was giving a lecture in the middle hall of the *Konzerthaus*. Both Professor and Frau Pötzl came to the lecture, and afterward she met Elly. And in her Bohemian accent, she said, *'Mein Mann da Pötzl...'* "— and the Frankls broke up laughing while I waited again to get it. Frau Pötzl never called her spouse "my husband" but "my man the Pötzl." Viktor chortled, "Don, can you imagine Elly calling me, *'Mein Mann der Frankl?'* " Elly howled, too.

This is what Frau Pötzl had said to Elly after Viktor's lecture: *"Mein Mann da Pötzl, der hat mir nach dem Vortrag von Ihrem Mann gesagt, 'Der Frankl ist kein Frankl. Er ist ein ProPHET!'* "—"My man the Pötzl, after the lecture, said, 'The Frankl is no Frankl. He is a proPHET!' " On that final word Viktor's voice broke into a loud, high falsetto. According to Elly that is exactly the way Frau Pötzl had spoken, and she avowed Viktor's imitation as a faithful one: "He is a proPHET!"

As soon as Viktor launched another story, Elly fell into anticipatory giggles. "One time Frau Pötzl met Elly in the passageway to Alser Strasse, and she said, 'Frau Frankl, you cannot believe what I am going through, that I have to carry all these things all day because my maid is ill. I have to do all the shopping!' And the only thing she had in her hands was a quarter pound of coffee!"

Heinz von Foerster, one of the pioneers of cybernetics and cognitive science, was a friend and contemporary of Viktor.[3] On an occasion shortly after the war, von Foerster was at the Mariannengasse flat with the Frankls and the Pötzls. Von Foerster, as he readily confessed, liked to entertain with magic tricks—for him only a hobby. In good-natured fashion he asked Mrs. Pötzl to hide a coin under the carpet, which she did dutifully. Then von Foerster—after some sleight of hand—told her to find the coin, but apparently it had disappeared. Viktor recalled, "She was so impressed by this that she whispered to me, 'Doesn't he make this by hypnosis? Otherwise it is impossible to explain this!' " While Professor von Foerster did not remember the specific incident, he laughed when I told him about it, saying that it sounded likely.

The Frankls found enormous enjoyment in this recollection and, after telling me about Frau Pötzl, Elly lamented, "But this cannot happen now. No one is such a funny person—at the same moment a great person with her own style." "Naive and very human, with a warm heart. And we enjoyed her," Viktor added.

IN THE MARIANNENGASSE *Haus* were other flats and residents, of course, but there was no neighbor who became as dear to the Frankls as Hermi Ecker. Hermi still lives in the ground-floor flat at Mariannengasse, where she has been caretaker of the building since before World War II. She remembered the living situation into which Viktor Frankl had come by himself in 1945. Later, after Elly moved into his flat, she and Hermi became the best of friends. They often visited with one another, especially when Viktor was extremely busy or away. He also loved Hermi very much and they all trusted her implicitly. The Frankls agreed that Hermi, a devout Roman Catholic, is the kind of person whose integrity and natural kindness cause one to think that her religion must be a great one indeed. They even trusted Hermi to sort their daily mail into piles in their apartment while they traveled. As for money, they quipped that Hermi would never steal a penny but might *add* some money to whatever she found in the flat! And it was Hermi who became Gaby's favorite babysitter, a godsend to both Gaby and her parents.

Of course Gaby had favorite places to play: the courtyard garden of the sprawling General Hospital just across Spitalgasse from their home; even more, the beautiful little garden of the Pötzls, who were living nearby in an apartment of the University Psychiatric Clinic (which no longer exists there). Professor Pötzl gave to the Frankls a key to this garden so that they could bring Gaby there to play whenever they wished. "Gaby practically grew up in that garden."

Before long Gaby was a schoolgirl and a good student. Early on she was confronted with anti-Semitism in public school. A certain teacher made damaging remarks about Jewish people, and Gaby told her parents about it when she came home from school. In response to this, Viktor did something new.

> I started applying corrective measures so that Gaby could say to herself, "I know better." If we had Jewish visitors from abroad or wherever, I noticed that Gaby was also impressed, and when they left our apartment I said, interspersing, "And you know, Gaby, that these people were Jewish." . . . I did this so that retro-

spectively she would believe that Jews are good people, and thereby I was counteracting any remark that would imply that Jews are bad people.

When the topic of conversation shifted back to the social circles of the medical/psychiatric establishment, Elly and Viktor remembered particular get-togethers, and Hans Hoff came to mind again. Following meetings of the Society for Medical Psychology, its leaders typically went to a restaurant to continue interacting with famous visitors and physicians. At one such gathering a Roman Catholic priest quietly pressed Viktor for an assessment of Hoff, whom the priest thought was too materialistic. At the time Hoff was a candidate to head up the Psychiatric Clinic and the priest was a relatively high-ranking churchman on the "search committee." Instead of answering directly, Viktor simply asked the priest how significant such a characteristic (materialism) might be in the actual practice of neurology.

Musing over the old days, Elly said, "Viktor, when I think back on all these people we have known—heads of the departments and their wives and families—you never really fit in this society." Viktor agreed, "They tended to be highbrow." "And I would have been very unhappy," said Elly. "I never would belong to this group. Their main wish was to get a larger villa and a larger car and so on. . . . Sometimes ladies on the street, the wives of wealthy doctors, told me, 'My goodness. I have a Porsche and now I have a swimming pool.' So what?"

Viktor elaborated, "The greatest rewards [that people desire]—money and things—I never aspired for these." When Elly said, "So we are free, and we enjoy it," Viktor roared joyfully, "Really!"

THROUGH THE YEARS, Elly went to Kaisermühlen to see her parents as often as she could and Viktor went with her on occasion. As her parents aged, Elly and her Tante Mitzi looked after their needs, but eventually Elly's mother was suffering from Alzheimer's disease and no longer recognized her own loved ones. As Elly was recounting those years and the passing of her parents, she pointed out family photographs of her father and mother. "Here is my father, approximately two years before he died. . . . He died in '75, and it was my greatest wish that father and mother should die in my arms. And you wouldn't believe that he did die in my arms." Leo Schwindt passed away at the age of seventy-four, and Viktor recalled the circumstances. "On a walk in the Vienna Woods he suddenly had pains in the abdomen. He was hospitalized, and people first thought it was kidney failure. But in half an hour it turned out to be something different. It was a rupture of the abdominal aorta . . . and when we talked with the surgeon he said that theoretically one can operate, but at Leo's age and under the circumstances it would most likely end with death on the operating table." "Today they could do more," Elly surmised, "but at that time the procedures were not so advanced. And then much later, in 1988, I was with my mother twenty minutes before she died—I had to leave because Viktor had to be at a reception with Kurt Waldheim [then Austria's president]. But my mother was already in a coma when I left her, and in a sense she was gone."

Viktor recalled that day as well. "Elly arrived at the reception at the court of the president—it was a reception for people who had emigrated and Waldheim had invited them back to Vienna." Their recollections synchronized as Elly added, "And Sissy Waldheim, his wife, kissed me and was so thankful that I came in such a situation—she knew that my mother was dying. . . . And it was at a time when Kurt Waldheim was being bombarded with hate from all over the world."

On an occasion when I was with Elly and Viktor for a visit with Tante Mitzi in her flat next to the old Schwindt family apartment in Kaisermühlen, Viktor sat with me at a small table while Elly and Mitzi chatted near her bed. He explained to me, "It was here in this apartment that Elly took care of her mother near the time of her death. From seven in the morning until ten at night Elly would be here." Elly overheard this and added a nuance, "It was Mitzi who took care of my mother when she was so sick, and this made it possible for me to travel with Viktor. What Mitzi has done is unbelievable."

IN AUGUST 1962 it had been exactly seventeen years since Viktor's return to Vienna from the concentration camps. He was fifty-seven and at the top of his form, prodigious in writing and lecturing, traveling the world, and heading up neurology at the Poliklinik. Visitors from near and far were coming to him, and the Frankls were constantly deciding which international invitations they could reasonably accept. The daily routines at home were well established as he and Elly managed the flow of work. Gaby was a teenager making her way through high school.

The only reason to tell my own early Vienna story is to provide a glimpse into the lives of the Frankls in the 1960s. I was a young student when I met Professor Frankl for the first time in September 1962. Earlier that summer I had graduated college and my professor had planted the idea of studying with Frankl or even pursuing a doctoral degree in Vienna.[4]

When I arrived in the city I was a naive and impressionable youth without a word of German. During the ten months of my stay I had only the thinnest grasp of the events in which the Frankls' lives were embedded. I recall being struck by how many disabled men were on the streets, and I assumed they were war veterans. It was nearly two decades since the defeat of Hitler, and these men for the most part were still getting by despite missing limbs and lost capabilities. It seemed so ironic that they had fought *for* the Nazi cause, however reluctantly or eagerly.

Austria was beautiful and its capital enchanting that fall. Soon I was renting a splendid room advertised by a kindly and quiet German widow. With no elevator in the building, I marveled that lame and aging people managed to climb the circling stairway daily. Upon leaving in the mornings I often passed older women carrying their cloth bags laden with groceries, pausing on landings to catch their breath as they ascended. Copying the neighbors, I learned to take my own empty milk bottle for refilling by ladle from an open tub at the store. In the little bakery on the corner they called me "Mr. Kennedy"—the locals were so proud of President Kennedy for facing down the Soviet Union in the Cuban missile crisis that October.

The apartment living I experienced that winter was much like that of the Frankls. My room had the mandatory creaking parquet floor and a chandelier hung from the center of the high ceiling. As in the Frankl flat the windows opened on the street below, which was bustling with commerce and traffic. In each flat was the typical coal stove—the only source of heat. The Frankls kept warm in their much larger flat as Elly carried wood and coal each day from the ground floor, then fired up the stove in Viktor's study. Keeping the doors open between rooms cut the chill throughout their apartment.

I attended Professor Frankl's twice-weekly lectures, in English and German, in the Poliklinik's lecture theater—the *Hörsaal*. Its white curving benches were arranged in steep rows, and we looked down to the front-center where Frankl paced as he lectured, scribbling on the chalkboard and occasionally projecting slides on the screen. Now and again he would integrate an interview of a psychiatric patient into his presentations. There was always an air of excitement in the room. Facing him from the left front rows were visitors from various countries, and sometimes he introduced or referred to them.

Though I was one among many students, Frankl and I became acquaintances and he arranged for me to be in his neurology department, with him on occasion but more often with his assistant, Kurt Kocourek. I sat in on sessions of small group psychotherapy and sometimes I observed Professor Frankl in his daily office interactions. I still have my notebooks from the lectures and memories of foreign visitors, including a particular American professor.

Ostensibly this professor was in Vienna to study with Frankl and, as I remember it, had some German or Austrian background himself. But it seemed that he was making the least of his opportunities as he quietly came and went. Following a lecture, Frankl typically stood around chatting with people who remained. On one occasion, when these interactions subsided, Frankl noticed that the American professor had slipped out again without a word. He turned to me and asked in a booming voice, "Where in the world is Professor _____?" "Sorry, but I have no idea." I was amused by the situation, but Professor Frankl was not amused that his mature American scholar had sneaked out while even I, the young student, had remained.

As it happened, one afternoon I spotted the American professor on Währinger Strasse near the formerly smelly Anatomical Institute. He was standing by the curb and looked very sad and lonely. When I greeted him I saw at once that he had been crying. I inquired, "How are you?" "You see, I have a broken shoelace but I don't know the German word so I can't ask for a new pair." This surprised me since he knew more German than I by far, but I urged him to come with me into a shoe repair shop. I simply lifted my foot, tugged at my own shoelace, and asked, *"Haben Sie so?"* The shopkeeper opened a box of assorted shoelaces and my professor-companion selected what he needed. Back out on the street he thanked me profusely. I recall thinking that the combination of loneliness in the unfamiliar city and Frankl's rambunctious manner had overwhelmed the poor guy. On the other hand, though I also was lonely at times, I was thriving—captivated by the city as well as by Frankl's unique style.

That fall I was unaware of Professor Pötzl and of the exceptional re-lationship between him and Frankl. In fact, Pötzl had died a few months earlier, April 1, 1962, at the age of eighty-four. I learned from Viktor and Elly that near the end Pötzl had lost his mental faculties. Viktor visited him in the hospital and returned to Mariannengasse deeply saddened that such a great man should die disoriented and demented. After witnessing Pötzl's decline, Frankl ever after wished and expressed to Elly his hope that—whatever suffering might accompany his own eventual passing—he might retain his mental capacities to the end.

Though the Frankls' personal lives were out of my sight that year, I was aware not only of international visitors but also of the periods when the Frankls were traveling abroad. For weeks at a time there would be no lectures, but I continued to go to the Poliklinik and also to attend lectures in the university psychology department.

My *Studienbuch* (a small student record book of courses with profes-sors' signatures and innumerable rubber stampings) for that year is the same format as Frankl's for his postwar PhD studies. And though I did not know it then, Professor Frankl's life and mine were intersecting with the person of Professor Hubert Rohracher (1903–72), head of the university psychology department. Rohracher was more scientist than philosopher and a pioneer in brain research. He authored textbooks and articles, many of them reporting his studies in neurological psychology. I faithfully at-tended Rohracher's lectures in the huge Auditorium Maximum. (Another student, of whom I was unaware at the time, also attended the Rohracher lectures in 1962–63—Franz Vesely, soon to become husband of Gaby Frankl.)

I knew that the university had been devastated by the loss of its many Jewish professors under Hitler and I knew that the Nazis readily had de-ported non-Jews for any resistance. But recently I learned much more from Giselher Guttmann, Rohracher's former student who succeeded him as head of psychology—the same Guttmann who had become Viktor's friend and rope comrade. During the Hitler years Rohracher was known to be anti-Nazi. In fact, he stopped his research completely during the war, refusing to resume it until after the Nazi defeat. Guttmann speculated that Rohracher had not only survived the Nazis but also remained in his uni-versity position because the Nazis were interested in Rohracher's research for their own purposes and considered him potentially useful.

In the years immediately after the war, it was University of Vienna philosophy professor Leo Gabriel who urged Frankl to pick up his philosophical and psychological studies for a PhD. Frankl had already completed some semesters under Karl and Charlotte Bühler—two leading lights in the history of psychology in Vienna—and needed only a couple of semesters more. And for the doctoral dissertation, Gabriel accepted Frankl's German manuscript for *The Unconscious God.* Frankl had oral examinations with Professor Kraft, a philosopher of language, and a second exam with Rohracher. As that oral exam went along, Frankl recalled, Rohracher was making notes on particular ideas they discussed, saying that these would be useful in his lectures. Nevertheless, in the end Rohracher did not give Frankl a high grade (*Sehr gut*), explaining that it should not appear that the PhD had been obtained easily (since Frankl was already a university lecturer). Viktor noted with a touch of amusement that this was a typically Viennese manner of doing things at that time. Professor Gabriel told Viktor that Rohracher confessed that he had underrated Frankl, who really should be acknowledged for adding a complementary new dimension to psychology. Viktor obtained his PhD in 1949 under Gabriel, Kraft, and Rohracher.

AS WINTER FELL on my student year in Vienna, the city turned damp, dark, and cold. In the fall sunshine and in my excitement over my new experiences, I had not noticed the marred face of the old city. Under gray and chilly skies the worn edges of Vienna's former greatness became apparent. Against winter snows the aging buildings with their caked-on soot appeared more black than gray. As soon as white snow accumulated on the streets it turned ugly with traffic grime and the coal dust spewing from thousands of chimneys.

By late winter I had decided to return to Connecticut at the end of the academic year. When I told Professor Frankl that I would be leaving Vienna in June, he offered me a chance to take in more of university psychiatry while there was still time. I responded with enthusiasm, and on the spot he telephoned his colleague, Professor Hans Asperger, chief of the University Children's Clinic. I went to Asperger's office where he arranged a "clerkship" for me. I was given a lab coat and assigned a locker at the *Heilpädagogischen Ambulanz* (outpatient remedial clinic for children).

For a couple of mornings each week for three months I observed (*hospi-tieren*) the treatment of children who had psychiatric disorders. To this day Professor Asperger is known for his identification of a pervasive developmental disorder similar to autism, which is called Asperger's Disorder.[5] The opportunity for me, a professional nobody, to be in Asperger's clinic I owed to Professor Frankl.

I continued into spring, attending all of Frankl's lectures. He invited me to his home, and there I met Elly for the first time, though I had seen her on occasion at the Poliklinik. I was in their flat only a couple of times but remember that Professor Frankl was particularly interested in what I thought of a manuscript he was drafting in English. I was quite at ease responding despite my youth and inexperience. I have no recollection of seeing the back room, which today is a makeshift storeroom cluttered with thousands of files, documents, trophies, certificates, awards, films, and photographs. Most of the time that large room was closed off like a closet, even to the end of Viktor's life. Much of its contents is now being archived with support from the city of Vienna.

When I left Vienna in June 1963, I carried away my *Studienbuch*, a certificate from Professor Asperger, and a longer letter of recommendation from Professor Frankl. Back in the States, I completed my education but my résumé only noted my year in Vienna. I had virtually no contact with the Frankls until our reacquaintance thirty years later. I say virtually because of some incidental contact during those decades.

In the mid-1960s when I was a student in Minnesota, I went to a packed lecture hall in the Twin Cities to hear Frankl speak, but there was no chance to greet him personally—he was swamped by people wherever he spoke. Then in the early 1970s my wife and I were living in Connecticut and occasionally went to New York City for a break. On one outing we were walking along Times Square where Seventh Avenue intersects Broadway. In front of the Metropole jazz club I spotted the Frankls walking toward us. We stopped them and, with the help of a few cues they remembered me. After introducing Jan to them, the Frankls said they were heading out the next day on a lecture tour. We chatted awhile, amused that we had met by chance at such a time and place. During our consultations for this book twenty years later, Viktor and Elly remembered that Times Square encounter.

On one other occasion I talked with Professor Frankl from a phone booth in central Vienna. It was 1990 and Jan and I were living in Chicago with our two sons, who were finishing high school. To mark that milestone we took a family motor tour of Europe that summer. In Vienna, I showed them my old haunts and wanted to visit the Frankls if possible. With a number from the telephone directory in the booth, I dialed. Viktor's voice was clear as he answered simply and characteristically, "Frankl." I explained that we were in the city and, if he had time, perhaps I or we could stop by. Either he did not remember me or for some reason seemed distracted. But he was cordial as usual, and with an apology summarized his obligations for the next few days. We concluded that there would be no chance for a visit, so I left my greetings with Professor Frankl and did not call again. I was aware that little had changed in his life, except that he sounded busier than ever.

FOR THE FRANKLS in the early years, their at-home routines were already well established. As Viktor awakened each morning, Elly brought him strong coffee to start his day—nothing else for breakfast. He remained in bed for half an hour or more, making notes or writing. Then he showered, shaved, and dressed. Before leaving for the Poliklinik he dictated to Elly, who took shorthand. During the morning, while Viktor was at the hospital, Elly typed the correspondence and then around noon took the letters over to Viktor for his signature. Sister Hilda at the Poliklinik typically took the letters from there to the post office as Viktor returned home for lunch with Elly and to continue his work there in the afternoon. Mail deliveries came twice a day, early morning and midafternoon, Elly remembered. "We had Gaby, who was very young, and there was so much to do. It was a very hard time. But I was so *full* of strength and energy." I guessed aloud that the load of work might have killed a frail or weaker person. "I think so," Elly agreed. "Over the years we learned a lot and got smarter. Otherwise even we would not have survived all the work. The mailman brought up the mail because it could not fit in the box downstairs. We have often wondered how we could do all this."

When Viktor was eighty-three and Elly sixty-three, people in Buenos Aires asked them for a description of their daily life. Together they made some notes about a typical day at home. That was in 1988, and the notes show that basically their routines were still similar, though breakfasts had improved and Viktor was retired from the Poliklinik. Here is a summary of what they wrote together.

Elly is up early and does some of the housework, and Viktor awakens between seven and eight o'clock. Elly provides him with very strong coffee and prepares a simple breakfast that they eat together, typically orange juice and some cereal with milk. Viktor returns to his bed to dictate manuscripts and correspondence and to read from the heaps of books piled on his desk. Because of Viktor's intense need for privacy and quiet while he works, for these hours no one is invited to the apartment and no one comes in to help with housekeeping either, though this is mostly because it is difficult for Viktor to trust other people with his papers. Everything has to be in its place, and Elly seems to be the only one who understands.

Each day typically two dozen letters arrive. They read all the correspondence and sort it into piles of priority. Then Viktor and Elly decide together how each letter should be answered, and he settles back in bed with a dictation machine on the chair beside him. He talks through the piles while Elly goes out for shopping and on other errands. When she returns, she and Viktor share a simple lunch: cheese or ham, fruits and vegetables, and very dark brown bread.

After lunch Viktor takes a short snooze and Elly begins typing the dictation of the morning. He rises again after his nap and takes more strong coffee before returning to his work on speeches and on the manuscripts, books, dissertations, and reprints that also arrived in the morning mail. Since Viktor's vision is starting to fail, increasingly Elly reads and underlines more and more of this material. The telephone interrupts many times during each day—invitations from all over the world, people wanting free logotherapy by telephone for half an hour or more, sometimes even calling collect!

Viktor and Elly work late every day, and he keeps going sometimes until 1:30 in the morning. No vacations ever, with the exception of those weekends mountaineering—though as the years passed even in the climbing season it might be several weeks between treks in the mountains. They might go two or three years between attending the theater or a concert or movie.

In the four years before the Frankls made these notes about their daily routines, Elly also was caring for her ill and aging mother—up at four o'clock to catch the early streetcar to Kaisermühlen. Before Elly returned to Mariannengasse around eight o'clock, when Viktor needed her, she would help her mother by preparing meals, cleaning the apartment, and so on. Then the normal day began for Viktor and her.

After Viktor's death, Elly reflected on those years of hard work. "Without a very deep love we never could have done it. It would have been impossible for me. Viktor was not a bad man, but he was out of touch and did his work with little understanding of practical things. To change a light bulb was almost too much."

Of the sacrifices they made, neither Elly nor Viktor was regretful. Here are the closing words of the notes on their 1988 routines: "Elly feels that she has to satisfy her conscience which commands her to offer all the sacrifices without receiving recognition or gratitude from others. Viktor feels more than ever in his life being responsible for keeping his work available to anyone who is in need of it and doing what he can so that others may take the torch and carry it on. . . . But it would mean doing injustice to our fate if we did not mention the great balm on our souls: our grandchildren, Katharina Rebekka and Alexander David!"

A MENTION OF the grandchildren was unusual for the Frankls outside of family and intimate friendships. Generally Viktor and Elly were private people when it came to family and, in fact, in thousands of lectures Viktor said no word about Elly, Gaby, or their grandchildren. But in the close-knit circle of their family Viktor and Elly were at home, and they relied on these few loved ones. Family, like faith, were bedrock for Viktor. So much so that he had little need to draw public notice to either.

Gaby was still a teenager when she first met Franz Vesely, a student working on his doctorate in physics. She herself became a PhD student in psychology, with particular interests in child and developmental areas, not psychotherapy. During their student years Gaby and Franz became close friends, and eventually she invited him home to meet her parents. At the Mariannengasse flat Franz was unnerved by the behavior of Viktor and Elly. Having grown up in a quiet family, where feelings were kept in check and voices were not raised, Franz was completely unprepared for the boisterous banter between Professor and Frau Frankl, and was surprised to find Gaby joining in! He watched as passionate feelings flowed out unchecked as the Frankls disagreed openly with one another, sometimes shouting in a manner that left Franz wide-eyed. His first thought was that the Frankls were kidding, putting on an act for him. But that thought was worn down over a period of weeks, as every time Franz visited he saw the same interactive style. To someone new, Viktor and Elly and Gaby even appeared rude to one another. Franz wondered if the Frankl marriage was in crisis. When Gaby slammed a door in frustration, Franz wondered what he was getting into. Later he joked about it, but at the time he actually weighed the wisdom of becoming part of such a family. In time he realized that the Frankls were just being themselves—literally and utterly. They actually seemed to thrive on cranked-up dialogue.

Before Franz met the Frankls he knew little or nothing about Viktor's work. The first time they met, Viktor gave him a copy of *The Doctor and the Soul* (in German, of course). Franz remembered that when he started to read it, "I couldn't put it down. It was wonderful writing and great ideas. And I wondered, 'Who is this guy, really?' "

Viktor and Elly took to Franz, and in 1968 they invited him and Gaby to accompany them on a United States speaking tour covering thirteen cities in twelve days. They would sleep in a hotel and leave early the next morning in a small plane for another nonstop lecture day. On the flights Franz sat behind Elly and she swore that he turned green. "I was laughing about Franz, and after our trip Gaby said she never would go on such a trip again—that she couldn't survive it." Franz, exhausted by the adventure, also vowed that this would be his only lecture tour with the Frankls.

FRANZ AND GABY married in July 1969 in a civil ceremony at the Währinger Strasse headquarters of the Ninth District—the very same building where Viktor and Elly had been married more than two decades earlier and where Viktor had done his suicide prevention work with students when he himself was still in medical school.

The wedding was a high point for the Frankls and Veselys, and for Franz it was a momentous day for two reasons. He married Gaby, actually overcoming his ambivalence about joining the outlandish and wonderful Frankl clan—having said earlier that "either I have to give up Gaby and get out or I must marry her and go into this family." Second, only a couple of hours after the marriage ceremony he received his PhD in physics at university ceremonies.

Franz and Gaby also had an ecumenical religious ceremony at Christ the King Church in Orinda, California, October 12, 1969. Many Jewish family friends attended and three clergy officiated: Tom MacDonald, a Catholic priest, George Vlahos, a Greek Orthodox priest, both friends of the family, and the pastor of the parish. Pregnant at the time, Gaby had to find a suitable wedding dress for the occasion.

Gaby resisted getting too involved with the work of logotherapy. Franz told me that she decided, when their children were born, that for her vocation she would be a mother. Taking a long "baby break" after the birth of Katja was consistent with Gaby's family commitment and gave her a chance to apply what she knew about human development. Viktor said, "And look at the result." The Veselys' two children are Katharina (Katja), born February 12, 1970, and Alexander, May 20, 1974. These two grandchildren opened up a new world of joy for Viktor and Elly. Their mother had completed her dissertation in 1973, but took her doctoral exams and obtained her PhD in July 1981.

When Katja was a little girl she was often with Viktor, listening to his stories and playing games. She wanted to marry him when she grew up, and Elly remembered that "she dressed up for him, putting on this and that, and they walked together throughout the whole apartment so proudly and holding hands. . . . She was so lively. How Viktor enjoyed this!" It was one of Katja's own favorite memories, too.

> In my preschool days I loved dressing up. When I was allowed to sleep over at my grandparents'—always a treat in itself—I used to wrap myself in my grandmother's dark red bedspread; then she would pin brooches all over my red "gown." I'd borrow all her long necklaces—very '70s—and play bride. Next, I would marry my grandfather by just walking through the whole flat by his side very slowly. Elly sang the wedding march and carried my train. I wonder what Freud would say about this one!
>
> My grandfather also invented two characters for us children. They were "Bof" and "Nebof" and were played by Viktor's feet. Lying in bed, he made his feet talk to one another under the covers. One with a very high-pitched voice, the other with a very low voice.

When little Alexander came along, he had his happy times with the grandparents, but not because Viktor was a wonder at the chores of child care. On one occasion when Elly and Gaby went out together they left Alexander at home alone with Viktor. Alex was about a year old and crawling about. As Elly told it, "We returned after one hour or so and Viktor opened the door, 'Thanks to heaven you are back!' So we asked, 'Why, what has happened?' " Viktor explained that little Alex was very unhappy. When Elly and Gaby entered the room, Alex was under Viktor's desk and they could smell the problem at once. He needed fresh diapers but Viktor seemed helpless—he had no idea what was wrong with the little boy. "Even his nose didn't notice it!" Elly said. Then her demeanor changed in the flood of memories. "Even now I can see little Alexander sitting here with his grandfather. . . . With both grandchildren Viktor played very often and, oh my, how they would laugh together!"

Viktor loved the spontaneity of the little children. He described an incident in which he took particular delight. "In the central synagogue of Vienna, we went together to a Friday evening service and took with us our grandson—maybe four years old or so. There was a ceremony where wine is served, and at the end one takes a sip. We were honored by the *shamas*, who seated us in the loge. And the *shamas* told Alexander to come and take a sip. When Alexander tasted the sweet wine, he held up the cup for more. The people who saw this were laughing. It was absolutely natural. This story we have not told."

Some time after Viktor's death I asked Alexander what he loved most about his grandpa. "Maybe his 'entertainer' abilities—as when he did impersonations or imitations of animals such as a rooster. I loved his dry humor—a funny comment on almost any situation. As you know, there are two telephones in the Mariannengasse apartment. When I was a kid, he would make calls from one room to the other, changing his voice and taking on two characters he had invented for us—'Bof' and 'Nebof.' One was a smart one and one was a stupid character. It was *so funny!*"

"Also," Alex went on, "my grandpa and I discovered strange similarities in behavior." They both could draw caricatures and did it well. And somehow, Viktor's gifts for impersonations turned up in Alexander. Neither had training in music nor could they read notes, yet both could sing—Viktor once was invited by his rabbi to be the cantor for synagogue worship, and Alex passed an aptitude audition for opera. There were little things, too, Alexander recalls: "We both spit after someone sneezed to avoid getting infected. And we held a fork in the same funny way." I noticed when we ate together that Viktor held his fork in the oddest way and learned that Alex did the same thing naturally. When Viktor tried to teach me to hold a fork that way he soon gave up in frustration and put me in my place, "This is something for which you have no capability." (But I was used to having him point out my inadequacies. Once when the Frankls were having coffee, I declined the offer of some by saying, "I never drink it, thank you." Viktor-the-coffee-addict rebuked me at once: "Then you shouldn't have been given a visa to visit Vienna.")

"And your grandma?" I asked Alex. "Her cooking! Spaghetti never tasted so good. Even vegetables that I did not like at home tasted great when she cooked them—and they still do. She was wonderful at playing with kids, and there was always so much at Mariannengasse to play with."

Once I asked Elly if Viktor ever did the cooking and she laughed. "Several times he tried to cook his 'Existentialist Stew.' This was a stew where you put in everything you can find and that is what he named it. It had potatoes, meat, *Wurst,* vegetables." "Did you eat it?" "I had to eat it," Elly snickered. "And once he prepared Mother's Day breakfast for me. Oh my goodness. It was coffee with sour milk and I didn't know; but I couldn't drink it. When he cooked I was behind him and everything was a mess, but this was no problem for him. I always thought he would start a fire— that he was dangerous in the kitchen. . . . But he enjoyed it, and he was always asking me how to do this or that." Again, that boyish delight in learning something new. Perhaps it was fortunate that he was not good at feeding the children—he then might also have cooked for them.

In Viktor's last year he spoke lovingly of his family, perhaps even more than usual. He said this of Franz Vesely: "The best son-in-law there can be, and I tell you that this is the first time that I ever said something like this." In times of crisis I watched Franz carefully advising and assisting the Frankls. At one of those times Elly said, "In a way our life together is very rich. To find a son-in-law of this caliber is a real gift. He has become like a son to us."

So with their family Viktor and Elly increasingly settled into a profound contentment after experiencing the devastation of war and hatred. Viktor never ceased to draw upon the memories of his father and mother and Tilly, but over time, since he was human, memories alone were not enough. He lived on with his memories and thrived in the loyal affection of Elly, Gaby and Franz, Katja, and Alexander.

OF COURSE, AS head of Poliklinik neurology, Frankl mentored many medical students and young physicians, mainly from Austria or nearby. During the course of my research I had the opportunity to interview Lotte

Bodendorfer and Alfried Längle. While I did not interview Elizabeth Lukas—my focus has been biographical—her outstanding work in logotherapy is widely known.

Lotte Bodendorfer was one of Viktor's earliest students. She went on to practice psychiatry in Sweden and, when we met in Uppsala, she was enthusiastic in her conversation about Frankl; she described the terrible postwar conditions in Vienna in 1947. At that time she was invited by another medical student to hear Frankl at the Poliklinik. They arrived early but there was only standing room in the lecture theater, which was abuzz until Professor Frankl walked in and took his place. Bodendorfer wrote of that lecture, "If this was part of medicine, then I wanted to become a psychiatrist. For the first time I heard how to help a mentally disturbed patient. But this was not the only gift of this lecture. In these depressing postwar times where it didn't seem worthwhile to make plans because everything was so meaningless, came a message of courage and hope."[6]

Of Elizabeth Lukas, a preeminent student of Frankl in a later era, he was enduringly very proud. She has distinguished herself by careful scientific work, publications, and the training of logotherapists at the Southern German Institute of Logotherapy in Munich, of which she is director. Frankl wrote this about her: "For Lukas there is no human being who does not retain a chance to grow, no situation which does not have its spark of meaning.... To elucidate meaning possibilities is the art of Elizabeth Lukas and entirely in the tradition of logotherapy."[7] Dr. Lukas lectures internationally also and her institute is one of the key training centers for logotherapy in the world. Her name turned up repeatedly in my conversations with Viktor and Elly, and their delight was apparent whenever we discussed the contributions to logotherapy Lukas has made across the decades.

Another who studied with Frankl is Alfried Längle, now head of a group psychotherapeutic practice in Vienna. Längle was associated with Frankl in the late 1970s and 1980s, has lectured and published regarding logotherapy and his own brand of psychotherapy, and also has written about Frankl. Before I met Längle, I was aware of the rift that had occurred between Frankl and him in the late 1980s. Across the years of my consultations with the Frankls, though Viktor himself rarely spoke of Längle, I came to understand that what the Frankls objected to was not Längle's integration of logotherapeutic elements into his therapy, but the ongoing use of "logotherapy and existential analysis" as the name for his approach. In Frankl's view, Längle had adopted components from other therapeutic schools that went far afield of logotherapy. Though Längle also calls his approach "Personal Existential Analysis," he retains the name of his organization, Society of Logotherapy and Existential Analysis—the terms Frankl coined.[8] That is the primary ongoing point of tension between the Frankls and Längle.

Of special biographical interest are Längle's recollections of Frankl in the 1980s, particularly on the scientific front. Längle remembers Frankl as a very serious physician, in both neurology and psychiatry, maintaining throughout his life a keen scientific edge. When Professor Frankl was well past his eightieth year, Längle recalled, he was still going every week to the library of the Society of Physicians in Vienna to read in neurology and psychiatry. That is the library where Freud and Frankl studied and where they lectured in an adjoining auditorium—and where for generations leading Viennese physicians have been doing their "homework." According to Längle, Frankl was at the library one to three hours at a time and that he was a "passionate neurologist, very bright and eager, a real genius." Elly remembered that it was Viktor's custom to study at the library, and often she waited for him or met him there. And Donald Tweedie, Jr., who was with Viktor daily in 1959–60, had many opportunities to watch him in neurological consultations. He remembers that other neurologists, stumped by a problem, would call Frankl in because he could get to the heart of a matter with his remarkable intuitive grasp of neurological function and dysfunction. Tweedie described Viktor as a "neurological troubleshooter" for his medical colleagues.

During his years at the Poliklinik, Viktor pioneered in the development of psychoactive drugs to reduce the symptoms and suffering of mental disorders. He was ever watchful for scientific studies of logotherapeutic techniques and concepts, and as these appeared he was fond of citing them and quoting them. Instruments for measuring aspects of logotherapy, developed by researchers in various countries, have given increasing credibility to Frankl's theoretical and applied work. The numbers of books and articles are increasing and it is difficult to keep track since they are written in many languages. Current bibliographies are available, however, on the Internet.[9]

In this connection it should be noted that, while Frankl is internationally famous as philosopher and psychiatrist, it is not widely known that he had a keen research orientation in medicine and neurology. His

1986 honorary doctorate from the University of Vienna came from neither the philosophical nor the medical faculty, but from the department of natural science—this in recognition of Frankl's scientific rigor and contributions through research. He wrote and published hundreds of articles in scientific journals.

In this chapter on the daily lives of the Frankls at home, it has not been possible to avoid Viktor's international influence. We look at his students and we are drawn to the impact of logotherapy. We pause on the family life of the Frankls and end up talking about Viktor as scientist. We consider the importance of human love in the Frankl family and story and the world elbows in. After all, it was love at home and the security of their base camp that made it possible for Viktor and Elly to venture away. The venturing went so far that, in the end, they belonged not only to Vienna, but to the world.

CHAPTER 15

They Belong to the World

WHILE VIKTOR HAD made some lecture trips during the period between the two world wars, the 1950s mark the beginning of global travel—tours to faraway places, sometimes with several international destinations on one itinerary. In 1954 he was preparing to go to Buenos Aires to lecture when he received a letter from New York's Norman Vincent Peale, the popular pastor, author, and media personality of "the power of positive thinking." Peale was already a force in the dialogue between psychology and faith, and had founded the American Foundation for Religion and Psychiatry in New York in 1937. Having discovered Frankl, Peale wanted him to come to Manhattan. To entice Frankl to come to New York on his way from Argentina back to Vienna, Peale offered him two hundred dollars for the entire detour. "And I accepted it. Then do you know what happened? The Marble Collegiate Church was filled with a thousand people or so . . . and tactfully they had removed all crosses or covered them with American flags, out of consideration for my Jewishness. And I gave a lecture, 'A Psychiatrist Looks at Religion.' "

In the same year Viktor traveled to Holland and London, and in the next he began lecturing at American universities. In 1955, *The Jewish Echo: Newsletter of Jewish Academics*' sent out a press release on Frankl, and widening media coverage was underway. Before the end of the 1950s, Frankl was flying around the world on schedules that would have exhausted a much younger man.

In 1957, Frankl made a major tour of the United States, speaking at medical schools and universities across the country, sponsored by the Religion in Education Foundation—an organization concerned with values in education. Randolph Sasnett made arrangements for the tour and accompanied Frankl from September 15 to October 17. Viktor lectured as many as several times each day for the entire period in auditoriums, class-rooms, dining, and conference rooms: at Boston and Brandeis Universities; Harvard University and Harvard Divinity School; Massachusetts Institute of Technology; and a Cambridge gathering of people from Andover-Newton Theological School, Brandeis, Boston University, Drew, Harvard, Tufts, Wellesley, Yale, and the University of Vermont; Columbia University Teachers College; New York University; and at Union Theological Seminary for participants from Protestant, Jewish, and Catholic theological schools in the New York area. He continued on to Princeton; Yale University and Yale Divinity School; University of Chicago (medical school and Federated Theological Faculty); Garrett, Seabury-Western, and McCormick Theological Seminaries; Loyola University (at both Chicago and Los Angeles); Marquette; Northwestern University and Medical School; Pacific University; University of Redlands; University of California at Los Angeles; Willamette University; and the University of Washington. Many of the lectures were to large audiences, but Frankl also made presentations in faculty colloquia where the interdisciplinary makeup of the gatherings was a unique feature. At some universities it was the first time various faculties met together (medicine, philosophy, and religion, for example). At the end of that tour, on October 18, Frankl continued on to Australia, India, and the Middle East, lecturing every day. In 1957, following another tour, Gordon Allport of Harvard moved to bring *Man's Search for Meaning* to English-speaking readers.

With *The Doctor and the Soul* already in print in the United States in 1955, three more United States tours were arranged in a similar way, after which Viktor and Elly did most of their tour planning. Press coverage of his travels swelled, and his writings were appearing in more languages. Recordings and films went into distribution. In a 1997 conversation with Giselher Guttmann in Vienna, he said, "The world was Viktor's lecture hall." In the Soviet Union and its satellite states, poor people actually studied German in order to understand Viktor when he came to speak and so they could read his books not yet translated into their languages. At San Quentin prison in California, inmates on death row listened intently to Viktor and interacted openly with him.

For many years Viktor and Elly kept a written record of their travels, but the little book was stolen on a break-in to their Mariannengasse flat. After that they discontinued logging their trips, but in 1993 estimated that they had flown more than six million miles together. To the United States

alone Viktor made ninety-two trips, and Elly accompanied him on all but
the first few. They traveled repeatedly to all five inhabited continents over
a period of fifty years. Hundreds of thousands have heard Viktor in person and millions more have read his lectures or heard him on recordings—
fortunately, many audio and video recordings of his lectures are preserved
and available.[2]

What was it that so captivated audiences that Viktor was invited again
and again to the same places as well as to more and more countries—even
where his German or English had to be interpreted to audiences sentence-
by-sentence? With a huge spread of photographs and text, *Pace* magazine
in 1967 reported Frankl's lectures under the title, "A human dynamo
sparks U.S. colleges" with the line, "They call him 'a real turned-on professor.'"[3] The photographs are from visits to Harvard and Suffolk
University, Boston; in one of them Elly is surrounded by smiling students,
and other photos show Viktor in action at chalkboards and lecterns.

Though it is impossible to convey in print the dynamics of a live
Frankl presentation, at least the content and interactions can be repre-
sented by looking at a lecture before a large audience of university students.[4] Mainly young people pack the house—a large auditorium in
Toronto. Frankl's topic is "youth's search for meaning" and he sits alone at
a table on the stage. On his lapel a microphone and behind him a large
chalkboard. In typical fashion he starts slowly, seemingly dependent on his
scribbled notes, but soon he is moving about and speaking extemporane-
ously. His use of language is complex, but invigorated with passion as he
proceeds. Before long—and typically with a jolt from some strong coffee—he catches his stride.

Ladies and gentlemen, recently I received a letter from an
American student and I would like to quote from this letter just
two sentences: "Dr. Frankl, I am a twenty-two-year-old with a degree, car, security, and the availability of more sex and power than
I need. Now I've only to explain to myself what it all means."

What is lacking, what is missing, what is the meaning of all
that he has in the midst of an affluent society? And this feeling of
meaninglessness is ever increasing and spreading today, particularly among youth. It's often associated with the feeling of emptiness in an inner void—what I've described in terms of "an
existential vacuum." This vacuum is the existential frustration of

a young person's search for a meaning that would make life worthwhile. Let me offer you a brief attempt at an explanation.

I would say that, in contrast to an animal, man is no longer told by his instincts what he *must* do. And, in contrast to former times, he is no longer told by traditions and values what he *should* do. So now sometimes he simply seems no longer to know what he thinks he basically *wishes* to do. Consequently he just wishes to do what other people are doing—conformism—or else he just does what other people want him to do—totalitarianism.

I would not subscribe to a sentence that Sigmund Freud once wrote to Princess Bonaparte when he said that at the moment a man doubts or questions the value, the meaning of his existence, he is sick. I don't think that he's really sick. I rather think that this is a manifestation of his being truly human. No ant, no bee, no animal will ever raise the question of whether or not its existence has a meaning, but man does. It's his privilege that he cares for a meaning to his existence. He is not only searching for such a meaning, but he is even *entitled* to it. If for no other reason, this would have to be recognized as a human achievement rather than a neurotic symptom. After all, it's a sign of intellectual honesty and sincerity. It's a prerogative of youth boldly to dare and venture rather than taking it for granted that there is a meaning to life— to question it, to challenge that such a meaning really exists. But I think this courage should be marked by patience. These young people should also see to it that they wait—patiently wait—until sooner or later meaning may dawn also on themselves, rather than impatiently taking their lives. Just consider the worldwide increase of suicide as young people take their own lives.

Or they take refuge by resorting to drugs because—once you take in certain drugs—suddenly the whole world takes on "infinite meaningfulness." You get feelings of meaningfulness, but these are merely subjective feelings, not backed by true meanings, actual meanings, real meanings. Real meanings are out there in the world, in store and wait for you, to be fulfilled by you, but they are not within your own psyche. The young people who resort to drugs, filling themselves with this subjective experience of infinite meaningfulness, are threatened and endangered in the same manner as those animals with which Olds and Milner[5] made their self-stimulation experiments. They put electrodes into the hypothalamus of the brain of the animals, and whenever they closed the electric circuit they observed that obviously these animals had experiences like sexual orgasm or the satisfaction of ingesting food. Then the animals learned to close the circuit themselves by jumping on the lever and then they became addicted to this business. These animals that were able to provide themselves with the subjective satisfaction, in sexual or nutritive terms, neglected and ignored the real sexual partners and the real food they had been offered. The electric current was enough. In a similar way I think that those who provide themselves with this feeling of meaningfulness by taking in drugs in the long run will bypass the true tasks, the true meanings that wait to be fulfilled by them—and exclusively by them. And those meanings will pass away forever if they are not materialized here and now by the specific person.

As Frankl's manner intensifies still more, the audience is quiet, respectful. The camera sweeps and picks up rows of students, intent as they listen and jot notes.

Unless we follow people into their human dimension, taking at face value the human phenomena rather than depriving them of their very humanness in a reductionist manner, we will not be able to cope with this worldwide state of affairs. Unless you recognize the truly human motivation, which is the search for meaning, you will not be able to understand its frustration. In other words, how will you be able ever to cope with or to help people overcome the ills and ailments of our age unless you've tried to overcome the old-fashioned motivational theories—the schemes and clichés of current academic psychology to whose indoctrination you are incessantly exposed on your campuses: that man is a closed system, like any animal, who tries to maintain all his store within himself in an equilibrium called in biology "homeostasis"? Unless you've overcome the view that man is satisfying his drives, gratifying his needs, even using people as partners for sex for the sake of his homeostasis? If you attempt to help people from such a caricature of man you are not able to help overcome this state of affairs.

A human being originally, basically, primarily, does not care for homeostasis. He doesn't care *primarily* for pleasure, happiness, or for the condition within himself. Originally, basically, he is not concerned with himself or anything within himself. But the true sign and signature of being human is that being human always points to and is directed towards something other than itself. Human existence always refers to something other than itself or someone other than oneself.

In other words, what I call self-transcendence means that man is basically concerned with finding and fulfilling a meaning in his life or loving and encountering another human being—not as a tool just to get rid of sexual tensions or aggressive drives or potentials, and so forth. But on the human, personal, level it means recognizing and getting hold of the unique essence of another human being as a person; and this means loving that person. Now self-transcendence means that man is basically, originally—unless his existence has been distorted in a neurotic way—out to serve a cause greater than himself or to love a person other than himself. In this service for the sake of a cause or for love of another person he is actualizing himself in terms of side effect, but not by aiming at it. Aiming for self-actualization proves to be self-defeating in the ultimate and final analysis.

Don't just dismiss the concept of a will to meaning that I am propounding, either by disposing of it or by conceiving of it as an idealistic, private assumption of some Dr. Frankl—that guy from Austria. My idealism is the real realism. The will to meaning, for instance, has been shown by a university department of experimental psychology study based upon 1,351 subjects; it turned out that there is a will to meaning, a primary motivational force in man. . . . In Europe, American adults are regarded as those who are just out to make a lot of money. But in another study of university students only 16 percent of students regarded their main goal in life to make a lot of money. And do you know what was the top goal? Seventy-eight percent of these American young people were concerned with finding a *meaning and purpose in their lives.*

If we take man as he really is we make him worse, but if we *over*estimate him—if we look at him high—we promote him to what he really can be. And do you know who said this? It was Goethe who said this.

If you don't recognize a young person's will to meaning you make him worse, you make him dull, you add and contribute to his frustration. In a so-called criminal or juvenile delinquent, or drug abuser and so forth, there must be, as you call it, a spark— yes, a spark of the search for meaning. Let's recognize this. Let's presuppose it. Then we will elicit it from him and help him become what he in principle is capable of becoming!

Let me use the eyes to explain this abstract problem of self-transcendence. In a way, your eyes are self-transcendent as well. Just notice that the capacity of the eye to perceive the surrounding world is ironically dependent on its *in*capacity to perceive itself, except in a mirror. At the moment my eye perceives something of itself, for instance a halo with colors around a light, it perceives its own glaucoma. At the moment I see clouding I perceive my own cataract, something of my own eye. But the healthy eye, the normal eye, doesn't see anything of itself. The seeing capacity is impaired to the very extent to which the eye perceives something of itself.

It is the same with human existence. Human existence is distorted to the very extent one is primarily concerned with oneself rather than letting happiness happen. People are striving for happiness by making it a target and thereby are missing what they are aiming at. You see today that sexual pleasure becomes a substitute when the original will to meaning is frustrated. In an age of the existential vacuum it is no wonder that sexual libido is thriving—it is exaggerated in an existential vacuum on a mass scale. An inflation of sex, I would say, is like other kinds of inflation, including the monetary market: it is associated with devaluation. Sex today is devaluated and it is dehumanized when originally sex was never just for the sake of fun. Human sex is always more than mere sex: it is more than mere sex to the very extent to which it is used as a physical expression of something meta-sexual—as an incarnation of love. Then ultimately it is rewarding to the same extent. I am not teaching as a moralist, but rather on the grounds of everyday office practice, clinical and hospital experiences. From these I have come up with such a conclusion.

ELLY, WHO ALWAYS accompanied Viktor after 1955, heard him lecture thousands of times. He remarked once how "scary it was that Elly knows so much; she could give my lectures herself." But she could never duplicate what Viktor did in his interactions with audiences. While some questions were asked time after time, often enough someone would raise an unusual question or test Viktor in a fresh way. When he was drawn out in this manner, pushed off the familiar and into something novel, Elly said he was at his best. He could handle any question and rise to any public challenge—here his real genius shone. Elly marveled at his responses, hearing things she had never heard before. On returning to their hotel, she said to him many times, "Viktor, that was wonderful. You absolutely must write what you said." Many of Viktor's papers, chapters, and whole books originated with that kind of urging from Elly.

Here are some edited excerpts from a question-and-answer period following a lecture[6] at Anaheim, California, in 1990. The first question is from a woman in the audience who is a professor.

"In my childhood I experienced the despair that comes from being victimized. I read your book many years ago and got a glimpse of hope. But I didn't quite understand it until today. I think I understood that what you said, that the meaning that you found had to do with a point of choice in the moment. That what you found for yourself inside was that you had that capacity, that ability no matter what else was going on externally, to make that choice. It seems like the absence of choice leads to despair. I was wondering if you could talk a little bit more about that." Frankl replied this way.

Professor, I could repeat something which has been laid down in the book, *Man's Search for Meaning*. This is that even in a situation where you have no freedom at all—including the freedom of choice—you still retain the freedom of decision. Every human being retains up to the last moment of his life the freedom to choose an attitude toward the tragic situation. The attitude I adopt toward a tragic situation may well save me from despair. For instance, if a woman believes that her absolute value—that the ultimate meaning of her existence—lies in cocreating life and having children, then she falls into despair if an obstetrician tells her that she will never bear children. Then she despairs because she absolutized the value of procreation.[7]

But if she is aware that life is full of potential meanings, then this is just one among a multitude of potential meanings to fulfill. She need not despair. For example, she can find meaning in helping others. She could set up a group of women who can never have children and who in spite of this limitation can find meaning in common efforts to help others. So meanings are always available under any conditions. The potential meaningfulness of life is an unconditional one.

A man in the audience refers back to something Frankl said in an earlier talk that same day. "Dr. Frankl, you said that believing is not knowing, that believing means thinking plus the existentiality of the thinker. I don't understand that yet." Viktor seems chagrined as he replies.

Ah, since I made this utterance I have felt deeply guilty because I was trying to say something that I know cannot be communicated in a few words. Now what I meant is the following. I said that believing is not some sort of thinking minus the reality of what I am thinking about. But it is some sort of thinking *plus* something. But this statement is not understandable unless I try to explain it.

In school in Vienna in the 1910s, we always used to say that believing means not knowing, and not knowing means you are an ass. [The audience laughs.] But you see it is not true. Believing is not just a lack of knowledge. It's something *more*. I hinted to this fact when I was quoting Blaise Pascal, the great philosopher. He spoke of the fifty-fifty possibility that God exists or that God does not exist. Most theologians today consent that there is no rational proof of the existence of God. That's why it is reserved to *believing* in God.

I cannot by discursive thinking—as it is called in philosophy—or by rational concepts decide what is true, whether God exists or not. But you may speak of God, or you may also speak of an ultimate meaning. There is a meaning we cannot get on the two-dimensional plane; we cannot understand it. So we are left to believe. Now if there is a fifty-fifty possibility—or be it probability—I can only try to put my whole existence onto one side of the scale.[8] That is to say, one option is possible and reasonable no more or less than the other one. And if both sides of the scale are on an equal level, then I make a decision that I wish that it be *that* way. That is, I put myself—my existence, my emotion, the depth of my heart, whatever I will, whatever I intend—I put it there on one side of the scale in favor of an ultimate meaning. I cannot get hold of it by mere rational means, but only by existential means. That is to say, I stand for it, that it should be that way. I wish out of the depth of my heart to decide that there *is* ultimate meaning. I decide against absolute meaninglessness in the world.

Further, I decide there is an ultimate meaning that is so rich that I cannot grasp it any longer in all my human finiteness, with all the limits of my intellectual capacities. Then I need not simply resign, but I may always say, "This is my wish from the depth of my heart. This is my whole existence. My belief permeates—that there should be an ultimate meaning, although I cannot get hold of it in rational terms."

Now what comes to mind is something I would like to give you. A wonderful simple sentence I came across in a book by Franz Werfel, the Austrian novelist. I think it was in one of the famous novels that he wrote: "Thirst is the most secure proof of the existence of something like water." [Audience laughs.] Do you follow? It would be inconceivable that nature had planted into ourselves the drive, the instinct, of thirst unless there were water for which I am compelled to search.

And now man's search for meaning. Unless there exists some meaning, some ultimate meaning, some meaning that is no longer rationally conceivable, how can you imagine that what I call will to meaning is so much rooted in the existence of every human being?[9]

There also were questions that Frankl was asked repeatedly on the road. A man asks: "Dr. Frankl, I have a question about your friend Martin

Heidegger. I understand he at one time joined the Nazi Party. Can you say something about this?"

Yes, he was a member of the National Socialist Party—you are absolutely right. He became a member in 1933 when Hitler took over in Germany. Now I wonder if you agree with my statement that Heidegger was a genius in his field—in philosophy. As it may be, let's take for granted he was a genius.

Why should each human being not be allowed to make mistakes, including mistakes in the political arena? And why should a genius not be allowed the privilege to make a mistake? You are fully entitled to now say, "Okay, but then sooner or later he should confess publicly that he made a mistake." Now Martin Heidegger, after one year, canceled his membership in the National Socialist Party. Thus at that time he publicly demonstrated his being disgusted by the National Socialist Party and by Hitler.

On many occasions Frankl was asked about the Holocaust. A questioner first explains that his friends, both Jews and non-Jews, often complain, "Why bring up this Holocaust business over and over again? Why not forget? Why not allow the pain to go away?" The questioner then asks Frankl what answer he would give.

I think we should see to it that the Holocaust is not forgotten. Forgetting something like this deprives us of the chance to see to it that it never is repeated. What happened in the Holocaust should be documented, and not only in archives of university departments of twentieth century history or in academic circles. It should also be in the newspapers—references to it so that it be not forgotten. . . .

But there is some sort of rehashing these stories and imposing them again and again on the public ad nauseam so that a negative effect is created and people get fed up. . . . We can fall prey to the old typically National Socialistic concept which today we call collective guilt. That is the concept I have been fighting against since the first day after the liberation from my last concentration camp.

A woman is recognized by the moderator and asks her question into the microphone. "Dr. Frankl, I want to ask about your sequel to *Man's Search for Meaning*—maybe 'Woman's search for meaning'?" [Audience laughs.]

Okay. You shouldn't forget that as an octogenarian I'm entitled to think and speak and write in the language of my time. And in that language, in German or English, the word "man" does not mean male but human being, and surely we would not deny that women are also fully human. So if I speak of "man's search for meaning" I mean a human being's search for meaning and not a male's search for meaning.[10]

Another woman asks Frankl to say more about dealing with anger as a victim, since she has had to deal with her own circumstances.

In principle, suffering has a meaning. But this is easily said, and I should say it more cautiously. Suffering may be bestowed by you with a meaning, but suffering can have meaning only if it is unavoidable. For instance, if your suffering is caused by a carcinoma, by a cancer, and it turns out to be operable—that is, there is a chance to remove it even forever and to prevent metastasis by surgical operation—then you have to take the courage to be operated on. In this case the cause of suffering can be removed. But if you have a cancer that is inoperable, then you need not the courage to insist on an operation, which would not be real courage anyway. In this case, what you are called upon to do in humility is to shoulder this terrible fate since there is a last chance to endure it by taking, by adopting, an attitude that gives meaning even to suffering. Suffering can be borne with courage and dignity. So if you shoulder this fate—and a Christian would say to take your cross upon yourself—with courage and dignity, you not only may squeeze out meaning from such a terrible event but even reach the highest possible level of meaning. You see, doing a deed or creating a work, or experiencing something or loving someone are also ways to find meaning. But to bear such a fate with dignity, this is something extraordinary. This is the highest-ranking value of meaning.

Recently in Linz, a city on the Danube in Austria, there was a public opinion poll. On the streets people were asked what they thought is the highest human achievement. The majority of the answers of the men and women were that the highest achievement is to master a very hard fate *plus* helping others who are afflicted to do so also.

I think of Jerry Long, Jr., a young gentleman who years ago wrote me a letter to Vienna, and therein he said, "Dr. Frankl: I read your book *Man's Search for Meaning* and I want to tell you that I was paralyzed from the neck down in a diving accident. And I'm writing this letter by typing with a wooden stick between my teeth. I broke my neck but it did not break me." What I want to convey to you is that this man squeezed out some meaning from this terrible thing. He became a student because he wanted to become a clinical psychologist. He said, "I think that my suffering will help me to help others who are involved in situations that cause them suffering." In the meantime this man has become a psychologist and married and so on, still paralyzed from the neck down. He is mastering his fate, and not only that. He is also helping others. So he is an example of fulfilling both ideals that were identified by the several hundred citizens interviewed in Linz.

HOW DIFFERENT FROM public lectures was the experience of the Frankls when they had an audience with Pope Paul VI (papacy 1963–78). Viktor spoke and wrote of this encounter, but I was interested in the details and the circumstances surrounding that meeting.

As the Frankls recalled it, in 1970 Viktor was invited to Rome to give a speech to a gathering of the Young Presidents' Organization (YPO), which annually convened economic and corporate leaders from around the world. Prominent people were always on the program, and Viktor had lectured at their meetings on several occasions before.¹¹ At the Rome YPO meeting there were two other speakers: Otto von Hapsburg, son of the last emperor of the Austro-Hungarian Empire (who together with his wife Regina shared a mutual acquaintance and admiration with Viktor and Elly); and Neil Armstrong, the American astronaut who in 1969 was first to set foot on the moon. The entire Hilton Hotel was reserved to host members and spouses for the gathering.

(Elly interrupted these recollections to say that Otto von Hapsburg was a humble and wonderful man whom they admired very much. Once they met him on an airplane, and he also was flying economy class and carrying his own luggage. The Frankls both reasserted a favorite motif: that some of the greatest people are the most humble and down-to-earth.)

In their Rome hotel room between YPO sessions the phone rang for Viktor. It was the Vatican calling. "We have heard that you are in the city and we wonder if you would like to pay a visit to His Holiness." "But of course, if I might be allowed to do so," Viktor answered, understanding the protocol that heads of state technically do not invite visitors but rather grant audiences on request.

On the day of their meeting with the pope, the Frankls also attended a luncheon for the founder of an apostolic order. As they entered an ornate room, Viktor did not realize that the hors d'oeuvres being served were simply a prelude to lunch. He thought the vast array of small sausages on toothpicks—a treat "just for us Viennese"—was the meal. He proceeded to eat nearly a whole platter of them, only to be ushered later into a great room where the real lunch was to be served. "But I was already full of the sausages I had been eating so much!"

In contrast to the luncheon setting, the pope's chamber was sparse and even stark in its simplicity. There was no throne for the pope to sit on, only a simple wooden stool. When Viktor and Elly entered this room they were introduced to Pope Paul VI in a few German words. Then His Holiness spoke in his native Italian, conversing with the Frankls through an interpreter. At the outset he pointed to Elly and Viktor in turn, saying, "I know that you are Catholic and that you are Jewish." Viktor explained his understanding of the pope's gesture: it was a kindly way for the pope to put the Frankls at ease in his presence, so that there need be no awkwardness over their interfaith marriage. The pope then proceeded to say that he knew Frankl's books and praised him for what he had done. Viktor later reconstructed how he had responded to the pope.

> The words by which you honor me make me simply sad, because the more you speak of what I may have achieved, I become at the same second ever more aware of what I *should* have accomplished but did not. Please understand that a man who has stood at the railway platform at Auschwitz and says to himself, "Who can tell me that there is absolutely no hope that I can survive this? And if there is only a 1 percent chance that I can survive this, I

have the responsibility to survive if I can because someone might be waiting for me at home." Nobody was in wait for me when I came back to Vienna, but there was some *thing* in store for me to do. And a man who has received God's grace to survive cannot avoid asking himself, day by day, whether he has been worthy of that grace, and daily to confess to himself that, if at all, only partially.

The audience lasted just under twenty minutes, and as Viktor and Elly were about to leave the room, suddenly Paul VI turned to them, switching into some simple German words: *"Bitte, beten Sie für mich"*—"Please, pray for me."

Viktor was astounded at this. "Imagine the pope asking a psychiatrist, coming from Vienna, *Jewish*, to pray for him! Again we see that some of the highest-ranking people are the most humble of all." Viktor was visibly moved as he described the gaunt figure of the pope: "Here was a man who, throughout nights lying awake, was thinking about unpopular decisions he had to make—still struggled with his conscience that he could not avoid it and that he simply had to stick to it—and this is admirable. The deep lines in his face, the sleepless nights . . ."

DURING HIS ABSENCES from Vienna for travels abroad, Frankl drew no salary from the Poliklinik—he was on leave without pay. Then in 1970 he retired as chief of neurology and finally was free to devote himself full-time to the expanding work of logotherapy—visitors, correspondence, writing, and lecturing locally and around the world. In the United States he became guest professor at Harvard, Duquesne, and Southern Methodist Universities. Following a lecture he gave in Los Angeles in 1970, Frankl was invited to United States International University (USIU) in San Diego, to give a lecture for the whole university. In the front row was Carl Rogers, one of America's most influential psychologists, who years earlier had written an endorsement for the first publication of *Man's Search for Meaning*. Rogers was also teaching at USIU and introduced himself to Viktor and Elly following the lecture. The next morning, before the Frankls left San Diego, the president of USIU approached Viktor. "Now that you are retired, would it be possible for you to come to our campus as part of a chair of logotherapy that we will establish here?" After thinking it over, Viktor accepted and started teaching at USIU one academic quarter each year—eight weeks, sometimes more—throughout the 1970s, lecturing, supervising students, and meeting with smaller seminar groups.

Viktor's courses were in high demand and at one point he had 365 students in one course, meeting in an auditorium. As usual Elly assisted Viktor, this time by reading countless academic papers written by students—"It was a hard time." Housing was provided to the Frankls in various homes and the pay was poor. The Frankls borrowed or rented a disintegrating old car, but it was the first time they had driven an automatic transmission. Students had automobiles much newer and more luxurious, and some of them expressed their embarrassment: "You are a famous professor, and you are driving a car like that?"

Often, and as their time allowed, the Frankls traveled from San Diego to give lectures in Canada, Mexico, and many places in the United States. But unlike the typical pressures at home in Vienna, there were spells in California that allowed them to meet extraordinary and ordinary people. For example, they were befriended by Vice Admiral Raymond Peet, commander of the American First Fleet in the Pacific. He took them by launch around the naval harbor and to see the carrier *Nimitz*. In a widening circle for the Frankls, many of the best-known people in psychiatry, psychology, theology, and religion as well as in leadership—in many other countries also—were with them socially and appeared together in public forums on relevant topics and issues.

The Frankls found the world relentlessly fascinating, although they were more interested in people than places. They thrived in and soaked up all they could of their opportunities abroad, spending time with students and relating easily with many ordinary people they met. They enjoyed immensely the richness and diversity of the human family in multicultural San Diego. For example, they discovered the celebrative music of African-American gospel choirs, occasionally attending services and concerts, drawn in by the outpouring of religious feeling among African-Americans that was so different from Vienna's sedate Jewish and Catholic traditions. "Viktor liked the spirituals, and so did I," said Elly. In 1970 all the Frankls were in San Diego—Viktor, Elly, and Franz and Gaby with their little daughter Katja. Katja had been baptized in Vienna by Juan Battista Torrello earlier that year, but two priests, close friends of the family, wanted to add their own blessings. So here, in an African-American church service in California, a white Greek Orthodox priest and a white

Roman Catholic priest conferred their blessings on the little girl, descendant of a Jewish psychiatrist from Vienna. Before the service, children were playing tag and hiding under the altar. Then drums and guitars accompanied the mainly black congregation as they belted out gospel music. Franz said afterward that the whole thing was "unbelievable for us staid Europeans."

Another particular San Diego expansion of personal experience delighted Viktor more than it did Elly. There was time—only in San Diego—for him to take flying lessons from David Klostermann, a flying instructor who became a friend. All his life Viktor had wished to do parachuting, but always was advised not to by his physicians because of his weak ankles. Consequently he was thrilled with the experience of flying a small plane. Elly described him as like a happy little boy, absorbed in the adventure and learning to calculate and prepare flight plans. "Where we were in California he couldn't do climbing, so he started flying. Oh, my goodness. He was so happy." He learned "crabbing" toward a destination to compensate for winds and weather, and analogies from flying turned up in more of his lectures. (His fascination with heights—whether climbing in the mountains or flying a small aircraft—were analogies for his "height psychology"; a lifelong motif was pushing back, farther and higher, the limitations or boundaries of human capability.) After Viktor obtained his flying license he went up at every chance, sometimes over the water toward Mexico, but never venturing far and always returning the little aircraft to the same small airport.

A unique adventure in Southern California allowed the Frankls a taste of another subculture. The Tweedies—Don, wife Norma, and their children who had moved to California—invited Viktor and Elly for a day at their ranch in the rugged hills above the desert in Anza. It was not a working ranch but had an interesting history. The Frankls heard stories of actual Wild West shootouts in the ravines and arroyos of the Tweedie ranch. Now it was quite safe among the few domesticated animals at the place— dogs, a couple of horses, barnyard chickens, and cats—and the wildlife generally stayed at a distance. The Frankls had a chance to go horseback riding, quite an adventure for Vienna city folk. But it became clear that Elly's love of animals was more for the smaller, gentler sorts.

Coyotes howled in the distance. "I was not happy at this ranch," Elly said. "In the kitchen, out from the drain in the sink, came a snake! Not only that but the two horses were behind me and one of them bit me."

Viktor emphasized it, "The horse really bit Elly on the upper arm, right through her clothing!" They did not stay overnight with the Tweedies or among the coyotes, but there are photographs of Viktor and Elly clowning on the ranch. They had been cowboys for a day, and when they told about it years later they did so with enthusiasm. Elly remarked that, at the ranch, Viktor simply had been himself and enjoyed it tremendously.

Viktor and Elly relished San Diego's warm January weather and there were other advantages of extended stays there. "I was forced to learn English, to run a household in America, to shop, and so on," Elly observed. Their competency in English returned rapidly on each trip to America, England, or Australia. By the end of their longer stays, both Viktor and Elly were dreaming in English. Within a couple of weeks back in Vienna, their dream content always reverted to German.

A COMMEMORATIVE BOOK, *Austrians Who Belong to the World,* was published in Vienna in 1979.[12] It presented eight living Austrians in historical photographs and text, with portraits made in 1978 by famed photographer Alfred Eisenstaedt. Among those honored in the book are Anna Freud, daughter of Sigmund; filmmaker Otto Preminger; statesman Kurt Waldheim; architect Friedensreich Hundertwasser; and Viktor Frankl.

When *Austrians Who Belong to the World* was published, no one imagined the international firestorm that would erupt and engulf one of the honorees just seven years later. It became known around the world as the "Waldheim affair." The affair can be understood only in the context of conflicts over Austria's Nazi past—including passionate accusations and denials—and the Allies' resolution of various issues following their defeat of the Nazis, which placed Germany and Austria in different positions despite Austria's complicity. The resolution cast Austria as Hitler's "first victim"—a slant that temporarily obscured Austria's responsibility while Germany was held accountable for the war and the Holocaust. For decades Austria had escaped international scrutiny for its own Nazi past.[13]

Kurt Waldheim was elected Austria's president in 1986 and, partly because of his fame as former secretary-general of the United Nations, the crisis over his alleged role as a Nazi military officer during the war went international. Jewish organizations expressed outrage and the controversies became bitter. Campaigns against Waldheim broke out. Nevertheless, a commission of historians assigned to investigate Waldheim found no cause for charging him and he was never convicted of any crime.

Yet Waldheim's reluctance to own up forthrightly to his past affiliations damaged him severely. When Viktor and Elly Frankl became social acquaintances of Kurt and Sissy Waldheim, it enraged some Waldheim enemies. Simply by their association with the Waldheims, Viktor and Elly were fiercely criticized. When Waldheim in his official position as Austrian president presented to Frankl one of the nation's highest honors, a few even suggested that Frankl should have shunned Waldheim and refused the award. But anyone who thought that Viktor Frankl would cave in to the politicized verdicts of others, that he would take seriously those who were deciding with whom he should or should not associate, simply had no clue about his character. Frankl would bow to no amount of pressure. He gave no quarter to spite or revenge. He was adamant and consistent in his refusal to give himself any license to hate and, ironically, for this some people apparently hated him.

Another ruckus, this time more confined to Europe, erupted in the mid-1990s over Jörg Haider and the Freedom Party in Austria. Due to democratic elections, this right-wing political faction became part of the Austrian coalition government. For inclusion of the Freedom Party, Austria came under sanctions by the European Community—controversial sanctions that the EC later lifted. Haider became notorious for his address to a reunion of Nazi SS in Krumpendorf. In remarks he later claimed to regret, Haider praised the former military officers.

Frankl had met Haider in 1995, the year Frankl received the highest civic award of the city of Vienna—honorary citizenship. The Freedom Party's nomination of Frankl for the honor was confirmed by a unanimous favorable vote in the large city council, though it irked some of Haider's foes who alleged some kind of connivance between Haider and Frankl. Fanning the flames, on public television Haider had shown a copy of a book written and inscribed by Frankl "to my friend, Jörg Haider." But Frankl across the years had autographed thousands of books for admirers, often using the word "friend" even for people he did not know well. In this case Haider used the autographed book opportunistically when he was under tremendous political fire.

The experience was painful for Viktor who—ever since his youthful involvement in the socialist movement in Vienna ended—was neither interested in nor savvy about politics. I was with Viktor and Elly during part of this crisis and, since Viktor kept his distance from politics, it was an unusual move when he prepared a press release regarding the Haider brouhaha. The press picked up the release, and *Der Standard*, for one, published its report (in German of course). The following translation shows Viktor's position balanced with a typical refusal to join in the politics of accusation or hate. The caption reads, "Viktor Frankl distances himself from Freedom Party Boss Haider."[14]

Vienna. Viktor Frankl, called by Jörg Haider a "personal friend," has declared that he has "no sympathy" for the appearance of the Freedom Party leader at a meeting of the SS in Krumpendorf. Frankl says that he is not happy to see his name mentioned in such a context. Haider had repeatedly emphasized that he "never had the heart to hurt the feelings" of Frankl, a survivor of the concentration camps, owing to their friendship.

On the subject of friendship Frankl had the following to say. Haider had been introduced to him in the spring of 1995. At an evening gathering in the summer Frankl had experienced serious blood-pressure problems and had to be taken to a hospital. Haider, who was also present, had gone to extra effort to help him. "For this I owe him my thanks. One must understand that I am not going to split hairs in public over whether this was an act of kindness by an acquaintance or proof of friendship. This would hurt the dignity of all persons involved."

Frankl simply stayed his course amid the new flare-ups of criticism directed at him.

AS THEY TRAVELED on intensive itineraries, Elly was always concerned about the strain on Viktor and about his health, and there had been a couple of occasions for genuine alarm. But the tables turned on a particular lecture tour to America. As part of the trip, Viktor and Elly stopped in Boston to celebrate his seventy-fifth birthday. They had fond memories of their visits to Boston and their time at Harvard. This time, however, it was Elly who became ill.

I was sick with a high-fever flu and could get no doctor to come. We went the next day to the Lahey Clinic and the red carpet was out for the Frankls. So I went in with Viktor and the doctor examined me and then sent me down for x-rays. And I thought everything was okay, but then they took more x-rays—fifth, sixth, seventh. Viktor asked why, and they said there was something not right. When we met with the doctor he said that I might be afflicted with a lung cancer, but not for certain. And Viktor was to give a lecture the next day in Washington and what should we do? Should we go back to Vienna right away? But we decided to go to give the lecture, and I was worried that I had cancer. Robin Goodenough was very kind to me. And then we flew back to Vienna on the Concorde supersonic plane.

They took the Boston x-rays to a pulmonary specialist at home and he confirmed the appearance of some kind of blood clot. Thankfully it turned out to be some harmless residue. The Frankls decided, "Instead of twice-a-year checkups for the rest of your life, always worrying about it, let's get rid of it." So Elly underwent lung surgery—"a terrible couple of days."

Son-in-law Franz said, "I have never seen Viktor so worried and edgy. He was incredible in his care for Elly. I went with him to a grocery store to buy something for him to eat, but he could never say exactly what he wanted. So he pointed to this and that, and then we had to wait for about thirty seconds for the cashier. But Viktor ran out of the store to go back to Elly and I ran after him, leaving the food behind, and then some other people came out after us. The next day I went back to the store and explained what had happened."

Another medical crisis hit the Frankls when Viktor nearly died from logotherapy. This takes a bit of explaining. Though paradoxical intention is the best known of the logotherapeutic techniques, another is what Viktor called "dereflection." This is an approach for remedying excessive attention on oneself, as when one obsesses about his own sexual functioning instead of focusing on his partner, or when someone anxiously centers on some insignificant physical symptom. In 1982, Viktor himself was troubled by a rhythmic scraping sensation in his left ear, but only when lying on his left side in bed. Aware of his own tendency toward hypochondria, he applied dereflection to himself—he talked himself out of hearing noises by focusing on something else. This turned out to be a dangerous move.

During a routine physical exam Viktor casually mentioned to his physician this scraping noise in his left ear. After listening closely to the areas around Viktor's ear and neck, the doctor became alarmed and recommended immediate closer examination and surgery. Viktor was rushed to the hospital to have a blockage in a carotid artery removed. The condition had been very serious, even life-threatening. After the episode, Viktor declared, "Never forget how dangerous it is to apply good logotherapy to all situations!"

While Viktor injected humor into this situation, it is essential to recognize the dangers of applying logotherapeutic techniques inappropriately. The risks in using dereflection are illustrated by Viktor's experience with the blocked artery. In the case of paradoxical intention (which encourages a sufferer to do the very thing that is feared), which is so effective in treating anxiety, obsessions, compulsions, and phobias, it would be not only foolhardy but potentially deadly if misapplied in cases of depression—no depressed person with a genuine desire to die should ever be urged to go ahead with suicide plans. We know now that the lines separating anxiety from depression are thin and that these problems often occur together. So both care and expertise are necessary in applying logotherapeutic, or for that matter psychotherapeutic, techniques.

NO ACCOUNT OF the worldwide travels of the Frankls would be adequate without including some of the ridiculous situations they confronted and the strange experiences they had. As the two native Viennese ventured across borders of culture and language, they had a roaring good time laughing at themselves.

In the Hilton Hotel, New York City, a big reception was set for the next morning. Elly needed to have her hair done and there was a hair salon in the hotel. During their travels they had become accustomed to having their choice of salad dressing and a favorite, in German, was *Knoblauch*—garlic dressing. So when the hairdresser asked Elly what kind of hair dressing (fixative) she would like, Elly reached into her English for her favorite dressing and asked for garlic. It was a great moment in the salon and, among the world's scents, a unique choice for a grand social event.

Viktor's observation was that "they would have put Elly in a room by herself at the reception."

In another time and place, Viktor liked a wonderful custard pudding served at a hotel luncheon. Later that day he requested room service for a black coffee with a "portion of that mustard that was served in the dining room at lunch." The waiter asked three times, "Are you sure this is what you want with your coffee?" Finally they figured out what was happening and the waiter joined in the fun. Elly, in telling this story, observed, "So you see we have always had the capacity to laugh." Viktor asked, "What else should we do, cry?"

In the United States at a roundtable event, Viktor and Elly were in a receiving line where they had to shake hands and greet a thousand people filing by at a reception. "It was hard to meet so many people," Elly said, "but we smiled and shook hands. After a few hundred it was terrible to continue." Viktor picked up, "To lift our mood and keep our spirits up we started talking with one another in the most extreme Viennese slang—nobody would understand this. I remember we were commenting on what was going on—for instance a lady came along, strangely dressed, and I said in this extreme slang, 'Look at this lady, dressed like a *Kasperl* [buffoon].' Of course we kept a straight face. Suddenly the man next to her started showing off a bit of German and said, 'But what is this word you used?' And then the man on the other side of the woman, who knew *Wienerisch*, translated it as 'clown.' What a terrible situation!" Elly recalled, "But when we were together we could take it."

On a stop in New York, Viktor and Elly went to Bloomingdales department store and there was a sale on men's underwear. Three-packs were strewn over the display tables and they thought it a chance to stock up at a good price. As they were deciding what color to buy for Viktor, he slipped into extreme Viennese slang again so no one who might overhear could possibly understand, "Elly, it's better to buy black just in case of accidents." Immediately a salesclerk nearby jumped in, "That is a good reason to buy dark colors, just in case one makes some shits." It was a clerk who knew *Wienerisch*.

One morning in Montreal's Queen Elizabeth Hotel the Frankls were at the coffee counter and Viktor was next to an espresso machine.

> Suddenly to my right a man sat down on the next stool. Then
> he took a napkin and cleaned off the bar first, about a square yard;

he took the knife and spoon and cleaned everything so carefully, putting them down in perfect order. And I whispered to Elly cautiously, in extreme Viennese slang, "Look at this guy—a severe repetitious compulsive individual." I always appreciate a beautiful, clear array of symptoms. When we had finished [Elly giggles] at the counter, we went away and I took my raincoat. All of a sudden I realized that I had left my umbrella at the counter and went back. At once this man turned to me in clear German, "Have you forgotten something?"—he was so friendly, and from Austria or Bavaria. What I had forgotten is that he might possibly have understood my Viennese slang! Automatically, we speak extreme slang and we don't think about it.

Viktor and Elly, on a visit to Israel in the 1980s, wanted to see the Sinai region during a couple of free days.

We flew over and went to the foot of the Sinai to the cloister there. But on this particular day it was closed, and even the military men had to bivouac overnight in the open. On this day the monks inside were not allowed even to speak. So we could not get in, and I talked with the doorman and offered him a copy of my book as a gift to the prior or library. And then we were allowed to enter and the abbot came in and said, "We know your book and have it already in our library but are happy to have another copy. And what can we do for you?"

Well, we had hoped to stay overnight so that early in the morning we can climb on the mountain. "We will make an exception and you will be our guest in the monastery. And I will organize an exploration with two camels so that you can see the Sinai, but it must be done at 3 A.M."

Elly picked up the story. "They brought us food and it was terrible—sour herring—and whenever this man turned away I put the fish in my pockets. So we went to our room, where the walls were covered with bedbugs, and there was no heat." "To protect us," Viktor said, "someone was patrolling outside our room—maybe to protect us from the bedbugs, I don't know. It was so cold we put on all the clothing we had." "Oh, it was cold and I was stinking from the fish," Elly stressed, "but at three in the morning the camels were waiting for us and there were no lights. So we had to feel our way along the walls, down the stairs. Two Bedouin were waiting with two camels outside. And Viktor got a good, large camel and I got a very lame camel—still with the fish in my pockets. I had no idea where I could throw the fish away."

It was Viktor's turn. "If you have ridden on a camel, you know it is easy to fall off when they stand up. We could see absolutely nothing and the Bedouin could not speak with us. But, suddenly one of them made two steps to the left and started urinating in front of me. After a while, thanks to heaven, the sun was coming up but the camels could not go beyond a certain place. We had to walk. But our plane was leaving that afternoon and a jeep was waiting for us, so we never got to the place where the Ten Commandments maybe were given to Moses. We simply had to return and went down to get the jeep for the airport."

"But I was stinking so that everyone moved away from me at the airport and I was sitting alone!" Elly remembered their arrival at the Hilton in Jerusalem. "Before dinner in the evening, I had to throw away everything I was wearing."

VIKTOR AND ELLY on their journeys to Buenos Aires in the 1980s became acquainted with President Raul Alfonsín. He always invited them to visit him and, keeping with state protocol, spoke only in Spanish through an interpreter. The president had read Viktor's writings in Spanish translations (more of Frankl's books are translated into Spanish than English). After a visit of about an hour, the Frankls were surrounded by a police guard and the press, inquiring about their conversation with the president. Since that time the president's sister has kept in touch with the Frankls, and with Elly even after Viktor's death. "So you see," Elly remarked, "we have met many wonderful people. And we have met thousands and thousands in many different cultures around the world. It would take years to tell about this—if Viktor were alive it would be nice to talk more about these things, but not for me alone. Anyway, people would not believe all that we have done. After all, Viktor came out from Czerningasse and was rather poor. And I came from Kaisermühlen, where I had almost nothing but my family and happiness."

CHAPTER 16

Love Beyond Darkness and Parting

VIKTOR SAID THAT there are three circumstances in which human beings should not be photographed: when they are loving, when they are praying, and when they are dying—these circumstances are too personal, too intimate for that. Oddly then, near the end of our story we are drawn to look at love, prayer, and parting. But not only at these; Viktor's sudden loss of eyesight approximately a month after his eighty-fifth birthday placed him in an irreversible darkness and its limiting consequences. For most of his last seven years Viktor was functionally blind, seeing only dim, distorted images with what vision remained in one eye. Though hampered, he was undaunted and learned without fretting to compensate for his loss in various ways. But with no slackening of the external demands on him, immense new burdens fell upon Elly.

The telephone, for example, kept ringing as much as ever. Describing this aspect of their lives, Elly said, "We live with telephone terror and doorbell terror. Seemingly Viktor is even less capable than I am to control it. He sees only the good in people, and I can see the bad. But he cannot see the bad—perhaps it has to do with his blindness." Viktor did not disagree, but entered the dialogue, "When I am on the phone and people are demanding that I do this or that, Elly is dancing around me in frustration, signaling that I should hang up the phone." "But Viktor, people are misusing you. The newspapers are writing things that are twisted and distorted, but what should we do? Anyway, we cannot change our life, so Don, you can write everything."

The loss of Viktor's eyesight occurred without warning one evening when, in typical fashion, he was watching the television evening news. Elly's recollection of the portentous moment was vivid.

It was 7:30 in the evening—April 11, 1990. I was in the kitchen and suddenly Viktor called out urgently, "Elly! Elly! Come here, please!" I went to him, and he spoke these four words to me: "Elly, I am blind." Immediately we took a taxi to the hospital and he was admitted and given medication. Only a little vision was left—one eye was useless and the little he could see with the other eye was only peripheral. . . . For nearly eight years he lived with this, and it was hard for both of us. I had to read everything to him, up to five hours each day, and sometimes I lost my voice. Katja and Alexander offered to come and read to him, but he said, "Elly, it is your voice I am used to." Sometimes I closed my eyes and said to myself, "Just imagine if this happened to you, and you are blind. Especially for someone so active and dependent on reading." But Viktor lived what he talked—absolutely, absolutely. . . . Never did he complain about his blindness. Not even once.'

Elly wearied in reading aloud psychology and philosophy in addition to all the mail. Sometimes in one week ten books would arrive, the senders naively hoping that Viktor would read them. Elly continued to read for him as much as time and strength allowed. If she had energy and eyes left for it, in the evenings she was happy to read something completely different for herself. Among her favorites were the English mysteries of Agatha Christie—"These I read for relief."

In such a bind, their affection for one another deepened and the whole family rallied around Viktor. So he remained hopeful and continued the pace of his work. When I saw the Frankls in Vienna in 1992, after decades with virtually no contact with them, I had little awareness of how serious was the loss of Viktor's sight.

IT WAS JUNE of '92 when I made a nostalgic stop in Vienna, hoping to touch base with the Frankls and revisit my old haunts. I knew Viktor was aging and I wanted to thank him for what he had done for me unknowingly. When I arrived in the city I phoned, and he answered as he always had, simply "Frankl." I refreshed him about who I was and asked if there might be a chance to see him, however briefly. He was busy and wondered how long I would be in town. Would it be possible for me to phone again on Monday morning?

So on June 22, I phoned and learned that there might be a chance that evening to greet one another at least. Viktor was to give a talk in Leopoldstadt on the topic, "Up to the Time of Deportation to the Concentration Camps"—in which he was to describe his early life and the menacing events that had taken place in that very neighborhood. After supper that day I arrived early at Praterstern 1, where a poster on the door verified that Frankl was due. By the time he showed up in an entourage of hosts and family, the place was packed with locals, many of them older and with memories of their own going back to the times Viktor was to recall. Following his talk, while interacting with the audience, he was asked by some if he knew anything about certain relatives they named. Fifty years after the Holocaust they were still hoping for some word about their lost loved ones. Present also was a person from Viktor's own past: Toni Grumbach himself, the former SA Brownshirt who had offered shelter to Viktor in the Hitler time. Viktor thanked Toni again, this time publicly. There was an older woman in the audience who, speaking into a microphone, explained that she too was a survivor of Theresienstadt. She remembered Viktor's efforts to help her and others in facing shock and the temptation to suicide, and thanked him for what he had done in Theresienstadt.

After the program I stood by watching as Viktor autographed books and articles that people brought to the stage. Finally we went outside into the night and Viktor, orienting himself to the distant lights, pointed in the direction of the Prater and the *Riesenrad* just beyond North Station. He commented on the landmarks, then started to edge away from the crowd. Elly flagged me over and, as we walked away together, Viktor said to me, "On Friday morning I give a lecture in English to a group of visitors. Will you still be in Vienna?" I told him that I was driving to Freud's birthplace in Pribor [Czechoslovakia] and perhaps on to Auschwitz, but that I had to return to Vienna for my Saturday flight home. So it might be possible to get to the Poliklinik Friday morning. Naturally, I liked the idea of sitting again in the *Hörsaal* for a Frankl lecture.

After visiting Pribor and Auschwitz, early Friday morning I drove from Olomouc back to Vienna and arrived at the Poliklinik in plenty of time. But as the lecture hour neared I was still alone as I explored the *Hörsaal*. So I returned to the doorman, who checked the board on the wall and found that the lecture had been canceled. Determined not to bother the Frankls, I decided simply to say good-bye to them by phone. The door-man dialed "Herr Professor" and politely explained my presence. Then he handed the phone to me and Viktor asked if I could possibly come to their apartment just down the block. "Of course," I said, "if only for a minute."

I rang at Mariannengasse 1 and the Frankls buzzed me into the build-ing. The interior seemed the same. That deafening doorbell at the Frankl flat summoned Elly, who welcomed and ushered me in. We sat down, Viktor behind his large old desk with the bright bay windows behind him, Elly on his couch/bed near the phone, and I in a chair facing them. The conversation ended three hours later.

Just before my arrival, Viktor and Elly had had a spat—in itself nei-ther unusual nor earthshaking—this time triggered by a just-published piece in a British magazine.[2] The reporter's article, based on an interview, appeared with a photograph of the Frankls and included a line about Elly giving Viktor "an occasional verbal prod." While it was not very impor-tant, and even though the Frankls did not fully understand it, that line un-corked Elly's frustrations with the workload—she had interpreted it as suggesting that she pushed her husband around. The notion was absurd, but Elly did not appreciate the printed insinuation. They asked me to ex-plain "prod" and I laughed, saying that it meant to jab someone; I said that "a cattle prod is a stick used to get cattle to move along." Viktor loved that one. Exuding enormous pride, he threw up both arms and shouted, "This means that I am the COW!" Elly thought that was funny, too, and our laughter seemed to vaporize the annoyance over the article.

Our spontaneous rapport metamorphosed a mere acquaintanceship into a friendship. I certainly was surprised to be joking with the Frankls about the "crisis" of the morning, as though I were a befuddled marriage adviser. Other interactions were moving, personal, but what struck me most was that these two people were still working together as they had continuously for nearly fifty years.

As the conversation wound down, to save Elly the trip, Viktor asked if I would accompany him on an errand. Elly and I said farewell with a hug and I left with him. It was then that I became aware of Viktor's vi-sual impairment. He took my arm as we walked, especially crossing busy Alser Strasse. After a stop at the bank, we walked together back to Mariannengasse. At the door of their building we parted, and his embrace surprised me, since Viktor typically was not demonstrative. He said simply as he entered the doorway, "Until we meet again, if heaven permits."

Back in Chicago, I followed up by doing two things. I wrote a brief article for the new Frankl journal, as Viktor had requested, and sent it to Vienna.[3] Viktor acknowledged it, adding, "Elly and I treasure the memory of your recent visit." Second, I went to David Horner, president of North Park University[4] where I teach, suggesting that North Park grant honorary doctorates to both Viktor and Elly in recognition of their mutual work throughout half a century. He sent the recommendation on and it made its way through the academic hoops. Before President Horner wrote the official letter, he suggested that I notify the Frankls about the North Park decision. So I informed Viktor and Elly that they would be invited to Chicago to receive doctorates in ceremonies May 22, 1993. Viktor wrote in response:

> Dear Don,
>
>   ... What a surprise is the honor extended to Elly, and I know better than anyone else how much she is worthy of it! It is, as you rightly assume, the first such recognition. ... I fully understand that North Park wishes to confer a doctorate on me too but, while I would appreciate it, I cannot accept it. As I see it, the more exclusively Elly is to be honored the more conspicuous it will be in making the occasion of special significance for her. ... She—still being overwhelmed by the honors you have triggered off—joins me in warmest regards to you and Jan.
>
>   Cordially yours,
>   Viktor

Then Elly, doubtless having typed the letter for Viktor, added her own handwritten postscript: "When I read your letter I was moved to tears and I still cannot believe that I really deserve such an honor. Once more, best wishes. Elly."

Viktor told me later that Elly had gone about the apartment weeping off and on for a period of days—the apartment where across the decades she had been caretaker of that storage room laden with honors bestowed on her husband. Always she had preferred to be out of the limelight, behind the scenes. Now she was overwhelmed by the one public thank-you of its kind to come her way. Their trip would be like no other: the only one on which he would accompany Elly. This time *he* would be in *her* shadow. Little did I understand at the time how much this meant to both of them.

After that response from Viktor, I wrote this paragraph in a letter to the Frankls.

As I thought about the praise that you, Viktor, have for Elly, to my mind came some lines by the English poet William Wordsworth, written in 1801. In the poem, "The Sparrow's Nest," he looks back upon his childhood and writes lovingly of his sister Emmeline. They are words that you, Viktor, might borrow even now for Elly:

She gave me eyes, she gave me ears;
And humble cares, and delicate fears;
A heart, the fountain of sweet tears;
And love, and thought, and joy.

JAN AND I met the Frankls on their arrival in Chicago on May 19, and we went directly to the Omni Orrington Hotel in Evanston, near our home. To protect their privacy I had made a reservation for them under fictitious names. When we entered their room the television screen was flashing the proper message, "Welcome to Mr. & Mrs. Don Lind"—that struck the Frankls as funny and the laughter was underway at once. They settled in.

Later that day we met to go for a walk. Viktor and Elly had no interest in doing anything fancy—they were happy to find a McDonald's restaurant right in the hotel building. They did want to pick up some snacks for their room, however, so we stopped at the Osco Drug store just a block from the hotel. There the Frankls selected their snacks and we met at the checkout counter. With my wallet I motioned to the cashier that I would be paying, but Viktor stopped me. To the befuddled cashier he said, pointing at me, "I am a psychiatrist and he is my patient. Furthermore, he is not allowed to handle money." So it was impossible for me to pay. After leaving the store I said to Viktor, "Now what am I supposed to do when I go back to this store to buy something on my own?" He laughed heartily and said heartlessly, "Good luck."

The next morning when I went to meet the Frankls, I found them laughing about their breakfast adventure. As they liked to do, they had phoned the hotel kitchen to order breakfast. Among their all-time favorites was raisin bran, but at the hotel they preferred pancakes with maple syrup—and strong coffee, of course. When room service arrived, the server wheeled in a breakfast cart and asked Viktor to sign the charge slip. Instinctively he signed his typical "DrVFrankl." The server objected that the signature was not correct for the order. Elly was in the bathroom at the moment, so Viktor shouted out, "Elly, what name are we using?" The server was unruffled but, after he left the room, Viktor and Elly laughed over possible conversations back in the kitchen about the old guy in the suite asking the girl in the bathroom what fake name they were using!

The next evening Viktor gave a talk in a packed auditorium at North Park with Elly at his side. (He had strictly refused any other appearances on this trip, in order to honor her.) Starting his talk slowly as usual, Viktor gained steam thanks to the substance of his talk and the strength of his coffee. He used a few notes—huge black marker scribbles on white paper, perhaps six lines on a page and only two or three words on each line. Even these he could make out only with difficulty, using the slice of blurry vision that remained in one eye. Elly prompted him when he could not see—I dare not write that she prodded him—and he reminisced about his long life. He also noted, from a Chicago visit many years earlier, that a local journalist had described logotherapy as a "mixture of psychiatry and prayer."

Using a slide show, Viktor introduced the audience to Freud, the Heideggers, Jaspers, Marcel, Buber, Adler, and others. He himself appeared in some of the slides with these famous people, and together with Elly at the audience with Pope Paul VI. The listeners seemed spellbound, silent except for instantaneous bursts of laughter whenever Viktor quipped. During the interaction time he handled questions from the audience like an old master. Hundreds attended the reception following, but no books were on display or for sale. As usual, in advance Viktor had forbidden us to peddle his books since he did not want his appearance to be used in that way.

On Saturday morning we drove the Frankls to the president's reception for those who were to be honored in the commencement ceremonies. Among the doctoral honorees was the provincial governor of Uppsala, Jan-Erik Wikstrom, former cabinet minister and member of the Swedish Parliament. He was dumbfounded that the Frankls were there, and he told Elly how honored he was to be in the same ceremonies with her. At the given moment, Elly was robed among the dignitaries in the procession of platform guests, faculty, graduating students, and bearers of banners and international flags. The line moved from outdoors into the hall, where nearly three thousand people had assembled. Finally, Elly was seated on the platform amid the pomp. To assure Viktor a clear vantage point, his seat was just offstage and out of view of the audience. Following the invocation the entire assembly joined in the Walter Chalmers Smith hymn, which in retrospect seems apropos both to Viktor's sense of mystery and to his actual visual impairment:

> *Immortal, Invisible, God only wise,*
> *In light inaccessible hid from our eyes,*
> *Most blessed, most glorious, the Ancient of Days,*
> *Almighty, victorious, thy great name we praise.*

After I presented her with a brief sketch of her life, President Horner conferred the doctor of laws degree *honoris causa* upon Eleonore Katharina Frankl, the first of the honorees. As she was invested with the hood signifying the degree, the audience rose instinctively in a prolonged ovation for her. Elly stood, holding back her tears—that is, until Viktor made a completely unexpected move. Since he had an unobstructed view and path from his seat to Elly, he rose and walked unaccompanied straight towards her at center stage. When she saw him coming, she broke down and wept. He walked up to her, took her head in his hands, and, as he put it later, "I was kissing away her tears from her cheeks." There were no other dry eyes in that assembly either as the ovation swelled.

WITH VIKTOR AND Elly—we are used to this by now—conversation could switch from the sublime to the ridiculous in a flash and back again. So prayer and cereal could meet in just a few moments of dialogue. I knew about the Frankls' fancy for raisin bran, but in Vienna I learned they could not obtain in it in stores there. So I promised to ship some from Chicago when I got home, telling them that I would even send some different brands—Post, Kellogg, Total—and they could set bowls side by side and have a tasting, as people do with fine wines. "Good, Don," Viktor said, with his research orientation, "but if we do this we must consider not only the pleasure going in but also the ease of coming out!"

I did ship some raisin brans, and upon receiving them Viktor and Elly phoned immediately from Vienna. He was exuberant. "Even though it is evening, we are having raisin bran!" he shouted into the phone. I told him, "Viktor, you can eat it now or whenever you wish! And in between you can even dream about it." "I HOPE so!" he bellowed, and I laughed at him.

One day in Vienna, Elly and I were chatting about Viktor, about the utter childlikeness that resided in him alongside intellectual powers and spiritual depth. She thought of Martin Heidegger, sitting next to her in a Vienna wine garden; when his meal arrived at the table, he turned to Elly rather timidly, "Do you think it will be alright if I eat with my fingers?" With her assurance, he delightedly picked up a piece of chicken and started to eat. "And you know, he was like a happy child," Elly continued. "Viktor was like that also. In many ways he was just like a child."

Though Viktor was not as taken with animals as Elly was, he became very fond of a certain cat. Sheila belonged to a neighbor in Hütteldorf, on the outskirts of the city where the Veselys lived and where the Frankls had a small apartment on the edge of the Vienna Woods. After their mountaineering days ended, Viktor and Elly went on many weekends to Hütteldorf to be near their family, to breathe the fresh air, and to escape the doorbell and telephone terrors. Whenever they arrived at the little place, Sheila would be waiting for them. During their afternoon naps Sheila would lie on Viktor's chest, facing downward with its tail near Viktor's face. He explained that "this *a posteriori* arrangement presented me with a view I did not prefer." Still, the affection they had for Sheila helped motivate the Frankls to make yet another visit to Hütteldorf.

IN THE VERY last years of his life, Viktor and Elly were still living out the themes of their decades together. While Viktor seemed at times to be self-promoting, he was more interested in logotherapy than in garnering praise and attention for himself. This is illustrated in their different responses to young people who approached them.

A group of American college girls arrived unannounced at Mariannengasse and rang for the Frankls. When Elly went to the intercom to respond, she heard the girls chatting loudly. She overheard one of the girls: "I'll make a bet that I can get a personal autograph from Frankl." The Frankls decided to make no response, to not answer the doorbell. The girl must have lost her wager.

How different Viktor and Elly were toward a high school boy from Graz. Stefan had lost his dad and it had plunged him and his mother into grief. Stefan reached a turning point, however, thanks to *Man's Search for Meaning*. As his despair lifted he read more and more of Frankl's writings. He told his story to his schoolmates, playing a recording of a Frankl lecture in class. The students were attentive, then aroused. Eventually Stefan wrote to Professor Frankl, hardly expecting any reply. The Frankls were touched by his story, and his letter showed an advanced grasp of logotherapy—the Frankls were impressed. So they phoned Stefan, inviting him to come to Vienna. Stefan was still flabbergasted as he scraped together the train fare. I was working with the Frankls the day he arrived at Mariannengasse.

The Frankls spent most of their afternoon with Stefan. The conversation ranged widely and, as always, there was laughter enough, too. The easy rapport between Stefan and the Frankls was remarkable to watch, and he was overjoyed with it. "I can't believe I am sitting right here, right now." When Stefan left for his return home, I told Viktor and Elly that it was good of them to call him and to spend so much time with him. Elly replied, "But Don, this is meaningful to do," and Viktor said it even more strongly: "Why *not?* Here is a boy who has lost his own father. Why should we *not* spend our time with him?"

That logotherapy speaks to people in despair is nothing new. Even in the extremes of the Nazi camps logotherapy kept on speaking—to those with enough strength left for hearing and thinking—long after the psychologies of Freud and Adler had gone speechless.

The Frankls also had no interest in accumulating wealth, or in spending it. They lived simply, without craving for things. Intuitively, at least after the Holocaust, they seem to have understood that—as social psychologist David Myers might put it—happiness comes not from pleasure but from kindness.[5] To Viktor, the "will to money" was a primitive form of the will to power,[6] and his only concern was that Elly and their family be provided for. When he once bought for himself a fine Rolex watch, he soon lost interest in it and regretted the purchase. He handed it to Elly saying, "You take it. I don't care for it." By contrast, when they came to Evanston, he was boyishly gleeful to find at Osco Drug a twenty-dollar Timex watch with big black hands and numbers on a large white face. But alas, his vision was so poor that ultimately the watch was not useful to him and he lost it.

In Viktor's own words, "money fulfills its meaning best when it avails somebody who needs it most." His family remembers that Viktor, upon seeing a poor person handling an item in a store and checking the price, would sometimes purchase the item and leave it at the cashier as a gift. On one occasion Viktor watched an old man asking the price of a newfangled little radio; the old gent gave up on purchasing one because he could not afford it. Viktor paid for it and asked the cashier to give it to the man.

On one of my trips I carried a book to Vienna protected in a Ziploc plastic bag for Viktor to autograph for someone. He accepted it, wrote in it, and returned it the next day—but without the Ziploc bag. So I asked for it. When the truth came out, Viktor had adopted the bag for himself. He was delighted to have a new one, since for years he had been using the same plastic bag to hold his medicine bottles. He kept all his prescriptions together and, holding the bag up to the light, he could even make out some of the bottles. When I accused him of stealing my Ziploc bag, he simply smiled and gave me his old one. It was so worn out, its texture was like that of facial tissue.

The Frankls were not very sentimental about things. The few objects that Viktor prized most were in that small cubicle which had been in his study since 1945—things practically worthless to anyone else, some of which had belonged to his father. After Viktor's death, according to Franz, Elly one day opened that little compartment and broke down, sobbing. Recovering, she commented on the pathetic little possessions Viktor had cherished—such simple things. Seemingly he cared for no other things, not even for the heaping piles of honors stored in the back room. Logotherapy, however, was his progeny and pride. But in a passionate moment he loosed his grip even on that.

Near the end he saw how weary Elly was, and his heart went out to her. His deep love and his compassion for her in her own need overwhelmed him. "Elly, when I am gone, take everything about logotherapy and throw it away. Get rid of it all, so that you can have your own life again at last." We who knew Viktor well might joke that he realized she would never do that—that she could not destroy the residue of all their work together. But we also know that he could be flooded with pity toward people who suffered, and he poured himself out to lift up people from their sorrows. So the sincerity even in so rash a suggestion may be trusted.

Oh, there was one honor that Viktor allowed to be displayed prominently in their home. Upon leaving the flat one day, he walked with me down the hallway toward the foyer. Midway he stopped and asked me, "Do you know what is the greatest honor given to me in my life?" "The trails in the Rax that are named for you?" I asked, reminding him of a conversation we had had about mountaineering. He smiled as if to acknowledge that he may have said such a thing once. But then he pointed to a framed certificate hanging on the hallway wall. "This is the greatest honor of my life." He waited patiently while I read and photographed it.

The certificate is framed in walnut, blending with the colors of a rendering of a large tree whose branches and leaves arch over the following words, as if to shelter them from the elements.

Ninety trees have been planted
by the students of St. Francis High School of
Calgary, Alberta, Canada
in honour of your 90th birthday
One for each year of your life
Dr. Viktor Emil Frankl
in Jerusalem, at the Children's Garden
within the Peace Forest
for you have guided a tremendous number of Calgary's
Catholic high school students for over twenty years and
will continue to do so for many more
generations to come

Then follow the names of the coordinating teacher of religious studies, the chaplain, and the principal, ending with the line, "And all of the Students." At the bottom left is a logo—one tree planted along a roadside and the words in both English and Hebrew, "Jewish National Fund of Canada."

"How beautiful, Viktor," I said. He said, quietly, "When I see this, I am ready to die."

THROUGHOUT THE FRANKL story there have been glimpses of the significance of prayer to Viktor. He was a deeply religious man whose faith is better described as high—that is, transcendent and monotheistic; and wide—that is, embracing all of humankind as one family ("monanthropism," he called it). Devout people of various faiths felt that he understood and encouraged them, that somehow he was in solidarity with them even though conventional boundaries cut off various faiths and denominations from one another. He adamantly refused to see the world divided into believers and infidels. Atheists, deists, polytheists, pantheists, monotheists, agnostics—all are human, all in the family. Viktor affected many people of faith as well as those who had only questions. While no one's journey is prescriptive for someone else, perhaps mine illustrates Viktor's influence. During my student year in Vienna, I was taking stock of life, as young people do. In my search, somehow my reading diet included Rabbi Abraham Heschel's[7] *God in Search of Man* and Karl Barth's *The Word of God and the Word of Man*—and from these I grasped the notion that it is not we who seek the answers in God, but rather God who seeks the questions in us. This was reinforced weekly by Viktor at the Poliklinik ("it is we who are questioned by life"), though he was talking about psychiatry and psychology, not theology. "Existence falters except in transcendence," he said, pointing beyond ourselves in unison with Heschel and Barth. For all of his intellectual powers and stridency, Viktor had a deep-seated humility and knew these words of the prophet: "For my thoughts are not your thoughts, and my ways are not your ways, says the Lord. For as the heavens are higher than the earth, so are my ways higher than your ways and my thoughts than your thoughts."[8]

I told Viktor that he unwittingly had encouraged me as a young student in my own search for faith, and he responded characteristically: "Good, Don. And why *not?* It *should* be that way!"

The certainty of his own faith in God may lie behind comments he wrote in the preface of a book while he was at Harvard in 1961.

> I personally doubt whether, within religion, truth can ever be distinguished from untruth by evidence which is universally acceptable to man. It seems to me that the various religious denominations are something like different languages. It is not possible, either, to declare that any of them is superior to the others. Similarly, no language can justifiably be called "true" or "false," but through each of them truth—the one truth—may be approached as if from different sides, and through each language it is also possible to err, and even to lie.
>
> The more weakly one stands on the ground of his belief the

more he clings with both hands to the dogma which separates it from other beliefs; on the other hand, the more firmly one stands on the ground of his faith, the more he has both hands free to reach out to those of his fellow men who cannot share his belief. The first attitude entails fanaticism; the second, tolerance. Tolerance does not mean that one accepts the belief of the other; but it does mean that one respects him as a human being, with the right and freedom of choosing his own way of believing and living.[9]

Viktor was a private person with regard to his own faith, his practice of prayer, his rootedness in Judaism, his sense of the holy. Ancient scribes, copying the manuscripts of Scripture, would leave blank spaces instead of writing the names of God—so great was their awe. Viktor had such a sense and seemed incapable of speaking in an offhand manner about the Incomprehensible One. Even to Elly he did not speak often of his faith, but she said, "There were times when I was sure that I was living with a holy man." He was absolutely grounded, fixed on something or Someone greater, and Elly marveled at it. He marched to a different drummer, as it were. That makes it difficult for most of us to understand him, and it is impossible for skeptics to comprehend how embedded he was in faith.

Somehow Viktor had retained or was given an enduring faith in a benevolent Providence in spite of all that had happened, a confidence that God suffers too and is indeed capable of infinite suffering—for us, because of us, together with and alongside of us.[10] And further, that suffering is now but not forever, that justice will come. Viktor placed his whole weight and (eschatological) hope with the prophet's words, apparently certain of an ultimate outcome:

The spirit of the Lord God is upon me
because the Lord has anointed me;
he has sent me to announce good news to the humble,
to bind up the broken-hearted,
to proclaim liberty to captives,
release to those in prison;
to proclaim a year of the Lord's favour
and a day of the vengeance of our God;

to comfort all who mourn,
to give them garlands instead of ashes,
oil of gladness instead of mourners' tears,
a garland of splendour for the heavy heart.[11]

Elly recalled an intimate conversation with Viktor shortly after the war in which he—inadvertently perhaps—confessed his trust in God. Of his mother he spoke often to Elly (she said that "Viktor must have loved his mother above all"). On this occasion, Viktor described seeing the newsreel in 1945 in the Munich cinema about Auschwitz, very close to the time he learned that his mother had perished there. He said passionately to Elly: "If it were not for my deep faith in God, at that time I would have hanged myself."

Because of his sense of privacy about faith and his aversion to speaking of God casually, not many know that Viktor emerged from the Holocaust a devout Jew or that he remained one to his death. From the crucible of the camps he emerged immovable. He could fuss over daily frustrations and fret or even fume over small irritations, but he seemed incapable of complaint with regard to true suffering, to bitterest memories, or to significant obstacles.

Though his Bar Mitzvahs are not widely known, they were no secret either since they were rites witnessed and celebrated in the Jewish community. As a thirteen year old, Viktor's Vienna passage into adult responsibility was a traditional one. Then he had his second Bar Mitzvah at the age of eighty-three—thirteen plus seventy years in Jewish tradition—and thus reaffirmed his "responsibleness." That second Bar Mitzvah was in Jerusalem, in a holy place near the great Wall of Tears beneath the Temple Mount. In a videotape of the ceremony, Viktor can be seen with the prayer shawl around his shoulders, and Elly—as a woman—is in the background, moved to tears as others were.[12] Viktor repeated the Hebrew prayers after the chief rabbi, completing some of the passages from memory, unaided. When the chief rabbi started to place the phylacteries on Viktor's forehead and arm, Viktor finished with the rapid, automatic motions of one who had done so thousands of times. He was addressed as Yitzhak Ben Gavriel—son of Gabriel—and, as the rabbi continued speaking sacred words, Viktor kept on saying, "How beautiful, how beautiful."

In his busy life back home, how often did Viktor pray? Following the Holocaust, every morning at the least. Upon arising each day Viktor closed himself in his study, put on the black leather straps and boxes containing the holy words, and said his prayers. After his death I asked Elly if he actually had made these prayers *every* day. "Absolutely. He never missed a day. Every morning for more than fifty years. But nobody knew this." As they traveled the globe Viktor took the phylacteries with them, and everywhere, every morning, he prayed. He uttered memorized words of Jewish prayers and Psalms, and daily he gave thanks for his mother and father, remembering them and their deaths. Whenever Viktor spoke, always rather awkwardly, of "improvising prayers," he meant simply that, in addition to ritualized prayers said in solidarity with all who pray, he also gave thanks and made petitions spontaneously and in his own words.

(After Viktor died I saw his phylacteries for the first time. Elly had placed them in the little cubicle with his few simple possessions. The leather straps and boxes were so frayed from over a hundred years of daily use that the black dye had worn off, the rust-brown natural color of the leather showing over long stretches. These were the very phylacteries that Viktor had seen on his father in morning prayers—"I approached him and asked him to allow me to kiss the Dear Lord. I was five or six years old.")

Viktor also developed a curious practice following the Holocaust, since after surviving he had "nothing to fear anymore, except God." Whenever he suffered a blow or hit an obstacle, he said, "in my mind, I go down on my knees as it were, and give thanks to heaven that this is the worst thing that has happened to me today." In that way he released himself from fretting about setbacks and losses. At one level it may appear a mere "cognitive strategy," but his faith in a Benevolent Providence was resolute. For Viktor, as for many devout people, with practice and the passage of years praying becomes more like breathing than talking. There is the growing sense that one's own best prayers are not made, but given; not offered up until they are first sent down. Words become fewer, silence more common, and listening more keen.

EVERYONE FOLLOWING THE Frankl story this far knows that Viktor and Elly moved seamlessly between domains Jewish and Christian, as though the two faiths were of one cloth. It was as natural when they spoke of Hanukah and Passover as of Christmas and Pentecost. For Hanukah and Christmas, instead of buying things and overeating, they would have potato soup for their holiday meal, remembering that others were in danger and in need, and recalling their own former desperation. Elly would go to synagogue with Viktor, sometimes together with Gaby or the grandchildren; Viktor would go to church with Elly, where both enjoyed choral and organ music, even sermons. The *Shema Yisrael* and the Lord's Prayer simply belonged with them both and in their marriage. But it was not easy for them, especially when they first married. They explained that, under Catholic rules, during the months Viktor was waiting for official Red Cross confirmation of Tilly's death so that he could remarry, Elly was a sinner (having a sexual partner outside of marriage). Later, in marrying a Jewish man she became a *public* sinner, a woman who—like a prostitute—was without shame. But Viktor and Elly *wanted* a religious wedding ceremony and, about the time of their thirtieth anniversary, they hoped that attitudes had changed enough to allow this.

A Catholic priest and friend of the Frankls contacted Cardinal König, and he approved a ceremony of marriage reaffirmation, requiring only that Viktor be willing to have the marriage entered in the church register. Viktor then approached the chief rabbi, asking if Jewish blessings could also be given to their marriage, under the *chuppe*. But the rabbi refused. So there was no ceremony, since the Frankls wanted their marriage—and their devotion to one another over thirty years[13]—blessed by both faiths. In his classic form, Viktor dismissed the refusal to bless their marriage: "It was no longer *our* problem."

Visiting with Franz and Gaby in their home one evening, I happened to tell them about being in the Soviet Union for Easter 1963—on an Austrian student tour during spring break at the University of Vienna. Franz urged me to tell the story to Viktor and Elly, so I did the next time we met.

As part of the tour, we students traveled by bus from Moscow to Sagorsk, a center of the Russian Orthodox Church. The church in the heart of Sagorsk that Easter Sunday morning was filled with mostly older Russian peasants. I understood nothing of the language and little of the liturgy with its incense and strange-sounding music—the "smells and bells." But I was acutely stirred by worshiping in such a strange way and place. We stood for the service—there were no seats—and upon leaving afterward I was followed by a few of the old Russians. When I boarded the bus for departure, I was amazed that these Orthodox pilgrims were standing outside looking at me. I exited the bus quickly and posed with them for a photograph, then took another picture from the window after I re-boarded. Since we could not converse I did not fully understand what was happening between those Russians and me, as the diesel engine roared and spewed out its pollution. When the bus lurched forward all of them waved goodbye to me by making the sign of the cross. Instinctively—but for the first time in my life—I returned the sign. I wondered if these folk had been watching me in the servie, if they had seen that I was deeply moved. When I told this to Viktor he was typically skeptical. "Someone might have told them you were an American—and perhaps they revered America, as many Russians did, as a kind of paradise." But I held out for some additional meaning in the signing of the cross, and Elly picked up on it first. "Though you had no language, you belonged together." Then Viktor relented his challenge, saying, "You were close to each other in Christ. They felt encouraged by this solidarity, by this gesture of solidarity with you."

Remembering their own travels, Elly explained, "We have been in several churches in Russia, where I put candles for my brother—churches full of old women who were very close to me, greeting me, and I don't understand Russian. I always have had the feeling with the Russian people that they are extremely warmhearted." "Deeply pious people," Viktor agreed, "even under Communism. Many Russian people are deeply religious, and even under the threat of their lives they still went to their churches or to underground masses. Even in the Communist camps in Siberia there were underground religious services."

SOME OF THE conversations with the Frankls resembled prayers or even became prayers spontaneously. Once, in some relevant context, we started singing together, "Nobody knows the trouble I've seen"—a spiritual that they had learned in California. On another occasion, the only one of its kind I can recall, we actually paused to share in a prayer. It was right on the street one cool, dark evening. At the end of one of my longer stays in Vienna, I was scheduled to fly back to Chicago the next morning. So the Frankls invited me to join them for dinner with friends Ludwig and Kitty Werber, who had come from London to visit in Vienna, as they often did. Ludwig had been Viktor's dentist in the years prior to Hitler and an enduring friend.

We walked several blocks to the restaurant where we met the Werbers and had a marvelous time at dinner, bantering and swapping stories. As with all good times the evening came to an end and we said good-bye to the Werbers, who were heading off in a different direction.

Viktor, Elly, and I walked arm-in-arm toward Mariannengasse in the darkness that had fallen while we were dining. Our conversation was serene—with the ever-recurring laughter occasionally—and, as usual, some sadness attended our imminent farewell. Viktor was the most keenly aware that we might not see one another again and he spoke of that freely. For the ride back to my room I was picking up streetcar #5 right where Lange Gasse ends at Alser Strasse and only a block from the Frankl home.[4] When I attempted to say good-bye they objected, since they wanted to wait with me for the tram. It was entirely natural in the mood of the moment when I told them about a prayer I remembered from my student days in Vienna—a prayer that I heard a few times at the end of late Sunday services in a little church on Mollardgasse. When I asked if I might offer this prayer, Viktor and Elly responded simultaneously, "Please, Don, please." Just as unselfconsciously as they had laughed at dinner, Viktor and Elly quieted themselves, and I uttered the words:

Lieber Gott:
Bleib bei uns am Abend dieses Tages.
Bleib bei uns am Abend unseres Lebens.
Bleib bei uns am Abend dieser Welt.
Amen.

Immediately Viktor and Elly responded, "Wonderful, Don. This prayer we have never heard until now. Wonderful."

As if on cue the big red streetcar rumbled around the corner toward us, prompting from the Frankls the familiar, "Until we meet again, if heaven permits. Bye-bye. Bye-bye"—and I boarded. I sat down where I could see Viktor and Elly and they had not moved at all. The streetcar jolted and we gestured our farewell with thrown kisses. (I know that in the parting our emotions were heightened, but I still believe those few minutes were among the most intimate I ever spent with Viktor and Elly.) Crossing Alser Strasse into Spitalgasse with the old General Hospital on the right, I bent to catch a glimpse of the bay windows of Viktor's study above and on the left. The short prayer kept circling in my head.

Dear God:
Stay near us in the evening of this day.
Stay near us in the evening of our lives.
Stay near us in the evening of this world.
Amen.

AMONG PRAYERS THAT Viktor loved very much is one from the revered Rabbi Leo Baeck, his former comrade in Theresienstadt. Viktor quoted this prayer, remarkable for having been written near the end of 1945. A copy of it was given to Viktor by Rabbi Pinchas Lapide and it bears the title "Prayer for Reconciliation and Peace Among Nations."[15]

Peace be with them who are of evil intent, and let there be an end to all revenge and to all talk of punishment and retribution.

Beyond all measure are the cruelties; they exceed all human power of conception, and too many are the martyrs. . . .

Therefore, O God, do not with the scales of justice measure their sufferings, charging them to their hangmen, taking a gruesome account; but let it be different. Ascribe and account instead to all the hangmen, informers, and traitors, and all evil humans, this: all the courage and spiritual strength of the others, their humility, their high-spirited dignity, their silent efforts in spite of everything, the hope that never gave in, and the brave smile that dried the tears, and all the love and all the sacrifice, all the fiery love . . . all the pierced and pained hearts that yet remained strong and confident, in the face of death and in death, yea, even in the hour of deepest weakness. . . .

All this, O my God, shall count for a resurrection of Justice— the good shall count, and not the evil; and to the memory of our enemies we shall no more be their victims, no more their nightmare, but rather their help, that they be able to let go the frenzy. . . .

Only this shall be demanded from them, that we, now that all is over, may live as humans among humans, and that there shall be peace again on this poor earth for the people of good intent, and that peace may also come to the others.

Why Viktor loved this prayer is not difficult to understand, given his stance against collective guilt, violence, and retribution.

IN 1994, VIKTOR gave a lecture in Lublin, Poland, not far from the former horrendous Nazi killing camp Majdanek, which like Auschwitz had been both a forced labor and extermination camp. The current Pope John Paul II—as Karol Wojtyla—had been professor of philosophy at the Catholic Lublin University and at Krakow University. Following Viktor's lecture, several people told him that many years earlier Professor Wojtyla often had quoted and referred to writings by Frankl.

Viktor was eighty-nine at this occasion, when he also received an honorary doctorate from the University of Lublin. At the ceremony the choir sang Mozart's *Ave Verum*, by which both Viktor and Elly were deeply stirred—Elly was "the ecumenical ingredient in logotherapy" as Rabbi Reuven Bulka once put it. While Viktor had not been especially fond of Mozart, upon hearing this piece while together with Elly, sung in Latin in Roman Catholic fashion, he loved it ever after. Among the words are these about an ancient Jew:

> *Thou who truly hangedst weary*
> *On the cross for sons of earth;*
> *Thou whose sacred side was riven,*
> *Whence the water flowed and blood,*
> *O may'st thou, dear Lord, be given*
> *At death's hour to be my food.*
> *O tender, O loving,*
> *O Jesus, Son of Mary,*
> *Show me thy mercy.*
> *Amen.*[16]

In Viktor's last years his family knew that *Ave Verum* had become one of his few favorites in the realm of music.

IN THE MID-1990S, Viktor was being hospitalized repeatedly with frightening symptoms—chest pain, shortness of breath, etc.—and betweentimes kept oxygen near at hand. These were the years of my visits and so I was aware of his series of medical emergencies. Eventually I learned from Viktor's physician and others that he had been a wonderful patient—cheerful, grateful for help, joking with staff. While no one wished him ill, the nurses were happy to have him when his return to the ward was prudent.

Harald Mori, a medical student who had befriended the Frankls, assisted them many times. He told me about these medical crises and about a particular one in 1995. The Frankls had called Harald and Claudia (his wife, a physician), requesting immediate help. At the Frankl home the Moris found Viktor in a serious state with lung edema. They administered oxygen and medication until the medics arrived with an ambulance. They stabilized the situation and rushed Viktor to the hospital. Harald and Claudia were in the ambulance and Viktor was desperate, apparently sensing that his own death might be imminent. Gasping for breath, the only words he said were these: "Take care of my wife. Please take care of my wife." Fortunately the medical interventions made it possible for Viktor to recover and even continue his work.

Elly's love for Viktor played out in her utter devotion to him in the final years, and there were many gestures of gratitude from him to her. Once Elly and granddaughter Katja made an overnight trip to Munich, and Viktor remained in Mariannengasse and in contact with the rest of the family. When the women arrived at their hotel a message was waiting for Elly. It was from Viktor and only three Latin words: *Cogito ergo sum.* These famous words of Rene Descartes mean "I think, therefore I am"— an odd message for a man to send to his wife. But for Viktor and Elly, it went way back to their early romance when he, the highly educated physician, was touched by Elly's guess at a translation: "I am thinking of you." Even after decades, *Cogito ergo sum* was code that had special meaning between them.

According to Elly, Viktor's health deteriorated dramatically immediately following the death of his sister Stella—October 1996 in Australia— only a month after cousin Fritz had died in Brünn. His response to her death signifies the depth of his love for her.

Upon Stella's passing, her daughter Liesl phoned from Australia and Viktor answered. Elly was in another room and all she heard was a loud cry from Viktor in his study. After hanging up the phone, he literally wailed out as he convulsed in grief. As usual, his crying was soon over, but the loss took its toll. Viktor was hospitalized that evening and never regained the health he had enjoyed up to that time. After that he did not speak so often of Stella. She now belonged to the past, to the world, and nothing could disturb her life and love ever again—those were now "sedimented," as Viktor put it.[7]

The last photographs taken of Viktor were in August 1997 at a back-yard party at the home of Franz and Gaby Vesely. It was in celebration of the marriage of Katja to Klaus Ratheiser, a physician specializing in intensive care. On a videotape Viktor is chatting and joking, as usual. "There were two Israeli soldiers in a military plane heading for Tel Aviv . . ." (see the prologue). Obviously Viktor was enjoying himself, surrounded by the people who loved him most and who would laugh yet again at that joke.

Later that month there was another emergency and this time it was more ominous. Viktor's heart was giving out and his demise seemed imminent. His physicians conferred with him and Elly, and it was Viktor's own decision to undergo bypass surgery—even at the age of ninety-two.[8]

The Frankls' son-in-law Franz and grandson-in-law Klaus visited Viktor in the hospital at this time. He had piercing chest pain despite medication, but did not complain. In fact, even in this situation Viktor was serene. Turning to the two men he said, "I cannot help myself, but I see nothing tragic in these circumstances."

Elly was with Viktor day and night, returning to Mariannengasse only in the late night hours to rest a bit and refresh as she was able. The medical staff expressed amazement at both her devotion and endurance. What they did not know was that, early each morning, Elly took to Viktor his phylacteries, closed his room door, then stood outside in the hall to ensure that no one entered. There in complete privacy Viktor, in his frailty, strapped on the leather bands and boxes and spoke the words as naturally as breathing, "*Modeh ani*—I thank you—King everlasting and eternal, for having mercifully returned my soul to me. Great is your faithfulness . . ." Only heaven knows what other prayers Viktor improvised in his most intimate dialogue.

WHEN THE TIME drew near for Viktor to be taken away for heart surgery, which he and everyone knew he was unlikely to survive, Elly was alongside the gurney on which he lay. With their parting at hand, Viktor said, "Elly, I have inscribed one of my books to you and I have hidden it in our apartment. There you will find it." When Viktor beckoned her to come closer, she bent down so that he could whisper into her ear, virtually his last words to her. "I want to thank you once more, Elly, for all that you have done for me in your life." The words echoed what Viktor had written in his 1978 book, *The Unheard Cry for Meaning*, on an otherwise blank page preceding the preface:

> A special word of gratitude to my wife, Eleonore Katharina, whom I thank for all the sacrifices she has made throughout the years for the sake of helping me to help others. Indeed, she merits the words that Professor Jacob Needleman once inscribed in a book of his that he dedicated to her on one of my lecture tours, which I made, as I always do, in her company. "To the warmth," he wrote, "that accompanies the light."
>
> May the warmth long persist when the light has dimmed away.[19]

Viktor survived the surgery but never regained consciousness. He lay for three days in intensive care with Elly at his side, alone. She had with her an audiocassette player and tape.

> You see, in the three days before Viktor died, Alexander was upset. And I had not allowed anyone to visit Viktor in this intensive care unit because he was no longer Viktor Frankl. Only Klaus was there, and Franz visited once in that unit. But Alexander told me, "Grandma, I bring you this tape recorder since I know grandpa liked Mozart and Mahler. So put this near his ear even if he is unconscious. Maybe he still can hear the music." And so I was holding the earphones for hours on Viktor's ears. And all the doctors and nurses remarked that they had never seen this before—all day I was speaking to Viktor and playing this music. Imagine in the last hours if he can hear his favorite music, *Ave Verum!* ["O may'st thou, dear Lord, be given, At death's hour to be my food."] This was Alexander's idea, and it was wonderful.

I asked Elly if Alex had visited, too, but she said, "Not in intensive care. It would have broken his heart. It was hard enough for me. Even though I had worked in a hospital, I had never seen something like this. Never in my life. To tell you the truth there was a conference, including Klaus, when they said Viktor's kidneys had shut down and it was only this machine that kept him going. And they said, if I say yes, they will turn off all the machines. And I said yes. But this was the hardest moment in my life." I said, "But Viktor would have wanted this." "Absolutely," she said, "he already had told me so."

Alexander's music was a tender story, I told Elly, and she continued. "Yes, he understood Viktor and they could talk with one another. If Alexander speaks of his grandfather, it is completely in tune with him. Both Alexander and Katja were extremely close to Viktor. It shows how close grandfather and grandchildren can be . . . how close old people and young people can be. It is wonderful. For both sides. Viktor was so proud of Katja and Alexander—you have no idea. . . . You have no idea." At these words Elly broke down and wept. Moved also, I waited quietly as the flood of feelings ebbed.

Elly remembered that when Viktor was old and very tired, he slipped into a vast sadness, and "he said, 'If I did not have these two grandchildren, I would not give a damn to go on with this life.' And he loved Gaby *very* much, and Franz was like a son to him. . . . In a way Viktor was embedded in this family."

We spoke also of Viktor's affection for people of many sorts, most especially for those who suffer, and Elly observed, "Yes, snobbish and shallow people he didn't like, but crazy people he loved." Then I returned to the main motif, "His family was his life. He could manage without other relationships as long as he had his family. All of this love made it possible for him to do his work—without love of his family he could never have done it. Yet he never spoke much about it." Elly agreed, "He never was public about his family. No one knew about us. Even in *Recollections* the editor had to push him to write something about the family."

ON TUESDAY, SEPTEMBER 2, 1997, Viktor died peacefully. News of his death went around the world, though it was barely noticed in the wake of the shocking death of Princess Diana. She had been killed in the Paris accident on Sunday—just two days before Viktor's death—and much of the world was transfixed by the tragedy. Then three days after Viktor's death, Mother Teresa died in Calcutta at the age of eighty-seven. His passing was overshadowed between and by the deaths of the two women, each far more famous than he.

Elly remembered a reception for Prince Charles and Princess Diana at the city hall in Vienna a long time ago, in fact early in the royal marriage. "Viktor felt sorry for Princess Diana. She was at that time only a young girl, and in such a gathering everyone was looking at her, and he said, 'It must be terrible for her.' She was to be seated at the head table, next to the Austrian president. When she came in she tried to sit down and seemingly there was something wrong with her chair, and she fell. Perhaps 500 or 600 people are looking at this, and we thought it was an awful situation. Viktor felt for her, very, very much." Seemingly he had feared for her in the frenzy of public attention.

Princess Diana—born and married into extreme privilege and celebrity—died before she could complete the good works that waited for her. On such a different journey, Mother Teresa—vowing poverty for the sake of the poorest of the poor—died full of years with a lifelong legacy of mercy. Mother Teresa and Viktor had been featured speakers on the same conference rosters at least three times—in Paris, Guadalajara, and Vienna—though they never met. Yet word reached Vienna that laureate Mother Teresa had written to the Nobel Committee in Sweden, urging them to award the Peace Prize also to Viktor Frankl, though nothing came of it.

That Viktor passed away in relative obscurity suited the manner of his burial. By virtue of the city's highest tribute, the honorary citizenship, Viktor had been offered a gravesite among the most elite in the Central Cemetery of Vienna. But he had refused absolutely a grave of honor and had been adamant that his remains be interred at the Lion (his mother's family name) plot in the Jewish section of the cemetery.

At an earlier time I had told Viktor and Elly about my visits to their family burial plots in Central Cemetery, on the main side of the Danube, and in Kagran Cemetery "on the other side." We all knew that religious convention would never allow Viktor and Elly to be buried in the same place as Jew and Christian. I pointed out that the Danube had flowed between them in their births in Leopoldstadt and Kaisermühlen, and that it would flow between them again when they were segregated in separate cemeteries at their death. Viktor jumped on it at once, "Who cares if we cannot be buried side-by-side? It doesn't matter a damn! What matters is that we have loved each other and worked together all these years. This can never be taken away!"

In his final parting, Viktor left to us what he long called the greatest human honor: to help wherever and however we can. To answer responsibly, no matter what the circumstances, as life calls out to us. To do everything we can to make the world a better place. And he wanted us to know by his loving union with Elly across half a century that we can only do so *together.* That, in a manner of speaking, no one defies the Danube alone.

When Viktor had finished his strident statements—about not giving a damn for the separation of graves, about what really matters, about wrongs forgiven, about sufferings borne, about loves loved and labors finished, which can never be taken away or erased from the world—Elly was ready to speak. She was sitting near Viktor but all she said was, "He is right. He is right."

The Jewish burial rite took place shortly after Viktor's death. Ten Jewish men were present, as required, and the prayers of the rabbi were nearly mumbled since Viktor had wished for silence more than words. (On a visit to the cemetery later I saw that only his name had been added to the humble family gravestone, with no reference whatsoever to his life or accomplishments. The surface of the marker was literally covered with little stones, each one placed by an earlier visitor in the Jewish custom.)

WHEN I RETURNED to Vienna a few weeks after Viktor's passing, the Mariannengasse home was eerie, strangely empty, silent. The former wellspring of its energy was gone. Elly and I sat in his study and chatted for many hours. She was very lonely, grieving. In the conversation I said, "It is good that Viktor can rest now. How could anyone keep going and going, with health failing. If he could no longer do what he loved to do, then it's enough." "It is enough," Elly replied, "and I told you that seemingly he was expecting his death and—in a way—wishing his death. He was ready for the end. He was ready." "Since that was so, then it was important for you who loved him most to let him go." "What a deep love we had," she continued, ". . . without a deep love we never could have done what we did. So it was much more than a marriage."

Then Elly told me about the book that Viktor had hidden in the apartment. Immediately after his death she had combed through the flat looking for it—over and over, trying to imagine each nook where he might possibly have hidden it. It was nowhere and Elly was frustrated. Viktor had been completely lucid up to the hour of his surgery and she was sure the book was somewhere in the flat, just as he had told her.

Eventually Elly came across the sought-for book when she was not expecting it at all. Viktor had been intimately familiar with her routines in

maintaining their household. Every few months Elly took down the treasured books from the case opposite Viktor's desk where he had carefully
arranged all the language editions of his books. These were not cataloged
in any systematic way, but Viktor knew each book and its place and trusted
only Elly to handle them. He apparently assumed that she would continue
to dust them carefully even after he was gone. That she did.

As Elly took down each row of books for dusting, behind a shelf filled
with editions of *Man's Search for Meaning*, one book was out-of-place—
perhaps it had been mistakenly pushed behind the others. But it was a
copy of his *Homo Patiens* (which means "suffering man") from 1950. In
this copy as in all others, following the title and copyright pages is a dedication page completely blank except for one word: Elly. When she opened
it the mystery was solved: this was the book Viktor had left especially for
her, inscribed during his last days or weeks—the inscription is undated.
Above the printed name, with his dark felt-tip pen he had inserted the
word *für*—so that the amended dedication begins "For Elly" (or "To
Elly"). Below this the scrawl of a man all but blind, the German lines
slanting irregularly but sharply upward to the right. The words are dis-
cernible perhaps only to those who know Viktor's handwriting intimately,
and even for them it takes some doing to read. But the words are these:

For Elly,
Who succeeded in changing a suffering man into a loving man.
Viktor

TO WRITE THIS story I had to replay and replay my recorded conversations
with Viktor and Elly. Because I had forgotten, I was quite surprised when
I listened to the words Viktor said to me the last time I saw him. It was unusual to be recording our dialogue as we walked down the hallway to the
foyer at Mariannengasse, but at this particular parting we all had a sense
that, though there were thousands of stories told and thousands more un-
told, it was enough.

As we were bidding farewell in the foyer and I was about to turn off
the recorder, Viktor said to me, "There, now you have it. The whole story
is sedimented, as it were."

Notes

INTRODUCTION

1. See D&SL (abbreviations of Frankl titles are listed in References). Appearing in German in 1946 under the title *Ärztliche Seelsorge* ("medical ministry"), it was one of the first books published in Austria following World War II. In 1955 the first English edition was titled *The Doctor and the Soul.* Currently an expanded and updated edition with the same English title is published by Vintage.

2. See MSFM. The original German title in 1946 was *Ein Psycholog erlebt das KZ*—literally, "a psychologist experiences the concentration camp"; later German editions bear the title,... *trotzdem Ja zum Leben sagen* ("... nevertheless we say yes to life"). The first English edition was *From Death Camp to Existentialism: A Psychiatrist's Path to a New Therapy* (Boston: Beacon Press, 1959). Over the years the book has appeared in a variety of English editions, the current expanded ones bearing the title *Man's Search for Meaning.* It is also available in Braille and on audiotape.

3. The first to use the tag "the third Viennese school of psychotherapy" probably was Soucek. See his 1948 article.

4. Frankl regarded Freud, as the founder of psychotherapy, as unique and irreplaceable; for example, see WTOM, p. 12.

5. The use of the term existential analysis requires explanation at the outset. Frankl started out labeling his theory "existential analysis" as distinct from psychoanalysis. Soon he coined the term "logotherapy" and for a time called his system "logotherapy and existential analysis." The two terms sometimes have been used almost interchangeably, but Frankl used existential analysis for his "anthropology" (used in German for his "concept of man") and its philosophical underpinnings, and logotherapy for his psychotherapeutic theory and practice—the methods and techniques. Over time, and for simplicity's sake in his lectures and writings, Frankl himself tended to use only "logotherapy" for his entire system. He never officially dropped "existential analysis" as such, but used it together with "logotherapy." "Existential analysis" was used also by Ludwig Binswanger and Medard Boss (the German *Existenzanalyse* and *Daseinsanalyse* are both translated existential analysis), and by Rollo May in America. The term is found in the writings of Heidegger, Sartre, and others (where it refers to the analysis of existence).

Today "existential analysis" is an umbrella term used by philosophers, psychologists, and historians for all sorts of developments whose threads tie in somehow to European existentialism. The term is used also in various countries and languages in the names of societies that may have little to do with one another. So as a practical matter, in this book I shall use "logotherapy" alone to refer to the entire body of Frankl's work, even though "logotherapy and existential analysis" was historically his own label. Fortunately, logotherapy is identified with Frankl consistently.

With advances in the prevention and treatment of psychological disorders, the techniques of logotherapy may be improved or even superseded. But logotherapy's future as a concept of human nature, as an approach that humanizes the treatment of people in a technological age, may be ever more important. That is, as cognitive science, brain science, psychosurgery, psychopharmacology, mind control, and even the technologies of destruction continue to develop, there will be more need, not less, to be reminded of the spiritual nature of persons—with inherent human dignity, freedom, and responsibility.

6. This is echoed by American psychologist Martin Seligman who writes that "rampant individualism carries with it two seeds of its own destruction. First, a society that exalts the individual to the extent that ours now does will be ridden with depression . . . Second, and perhaps most important, is meaninglessness [which occurs when there is no] attachment to something larger than you are." Cited in Myers, 1992, p. 148.

7. WTOM, p. 96; P&EX, p. 125.

8. The term "selfism" is used by Paul Vitz in his critique, *Psychology as Religion: The Cult of Self-Worship.*

9. By the 1980s the trend toward individualism, materialism, and self-gratification in America was pointed out by Americans also. For example, from psychological-religious perspectives, in 1977 came the first edition of Vitz's *Psychology as Religion: The Cult of Self-Worship;* and in 1980 Myers' *The Inflated Self: Human Illusions and the Biblical Call to Hope.* From a psychoanalytic perspective—with Freudian overtones even in its title—there is Stern's *ME: The Narcissistic American* from 1979.

10. This is a widely used mantra in publications and speeches, and it is often used for prophetic and religious challenges to contemporary society.

11. For a sociological study of American society see Bellah's *Habits of the Heart.* For an overview of the spiritual quest from the perspective of research in social psychology see Myers' *The American Paradox: Spiritual Hunger in an Age of Plenty.* For an analysis by an economist, see Lane's *The Loss of Happiness in Market Democracies.*

12. As early as 1929 Frankl used the term logotherapy, and in 1938 he published an article in which he explored logotherapy, existential analysis, and "spiritual problems in psychotherapy"—though he was not writing about religion. That original article was, "Zur geistigen Problematik der Psychotherapie." See Frankl, 1938.

13. Frankl understood the problems of translation and preferred in English to refer to the spiritual dimension as "noetic"—from the Greek *nous* for mind, intellect, including the human moral component. See P&EX, pp. 73–74.

14. See *Religion and the Clinical Practice of Psychology,* 1996; Richards and Bergin, 1997; and *Integrating Spirituality into Treatment,* 1999.

15. See D&SL, p. 29.

16. Again, for Frankl's own words, see "Self-transcendence as a human phenomenon," in WTOM, pp. 31–49.

CHAPTER 1

1. The word "holocaust" was applied some time after the Nazi era, and it is now common practice to capitalize it when referring to the genocide under Hitler. Often "Holocaust" is used

solely for "the Jewish Holocaust." But I use the capitalized "Holocaust" consistently for the Nazi abuse of all victims and the murder of what actually may have been tens of millions (excluding war casualties). Five million is a figure sometimes used for the number of non-Jews murdered under Hitler, but there is evidence that genocide by the Nazis actually may have taken *twenty-one million* lives or more, including the widely accepted estimate of six million Jews (see Rummel, 1997). In this book, when the term "holocaust" is not capitalized, it refers to mass killing by governments in the twentieth century—see chapter 12 especially—and to the potential for future mass atrocities.

2. Baedeker, 1905, pp. 64–65.

3. There are many biographical studies of Freud, but I have relied on the scholarly, sympathetic, and readable biography by Peter Gay, *Freud: A Life for Our Time.* The earlier three-volume work by Ernest Jones, a close Freud associate, contains many personal details: *The Life and Work of Sigmund Freud.*

4. Among few biographical sources on Adler are: the enduring study by Heinz and Rowena Ansbacher, *The Individual Psychology of Alfred Adler;* the chapter on Adler in Henri F. Ellenberger's *The Discovery of the Unconscious: The History and Evolution of Dynamic Psychiatry;* and Edward Hoffman, *The Drive for Self: Alfred Adler and the Founding of Individual Psychology.* An attempt to revive interest in individual psychology is Loren Gray's *Alfred Adler, the Forgotten Prophet.*

5. Today the visitor to Vienna, upon entering Czerningasse from Nestroyplatz, will find plaques in German denoting these residences of Adler and Frankl. The plaque on the building at number seven reads: "In this building lived and worked ALFRED ADLER, born 2/7/1870 died 5/28/1937, Founder of Individual Psychology." Across the street at number six the tablet reads: "The Neurologist and Psychiatrist VIKTOR E. FRANKL lived and worked in this building 1905–1942, from the day of his birth to the day of his deportation to the concentration camps."

6. In 1997, thanks to Austrian medical student Harald Mori, I had an extensive personal tour of the *Männerheim* (men's home), which is remarkably unchanged. The rooms which Hitler occupied are intact and our guide told us that documentaries on Hitler's life have been filmed therein.

7. Philosopher Jonathan Glover points out that we are shocked by the scale of twentieth century barbarism and atrocities, but that these "also contrast with the expectations, at least in Europe, with which the twentieth century began." See Glover, 1999, p. 3.

8. Gay, 1988, pp. 19–21.

9. *The Tenth Man* was written by Paddy Chayefsky and first performed at the Booth Theater in New York on November 5, 1959. It was then published by Random House, New York, 1960.

10. Frankl described his interaction with a psychoanalyst at a coffeehouse regarding the hated hikes in P&EX, p. 60.

CHAPTER 2

1. Carsten, 1986, pp. 1–18.

2. MSFM, p. 23; see WTOM, p. ix and p. 73 where Frankl describes logotherapy itself as optimistic.

3. Republished in 1997 as *Man's Search for Ultimate Meaning*—MSUL.

4. RECL, p. 32.

5. See UHCM, p. 41.

6. Frankl, 1924.

7. See P&EX, p. 121 for Frankl's definition of nihilism. The aspect most significant to him was its assumption that life has no meaning and, therefore, no value.

8. For a detailed review of the possible philosophical influences on Frankl, see Gould, 1993. Two other reviews, more critical of logotherapy from religious perspectives, are Tengan, 1999, and Tweedie, 1961.

9. *Analecta Frankliana,* 1982, pp. 8–9. Frankl referred his audience to his own UHCM. The extended quotation is also found in WTOM, pp. 166–67, from a 1966 Frankl lecture.

10. D&SL, p. xxvii.

CHAPTER 3

1. See Lukacs, 1997, especially chapter 2, and Fleming, 1982, "The Growth of an Obsession," pp. 1–16.

2. Toland, 1976, pp. 181ff.

3. See Freidenreich, 1991; Berkley, 1988; and Carsten, 1986.

4. Freidenreich, 1991, pp. 213ff.

5. Frankl, 1926, "Zur Psychologie des Intellektualismus," pp. 332–33. This quotation Frankl attributes to Goethe, who in *Faust* dared to change the words of the Gospel of John ("In the beginning was the deed").

6. Gay, 1988, pp. 391ff.

7. Cited in *Sigmund Freud: His Life in Pictures and Words* (1985), p. 229. In this book are photographs of Heinele among many other pictures of Freud and his grandchildren.

8. Gay, 1988, p. 418.

9. Appignanesi and Forrester, 1992, p. 21.

10. Schur, 1972, chapter 13.

11. Gay, 1988, pp. 420–21.

12. Hoffman, 1994, pp. 143ff, dates the fateful meeting and departures of Allers and Schwarz in 1925. Frankl stayed with the Adlerians for at least some months following the de-fection of Allers and Schwarz; his own recollections, and his ongoing lectures in Adlerian cir-cles in 1926, place both the fateful meeting and his own expulsion by Adler in 1927. Across the decades Frankl consistently dated these events to 1927 (see WTOM, p. 166; RECL, pp. 60–62). But most important for the story here, Frankl's memories and the Hoffman account of what happened at the meeting are in harmony.

13. Adler, in *The International Forum for Logotherapy,* 1980, p. 35.

14. *Zur Geschichte der Psychiatrie in Wien,* 1883, pp. 28–33.

15. See Ellenberger, 1970, pp. 585–86.

16. *A History of Psychology in Autobiography,* pp. 7–8. Social psychologist David Myers made me aware of the anecdote.

CHAPTER 4

1. RECL, p. 74.

2. D&SL, p. 19.

3. Frankl suggested that humor is also a divine attribute, citing certain passages in the Hebrew psalter; see P&EX, p. 147 note, and also WTOM, p. 17.

4. D&SL, p. 216.

5. Freidenreich, 1991, p. 187.

6. *Conquering the Past: Austrian Nazism Yesterday and Today*, 1989, pp. 137–48.

7. RECL, p. 34.

8. Bullock, 1952, chapter 6.

CHAPTER 5

1. Quoted in *Sigmund Freud: His Life in Pictures and Words*, p. 269.

2. Gay, 1988, p. 592.

3. Stürmer, 1999, p. 164.

4. Quoted in *Sigmund Freud: His Life in Pictures and Words*, p. 283.

5. Ibid., p. 263.

6. Freidenreich, p. 206.

7. Quoted in Gay, 1988, p. 615.

8. The SS, the SA, and the Gestapo were parts of the immense organization of the National Socialist system in Germany. There were many other components, but in this story these three will turn up repeatedly. The SS (*Schutzstaffel*), which Hitler himself founded as a personal protection force, swelled to many subunits and divisions comprised of thousands of black-uniformed state and military police. Among their numbers were those responsible for the implementation of brutal Nazi policy and for the concentration camps. The SA (*Sturmabteilung*) began as a paramilitary force but used brutality freely to assist Hitler's rise to power. Known as the "brownshirts," they may have numbered two million by 1933. After 1935 the SA was emasculated by SS forces and never regained its former clout. The Gestapo (*Geheime Staatspolizei*), on the other hand, was one bureau of the Central Security Office—essentially the national secret police. The Gestapo did the dirty work of eliminating elements the Nazis considered undesirable and dangerous. The Gestapo also were responsible for deportations of Jews to the extermination camps, so are highly relevant to the Frankl story.

9. Bullock, pp. 395–97; and *Chronicle of the 20th Century*, pp. 479–80.

10. For the events of the *Anschluss*, see Kershaw, pp. 65–86; Bullock, pp. 387–402; Toland, pp. 432–58; and Berkley, pp. 301–36.

11. Berkley, 1988, p. 260.

12. Carsten, p. 281.

13. *The Diary of Sigmund Freud*, pp. 229–37.

14. *Encyclopaedia Britannica*, 2000. "Kristallnacht."

15. Gay, 1988, note p. 649.

16. Berkley, 1988, pp. 277ff.

17. In 1960 in Chicago, Frankl told about "Dr. J., the mass murderer of Steinhof"—apparently the zealous head of the euthanasia program; see P&EX, pp. 62–63. Today the only public tangible reminder of the ghastly goings-on at Steinhof is a very general one: a stone marker near the Steinhof Church with this inscription (in German): "In remembrance of the victims of the National Socialist State at the Psychiatric Department—and as a warning. Erected in the year 1988."

18. Bukey, p. 166.

19. RECL, p. 82.

20. Most probably Gabriel found the stone amid the ruins of the Leopoldstädter Tempel at Tempelgasse 3, just around the corner from Czerningasse.

21. Jews were not permitted to use taxis in the city but in this case, for a medical emergency, Frankl did secure a cab ride.

CHAPTER 6

1. Actual identifiers are displayed in Holocaust museums. The United States Museum publishes an illustrative poster and explanatory materials: *Artifact Poster Set Teacher Guide*.

2. *Ghetto Museum Terezín* and *The Small Fortress Terezín, 1940–1945*.

3. *Encyclopaedia Britannica*, "Theresienstadt."

4. Troller, p. xxii.

5. An English rendering that I once used in an article is, "Be cheerful now and every day, for God will help us on the way." That is the meaning, but the German is more clipped.

6. Music was prominent in Theresienstadt and some was composed there. Recorded albums of music and satire from the ghetto are available. In the United States *"Bei mir bist du schön"* became one of the Andrews Sisters' greatest hits.

7. RECL, p. 93.

8. See Bondy, *"Elder of the Jews": Jakob Edelstein of Theresienstadt*.

9. See Berkley, 1993.

10. Berkley, 1993, pp. 161–62.

11. Bondy, pp. 374–75.

12. The book is *Das Leiden am sinnlosen Leben: Psychotherapie für Heute* (1977). Freiburg: Herder.

13. RECL, p. 26.

14. Berkley, 1993, pp. 123–24.

15. Bondy, p. 384.

CHAPTER 7

1. See *Historical Atlas of the Holocaust*.

2. For the transports of the family from Theresienstadt, see *Totenbuch Theresienstadt*, pp. 32, 45, and 1.22.

3. *Totenbuch Theresienstadt*, pp. 1.21, 1.22, 32, and 45.

4. *Auschwitz-Birkenau Guide-Book*.

5. For example, on the museum controversy see *Speaking Out: Jewish Voices from United Germany*, 1995, particularly the chapters by Hanno Loewy ("Thanks for the Memories: Reflections on Holocaust Museums") and Cilly Kugelmann ("Jewish Museums in Germany: A German-Jewish Problem").

6. See *Historical Atlas of the Holocaust*, pp. 142, 165–66.

7. No reader of Frankl should be surprised that he told the same anecdotes in different versions, since earlier in his postwar speeches and writings he avoided personal references. Later on he told of the same incidents in the first person, so we know that he was, in fact, the one of whom he spoke in third-person accounts. An example is this story of a prisoner at Auschwitz

who urged his young wife to grant sexual favors to Nazi SS men who might demand such, if by so doing she could save her own life; in this way the husband forgave his wife in advance for such an eventuality (see WTOM, p. 64). In another context Frankl wrote the same story autobiographically; that is, he identified himself as the prisoner-husband who frees his prisoner-wife Tilly from her obligation of sexual faithfulness to him in advance of a life-threatening situation (see RECL, p. 90). Another example is the story of a typhus victim (D&SL, p. 91 and RECL, p. 95); another is of a prisoner fortifying himself by imagining a lecture he might give after the war (D&SL, p. 100 and P&EX, p. 102); and yet another is the psychiatrist giving encouragement to fellow prisoners in the huts of the concentration camps (D&SL, p. 103; RECL, pp. 95–97).

8. In the biographical notes by Christian Handl, 1992, in Frankl, *Bergerlebnis und Sinnerfahrung*, p. 39.

9. MSFM, pp. 24–25.

10. P&EX, pp. 25–26.

11. MSFM, pp. 53–54.

12. RECL, p. 93. In my own audio recordings there is a version of this story also.

13. MSFM, pp. 44–45.

14. MSFM, p. 56.

15. MSFM, pp. 40–41.

16. See also P&EX, pp. 97–98.

17. RECL, p. 95.

18. MSFM, p. 66.

19. D&SL, pp. 90–91. Some of the notes on these scraps survived Türkheim with Frankl and are today in the Vienna archives.

20. MSFM, p. 93.

21. MSFM, p. 93.

22. *Chronicle of the Twentieth Century*, pp. 588–93.

23. MSFM, pp. 69–72.

24. In this passage Viktor offers a possible rendering of Psalm 118:5, which can also be translated: "Hard-pressed, I cried out to the Lord; and he answered me by setting me in a broad place." See MSFM, pp. 96–97.

CHAPTER 8

1. After Viktor's marriage to Elly Schwindt in Vienna in 1947, he took Elly with him on a visit to Munich—her very first journey outside Austria. They were poor and walked very far to the outskirts of Munich in search of this place. They finally found Zaubzerstrasse 36.

2. Anne Frank was a child deported with her family from Amsterdam in 1944 after keeping diaries during the more than two years they were in hiding. She, as one might guess, was sent to several camps—in her case to Westerbork, then Auschwitz, and finally to Bergen-Belsen. Anne and her sister died of typhus in horrendous camp conditions only a month before the liberation of Bergen-Belsen by the British in April 1945. In just a few months the epidemic may have claimed as many as thirty-five thousand lives there. See Anne Frank's *Diary of a Young Girl*. At least two major motion pictures tell her story.

3. At the University of Vienna, the "habilitation" was the first step on the way to a professorship. A major paper was required, and for this Viktor used his *Ärztliche Seelsorge* when he had completed it. Thus he became a *Dozent*—a lecturer in the medical school.

4. Under this arrangement the entire apartment was rented in Viktor's name. So he was in effect the manager and could sublet space, though he had no authority to evict anyone.

5. This may be the same journey that Frankl describes in RECL, p. 88.

6. RECL, p. 101.

7. It was Robert C. Barnes who, in planning the congress, located the family of Sergeant Barton T. Fuller, the soldier in this story, and arranged for the display of his uniform. See RECL, p. 137.

8. MSFM, p. 45.

9. A text and photo book by Gernot Römer.

CHAPTER 9

1. A good map for tracing the Frankl story is "Wien Gesamptplan" from Freytag & Berndt.

2. http://www.timeout/vienna/sight/the_danube.html (19 July 2000).

CHAPTER 10

1. For photographs of the Rotunda before and immediately following its destruction, see *Wien*, 1992, pp. 18–19.

2. See Gay, 1988, pp. 425–27 and 634–35; and *The Diary of Sigmund Freud, 1929–1939*, pp. 48, 84–85, 248.

CHAPTER 11

1. http://www.austria.org/aproo/thirdman.html (26 July 2000).

2. Ebert, *Chicago Sun-Times*, http://www.suntimes.com/ebert/greatmovies/third_man. html (12 July 2000).

3. See *The Third Man* (1949).

4. To translate and nuance this text is very difficult because of corrections and scribbles on the original. Perhaps no one could do better than Franz Vesely has done here, both because of his language skills and his intimate familiarity with Frankl's penmanship. I happen to know that Vesely was deeply moved as he worked on the translation.

5. For example, see Myers, 1992.

CHAPTER 12

1. A close association with Freud was possible even for a critic. Ludwig Binswanger (1881–1966), the Swiss psychiatrist who separated from psychoanalysis and developed his own existential analysis, proved that it was possible to be critical of psychoanalysis and yet remain "on the most amicable footing with Freud across the decades." Gay, 1988, p. 243.

2. Walter Spiel and Hans Strotzka are among the coauthors of *Zur Geschichte der Psychiatrie in Wien*.

3. May is credited with introducing European existential psychology to American readers

with *Existence,* a book he coedited and first published in 1958. In his *Existential Psychology,* 1961, May states that logotherapy hovers close to authoritarianism, p. 42.

4. "Is Logotherapy Authoritarian?" in Bulka, 1979, pp. 5–20. In this chapter Bulka also published responses from May and Frankl.

5. DuBois, in *Logotherapy and Existential Analysis,* p. 60.

6. Yalom, 1980, p. 442.

7. Gardner, pp. 364–65.

8. Bulka, 1980.

9. WTOM, p. 143, note 2.

10. While at first the election of Jewish-born Kreisky as chancellor might have been interpreted—by Frankl and others—as a sign of diminishing anti-Semitism in Austria, Kreisky's accession to political power and his subsequent actions did little to push Austria toward acknowledging its own Nazi past or toward facing up to its full complicity with Germany in the Holocaust.

11. Wiesel in this speech showed his understanding of the growing ties between Germany and Israel, between Germans and Jews—ties that some American Jews, focused on the Holocaust, may not yet comprehend or accept.

12. http://www.germany-info.org/newcontent/gp/Thierse_01_27a_ 00.html.

13. Wiesenthal has written of his own Holocaust experience and of the problem of forgiveness in a small book, *The Sunflower.*

14. Frankl recognized that the matter of apologies and restitution by governments for injustice is both emotionally loaded and complex. For a balanced and helpful analysis of restitution issues see Barkan, published after Frankl's death.

15. In personal correspondence (Feb. 12, 2001), Nurmela cited Frankl's *Der Wille zum Sinn,* 1997, pp. 96–99.

16. UHCM, p. 37.

17. MSFM, p. 17. In retrospect, Frankl's line about the small camps "where most of the real extermination took place" seems odd. But he wrote this in 1946, when his own knowledge of the extent of the Holocaust was still limited; further, he may have known only a little about the extermination process at Auschwitz, where his own mother perished—the time between a prisoner's arrival and death in a gas chamber there was a matter of hours. In contrast, Frankl knew intimately from his time in the Dachau camps how death typically followed many months of torture, forced labor, starvation, exposure, and illness—hence "the cold crematoria."

18. MSFM, pp. 44–45.

19. UHCM, p. 37, italics mine.

20. UHCM, p. 37 note.

21. MSFM, p. 19.

22. MSFM, pp. 9, 22, 31, 33–40, 72, and 94–99.

23. MSFM, p. 12.

24. See MSUL, pp. 77–81.

25. See, for example, WTOM and MSUL.

26. Freud did so in a letter to his clergyman friend Oscar Pfister, October 9, 1908; see Gay, 1987, p. 37.

27. Freud, 1961 and 1939; Jung 1938.

28. Jung's somewhat obscure views may be found in his Yale University lectures, given not long before Freud's death, and published as *Psychology & Religion.*

29. Fromm's popular writings include *The Art of Loving, Man for Himself,* and *Escape from Freedom.*

30. See Fromm, *Psychoanalysis and Religion,* especially pp. 96–97.

31. MSUL, p. 71.

32. Yalom, p. 442.

33. In this connection, it may be noted that at a personal level Elly had little use for psychotherapy, though she recognized the importance of medical-psychiatric interventions for serious psychological disorders. But to her it was unthinkable that she would ever pay a stranger to listen to her most personal, intimate struggles. "I have family and friends for that, and never in my life would I go to a psychotherapist to talk about my personal life." When I asked Elly how, or why, she devoted her life to promoting even her husband's brand of psychotherapy, she replied: "I cannot argue with the mail—thousands of letters over the years from people who had conquered their despair with the help of logotherapy. And I cannot argue with the hundred of patients Viktor treated who turned away from suicide or despair, became hopeful again and went on with their lives. So if I had to go to a psychotherapist, it would only be for logotherapy."

CHAPTER 13

1. Lukan, 1978, *Schneeberg und Rax: Hochgebirge für Jedermann (High Mountains for Everyone).* See p. 123. In this passage, "Dr. Dr." is simply the Austrian way of indicating that a person has more than one doctorate.

2. See Frankl, 1991, *Bergerlebnis und Sinnerfahrung.* Photos by Handl.

3. Selye's 1956 classic led to contemporary research on and understanding of stressors and stress. See Selye, 1978.

4. WTOM, pp. 44–45.

5. Csikszentmihalyi, 1990.

6. Frankl, 1992, p. 31.

7. UHCM, p. 42.

8. Frankl, 1992, p. 35.

CHAPTER 14

1. *C. G. Jung: Word and Image,* p. 131.

2. *Zur Geschichte der Psychiatrie in Wien,* p. 14.

3. Von Foerster left Vienna in 1949 for the United States where he taught at the University of Illinois and ultimately retired in California. In an interview with the *Stanford Humanities Review* he reported that it was Viktor Frankl who called his own publisher, Franz Deuticke, urging him to look at von Foerster's short German manuscript, *The Memory: A Quantum Mechanical Treatise.* That resulted in its publication. In 2000, I telephoned von Foerster at his California home. At the age of ninety, he burst with enthusiasm at the mention of the name Frankl. Von Foerster had been responsible for a radio discussion program in Vienna right after the war, *Fragen der Zeit (Questions of the Time).* The program was aired every Friday and featured a small panel of leading lights interacting on crucial issues. Von Foerster sent me some

old documents, in one of them a photograph of four people around a microphone: Dr. Diego Hanns Goetz, a Dominican priest; Frankl; character-researcher Margarete Bauer-Chlumberg, and their interviewer. See *Die Radio Woche*, 1948; and "Heinz von Foerster," 1995.

4. My professor was Donald Tweedie, Jr., who had studied with Frankl during the 1959–60 academic year, after which he wrote his book on logotherapy. See Tweedie, 1961. Others who wrote books in English after spending time with Frankl in that era were Aaron J. Ungersma, *The Search for Meaning*, 1961; and Robert C. Leslie, *Jesus and Logotherapy*, 1965.

5. Asperger's Disorder receives expanded research coverage in the latest manual of the American Psychiatric Association. See the 2000 revision of the *Diagnostic and Statistical Manual of Mental Disorders*, DSM-IV-TR, code 299.80.

6. See Bodendorfer, 1985, "Recollections from the Early Days" in *The International Forum for Logotherapy*.

7. From the cover endorsement of Lukas' *Meaning in Suffering*.

8. From Längle's writings and my discussions with him, it was apparent that, in his psychotherapeutic approach, logotherapy is now one among the supplements incorporated in a much more complex eclectic system; when I suggested this assessment to him, Längle agreed that it is a fair one. But Längle has also embraced therapeutic elements that Frankl actually set out to counteract, such as focusing on oneself, on feelings, etc. When asked publicly about the therapeutic approach of Längle, Frankl made an extremely terse response: "I am not responsible for what is not logotherapy and existential analysis." Further, the 1998 German book by Längle, *Viktor Frankl: Ein Portrait*, has been reviewed critically in German by Franz Vesely from his perspective as a close Frankl family member; see *"Bemerkungen zu Alfried Längles Buch 'Viktor Frankl—Leben und Wirkung'"* in *The International Journal of Logotherapy and Existential Analysis* 6, no. 2, fall/winter 1998. Another scholarly perspective on the issues is a dissertation under Eugenio Fizzotti by his student Ivan Stengl: *Selbstefahrung: Selbstbespiegelung oder Hilfe zum Erreichen der noetishcen Dimension?* ("Self-experience: Self-entanglement or Help in Attaining the Noetic Dimension?") Universita Pontificia Salesiana, Rome, 2000.

9. Specifically, Eugenio Fizzotti of Rome compiles a comprehensive bibliography of Frankl's writings; the books of Frankl are often republished without updating bibliographies. The surest path to the most complete information about Frankl and up-to-date bibliographies is the website of the Viktor Frankl Institute Vienna, http://www.viktorfrankl.org.

CHAPTER 15

1. *Das Judische Echo: Zeitschrift Judischer Akademiker*, Nummer 2/3, Vol. IV, 1955.

2. The Viktor Frankl Institute in Vienna has cataloged recordings of Frankl's lectures and can provide information on how to obtain electronic copies. Go to http://www.viktorfrankl.org for details.

3. "A Human Dynamo Sparks College America," *Pace*, May 1967.

4. Here I have taken excerpts from a typical lecture and combined them with some content from other presentations. My editing smooths the English reading. Naturally, the content of Frankl's thousands of lectures was repetitious since he also had thousands of different audiences. The material used here is based mainly on a lecture sponsored by the Toronto Youth Corps, February 11, 1973, at Massey Hall.

5. The famous study is James Olds and Peter Milner (1954), "Positive reinforcement produced by electrical stimulation of septal area and other regions of the rat brain," in *Journal of*

Comparative and Physiological Psychology, vol. 47, pp. 419–27. The study inspired research on some of the biological mechanisms in addictions.

6. These edited excerpts are from the question-answer session following a Frankl lecture at the "Evolution of Psychotherapy" Conference in Anaheim, California, December 12–16, 1990, used with permission from the Milton H. Erickson Foundation, Inc., Phoenix, Arizona.

7. See also D&SL, pp. 67–69.

8. Psychoanalyst Erich Fromm (1900–80), himself an atheist who renounced his Jewish faith in 1927, put his weight on the other side of the scale. He held to the Freudian line that God is merely a human invention to meet a human need and that it does *not* follow that God actually exists. See Fromm, pp. 54–55.

9. Of course, Frankl objected to the notion that there is an instinctual drive toward religion, and in these comments he uses thirst—a biological drive—only as an analogy for the orientation of the human spirit toward transcendence.

10. Frankl was not aware of the research, much of which was taking place during the final years of his life, on the relationship between language and thinking. It is now clear that the words we hear and use do influence how we think; hence, male nouns and pronouns, used predominantly, are not neutral or inclusive of female in their effect.

11. I sought to obtain the dates of all Frankl lectures for the Young Presidents' Organization. A cordial response came (e-mail October 19, 2000) from Ann Lovasz, YPO communications manager. But due to the move of their headquarters office she was unable to locate the records.

12. *Österreicher, die der Welt gehören,* pp. 44–53.

13. See *Conquering the Past: Austrian Nazism Yesterday and Today.*

14. *Der Standard,* 13/14 January 1996, p. 4.

CHAPTER 16

1. Viktor's blindness was attributable to age-related macular degeneration (AMD) over a period of years. The sudden loss of vision on the fateful evening, according to two ophthalmologists consulted, may have been due to the rupture of blood vessels in the eye(s). Because of genetic and other factors it is not likely that Viktor's blindness was caused by prolonged exposure to intense sunlight in mountain climbing, but that may have been a contributing factor. He did not wear sunglasses while climbing; at the time less was known about the sun's harmful rays, and sunglasses were rudimentary compared to today's protective eyewear.

2. "Viktor's Choice," 1992.

3. The article, "Logotherapy Then and Whenever: A Personal Reflection," was published in a new venture, the *Journal des Viktor-Frankl-Instituts* (1993)—the first writing I had ever done on the Frankls. Subsequently I wrote two more articles for the journal, one for a special issue commemorating Frankl's ninetieth birthday (1995), the other for the commemorative issue following his death—the latter based upon a chapter of this book in progress and titled, "Viktor and Elly Frankl: Defying the Danube" (1998).

The bilingual *Journal des Viktor-Frankl-Instituts* ceased publication in 1998 and in 2000 was succeeded by a new journal, *Logotherapy and Existential Analysis,* published by the International Association for Training and Research in Logotherapy and Existential Analysis, Bad Ragaz, Switzerland.

4. Technically, at that time the institution's name was North Park College and Theological Seminary—legally changed in 1997 to North Park University.

5. See Myers, 1992. In a materialistic society, living simply and being happy seems an odd mix. But as social psychologist David Myers writes, "the *less* expensive (and generally more involving) a leisure activity, the *happier* people are while doing it. Most people are happier gardening than power boating, talking to friends than watching TV" (p. 137).

6. See WTOM, p. 96; P&EX, p. 125.

7. Frankl knew and admired Rabbi Heschel. At a Jewish seminary in New York they once had discussions together, which Elly remembered well: "Rabbi Heschel and his wife were both warmhearted, kind people. They were wonderful, not only to Viktor, but to me also."

8. Isaiah 55:8–9.

9. Tweedie, p. 6.

10. See Fretheim, 1984, *The Suffering of God: An Old Testament Perspective.*

11. Isaiah 61:1–3, this translation from *The Revised English Bible,* 1989, Oxford University Press.

12. Mignon Eisenberg wrote an account of the Bar Mitzvah, "With Viktor Frankl in Jerusalem." Also present were Max Eisenberg of the Viktor Frankl Institute of Israel and David Guttmann, dean of the School of Social Work, Haifa University.

13. Once, in an almost offhanded way, I asked the Frankls if either of them had ever had an extramarital affair (explaining exactly what I meant). They both laughed and asked, "Where? When? There was never time and we were always together anyway." Because they were accustomed by then to distortions by some journalists and critics, they conceded that someday someone might make up a story, "but that would not be *our* problem!"

14. After Viktor's death a pathway in the vast courtyard of the three-hundred-year-old former General Hospital was named Dr. Viktor Frankl Way. It is the longest of the paths between the buildings, where formerly patients were wheeled outdoors. The pathway is marked today by a plaque just inside the gateway at the corner of Alser Strasse and Spitalgasse—a gateway that is visible from the bay windows of the Frankl study at the corner of Spitalgasse and Mariannengasse.

15. The translation from German here is by Franz Vesely.

16. Translation by H. N. Oxenham.

17. Even as a younger man Frankl wrote about the meaning of death. See D&SL, pp. 63–92.

18. After Viktor's death I conferred with his physician and learned that the justification for bypass surgery was that Viktor's general physical condition was excellent, that of a much younger man. The problem was his heart, and there might be only days to live; the one hope of prolonging his life was to attempt the surgery, though the risks of doing so were understood.

19. UHCM, p. 8.

References

ABBREVIATIONS FOR BOOKS IN ENGLISH BY VIKTOR E. FRANKL

D&SL   *The Doctor and the Soul.* New York: Vintage Books, Random House, 1986.

MSFM   *Man's Search for Meaning: An Introduction to Logotherapy.* Fourth edition. Boston: Beacon Press, 1992.

MSUL   *Man's Search for Ultimate Meaning.* New York: Plenum Press, 1997.

P&EX   *Psychotherapy and Existentialism.* New York: Washington Square Press, 1967.

RECL   *Viktor Frankl Recollections: An Autobiography.* New York: Plenum Press, 1997.

UHCM   *The Unheard Cry for Meaning.* New York: Washington Square Press, 1978.

WTOM   *The Will to Meaning.* New York: Meridian, Penguin Books, 1988.

OTHER REFERENCES

Adler, Alexandra (1980). "A Personal Recollection." *The International Forum for Logotherapy,* vol. 3, spring, p. 35.

A History of Psychology in Autobiography, vol. V (1967). Edited by Edwin G. Boring and Gardner Lindzey. New York: Appleton-Century-Crofts.

"A Human Dynamo Sparks College America" (1967). By John McCook Roots in *Pace* magazine, May 1967, pp. 36–41. Los Angeles: Pace Publications.

Analecta Frankliana: The Proceedings of the First World Congress of Logotherapy, 1980 (1982). Edited by Sandra A. Wawrytko. Berkeley, CA: Institute of Logotherapy Press.

Ansbacher, Heinz and Rowena (1956). *The Individual Psychology of Alfred Adler.* New York: Basic Books.

Appignanesi, Lisa and John Forrester (1992). *Freud's Women.* New York: Basic Books.

Artifact Poster Set Teacher Guide (1993). Washington: United States Holocaust Memorial Museum.

Auschwitz-Birkenau Guide-Book (1996). Oswiecim: Publishing House of the State Museum in Oswiecim.

Baedeker, Karl (1905). *Austria-Hungary Including Dalmatia and Bosnia: Handbook for Travellers.* New York: Charles Scribner's Sons.

Barkan, Elazar (2000). *The Guilt of Nations: Restitution and Negotiating Historical Injustices.* New York: W. W. Norton.

Bellah, Robert N. *et al* (1996). *Habits of the Heart: Individualism and Commitment in American Life.* Berkeley: University of California Press.

Berenbaum, Michael (1993). *The World Must Know: The History of the Holocaust as Told in the United States Holocaust Memorial Museum.* Boston: Little, Brown and Company.

Berkley, George E. (1988). *Vienna and Its Jews: The Tragedy of Success, 1880s–1980s.* Cambridge, MA: Abt Books.

Berkley, George E. (1993). *Hitler's Gift: The Story of Theresienstadt.* Boston: Brandon Books.

Bodendorfer, Lotte (1985). "Recollections from the Early Days." *The International Forum for Logotherapy,* vol. 8, no. 1, spring-summer, pp. 5–6.

Bondy, Ruth (1989). *"Elder of the Jews": Jakob Edelstein of Theresienstadt.* New York: Grove Press.

Boring, Edwin G. & Lindzey, Gardner (eds.) *A History of Psychology in Autobiography, Volume V* (1967). New York: Appleton-Century-Crofts.

Bukey, Evan Burr (2000). *Hitler's Austria: Popular Sentiment in the Nazi Era, 1938–1945.* Chapel Hill: University of North Carolina Press.

Bulka, Reuven (1979). *The Quest for Ultimate Meaning.* New York: Philosophical Library.

Bulka, Reuven (1980). "Frankl's Impact on Jewish Life and Thought." *The International Forum for Logotherapy,* vol. 3, spring, pp. 41–43.

Bullock, Alan (1952). *Hitler: A Study in Tyranny.* New York: Harper & Brothers.

C. G. Jung: Word and Image (1979). Edited by Aniela Jaffé. Princeton, NJ: Princeton University Press.

Carsten, F. L. (1986). *The First Austrian Republic, 1918–38.* Brookfield, VT: Gower Publishing.

Chayefsky, Paddy (1960). *The Tenth Man.* New York: Random House.

Chronicle of the Twentieth Century (1995). Edited by Clifton Daniel. New York: Dorling Kindersley.

Conquering the Past: Austrian Nazism Yesterday and Today (1989). Edited by F. Parkinson. Detroit: Wayne State University Press.

Csikszentmihalyi, Mihaly (1990). *Flow: The Psychology of Optimal Experience.* New York: Harper & Row.

Diagnostic and Statistical Manual of Mental Disorders, Fourth Edition Text Revision (2000). Washington, DC: American Psychiatric Association.

Die Radio Woche: Österreichische Programmzeitschrift, 21–27 Marz 1948, Vienna.

DuBois, James (2000). "Psychotherapy and Ethical Theory: Viktor Frankl's Nondirective Approach." In *Logotherapy and Existential Analysis,* vol. 1, no. 1 & 2, pp. 39–65.

Ebert, Roger. *The Third Man.* http://www.suntimes.com/ebert/greatmovies/third_man.html (12 July 2000).

Eisenberg, Mignon (1990). "With Viktor Frankl in Jerusalem." *The International Forum for Logotherapy,* vol. 13, no. 1, spring 1990, pp. 32–33.

Ellenberger, Henri F. (1970). *The Discovery of the Unconscious: The History and Evolution of Dynamic Psychiatry.* New York: Basic Books.

Encyclopaedia Britannica DVD 2000 (1994–2000).

Encyclopedia of Psychology (2000). Alan E. Kazdin, editor in chief. Washington: American Psychological Association and Oxford University Press, Inc.

Fabry, Joseph B. (1980). *The Pursuit of Meaning: Viktor Frankl, Logotherapy, and Life.* New York: Harper & Row Publishers.

Fowler, James W. *Stages of Faith: The Psychology of Human Development and the Quest for Meaning.* New York: HarperCollins Publishers.

Frank, Anne (1995). *The Diary of a Young Girl: The Definitive Edition.* New York: Doubleday

Frankl, V. E. (1924) "Zur mimischen Bejahung und Verneinung." *Internationale Zeitschrift für Psychoanalyse,* 10, pp. 437–38.

Frankl, V. E. (1925). "Psychotherapie und Weltanschauung." Vienna: *Internationale Zeitschrift für Individualpsychologie*, 3, pp. 250–52.

Frankl, V. E. (1926). "Zur Psychologie des Intellektualismus." Vienna: *Internationale Zeitschrift für Individualpsychologie*, 4, pp. 326–33.

Frankl, V. E. (1938). "Zur geistigen Problematik der Psychotherapie." *Zeitschrift für Psychotherapie*, 10, 1938, pp. 33–45. Reprinted in the *Journal des Viktor Frankl Instituts*, vol. 1, no. 1, spring 1993, pp. 125–36.

Frankl, V. E. (1946). "Lebenswert und Menschenwürde." In *"Niemals Vergessen!": Ein Buch der Anklage, Mahnung und Verpflichtung*. Vienna: Verlag für Jugend und Volk, Gesellschaft M. B. H.

Frankl, Viktor E. (1992). *Bergerlebnis und Sinnerfahrung*. Photos by Christian Handl. Vienna: Tyrolia-Verlag.

Freidenreich, Harriet Pass (1991). *Jewish Politics in Vienna, 1918–1938*. Bloomington, IN: Indiana University Press.

Fretheim, Terence E. (1984). *The Suffering of God: An Old Testament Perspective*. Philadelphia: Fortress Press.

Freud, Sigmund (1959). *Moses and Monotheism*. New York: Vintage Books.

Freud, Sigmund (1961). *The Future of an Illusion*. New York: W. W. Norton & Co.

Friedlander, Henry (1995). *The Origins of Nazi Genocide: From Euthanasia to the Final Solution*. Chapel Hill: University of North Carolina Press.

Fromm, Erich (1950). *Psychoanalysis and Religion*. New Haven: Yale University Press.

Gardner, Howard (1993). *Creating Minds*. New York: Basic Books.

Gay, Peter (1987). *A Godless Jew: Freud, Atheism, and the Making of Psychoanalysis*. New Haven: Yale University Press.

Gay, Peter (1988). *Freud: A Life for Our Time*. New York: W. W. Norton.

Gay, Peter (1998). *My German Question*. New Haven: Yale University Press.

Gesellschaft der Ärzte in Wien, 1837–1987 (1987) Karl Hermann Spitzy, editor. Vienna: Christian Brandstätter Verlag.

Ghetto Museum Terezín. Published by Terezín Memorial.

Glover, Jonathan (1999). *Humanity: A Moral History of the Twentieth Century*. New Haven: Yale University Press.

Gould, William Blair (1993). *Frankl: Life with Meaning*. Pacific Grove, CA: Brooks/Cole.

Gray, Loren (1998). *Alfred Adler, the Forgotten Prophet: A Vision for the Twenty-first Century*. Westport, CT: Praeger.

Hamann, Brigitte (1999). *Hitler's Vienna: A Dictator's Apprenticeship*. New York: Oxford University Press.

Hammarskjöld, Dag (1965). *Markings*. New York: Alfred A. Knopf.

"Heinz von Foerster" (1995). Interview in the *Stanford Humanities Review*, vol. 4, issue 2, 26 June 1995. http://www.stanford.edu/group/SHR/4-2/text/interviewvonf.html (4 August 2000).

Historical Atlas of the Holocaust (1996). United States Holocaust Museum. New York: Simon & Schuster Macmillan.

Hoffman, Edward (1994). *The Drive for Self: Alfred Adler and the Founding of Individual Psychology*. New York: Addison-Wesley.

Integrating Spirituality into Treatment (1999). William R. Miller, editor. Washington: American Psychological Association.

Is the Holocaust Unique? Alan S. Rosenbaum, editor (1996). Boulder, CO: Westview Press.

Jones, Ernest (1953). *The Life and Work of Sigmund Freud.* New York: Basic Books.

Jones, Sidney (1983). *Hitler in Vienna, 1907–1913.* New York: Stein and Day.

Jung, C. G. (1938). *Psychology and Religion.* New Haven: Yale University Press.

Kershaw, Ian (1998). *Hitler, 1889–1936: Hubris.* New York: W. W. Norton.

Klingberg, Haddon, Jr. (1993). "Logotherapy Then and Whenever: A Personal Reflection." *Journal des Viktor-Frankl-Instituts,* vol. 1, no. 1, spring 1993.

Klingberg, Haddon, Jr. (1995). "Tracing Logotherapy to Its Roots." *Journal des Viktor-Frankl-Instituts,* vol. 3, no. 1, spring 1995.

Klingberg, Haddon, Jr. (1998). "Viktor and Elly Frankl: Defying the Danube." *Journal des Viktor-Frankl-Instituts,* vol. 6, no. 1, spring-summer 1998. This article was reprinted in *Journal of the Viktor Frankl Foundation of South Africa* in 2000, and in *The International Forum for Logotherapy* in 2001.

Lane, Robert E. (2000). *The Loss of Happiness in Market Democracies.* New Haven: Yale University Press.

Lukacs, John (1997). *The Hitler of History.* New York: Alfred A. Knopf.

Lukan, Karl. (1978) *Schneeberg und Rax: Hochgebirge für Jedermann.* Vienna: Verlag Anton Schroll & Co.

Lukas, Elisabeth (1986). *Meaning in Suffering: Comfort in Crisis through Logotherapy.* Berkeley: Institute of Logotherapy Press.

May, Rollo (ed.) (1961). *Existential Psychology.* New York: Random House.

May, Rollo, Ernest Angel, & Ellenberger, Henri (eds). *Existence: A New Dimension in Psychiatry and Psychology* (1958). New York: Basic Books, Inc.

Myers, David G. (1980). *The Inflated Self: Human Illusions and the Biblical Call to Hope.* New York: The Seabury Press.

Myers, David G. (1992). *The Pursuit of Happiness: Who is Happy and Why?* New York: William Morrow and Co., Inc.

Myers, David G. (2000). *The American Paradox: Spiritual Hunger in an Age of Plenty.* New Haven: Yale University Press.

Novick, Peter (1999). *The Holocaust in American Life.* Boston: Houghton Mifflin.

Nurmela, Risto (2000). "Viktor E. Frankl on the Holocaust." Paper presented at the Thirtieth Annual Scholars' Conference on the Holocaust and the Churches, Philadelphia, March 5, 2000.

Nurmela, Risto (2001). *Die innere Freiheit: Das jüdische Element bei Viktor E. Frankl (Inner Freedom: The Jewish Element in the Thought of Viktor E. Frankl).* Frankfurt am Main: Peter Lang.

Österreicher, die der Welt gehören (1979). Vienna: Mobil Oil Austria AG, Verlag Brüder Rosenbaum.

Psychiatry in Vienna: An Illustrated Documentation (1983). Contributions by Peter Berner, Walter Spiel, Hans Strotzka, and Helmut Wyklicky. Vienna: Verlag Christian Brandstätter.

Religion and the Clinical Practice of Psychology (1996). Edward P. Shafranske, editor. Washington: American Psychological Association.

Richards, P. Scott and Allen E. Bergin (1997). *A Spiritual Strategy for Counseling and Psychotherapy.* Washington: American Psychological Association.

Römer, Gernot (1984). *Für die Vergessenen.* Augsburg: Presse-Druck-und Verlags-GmbH.

Routledge Encyclopedia of Philosophy (1998). Edward Craig, editor. London: Routledge.

Rummel, R. J. (1994). *Death by Government.* New Brunswick, NJ: Transaction Publishers.

Scheler, Max (1960). *On the Eternal in Man.* London: SCM Press Ltd.

Scheler, Max (1973). *Formalism in Ethics and Non-Formal Ethics of Values.* Evanston, IL: Northwestern University Press.

Schur, Max (1972). *Freud: Living and Dying.* New York: International Universities Press.

Selye, Hans (1978). *The Stress of Life.* New York: McGraw-Hill Book Co.

Sigmund Freud: His Life in Pictures and Words (1985). Edited by Ernst Freud, Lucie Freud, and Ilse Grubrich-Simitis. New York: W. W. Norton.

Soucek, Wolfgang (1948). "Die Existenzanalyse Frankls, die dritte Richtung der Wiener psychotherapeutischen Schule." In *Deutsche Medizinische Wochenschrift,* 73, p. 594.

Speaking Out: Jewish Voices from United Germany (1995). Edited by Susan Stern. Chicago: edition q, inc.

Stern, Aaron (1979). *ME: The Narcissistic American.* New York: Ballantine Books.

Stürmer, Michael (1999). *The German Century.* New York: Barnes & Noble.

Tengan, Andrew (1999). *The Search for Meaning as the Basic Human Motivation: A Critical Examination of Viktor Emil Frankl's Logotherapeutic Concept of Man.* Frankfurt am Main: Peter Lang.

The Diary of Sigmund Freud: 1929–1939, A Record of the Final Decade. Translated, annotated, with an introduction by Michael Molnar (1992). New York: Charles Scribner's Sons.

The Small Fortress Terezín 1940–1945 (1996). Published by Terezín Memorial (Theresienstadt).

The Third Man (1949). Canal+ Image U. K. Ltd.; DVD ©1999 The Criterion Collection, cat. no. TH1060.

Toland, John (1976). *Adolf Hitler.* New York: Doubleday.

Troller, Norbert (1991). *Theresienstadt: Hitler's Gift to the Jews.* Chapel Hill: University of North Carolina Press.

Totenbuch Theresienstadt [Book of the Dead] (1987). Wien: Junius Verlags–und VertriebsgesellschaftmBH.

Tweedie, Donald F., Jr. (1961). *Logotherapy and the Christian Faith.* Grand Rapids, MI: Baker.

"Vienna and the Third Man." Austrian Information, Washington, DC, vol. 53, no. 4. http://www.austria.org/apr00/thirdman.html (26 July 2000).

Vitz, Paul C. (1994). *Psychology as Religion: The Cult of Self-Worship.* Second edition. Grand Rapids: Eerdmans Publishing Company.

Watts, Janet. "Viktor's Choice," *Observer Magazine,* 21 June 1992, pp. 46–47.

"Wien Gesamptplan 1:25,000." Vienna: Kartographie, Druck u. Verlag: Freytag-Berndt u. Artaria.

Wien: Metamorphosen einer Stadt in Fotografien von Gestern und Heute (1992). Text by Bartel F. Sinhuber, photos by Fritzkarl Stumpf. Munich: Heinrich Hugendubel Verlag.

Wiesenthal, Simon (1997). *The Sunflower: On the Possibilities and Limits of Forgiveness.* New York: Schocken Books.

Wulff, David M. *Psychology of Religion: Classic & Contemporary.* New York: John Wiley & Sons, Inc.

Yalom, Irvin (1980). *Existential Psychotherapy.* New York: Basic Books.

Zur Geschichte der Psychiatrie in Wien (1988). With contributions by Peter Berner, Walter Spiel, Hans Strotzka, and Helmut Wyklicky. Vienna: Verlag Christian Brandstätter.

Acknowledgments

THANKS TO JAN, love of my life, who bore patiently my long stays away from home and my emotional distance, even at home, when I was preoccupied with this project. She also helped immensely by putting her own editing and intuitive skills to work whenever I needed them.

Our adult sons, Jess and Travis, kept cheering me on, each in his way. Jess sheltered me from intrusions, even when we both wanted to simply chat or take a walk. Trav read and advised, designed the two maps, and engaged in impassioned conversations on key issues.

The person who, in 1959, first made me aware of Viktor Frankl is my teacher and mentor, Donald F. Tweedie, Jr. He and his wife Norma, enduring friends of Jan and me, also had many a Frankl story to tell.

My critical readers in the manuscript's formative stages were Barbara Cleveland, and my students Chris Newhouse and Liz Smith. In later stages, Carl Racine (Boston) and Rabbi Reuven Bulka (Ottawa) gave crucial feedback. Joseph Alulis, David Koeller, and Greg Clark, my faculty colleagues at North Park University, read with the critical eyes of their particular disciplines; the wisdom of Fred Holmgren opened some new perspectives.

Thanks to Tom Zelle and Mark Seidel for translations from the German, to Ingrid Hjelm for videotape transcriptions, and to Eric Erickson for inciting new ideas following his visit in Vienna.

North Park University made the project possible. So I thank its Board of Trustees for the privilege of teaching and for academic leave for research and writing. President David Horner and Dean Daniel DeRoulet were genuinely interested and encouraging, start to finish. Katie Cook, colleague in psychology, cheerfully took on tasks that were technically mine, as did Jay Oleniczak, psychology assistant. At a critical time, Alexandria

Taylor and Mark Duncan shared the load of responsibility for the 2001 South Africa study tour. Student advisees in "the Arena" released me from routine demands so that I could keep my focus.

Three research grants were given, each just in time. The first resulted from a contact by Lloyd Ahlem with Bernice Brandel, whose grant enabled me to launch the project. The second grant came from Swanee Hunt, whom I met when she was United States Ambassador to Austria; the Frankls spoke often of the kindness of Ambassador Hunt to them. James M. and Arlyne Lane made the third grant possible near the end of the research phase.

In the course of gathering the Frankl story, there were many people in Europe and beyond—some of whom visited Vienna while I was there—all contributing perspectives, knowledge, and memories. Most I interviewed face-to-face, including Klaus Bühler, mayor of Türkheim; Ludwig and Kitty Werber, London; Alfred Schoenfeld, Paris; Lotte Bodendorfer, Uppsala; Liesl Bonday, Australia; Gerald Kriechbaum, Austrian Consul General (Chicago); Professor Risto Nurmela, Finland; Stefan Strahwald, Graz, Austria; and Patti Havenga Coetzer, South Africa. Among the Viennese, Hermi Ecker; the late Helene Eisenkolb; Professor Wilhelm Holczabek, former president (*Rektor*) of the University of Vienna; Helene Fischer Puhm; the late Gustav Baumhackl; Professor Giselher Guttmann; historian Gerhard Benetka; and physicians Wolfgang Base, Wolfgang Aulitzky, and Alfried Längle. Thanks also to the staff at the *Institut für Zeitgeschichte*, Vienna.

Harald Mori, a medical student who was assisting the Frankls in various ways when we met, became singularly helpful to me also. Harald and Claudia entertained me in their home, and it was he who took me to the Rax and the Hohe Wand, the Hitler dormitory, and other venues in Vienna; arranged accommodations for me; and provided information, documents, and materials.

Similarly, willing assistance was given by people in the United States: Lucinda Glenn Rand, archivist, Graduate Theological Union, Berkeley; Jeffrey Zeig, Director, Milton Erickson Foundation; Professor Heinz von Foerster; Robin Goodenough, Washington; Robert Barnes of the Viktor Frankl Institute of Logotherapy, Abilene; Robert Hutzell, editor of *The International Forum for Logotherapy*, and his spouse Vicki; Robert Leslie and the late Joseph Fabry, Berkeley. Archivists at the United States Holocaust Museum and the National Archives, Washington, guided me to relevant sources. Photographer Inge Mörath, New York, showed me pictures and talked about her very long friendship with Elly and Viktor.

I thank the Frankl family for their generous and assiduous help in putting together the story, and for unlimited access to the archives of the Viktor Frankl Institute, Vienna. I spent significant hours with the late Tante Mitzi Havlick, and with the late Fritz Tauber. What Franz and Gaby Vesely contributed to the story is extraordinary—they shared both knowledge and wisdom freely, and remained as gracious in hospitality as in tracking down a detail. Their adult children, Katja and Alexander, assisted each time I asked. I treasure the friendships with all of these good people.

If the editors at Doubleday Religion had merely done their jobs, I would not mention them here. But Editor Andrew Corbin—inheriting this project from the astute Mark Fretz, his predecessor—not only understood the story, but with tough mind and hand helped shape its telling while safeguarding its integrity. From our first meeting in New York, Andrew Corbin was a professional and a genuine collaborator. His assignment of Frances Jones to work with me on the details of the manuscript was a stroke of genius.

A disclaimer is due. Though the sources and helpers are many, the content of the book is my responsibility, since I did not accept all suggestions from my readers and critics, who at a few points still disagree with one another and with me.

Finally, my gratitude to the late Viktor Frankl and to Elly Frankl. Though Viktor lived to tell the story, he did not live to see it in print, so Elly was left with checking the accuracy of details in the manuscript. In doing so she was fascinated and moved to read about Viktor, but said, understandably, that "reading about one's own life is a strange experience." Herewith I thank them both for the honor of so challenging and meaningful a task.

Index